ALSO BY HERBERT LEIBOWITZ

Hart Crane: An Introduction to the Poetry

Fabricating Lives

FABRICATING LIVES

Explorations in American Autobiography

Herbert Leibowitz

Alfred A. Knopf   New York   1989

For Susan

Contents

	Illustrations	ix
	Acknowledgments	xi
	Preface	xv
1.	Style and Autobiography	3
2.	"That Insinuating Man": *The Autobiography of Benjamin Franklin*	29
3.	Reveries of an "Incorrigible Romanticist": Louis Sullivan's *The Autobiography of an Idea*	71
4.	The Sheltering Self: Jane Addams's *Twenty Years at Hull-House*	115
5.	The Shelterless Life: Emma Goldman's *Living My Life*	157
6.	"Principled Hedonism": Gertrude Stein's *The Autobiography of Alice B. Toklas*	197
7.	"You Can't Beat Innocence": *The Autobiography of William Carlos Williams*	229
8.	"Arise, Ye Pris'ners of Starvation": Richard Wright's *Black Boy* and *American Hunger*	269
9.	Stoking the Oedipal Furnace: Edward Dahlberg's *Because I Was Flesh*	307
	Notes	329
	Selected Bibliography	367
	Index	373

Illustrations

Benjamin Franklin Drawing Electricity from the Sky,
Benjamin West, c. 1805 (Mr. and Mrs. Wharton Sinkler
Collection; © 1984 Philadelphia Museum of Art)   31

Louis Sullivan, age sixty-four (© 1989 The Art Institute of
Chicago. All rights reserved)   73

Louis Sullivan, age fourteen (© 1989 The Art Institute of
Chicago. All rights reserved)   73

The Auditorium Building (© 1989 The Art Institute of Chicago.
All rights reserved)   73

Jane Addams, c. 1895 (Chicago Historical Society)   117

Ben L. Reitman, c. 1912 (International Institute of Social History) 156

Emma Goldman, 1906 (Chicago Historical Society)   156

Emma Goldman and Alexander Berkman, 1917
(The Bettmann Archive, Inc.)   156

Gertrude Stein and Alice B. Toklas on a
1934 U.S. visit (Culver Pictures)   199

William Carlos Williams, 1956 (John D. Schiff)   231

Richard Wright, 1945 (AP/Wide World Photos)   271

Edward Dahlberg, 1960 (Jonathan Williams)   309

Acknowledgments

ANYBODY WHO EMBARKS on a study of autobiography quickly learns that he or she cannot go far without frequently consulting the vast number of scholarly and critical works on the subject that serve as navigational charts. The last twenty-five years have seen a surge of interest in autobiography in general and American autobiography in particular. There are now thirteen hundred ways of looking at the blackbird, not thirteen. Even though I may not refer to all these secondary sources in *Fabricating Lives,* or engage in a game of polemical hardball with my colleagues, I could not have gotten far without standing on their shoulders. The reader who wishes to investigate these sources further can begin with my notes and selected bibliography and go on to more exhaustive bibliographies.

Several chapters were first delivered as papers or lectures. I would like to thank the following people for inviting me to test my ideas before stimulating audiences: the late Dr. Bernard Meyer and the members of his seminar on psychoanalysis and literature where I spoke on Emma Goldman and Edward Dahlberg; Professor David J. Gordon and the CUNY Forum where I discussed "The Centrality of Style in Richard Wright's *Black Boy* and *American Hunger*"; Professor Carol Berkin and the Columbia University Seminar on Early American History and Culture where I talked about *The Autobiography of Benjamin Franklin;* the American Studies Association where I sketched out my initial theories about the Jane Addams and Emma Goldman autobiographies, and Robert Boyers and Skidmore College where I presented my first tentative thoughts about Gertrude Stein's *The Autobiography of Alice B. Toklas*. My students at the University of Illinois, The College of Staten Island, and the CUNY Graduate Center who sat in classes and seminars about American autobiography have influenced and shaped my ideas and interpretations. I would also like to thank The Center for Advanced Study at the University of Illinois for giving me a post-doctoral fellowship that allowed me to begin this book.

During the course of writing *Fabricating Lives* I have had the good fortune of talking about American autobiography with many wonderful people, who took time out of busy schedules to scrutinize my essays. Sherman Paul read early drafts of the Stein, Franklin, Sullivan, and Williams chapters. His astute comments helped me correct errors of fact and interpretation. R. W. Flint's generous and detailed criticism of the Franklin, Sullivan, Stein, Williams, and Dahlberg chapters functioned as exuberant dialectical parries and thrusts. His letters over the years have constituted an informal literary tutorial for me. Judith Gleason, David J. Gordon, Cynthia Macdonald, and Virgil Thomson all read the style chapter and their varied responses enabled me to clarify issues and improve both prose and organization. Edward Burns read my chapter on *The Autobiography of Alice B. Toklas* and gave me the benefits of his deep knowledge of Stein's works. Suzanne Fox's canny sense of structure helped me redesign the Preface, the style chapter, and especially the Emma Goldman essay; she also compiled the bibliography and enthusiastically tracked down missing persons and tricky clues. Morris Dickstein reinforced my occasionally wavering faith that in an age of deconstruction there was still room for a book of belletristic criticism. Richard Lavenstein generously shared with me his knowledge of architecture and literature. Joyce Berkman's thoughtful comments on the Jane Addams chapter led me to revise certain assumptions. David Nasaw read the entire manuscript and engaged me in numerous conversations, on the Staten Island Ferry and in cars stalled in New York traffic, about the historical conflicts and ideas that marked the careers of Franklin, Goldman, and Jane Addams. Ross Feld's trenchant, supple, and unorthodox literary mind kept pushing me, by his challenging and sympathetic readings of my essays, to reopen discussions I had thought closed or to examine a work by Bakhtin that might shed added light on an analysis of autobiographical strategies. My long and leisurely discussions with Nick Lyons about matters literary, from big fish like Moby Dick to the exquisite music of sestinas, began in 1961 and have continued with undiminished pleasure up to the present day. He is the godfather of *Fabricating Lives,* having taken a lively interest in the book from its conception through its long gestation and growth to its birth. Dr. Leslie Seiden Gallo taught me much about intimacy and self-assertion and Dr. Marianne Horney Eckardt about the myriad ways identity is shaped by passion and the will, by nurturing or its absence. My agent, Gloria Loomis, lent the book strong support at all stages. I am very grateful to Judith Jones, my editor at Knopf, for reading the manuscript with meticulous eye, keen ear, disinterested mind, and warm advocacy. I would like to thank my copyeditor, Marjorie Horvitz, for her scrupulous attention to detail. Sarah Paul and Carl Paganelli did valuable research for me, and Carl and Laura J. Smyth, deciphering my squiggles and arrows, ably typed several chapters. My son, Gabriel Sky-Leibowitz, coped heroically with my having at times to break off a comparison of the pitching records of Orel Hershiser, Danny Jackson, and David Cone in order to return to my study. But the soul of *Fabricating Lives* is my wife and loving friend, Susan Yankowitz, who has entered so completely into the composition of the book. She has patiently read and edited draft after sweaty draft, removing obscurities and purple patches; talked animatedly about style or women's rights, an autobiographer's feelings of power and powerlessness, or a structure that can occlude meaning; joked me out of a morose mood and nudged me back to the word processor for one more revision. My debt to her for her collaboration cannot be adequately conveyed in words.

Preface

MY EARLY INTEREST in autobiography began innocently with Walt
Whitman's *Song of Myself.* Having been reared in an Orthodox
Jewish household where tradition, ritual, and law ruled absolutely,
I was unprepared for a poet unfazed by totems and taboos. When I
read the opening lines of Whitman's poem (his status as crackpot
bard endeared him to me—in 1954, he was not yet an academic
idol), a shudder of complicit recognition passed through me:

> *I celebrate myself, and sing myself*
> *And what I assume you shall assume,*
> *For every atom belonging to me as good belongs to you.*
> *I loafe and invite my soul,*
> *I lean and loafe at my ease observing a spear of summer*
>   *grass.*
>
>   *.   .   .*
>
> *Creeds and schools in abeyance,*
> *Retiring back a while sufficed at what they are, but never*
>   *forgotten,*
> *I harbor for good or bad, I permit to speak at every hazard,*
> *Nature without check with original energy.*[1]

To an earnest, self-conscious adolescent, Whitman's voice and icon-oclasm were liberating. He did not feel intimidated by authority; he shunted aside "Creeds and schools" with a humorous swat; he lived at ease inside the Zion of his body—a miracle: no guilt!—and he had the chutzpah to invite his soul, thus not only disobeying but teasing the Puritan censor . . . and going unpunished for his brazen transgressions. Though he started with "I" and punned slyly and bossily on the verb "assume," he ended with "you," establishing a sociable relation with the reader and asserting the value of intimacy. The conjunction "and" along with the verb "belongs" soldered to-gether self and society in a covenant of equals. Despite his brash investiture of himself as the American troubadour-seer celebrating the young country's democratic potential in a new vernacular, Whit-man did not settle for parochial egotism or bombastic chauvinism. His emotional generosity, as large as the continent whose physical lineaments and names he loved to catalogue, took in those cast out or despised by respectable society. It did not occur to me then that Whitman might have been enamored of duplicity and rhetorical games. Through *Song of Myself,* my "forbidden voices" could also speak unchecked with "original energy." Whitman gave me my first inkling of autobiography's renegade power—and its multiple forms of self-disclosure and self-concealment.

Many years later, I realized that my encounter with Whitman's poem had been a decisive turning point in my life, a lucky alignment of constellations that awakened me from a deep slumber and let light flood into my consciousness. Although I could not rig up a Richter scale that would measure the ramifying waves of this tremor, I was launched on that quixotic and murky enterprise, self-searching, that writers from Saint Augustine to Jane Addams, Henry Adams, and Maya Angelou have undertaken. Autobiography offered privi-leged glimpses of the past, flares in the metaphysical darkness before death extinguishes the remembering self. And it appeased my hunger for news of other people's childhoods and cultures. Edwin Muir could transport me to the Orkney Islands,[2] Konstantin Paustovsky to Kiev,[3] Jean-Paul Sartre to Alsace,[4] and Benjamin Franklin to co-lonial Boston,[5] worlds that resembled fairy tales in their mingling of enchantment and grim tragedy, powerlessness and personal hero-ism—worlds where the routine was transfigured into the glamorous and the sublime.

A subsequent immersion in autobiography confirmed what a complicated genre it was. Autobiography seemed the foster child of literature: Nobody could certify its parents. Was it the scion of history or of fiction—or, more probably, a hybrid, like an exotic orchid or a mule? Its forms fluctuated from eccentric designs like a folly to boxlike or jerry-built edifices. Under the pressures of memory, personal ideologies splintered. Retrieving the past frequently proved unreliable, as though an unstable conjuror had his finger on memory's switch.[6] Blank or faded pages got sewn into the book of every life. A detailed reconstruction of the historical past or a plunge into the psyche's abysses supplied only a portion of truth's dowry. To buttress this ambiguous limbo, autobiographers might frantically pile up sandbags of historical facts (the utilitarian solution) or twist fictional tubing together into a Beaubourg of *objets trouvés* and fabricated dramatic scenes (the imaginative solution). But the authors themselves are seldom satisfied with their experiments: The past as archaeological site yields an incomplete record even after sustained excavation. Nathalie Sarraute's rueful confession, in *Childhood,* can symbolize the favorite litany of the guild of autobiographers: "this reconstitution of what I must have felt is like a cardboard model that reproduces on a small scale what the buildings, houses, temples, streets, squares and gardens of a submerged town must have been like."[7]

It is entirely logical that because of these generic obstacles, autobiography has built up its long common boundary with fiction and that over the last century it has annexed—or had ceded to it—vast tracts of land formerly belonging to novelists. Character in autobiography, as in fiction, is the invented equivalent of men and women, dressed up in words, who move through time and live in a physical world that confines and presses hard on them, whether in the Mississippi Delta or in a leafy New Jersey suburb. In the vignettes of *Twenty Years at Hull-House,* her autobiography, Jane Addams reveals a strong gift for psychological analysis and moral imagination, as if she were George Eliot's American disciple. The rich anecdotal material about his medical and literary careers that William Carlos Williams sports with in his *Autobiography* is rendered with the "solidity of specification"[8] that Henry James demanded of the nineteenth-century realistic novel. Emma Goldman, by contrast, in *Living My Life,* is nearly swamped by the sheer quantity of events in her life; trying to find—or impose—patterns that might explain her character and behavior to herself eludes her.

But sometimes literary invention can have the opposite effect and overwhelm a life. In his book *Autobiographical Occasions and Original Acts,* Albert Stone stakes out a cautious position on this question:

> I remain uneasy over the tendency to treat autobiography chiefly as a branch of imaginative literature and thus to stress artistic creation over the equally complex processes of historical recreation, ideological argument, and psychological expression. *Life* is the more inclusive sign—not *Literature*—which deserves to be placed above the gateway to the house of autobiography.[9]

Only the most fanatical devotee of literary artifice would quarrel with Stone that we must assign supremacy to Life, in all its rugged diversity, not to Literature. But autobiography is not a foot soldier serving humbly in imaginative literature's army. It draws its strength, like Antaeus, from renewed contact with the vital earth of "artistic creation." Saint Augustine's *Confessions* is a brilliant amalgam of all the complex processes Stone mentions, but were it lacking in imaginative authority, the book would be of interest only to theologians or historians of the waning of the Roman Empire. Similarly, in *The Education of Henry Adams,* Adams, an epistemological Ahab, hunts for threads of relation in the bumbling drift of Grant's administration and in the godlike power shut up in the dynamo. In the last eleven chapters, Adams plays our Thucydides, monopolizing an imaginary conclave of intellectual historians gathered to discuss the effect of "unlimited power" on "limited mind" and the chronic fall of political virtue in a blundering and complacent, if nervy, America. But all his theorizing would sink his autobiography like the *Pequod* if it weren't piloted by his novelistic instincts. As V. S. Pritchett reminds us, "Nothing in this genre lasts unless it is done with art. . . . There is no credit in living; the credit is in being able to specify experience."[10] And this art is not the exclusive property of Brahmins like Henry Adams or literary Suleimans like Gertrude Stein. It is found equally in the comfortable bourgeois parlor of Jane Addams, the slum tenements of Richard Wright, or the outlaw territory of Edward Dahlberg.

Nonetheless, the other half of autobiography's Janus face stares at history. The intricate synapses of autobiography transmit private emotions and public events, registering how history forges identity and character makes history. The story of a single life is always entangled in the complex folds of a culture.[11] If American autobiographers occasionally flirt, as Gertrude Stein and Edward Dahlberg do in *The Autobiography of Alice B. Toklas* and *Because I Was Flesh,* with the dangerous idea that we can dispose of history altogether, history enters their autobiographies through back doors or on parapets like a cat burglar: World War I and the Great Depression are dark presences revealed through backlighting on the fictive stage. Most American autobiographers in fact have, as Robert F. Sayre points out in his valuable essay "Autobiography and America," "generally connected their own lives to the national life or to national ideas."[12] This includes men and women whose lives have been considered marginal, written off rather than written up. Over the last twenty years, everybody seems to be setting down his life and struggles, triumphs and defeats: a steelworker and Lauren Bacall, southern farmers and members of the Abraham Lincoln Brigade, biologists and biofeedback faddists, Lee Iacocca and residents of old-age homes, ethnics of every persuasion, jazz musicians, even criminals. In libraries and attics, in yellowed letters and on magnetic tape, forgotten selves are being recovered. Viewed cynically, this proliferation of autobiographies is merely another episode in America's insatiable appetite for gossip about any celebrity. But in telling their lives, American autobiographers put together a composite serial document, a Smithsonian Institution of necessary artifacts, which furnishes an unofficial history of American identities.

The grand theme of American autobiography, almost its fixation, is the quest for distinction, a quest that has shaped and deranged American identity throughout our history. In Puritan spiritual autobiographies, distinction meant one thing: election to the company of visible saints. The New World was both Promised Land and vestibule to the Palace of Heaven. But the light of conversion, the longed-for happy ending in which the soul was anointed with God's grace, did not touch all. This fact led to an anxious scrutiny of signs that indicated the person was one of the chosen—and neglect of the Puritan's daily life as merchant, judge, husband, father, and friend (there is a paucity of autobiographies in this period by women). If the idea of America's special destiny originated with the Puritans, it survived the crumbling of their theocracy. Benjamin Franklin enjoyed enormous repute at home and abroad as an advertisement of the opportunities for distinction in colonial America; he did not worry overly much about the nettles of limits as he grasped for himself the blossoms of power. (Although he bombarded the common people with facetious advice on getting ahead, he often viewed them as churlish and narrow.) One cannot write about American autobiography without taking the measure of Franklin's character and drive for success. He fashioned the American dream in his own spacious, guileful image: Hard work and shrewd will would ensure that an ambitious man would rise out of the bog of anonymity. America has not shed Franklin's belief in the benevolence of his own—and the country's—power; the jargon of virtue still permeates our politics. But Franklin failed to foresee what his astute rival John Adams did, "that the revolutionary abandonment of inherited titles and aristocratic rank makes everyone compete all the more fiercely for the *'distinction'* that can only be received from other people,"[13] and that "worse than poverty and as painful 'as the gout or stone,' is neglect. The poor man suffers most because *'he is only not seen.'* "[14] American blacks, forced to wear the galling shackles of slavery and suffering worse indignities than physical pain, were not even permitted to compete for distinction. But even out of such desperate circumstances, slave narratives (and, later, autobiographies by minorities) were written in eloquent protest against just that invisibility, supporting the cardinal tenet of Whitman's idealistic democratic creed, that distinction was possible for anybody.[15]

Whitman himself, however, at first ignored John Adams's forebodings. In the preface to *Leaves of Grass,* he "sees health for himself in being one of the mass,"[16] and remains unworried that individuality will be submerged by the crowds with whom he mingles, "mad for contact."[17] But the Civil War and Lincoln's assassination almost broke the neck of Whitman's faith in "amativeness." The twenty-eight bathers of *Song of Myself,* his cameradoes, began shouldering muskets and shooting at each other with deadly accuracy. American society, numb and divided, no longer corresponded to his bright, gabby "I" and his countless improvised identities in *Song of Myself;* all the jaunty humor of his rigmarole about "the pass-word primeval, . . . the sign of democracy,"[18] yielded to dazed maneuverings in search of a mended national purpose and unity. The perfume of quirky selfhood that permeates this autobiographical poem is overpowered by a stench of corruption from the corpses of European "feudal" forms still unburied on American soil: social rank, economic caste, racial hatred, religious bigotry. Whitman had failed to reckon with what Emerson called the "mountainous load of the violence and vice of society"[19] that never seemed to diminish. Sobered, he defers "man's free play of special Personalism"[20] (distinction) to a future America.

This crisis intensified throughout the Progressive Era, when industrialization and immigration, two gigantic pincers, threatened to bend democracy out of shape and pervert the American dream. Emily Dickinson's shy teasing question "I'm Nobody, Who are You?"[21] expressed a painful and pervasive dread in the American psyche. Louis Sullivan, echoing Whitman, might proclaim in *The Autobiography of an Idea* "the richness of the soul-life of the multitudes,"[22] but what kind of "soul-life" could flourish in a sunless rear tenement, where space for an expansive identity shrank to the size of a grave plot? Distinction seemed an unlikely goal to powerless workers assaulted daily by poverty and with the din of machines pounding in their heads.[23] Anarchists like Emma Goldman and Alexander Berkman argued that because real economic power rested in the hands of a corporate plutocracy, all promises that democracy would liberate the faculties of mind and spirit for the working class were mendacious rhetoric; their autobiographies did not modify this view. The cure they prescribed for social and economic disease was radical surgery: revolution and a new order. To muckrakers like Lincoln Steffens and Jacob Riis, progressives like Jane Addams, Alice Hamilton, Ida Wells, Charlotte Perkins Gilman, and Lillian Ward, and a socialist like Florence Kelley, however, America had come down with a bad case of what Huck Finn called the "dreadful pluribus-unum mumps."[24] The patient, if treated with a heavy dose of self-government, could regain his health. This required that the urban poor, the Irish miner, the Italian stockyards hoser, the Russian-immigrant sweatshop girl, the black sharecropper, so often neither seen nor heard but merely used up for economic gain, be rendered visible and their grievances addressed.

"To look at the agony of a fellow-being and remain aloof means death in the heart of the onlooker,"[25] John Jay Chapman once observed, and this moral apothegm might have been engraved on the consciences of those, like Jane Addams, who made it their lifework to combat an ethic of selfishness so toxic that it seeped into the social fabric, not only disfiguring individuals but causing damage to the body politic. With their faith in the possibility of steady change, in the efficacy of the trained will, these reformers and journalists, socialists and economists, recounted in their autobiographies how they strove to make democratic institutions serve the struggling poor and assure them lives of dignified autonomy and self-respect. Ignoring social taboos and refusing to accept passively the domestic sphere as their socially ordained jurisdiction, an entire generation of remarkable women led strikes, became authorities on lead poisoning, child abuse, generational conflicts, wages, and unemployment, built political coalitions and settlement houses, even, like Florence Kelley, translated Engels. In their autobiographies, they were often reserved about their private lives but passionately articulate about "their work life, their professional success, or their connectedness to current political or intellectual history."[26] In ministering to others, they paradoxically empowered themselves and achieved distinction.

Such autobiographies speak to the urgent issues of our time, to conflicts over class, sex, and race. A history of the self, however populated with marvelous particulars, would be incomplete if it did not lift its eyes from an engrossed pursuit of personal salvation to experiences and problems shared with others, such as wars, technological disruption, poverty, and child rearing. *Fabricating Lives* examines autobiographies that passionately debate the efforts—and failures—of America to live up to the high ideals inscribed in the Constitution, taught in the schools, and declaimed noisily and with self-congratulation on the stump. Jane Addams, Louis Sullivan, and Emma Goldman—a liberal reformer, an architect, and an anarchist—believed that the future of the American experiment hinged on wakening the masses from apathy to social initiative and political self-determination. Acutely aware that the chasm between democratic theories of equality and the harsh daily life of the overburdened worker could not be crossed by uttering fatuous slogans or defending the status quo, Addams never lost her unillusioned trust in the essential decency of the people. She entered into ethical and practical relations with them. Sullivan, by contrast, felt betrayed by what he deemed their herd acceptance of mediocrity in architecture and public policy, though as consolation in his *Autobiography of an Idea,* he designed a substitute visionary community of large-souled men and women, declaring that it was possible to put the round peg of elitism into the square hole of democracy. Goldman, who found American politics shallow and coarse, and democracy a system that sanctioned or abetted economic exploitation, felt an exasperated love for the young unruly country, as if believing, against the evidence of her head, that its openness might eventually nurture equality and cherish individuality. What is fascinating about the autobiographies of Addams, Sullivan, and Goldman is the complex mythologies of self they project onto the stage of history—in particular, their various idealisms, rooted in childhood experiences, evolving slowly and slantingly, digging channels for expression in an often crude America, faltering, righting themselves, surviving despair, indifference, self-destructive acts, but ultimately attaining distinction.

Distinction in life, however, is no guarantee of distinction in autobiography. Richard Wagner, a musical genius, won all the glittering prizes that the world dangles before us—power, wealth, fame, influence—yet his autobiography, *My Life,* is mainly a turgid monument to a colossal ego, a massive documentary gloss on the music. Florence Kelley's *Autobiography* is a hastily sketched self-portrait that barely hints at her resourceful character and the personal motives that inform her political commitments. Show-biz autobiographies that regale us with scandal and gossip and tales of backstage romances—the vicissitudes of stardom—usually offer a version of distinction as phony as canned laughter. But the genuine article, what rouses us from "the anaesthetic effect of habit,"[27] is style, a mysterious presence in words like the debonair grace of Fred Astaire as he dances on ceilings or partners a hatrack. Style mediates between fact and the interpretation of fact. When the particulars about a parent, a failed relationship, a career setback, or a political decision like the bombing of Cambodia during the Vietnam War tell us one thing, the style often supplies emotions and attitudes not reported, undermining the "objective" account. Identity is a matter of paragraphs and presentation. Franklin's plain style, compounded of eighteenth-century conventions and his own possum's wit, is the proxy for a more problematic character than legend and his wily embellishments allow, whereas Dahlberg's baroque style, subjectivity on a linguistic binge, dares the reader (and himself) to drive the proud artificer out of hiding into the glaring light of unpleasant truths.

Style is crucial interpretive evidence about any autobiography. Out of fairness, we do not expect public figures to be polished writers, but their literary styles, whether fluent or inept, magnify character so that we can study it close up. Emma Goldman's overheated style, for example, left its mark on her political ideals as well as on her conduct of love affairs and her fondness for combustible polemics; it infuses her attitudes on every subject from authority to violence; it is a major clue to the causes of excess in her psyche; it helps explain her behavior in times of crisis—and it vehemently insists that she would not be ignored. Several of the autobiographers that I discuss in *Fabricating Lives* (Franklin, Sullivan, Williams, Addams, Wright, Dahlberg, even the archsophisticate Gertrude Stein) pass themselves off in their prose with a crooked or sheepish grin as homemade innocents.

American autobiographers enjoy writing in a variety of styles. To claim this feature is exclusively American would be foolish jingoism, but perhaps because democratic ideology and folklore decree equality as a sacred value, our writers pursue an eccentric style as the means of asserting their singularity. Uncovering their "stylistic subterfuges" is a basic task for the literary critic and historian, who must read these texts with a strong sense of irony. Although I do not scant psychological and historical analysis in *Fabricating Lives,* I have moved style from the circumference to the center of interpretation. That is why in my first chapter, "Style and Autobiography," I draw my examples from many corners of the literary world as well as from the rich archive of American autobiography.

Why did I choose these eight people, five men and three women, for close scrutiny in *Fabricating Lives?* Because they represent a cross-section of American experience, a self-portrait gallery spanning almost two centuries. (Another curator might wish to exhibit other works and styles, which could equally illuminate the genre.) Whether scrambling for distinction or plotting to escape an unbearable loneliness, these autobiographers, like a close extended fractious family, fought over what America has been, is, or might be, sought its rewards, arraigned its injustices, jeered at its pretensions, and applauded its successes. In the tapestry of this book, each idiosyncratic voice speaks as one strand in the varied American skein; each vision of the good life is a patch in the quilt of American themes; and each telling of a life story, whether artistic, public, or political, annotates the peculiarly American ambivalence toward the self and society. Every one of these autobiographers, having the opportunity to read the other seven, would have to marvel at the forceful personalities and stylistic gamut of the group, concurring with Wallace Stevens that

> . . . *out of what one sees and hears and out*
> *Of what one feels, who could have thought to make*
> *So many selves, so many sensuous worlds,*
> *As if the air, the mid-day air, was swarming*
> *With the metaphysical changes that occur,*
> *Merely in living as and where we live.*[28]

NOVEMBER 1, 1988

Fabricating Lives

I

Style and Autobiography

The man is only half himself, the other half is his expression.
—EMERSON, "The Poet"

I

A WRITER HAS more than one mind, V. S. Pritchett once said, and nowhere is the truth of this remark more evident than in autobiographies. Because the autobiographer often dresses up in fictions and disguises himself in slanted fact, the reader must pass like a secret agent across the borders of actuality and myth, following a winding trail of hallowed lies and profane truths. "Our deeper intentions are plans and evasions inseparably linked,"[1] Sartre warned in *Les Mots,* so the task of the literary sleuth is to sift and analyze the slippery clues that the autobiographer leaves behind about childhood, family, race, sex, work, class, the errors of commission and omission smudged on the page and hastily or carefully rubbed out. Autobiographers and their exegetes agree on one point, that the truth is a cunning snare, sometimes "a crystal residue, indissoluble in memory's stream,"[2] as Virgil Thomson puts it, and at other times a comedy of delusions that also bears witness to a historical epoch's contradictions.

We are interested in the man or woman who, Henry Adams observes, can steal the bells of Notre Dame for the sheer adventure of it, but we also wish to probe the character and childhood of the person who would undertake such a daring theft.[3] What would the

3

style of such an individual's autobiography be? Purple and jittery and overwrought, or restrained and terse? Clear about public events and murky about private feelings? The self reveals itself through style. Neither mere ornamentation nor some obtrusive obbligato marring a true music, style is a dye introduced into the body of a life to uncover what lies beneath the surface, cell and organism, pathology and health. A reader stumbles upon the self hiding in a secret fold of syntax, grotesquely elongated or shrunken, as in a fun-house mirror, or disclosed in a rhythmical swerve, a fondness for the passive voice, short sentences that permit no qualification, repetitions of adjectives that escape the author's censor.

Consider the first paragraph of *The Education of Henry Adams:*

> Under the shadow of Boston State House, turning its back on the house of John Hancock, the little passage called Hancock Avenue runs, or ran, from Beacon Street, skirting the State House grounds, to Mount Vernon Street, on the summit of Beacon Hill; and there, in the third house below Mount Vernon Place, February 16, 1838, a child was born, and christened later by his uncle, the minister of the First Church after the tenets of Boston Unitarianism, as Henry Brooks Adams.[4]

Adams's style alerts us that his was no ordinary birth. If Christ was born in a manger, this American Adams has his peculiar though not obscure beginning in sumptuous troglodyte quarters. The pompous array of capitalized names, the slow, stately procession of phrases and clauses, arrested by the profusion of commas, as numerous as his kin and sponsors, which swaddle his brash energy and never let momentum build, the substitution of streets, place names, and institutions for his parents—these convey Adams's ironical view of his weighty, illustrious past, a legacy he was to judge harshly as unhorsing him at the starting gate for the American steeplechase in which he wished to contend. History imprisons the infant inside the walls of a fortress he cannot escape, every inch of which he measures with punctilious accuracy. When the child's name is finally officially recorded in the registry, both ceremonial flourish and anticlimax, Adams has cleverly insinuated his major theme: the past as guide and impediment. But despite the endless self-deprecations to follow in *The Education of Henry Adams,* the mannered avowals of failure and powerlessness, Adams's ornate supple style, like a consolation prize the gods bestowed on him at birth, instructs us that his ego is not going to be effaced. Style is, for Adams, an instrument of subtle penetration and unremitting clarity.

The range of styles available to the autobiographer is as varied and distinctive as consciousness itself: the gossipy ventriloquism of Gertrude Stein's *The Autobiography of Alice B. Toklas* and the gilded abstractions of Louis Sullivan's *The Autobiography of an Idea,* so like the foliage that embellishes the facades of his buildings; the absentminded, diffuse polemics of *The Autobiography of Big Bill Haywood*—a collage of IWW manifestos, newspaper reports, legal transcripts, and Marxist jargon—and the maudlin, conniving language of Richard Nixon's *Six Crises,* which mirrors his manipulative behavior and threadbare morality; the alternating folksy and clinical dissections of William Carlos Williams's *Autobiography,* a sequence of grumpy clowning and serious analysis of his roles as poet, doctor, husband, son; the tortured convolutions of Conrad Aiken's *Ushant* and the impassioned directness of Frederick Douglass's *Narrative.*

Although the elements of style can be isolated and classified—diction (colloquial, formal, euphuistic, detached), syntax (long or short, periodic or declarative), rhythm (muscular or dreamy, syncopated or neutral), form (linear, spiral, circular)—it is the ways in which they interact that give detail emotional impact, so that certain events, scenes, persons, in autobiography stay with us. Style is consciousness in reverie, in terror, in social repartee, in courtship and philosophical dispute, wheedling, telling a risqué joke, plotting revenge, rationalizing mistakes, rebuking real and imagined foes. But style can also represent the voices, the substance and motion, of other people, from parents to town bum, from commissars to poets.

The "I" cannot be conjugated without the world outside it, as Douglass understood. When he was working for Mr. Freeland, a relatively benign slave master, he resolved to flee bondage and broached the scheme to a select group of friends. The section of the *Narrative* that deals with this crucial period in 1835 stretches unbroken over three pages:

Our path was beset with the greatest obstacles; and if we succeeded in gaining the end of it, our right to be free was

yet questionable—we were yet liable to be returned to bondage. We could see no spot this side of the ocean where we
could be free. We knew nothing about Canada. Our knowledge of the north did not extend farther than New York; and
to go there, and be forever harassed with the frightful liability
of being returned to slavery—with the certainty of being
treated tenfold worse than before—the thought was truly a
horrible one, and one which it was not easy to overcome.
The case sometimes stood thus: At every gate through which
we were to pass, we saw a watchman—at every ferry a
guard—on every bridge a sentinel—and in every wood a pa-
trol. We were hemmed in upon every side. Here were the
difficulties, real or imagined—the good to be sought, and the
evil to be shunned. On the one hand there stood slavery, a
stern reality, glaring frightfully upon us, its robes already
crimsoned with the blood of millions, and even now feasting
itself greedily upon our own flesh. On the other hand, away
back in the dim distance, under the flickering light of the
north star, behind some craggy hill or snow-covered mountain, stood a doubtful freedom—half-frozen—beckoning us
to come and share its hospitality. This in itself was sometimes
enough to stagger us, but when we permitted ourselves to
survey the road, we were frequently appalled. Upon either
side we saw grim death, assuming the most horrid shapes.
Now it was starvation, causing us to eat our own flesh;—now
we were contending with the waves, and were drowned;—
now we were overtaken, and torn to pieces by the fangs of
the terrible bloodhound. We were stung by scorpions, chased
by wild beasts, bitten by snakes, and finally, after having
nearly reached the desired spot,—after swimming rivers, en-
countering wild beasts, sleeping in the woods, suffering hunger and nakedness,—we were overtaken by our pursuers, and,
in our resistance, we were shot dead on the spot! I say this
picture appalled us, and made us

"rather bear those ills we had,
Than fly to others, that we knew not of."[5]

As a piece of extended storytelling, this passage cannot be sur-
passed. But it also depicts the cruelty of a specific historical condi-

tion, slavery, which can produce in a generous, "life-giving" man a temporary paralysis of the will. Like a poet holding the mead hall in his palm, Douglass recounts an imagined journey and combat with the chimeras as if it had already taken place (fantasy coexists with moral and psychological realism). He is both Frederick Douglass and black Everyman undergoing a supreme test of his courage and manhood. With the trenchancy of a seer and the prudence of a leader, he appraises the restricted choices available to him and his friends. His leadership is not based on an icy will to dominate others; he is flexible and sympathetic, aware of his own weaknesses, wary of bravado. The humble image of walking down a road turns into a series of adventures an Odysseus or a Lancelot might have met, with dangers to overcome—wild beasts, cannibals, buffeting waves, evil knights (bounty hunters). The path also leads down into the stressful mazes of the mind in which demonic images throng, as frightful as the slaveowner and the "snow-covered mountain" vaguely beckoning, its "half-frozen" hospitality a dubious boon to the prospective runaways. Douglass sets forth the pros and cons of the slave's quandary like an eminent legal scholar arguing before a tribunal: "The case sometimes stood thus," he explains: on the one hand slavery, and on the other, freedom. This logic helps prove that his fears are grounded in the real horror stories any slave could recount.

It is Douglass's poetic style, however, that pulls the reader into the undertow of awful events, to turn ninety degrees with each dash and find the route of escape—gate, ferry, bridge, wood—blocked. The syntax hems in the rebellious soul searching for deliverance. Through personification, slavery becomes a repulsive brute, its robes "crimsoned" by the blood of innocent blacks it has ritually and gluttonously devoured. A moment later, starvation compels the slaves who have ventured the road to liberty to eat their own flesh. Douglass's pictorial imagination fashions the ugly shapes of "grim death," which swarm in the minds of the escaping slaves as the ultimate penalty for resistance. Slavery is a predatory institution, and the slave, its victim, prey; slaves were continuously reduced to an animal existence, so Douglass, quite naturally, conceives of tribulations physically (bloodhounds, scorpions, wild beasts, snakes). Each trial is at first lengthened and separated by both semicolon and dash, as if Douglass and his companions paused to catch breath, only to plunge into a sequence ("stung," "chased," "bitten") that culminates

7

in their being shot to death. But even before the period cuts off their bid for freedom, Douglass inserts another vivid cluster of participles within the parenthetical dashes, which makes the runaway slaves' ghastly end the more ironical and appalling because their strenuous self-assertion falls just short of success. Slaves were schooled in the imagination of disaster by their daily commonplace brushes with death and wanton cruelty, and Douglass draws on this communal oral tradition, but to it he adds his own literary skills, in particular a masterly control of pacing. By boldly appropriating Hamlet's lines as a legitimate symbol of the slaves' plight, Douglass further foils his audience's racist assumption that blacks were ignorant and inferior.

In fiction, the novelist may assign a quick recognizable identity through the use of verbal tags like mug shots (Dickens's "Barkis is willin'," for example, or Dostoyevsky's Underground Man, who whines and grovels nastily, while insisting with superior airs that two plus two equals five), construct identity in layers of grandiloquent language, as Melville does with Ahab in *Moby Dick,* or engage in a contest of vernacular and rhetoric, dialect and stagy, long-winded poeticism, such as animates *The Adventures of Huckleberry Finn.* In autobiography, a style may be as functional as a pair of sturdy brogues, but in order to give full pleasure it must produce the sorcery and presence of an unerasable voice.

Etymologically, "style" derives from the Latin word *stylus,* a writing implement, the nib of a quill scratching the soft surface of wax or the skin of parchment and leaving an imprint or incision. That controlled maneuver of the hand is a synechdoche for the indentation made on a portion of the world: the mind's conjectures about its own identity or the gravitational pull of moon and tides or a society's injustices, as systemic as cancer; or on a more domestic and emotional scale, a father's desertion of his family, a rape, sibling rivalry, or a chance encounter with books, any of which can alter the trajectory of a life. Here is Zora Neale Hurston, in *Dust Tracks on a Road,* remembering the Norse fairy tales she read as a girl:

> In a way this early reading gave me great anguish through all my childhood and adolescence. My soul was with the gods and my body in the village. People just would not act like gods. Stew beef, fried fat-back and morning grits were no

ambrosia from Valhalla. Raking back yards and carrying out
chamber-pots were not the tasks of Thor. I wanted to be
away from drabness and to stretch my limbs in some mighty
struggle. I was only happy in the woods, and when the ecstatic Florida springtime came strolling from the sea, trance-
glorifying the world with its aura. Then I hid out in the tall
wild oats that waved like a glinty veil. I nibbled sweet oat
stalks and listened to the wind soughing and sighing through
the crowns of the lofty pines. I made particular friendship
with one huge tree and always played about its roots. I named
it "the loving pine," and my chums came to know it by that
name.[6]

The worldly ironist revisiting the scene of her childhood, and a rich
field in which she foraged for folkloric material, savors the "great
anguish" of her early reading, reluctant to surrender her thrall to
the outsize storybook deeds of the gods, which roused in the girl a
sense of the marvelous and prepared her for a "mighty struggle":
She would be one of the "smiters," not a victim of the gods' high-
handed treatment. Like a woodland creature or shy pagan reveler
whose senses are open to "trance-glorifying" nature, a friendly deity
who comes "strolling from the sea," she is under a spell as if she
had swallowed a potion and fallen in love with Thor. The sweet oat
stalks are closer to ambrosia than the "Stew beef, fried fat-back and
morning grits," the diet of poor mortals, yet Hurston does not convert the chamber-pots into Greek amphora, as Edward Dahlberg
would, or fan the bellows of the romantic sublime until it produces
a mystical wind, as Louis Sullivan did in telling about his "loving
pine" in *The Autobiography of an Idea*. She shares the secret totem
with her chums. The mature woman feels both separation from
and attachment to the humdrum villagers going about their un-
forgettably human business, and her autobiography was to draw
nourishment from their sassy and plaintive wisdom—she had
"been in Sorrow's kitchen and licked out all the pots"[7] with them—
expressed in a speech she "rubbed with a soft cloth" in order to
preserve its music and its sheen. The ambiguities of her communion with her kin were most often straightened out by this stylistic
bonding.

Differences in temperament, of course, determine discrepancies of style. "The point of style is character,"[8] Howard Nemerov wittily remarks in his poem "Writing," so that even when hesitant, swaggering, furtive, or engaging in public polemics, autobiographers expose what they seek to conceal from themselves or the reader. Character revelation should not be confused with the superficial trappings and antics of personality—"life-style," that scrip of a consumer society's fantasies. Style is, to borrow Henry James's famous statement about experience, "the very atmosphere of the mind; and when the mind is imaginative . . . it takes to itself the faintest hints of life, it converts the very pulses of the air into revelations."[9] Whether the author claims she is a multitude of fluid selves, as Hurston does in *Dust Tracks on a Road,* or cannot free himself from a carapace of early traumas, as Aiken sometimes confesses in *Ushant,* style is the skin of identity into which all writers are laced. "The unity of style and meaning," William Gass says, "is a profound social and psychological truth"[10]—a proposition that can be examined by juxtaposing a few paragraphs of the autobiographies of Virgil Thomson and Edward Dahlberg. Both men begin their books with an evocation of Kansas City, Missouri, the city of their birth, at the beginning of the twentieth century. In *Virgil Thomson,* the composer disclaims any "gift for imaginative writing" or for making "a language change its sound or words their meaning, which is the faculty of poets." "I can describe things and persons, narrate facts,"[11] he avers modestly, and indeed he does not milk any moments, setbacks or triumphs, for weighty self-revelations. Even the ecstatic visionary pictures he saw after taking peyote while at Harvard are described with a levelheaded verve.

But fact is not simple, either by itself or in the aggregate, as Thomson's opening paragraphs argue:

> To anyone brought up there, as I was, "Kansas City" always meant the Missouri one. When you needed to speak of the other you used its full title, Kansas-City-Kansas; and you did not speak of it often either, or go there unless you had business. Such business was likely to be involved with stockyards or the packing houses, which lay beyond the Kansas line in bottom land. The Union Depot, hotel life, banking, theaters, shopping—all the urbanities—were in Missouri.
>
> So was open vice. One block on State Line Avenue showed

on our side nothing but saloons. And just as Memphis and St. Louis had their Blues, we had our Twelfth Street Rag proclaiming joyous low life. Indeed, as recently as the 1920s H. L. Mencken boasted for us that within the half mile around Twelfth and Main there were two thousand second-story hotels. We were no less proud of these than of our grand houses, stone churches, and slums, our expensive street railways and parks, and a political machine whose corruption was for nearly half a century an example to the nation.

Kansas, the whole state, was dry. And moralistic about everything. There was even an anticigarette law. Nearly till World War II, one bought "coffin nails" under the counter and paid five cents more per pack than in Missouri. Though Kansas had always been a Free State and supported right in Kansas-City-Kansas a Negro college, most of our colored brethren preferred Missouri, where life was more fun. The truth is that Kansas was Yankee territory, windy and dry, with blue laws on its books; and the women wore unbecoming clothes and funny hats.[12]

Thomson's style is crisp and "plain-as-Dick's-hatband,"[13] with the journalist's ear for the offbeat phrase ("coffin nails" for cigarettes). Urbane democrat that he is, Thomson relishes the "joyous low life" of saloons, jazz clubs, and brothels as well as the "grand houses" he later frequented and the "stone churches" in whose choir lofts he would earn his living playing the organ and whose hymns he incorporated into his music. No moralist seated on his high throne, he is discriminatingly worldly: If virtue is dowdy, "windy and dry," even the beneficiaries of rectitude will cross state lines in search of fun. The chapter title, "Missouri Landscape with Figures," tells a great deal: Landscape is dominant, and figures, including the author's ego, are secondary. In the passage quoted above, there is an immediate refusal of the first person; the "I" entering as the curtain rises in a subordinate clause and not clamoring for attention is quickly subsumed in the general "anyone," "you," "we," and "one." Yet the style makes clear his assurance (throughout the autobiography Thomson prizes his "unhesitating disobedience," "unconquerable rebelliousness," and impudence), which parallels his ease at hobnobbing with duchesses and musical royalty and Queen Gertrude Stein.

The rhythms of his prose, like his identity, are never flustered. His cantabile style springs from a privileged childhood: "I was precocious, good-looking, and bright. My parents loved me for all these things."[14]

The life in music, one of the autobiography's major themes, is introduced in the second paragraph without fanfare; expecting the atmosphere of high art, Mozart or Debussy, the reader is treated to a brief riff of ragtime and blues. Though Thomson confesses to an infatuation with Wagner's *luxe et volupté* of sound, his own verbal and musical practice is more understated. "New York, a boastful city, let one swell up,"[15] Thomson explains, but his prose never puffs itself up or loses its graceful composure, even when he records the nasty judgments of musical colleagues about the daringly unadorned harmonies of *Four Saints in Three Acts*. Thomson places himself in the tradition of midwestern humorists, Twain, Ade, and Tarkington, rather than in the "worried and preachy" tradition of Sinclair Lewis, Sherwood Anderson, and Hemingway. With his conspiratorial wink and impish voice of innocence,[16] those registered Americans trademarks, Thomson dodges the Puritan's blue laws and hectoring creeds—Thomson's family came from the South—in order to dance all night and sup on oysters and champagne. (Thomson does not share Twain's philistine suspicion of Europe or Tarkington's boyish sentimentality.) The spectacle of life, high or low, like the longevity of the corrupt Pendergast political machine, which produced Harry Truman, amuses him. In this balanced ebullience Thomson follows Franklin, Jane Addams, and Gertrude Stein, who also expressed strong opinions in reasonable prose.

Edward Dahlberg's Kansas City is as different from Thomson's as a John Sloan painting from an Eakins. Dahlberg grew up, so to speak, on the wrong side of the tracks, and he contrived his mannered style as a means of presenting both his "cut and bleeding soul" and the cityscape he roamed in as a boy, half Dead End Kid and half sniveling schlemiel. For Dahlberg, a nondescript style is the sign of an untrustworthy person and a feeble identity. Here are the first four paragraphs of his autobiography, *Because I Was Flesh:*

> Kansas City is a vast inland city, and its marvelous river, the Missouri, heats the senses; the maple, alder, elm and cherry trees with which the town abounds are songs of desire,

and only the almonds of ancient Palestine can awaken the hungry pores more deeply. It is a wild, concupiscent city, and few there are troubled about death until they age or are sick. Only those who know the ocean ponder death as they behold it, whereas those bound closely to the ground are more sensual.

Kansas City was my Tarsus; the Kew and the Missouri Rivers were the washpots of joyous Dianas from St. Joseph and Joplin. It was a young, seminal town and the seed of its men was strong. Homer sang of many sacred towns in Hellas which were no better than Kansas City, as hilly as Eteonus and as stony as Aulis. The city wore a coat of rocks and grass. The bosom of this town nursed men, mules and horses as famous as the asses of Arcadia and the steeds of Diomedes. The cicadas sang in the valleys beneath Cliff Drive. Who could grow weary of the livery stables off McGee Street or the ewes of Laban in the stockyards?

Let the bard from Smyrna catalogue Harma, the ledges and caves of Ithaca, the milk-fed damsels of Achaia, pigeon-flocked Thisbe or the woods of Onchestus. I sing of Oak, Walnut, Chestnut, Maple and Elm Streets. Phthia was a bin of corn, Kansas City a buxom grange of wheat. Could the strumpets from the stews of Corinth, Ephesus or Tarsus fetch a groan or sigh more quickly than the dimpled thighs of lasses from St. Joseph or Topeka?

Kansas City was the city of my youth and the burial ground of my poor mother's hopes; her blood, like Abel's, cries out to me from every cobblestone, building, flat and street.[17]

From the first words, Dahlberg puts in his bid for literary immortality, singing out his epic theme—sensuality, sex, flesh—and embedding his words, the jewels of a bankrupt character, he would say, in a mythic setting. Those homely Middle American streets he played on as a child compete with the place names of antiquity; Kansas City and Smyrna exist on the same latitude, sister towns. The reader is at first disconcerted by Dahlberg's ostentatious learning, as if culled from an atlas of the ancient Middle East—why are the sheep in the Kansas City stockyards labeled the "ewes of Laban," three-thousand-year-old mutton?—but soon realizes that Dahlberg is the kind of storyteller Thomson describes, who assembles pictures and people "into situations where they take on memorability."[18] Dahlberg's aggressive style is a species of prophetic poetry storming the heavens with song, erudition, and beseechings but coming back to earth in a "livery stable" or a "buxom grange of wheat." A sensual crank, this autobiographer pelts the reader with bilious and randy opinions delivered from his portable pulpit; even his questions are certitudes. His mother Lizzie's long nose will call forth a quotation from Lucian. When the temperature dips to zero in his soul, words alone can heat the senses or tender alms to the beggarly emotions—disloyalty, selfishness—for which he upbraids and flagellates himself. Dahlberg's style, so "wild, concupiscent," excessive, its assertive rhythms tempered by the sonorous substantives and abundant abjectives (Thomson is sparing of adjectives[19]) with which he likes to populate his sentences, seems a calculated form of literary reparations for the emotional penury of his upbringing. Thomson and Dahlberg, like twins parted at birth, illustrate how character determines style and style negotiates what Saint Augustine called the "mysterious alliance of intellect and feeling."[20]

II

A GRID IS a formal plan that imposes a strict pattern on events, thoughts, spaces, or materials. The appeal of the grid to city planners from ancient Kyoto to the newest suburban town is that it promises to confine human contrariness within rational boundaries. A walker in the city can move about in purposeful directions; fixed points and intersections facilitate the delivery of goods, social visits, and the circulation of ideas. Yet cities, like individuals, deform, transform, and defeat the grid because its uniformity is often dull. The grid presupposes that an unruly mind can be tamed by adhering to principles of objective order, a comforting structure that welds together material that might otherwise scatter like bombarded molecules. Sequences linking large blocks of experience—childhood, youth, adulthood, middle age, old age—are commonplace in autobiographies: the sovereign convention. Chronology, a temporal grid, is especially popular with statesmen writing their memoirs, because it neatly satisfies their assumption that political decisions ultimately follow the rules spelled out in manuals of *realpolitik:* the slow, patient wearing down of an opponent in negotiations, the cautious probing for small advantages, as in a stalemated chess game (the chessboard is also a grid). That is why most diplomats' autobiographies seem interchangeable: Any hint of spontaneity or heterodoxy has been suppressed, and the bureaucratic mentality requires that the language of passion and self-doubt be replaced by a pedestrian style pretending to be impersonal law. Consciousness becomes a minor actor in the behind-the-scenes maneuverings and public actions that take up most of the space in a Carter's or a Kissinger's memoirs.

The grid raises the crucial question of autobiography: What is the relation between depth and surface, insides and outsides? The quarrel is long-standing and bitter, and probably cannot be reconciled because so much depends on historical accident and the temperament of each autobiographer. Roland Barthes argues in *Empire of Signs* that the inside as a favored model is blatantly a Western bias:

> Topologically, Western man is reputed to be double, composed of a social, factitious, false "outside" and of a personal, authentic "inside" (the site of divine communication). According to this schema, the human "person" is that site filled by nature (or by divinity, or by guilt), girdled, closed by a social envelope which is anything but highly regarded: the polite gesture (when it is postulated) is the sign of respect exchanged from one plenitude to the other, across the worldly limit (i.e., in spite and by the intermediary of this limit). However, as soon as the "inside" of the person is judged respectable, it is logical to recognize this person more suitably by denying all interest to his worldly envelope.[21]

That the inside has more moral prestige than the outside is probably true, but Barthes's analysis is too schematic. In autobiography, many writers regard the inside as a void or a hieroglyph or a distracting nuisance and the "social envelope" as the self's true habitat. Benjamin Franklin, for example, prizes the public world because it affords him a large, convivial stage on which to compete for fame, wealth, power, and the pleasures of intellectual puttering. And Gertrude Stein, in *The Autobiography of Alice B. Toklas,* despite acknowledging in passing the sorrows and "tragic unhappiness" of great artists, cares little for the "dynamics of the soul" and much for the social pleasures of her Parisian milieu. Not all autobiographers embark on a journey to the Delphic oracle and spend time trying to obey its injunction, "Know thyself." Puritan autobiographies of the seventeenth century come closest to denying the "worldly envelope," but not even their intense spiritual self-examination, whether undertaken in a farmhouse or in a Plymouth counting room, and their allegiance to a closed doctrinal system can get rid of the outside and its seductive claims.

No autobiographer has dropped a plumb line deeper into the soul or searched memory more painstakingly for the causes of an infirm and sinful will than Saint Augustine in his *Confessions;* the inside is, for Augustine, the site of divinity and guilt, friendship and carnal desire, a sacred space overcast by the clouds of a corrupt world and a fractious will. Yet that tempting outside, however much it interferes with the access of God's grace, is never wholly repudiated. Saint Augustine's conversion to Christianity takes place in a real garden (a pear orchard), even as the gardens of Eden and Gethsemane hover figuratively in the air; and illnesses of the spirit break out in illnesses of the body. The spirit (the inside) needs the letter (the outside) to define its dilemma, but the heart and the self constitute "a house divided against itself." When Augustine likens memory to "a great field, a spacious palace, a storehouse for countless images of all kinds which are conveyed to it by the senses,"[22] or quotes from the Psalms to establish the authoritative fervor of belief that contrasts dramatically with the "agony of indecision" or the lapses and inner commotions he reviles himself for, he tacitly concedes that the outside is a plenitude useful to the self questing for spiritual peace. Although the bishop of Hippo must shun the pagan literature that initially inspired him—he can no longer weep for Dido—he never renounces his rhetorical and allegorical skills; he assimilates them into a new genre.[23] In the *Confessions,* the inside is the protagonist in the drama of the reborn or cleansed second self, the struggle to achieve an untroubled faith in and pious submission to God, and it is style that plays the crucial role in unifying Augustine's self-presentation: philosopher and theologian, teacher, son, friend, diagnostician of the sinner's perverse will, anxieties, and eternal war with base impulses, culprit, reluctant lover of the good, visionary, and healer of internal divisions. Even in its most liturgical and analytical passages, the *Confessions* is saturated in the language of feeling, intimate, pleading, and majestic; Augustine weeps frequently, quivers with fear, burns with shame, glows with hope, or sits with Monica at the window in an extraordinary silent communion. That window, while facing onto the street, does not hold his gaze; he peers inside: "For those who try to find joy in things outside themselves easily vanish away into emptiness. They waste themselves on the temporal pleasures of the visible world. Their minds are starved and they nibble at empty shadows,"[24] Augustine warns, but that outside world had entranced him and was the starting point for his difficult journey inward to the discovery of the atemporal pleasures, which he identified as the soul's terminus: salvation.

In contrast to those autobiographers who chart the torments of the soul's peregrinations, many others circumvent the inward journey by staying within the confines of the external. When the conceptual artist Sol LeWitt published his *Autobiography*[25] in 1980, he constructed his visual narrative with witty literalness along a series of grids, each containing nine images, which change as we turn the page: tools, pipes, tapes, artist's supplies, books; rugs, pillows, throws; the contents of bathroom, kitchen, and studio; scissors, large and small, open and closed; foods from Dundee Orange Marmalade and B&M Baked Beans to Bufferin, Ritz Crackers, and a bottle of Brunello di Montalcino. Each image is framed like a window, independent, though sometimes linked to the image next to it, or the one above or below. Occasionally, without explanation, a pane of glass is missing or dark, like a memory lapse or a photographic contact sheet that was dipped into the wrong chemical solution and did not print. Accident artfully disarranges rigid order. Then the viewer's eyes, momentarily blocked, resume their scanning of the grids.

In clustering his images along the grid, LeWitt seems uninterested in documenting his possessions or confiding his tastes, though at moments one cynically notes that an appraiser sent by a bankruptcy court might take similar pictures. Rather LeWitt wishes to explore the freedom that is available in fixity. One grid may reproduce details of larger grids—of African masks, Egyptian motifs, numbers, jokes, even what looks to be a scratch sheet for the three-by-three proportions. Grids multiply. Postcards form ad hoc grids, cropped at odd angles, or crates stacked like wine racks beseech the eye to notice a spatial pattern that is not just a geometer's or an artist's fancy but a law of nature. The eye travels the grid, pausing before one frame or, bored, hurrying on, picking out details of textures and surface—Formica, wood, the skin of a nude in a photograph—or the shapes lamps can take (twisting, looped, robotlike, a head swiveling on a neck). Some images juxtapose gracefully into elegant compositions, as in a still life: Moccasins, ice skates, and sneakers, functional objects, point in different directions, lying flat or on end.

In LeWitt's *Autobiography,* the imperial eye is the "I," self (auto) and life (bio) disappearing into the graphics. Time is dismissed as irrelevant (the several clocks in his loft have stopped at different hours) or survives as historical artifacts, like the model of a World War II airplane or the old hammer in a Peace jar. Family memorabilia, brooches, signs (DOCTOR A. LEWITT WALK IN), appear briefly to suggest the artist's past, as do pictures of friends, cats, and artists. Although the *Autobiography* finally breaks out of its domestic claustrophobia and welcomes other cultures as honored guests (Hokusai is given an entire page), the principle of selection or etiquette that went into the placing of *Le Vrai Portrait Du Juif Errant* next to a man with a scythe cutting reeds, and intersecting with a black couple and Chinese figures on adjacent planes, remains obscure. There is no way of reversing events in our lives, but the reader wonders why the images inserted by LeWitt on the grid took just that sequence. If the nine images were shuffled in another order, would the pattern be more revealing or less aesthetically pleasing?

LeWitt has sentenced consciousness to imprisonment in objects. His *Autobiography* is radical in its calm suppression of the self. Even his name is rarely seen, except on posters for an exhibit of his paintings. Childhood is passed over without comment, a Humpty Dumpty that fell off the grid unnoticed, and his development as a painter is ignored, scarcely to be inferred from the clippings, titles of books, maps, and prints hung on walls and doors. Who, then, is Sol LeWitt? The Garbo of autobiographers? No, he invites us into his home. A composite of household commodities, hobby shop icons, and souvenirs from travels in Europe and America? A ghost in the machinery of his conception? There is an undeniable pleasure in deducing the presence of the autobiographer from his possessions, the residual mystery of familiar objects, which is like putting Hamlet together from his doublet, buskins, sword, and books purchased in Wittenberg. But despite the charms of poring over his diagrams, in its undeviating faith in the grid, LeWitt's *Autobiography* points up the chief liability of this structure: It lacks depth. Though theoretically the vertical lines support the grid as the legs do a tripod, in practice there is no inside, little intimacy, just a generic style. The life of the emotions stands apart from the objects of the life and the array of cultural signs.

To many autobiographers, such as Franklin, Stein, and Thomson, who are not programmatically wedded to the grid, the two-dimensional surface is sufficient space for the account of their fascinating lives. What they tell, messily or elegantly, so their claims run, is what is there.

In her account of the rowdy banquet for the Douanier Rousseau, a legendary evening in the annals of the Parisian avant-garde, Gertrude Stein does not "gape and dawdle" as Henry James doubtless would have in his autobiography had he been invited to the ramshackle Montmartre studio. Stein assembles the long vignette anecdote by anecdote into an unframed sequence: speeches, songs, food, lovers' quarrels, spicy gossip, drunken improvisations, blows struck, an apache dancer and his donkey who wander in and out. Stein is simply a guest at the festivities who happens to be its chronicler. She adds no moral reflections. Indeed, viewing subjectivity as a gilded trap, she declares provocatively: "Gertrude Stein never had subconscious reactions."[26] By playing with narrative time in a casual manner, like an aleatoric composer or a speaker losing her place, shuttling back and forth between present and past, she avoids a merely linear movement and concentrates on an external reality as wide as the boulevards of Paris she loved to stroll—and ignores or stifles any urge to dive into consciousness itself. "Why is grief," a Stein maxim, builds an electrified fence around her "inside," blocking entrance to herself and the reader. And the style of *The Autobiography of Alice B. Toklas* ratifies this decision. Its limpid syntax tolerates few subordinate clauses or the hesitations and refinements of the periodic sentence in which consciousness corrects and revises and amplifies itself.

It is not surprising that Virgil Thomson should have been Gertrude Stein's close friend and collaborator, for he, too, is a notable skeptic of psychological analysis, dismissing the question "why" with testy humor as unanswerable or impertinent. "Ask me how," he will say, and indeed for engaging clarity as an expositor of musical practices and ideas he has few peers. In *Virgil Thomson,* he seldom ventures into introspection. When he does, he grows quizzical, gingerly, as though flexing a rusty skill again. Recalling his attack on Igor Stravinsky on the Russian composer's eightieth birthday, he assesses his possible motives. He found Stravinsky's "twelve-tone sanctimoniousness distasteful" and "deplored the celebrity apotheosis he had undergone."[27] To dispel the unctuous aroma clinging to his friend, Thomson delivered two blasts in print, calling Stravinsky "a manneristic composer in a manneristic age" and, more tartly, citing Metastasio's self-judgment, "a tolerable poet in an age of mediocrities."[28] (Thomson infuriated Stravinsky's wife, Vera, who subsequently snubbed him, but the composer seemed unruffled. In the photographs accompanying Thomson's text, we see the two composers sitting cozily together like old friends, as if nothing had happened.) Thomson sees that "My attack's chief interest is its seeming lack of motivation. I had no reason for diminishing a composer I profoundly admired, but we know what men will do to public monuments. And I do not regret it. Or do I? No, I can't. Living monuments are insupportable."[29] Since Thomson's criticism and autobiography are notable for their lack of petty malice toward rival composers, his brief self-interrogation is plausible, humorous rather than breast-beating, but it does not satisfy him, so he essays another explanation: "The purpose of my move *was* to test our friendship, to see if under blows it would survive."[30] But what causes this sudden spasm of doubt about a long friendship Thomson does not say. The reader is tantalized, confused, by this breach not of manners but of consistency, of surefootedness. In the last chapter of *Virgil Thomson,* the composer unexpectedly drops his temperate "I" and adopts the third person again ("he," "the musician," "your observer"), as if uneasy about this book's reticences and defecting to the camp of the self-examiners.

His only effort toward consistency has been to leave out things not actually seen by him. However, what he did see, and on

some evidence remembers, is not quite the whole of this recounting, for verity required that he explain just why it was
that he was where he was and how he happened to be looking
at what he saw. Which raised the question: Who was he anyway?[31]

This is a mischievous confession to make so late in the book, as if
Thomson wished to sow doubts about the authenticity of his record.
Does he not really know the centered man whom he has described
so ably for four hundred pages? His conversion to a self-dissecting
autobiography would be as suspicious as his writing twelve-tone
music after a lifetime of shunning it. The choice of the old-fashioned
word "verity" instead of the expected "truth" and the judicious legal
style of the paragraph (not the composer's normal voice) sound like
a comic hoax. Because Thomson is not a penitent type, or a dogmatic one, he probably felt the misgivings of other autobiographers
before him when they came to the end of their narrative and began
defending what they suspected was an exposed flank.

III

"THE MORE I squeeze the sponge of memory the more its stored
secretions flow,"[32] Henry James muses in *A Small Boy and Others*.
Where many autobiographers experience dearth or diffidence, James
has easy access to his unconscious; the sponge never runs dry. In
fact, he even apologizes for the constant high tide: "I confess myself
embarrassed by my very ease of recapture of my young consciousness; so that I perforce try to encourage lapses and keep my abundance down."[33] But the voices of the past are importunate, like fish
begging the fishermen to net them: "the names, as for fine old confused reasons, plead alike to my pen."[34] Impressions crowd in. The
words swarm. Sentences swell. For James, memory is phosphores-
cent. Any incident or figure or place from his childhood—a trip with
his father, a grotesque dowager aunt, a shop window, a classroom—is a treasure box to take out and turn over and sink with
into blissful speculation, into "rich awareness" of the settings, the
people, the stories attached to the original incident. James finds these
crannies of his mind covered with webs and tenderly brushes them

off for better viewing of the "rich and rounded picture"[35] that has cracked its frame, its grid, so that life pours in. James's circuitous style is the perfect image of his "rich and weighty consciousness," but he does not dissolve the outside so much as reconstitute it magically inside the imagination, offering a full fresco of his haunted past and its startling value to the mature artist appraising it. (The adjective "rich" takes pride of place so often that it must testify to James's unconscious faith in the abundance of his memories, like capital in the imagination's bank, even while he deprecates his early self.) Because he dotes on his memories, he indulges consciousness and catches himself lost at sea, temporarily without compass and sextant, trying to straighten out his course: "The point of my divagation, however, is," "I wander," "I stray," and similar locutions are signals to avoid capsizing his paragraphs. When James loiters over old posters and gives a voluminous recital of all the plays he attended as a boy, retrieving that seduction which led to the "shame of my sad failure" as a playwright, consciousness slides from the vivid to the vague (two of James's favorite adjectives), and the reader sympathetically balks at the tedious detail, which could, he thinks impatiently, be dispatched more quickly.

Nevertheless, it is the "wonder of consciousness in everything,"[36] James's grand theme in his *Autobiography,* that opens up vistas, "leads my imagination almost any dance."[37] "No particle that counts for memory," James insists, "or is appreciable to the spirit can be too tiny, and that experience, in the name of which one speaks, is all compact of them and shining with them."[38] From these particles—a quaint corner of Washington Square or John LaFarge's Newport studio, the delineation of his brother William's character or his father's unsystematic plan of education, for example—James, with one of the keenest "contemplative noses" among autobiographers, searches for "the representative design,"[39] "the aesthetic clue,"[40] and constructs the majestic, if unfinished, architecture of his consciousness—and his *Autobiography.* James's love of the "old surface" and psychological complexity is inexhaustible. The patterns he uncovers are not consecutive but periodic, like his sentences, but in addition to pacifying his memories of playing second fiddle, in an "ecstasy of resignation," to his gifted older brother, they prove he has broken out of the magnetic field of William's planetary influence and assumed proprietorship of his own life. One is struck by the suffusion of feeling in James's reminiscences, which usually prevents the dry rot of overrefinement from setting in. The Master of the House of Fiction maintains a strategic distance from the boy, his apprentice self, but also feels an intimate kinship with him.

It is in James's style that one sees enshrined—his detractors would say embalmed—his triumphant struggles. The length of his paragraphs permits him as autobiographer to reenact consciousness's amblings, to stare and absorb the groupings of facades, to enter a doorway richly ornamented or sit on a terrace sipping a drink while the mind plays with what the eye feasts on, then to digress, falter, and retrace his steps; the fugitive events and their attendant mysterious feelings linked in this elaborate circuit of suggestive syntax at last compose into a finely discriminating picture. James lavishes this attention to detail on obscure figures as much as on his brothers and sister. Here, for example, is an excerpt from James's sketch of Louis De Coppet, a boyhood chum who embodied "that 'sense of Europe' to which I feel that my very earliest consciousness waked":

The most vivid mark of the [De Coppet] brothers, and vividest on the part of the supersubtle Louis, was his French treatment of certain of our native local names, Ohio and Iowa for instance, which he rendered, as to their separate vowels, with a daintiness and a delicacy invidious and imperturbable, so that he might have been Chateaubriand declaiming Les Natchez at Madame Récamier's—O-ee-oh and Ee-o-wah; and proceeding in him, a violence offered to his serried circle of little staring and glaring New Yorkers supplied with the usual allowance of fists and boottoes, which, as it was clearly conscious, I recollect thinking unsurpassed for cool calm courage. Those *were* the right names—which we owed to the French explorers and Jesuit Fathers; so much the worse for us if we vulgarly didn't know it. I lose myself in admiration of the consistency, the superiority, the sublimity, of the not at all game-playing, yet in his own way so singularly sporting, Louis. He was naturally and incorruptibly American; the appearance being thus that the possession of indigenous English alone forms the adequate barrier and the assured racial ground. . . .

If I drop on his memory this apology for a bayleaf it is

from the fact of his having given the earliest, or at least the most personal, tap to that prefigurement of the manners of "Europe," which, inserted wedge-like, if not to say peg-like, into my young allegiance, was to split the tender organ into such unequal halves. His the toy hammer that drove in the very point of the golden nail.[41]

This homage to Louis De Coppet is a suave comic variation on the theme of European sophistication of (linguistic) manners versus American innocence and relative vulgarity. The correctness of this little Chateaubriand's pronunciation elicits from James a tribute that shades off into delicious lampoon: The "serried circle of little staring and glaring New Yorkers" stand on their native ground in the vulnerable armor of "fists and boottoes," poorly equipped for their jousting with the baronial De Coppet in the lists of idiom and pronunciation. The impressive pedigree of the European manner is rendered in sleek polysyllabic phrases, a Latinate musicality: "with a daintiness and a delicacy invidious and imperturbable," Louis changes the simple Indian names, Ohio and Iowa, into exotic American English. James writes sentences almost to a pitch pipe, dividing the sonorous abstract nouns and adjectives, like clusters of notes, into sparkling inflected rhythm: "the consistency, the superiority, the sublimity, of the not at all game-playing, yet in his own way so singularly sporting, Louis." Louis is placed perfectly at the end of the sentence with gracious deportment to receive and be anointed with the boys' admiration. (James is also a master of echoes.) In the coda, where James drops his bayleaf (a charming substitute for laurel leaf) on Louis's memory, he can revert to a simpler, more democratic diction—"tap," "wedge," "peg," "split," "toy," "nail"—which asserts the vigor of the domestic language. Style is the hammer that taps the pieces into perfect shape.

James's *Autobiography* is the epitome of the representation of consciousness in memory. Most American autobiographers have been reluctant to imitate or rival James, with the exception of Conrad Aiken in *Ushant*. Like a literary geologist, Aiken drills for meaning through the granite layers of the psyche and patiently explores the seams of experience and dream, refining so minutely the raw data he unearths that often the gritty acts, the materiality, of his life evaporate into trance. Aiken's model for consciousness is a Freudian one, which means that the route back and down to the trauma that decisively formed his emotional patterns, his parents' double suicide, is frequently blocked by impassable rock slides. Aiken soldiers on, digging and clearing a pathway through the palimpsest of consciousness, consulting the map of motifs thrown up by his dreams and art, and examining the gaps in the evidence, like a cryptic genetic code he cannot quite decipher. Disguise is symbolized by the list of dramatis personae he appends before the epigraphs as the key to this closet drama: Ezra Pound is called Rabbi Ben Ezra, T. S. Eliot Tsetse, Malcolm Lowry Hambo, etc.

What Aiken intends in *Ushant* is to capture consciousness as it plunges forward and back like a ship through angry oceanic waves. These "fettered leewardings" (to paraphrase Hart Crane) threaten wreckage, but emerge at last into serene, still harbors. Aiken is an extreme case among autobiographers: He virtually spurns verisimilitude; his narrative is a *"passacaglia* of symbols."[42] His three wives seldom appear in their own bodies or speak in their own voices; they are simply the three Loreleis (sirens) viewed from the deck of a ship through a fountain of sea spray. It is as though only the lyric consciousness can navigate the unsafe troughs of infidelity and deaths, and the voyage out:

—beginning without beginning, water without a seam, or sleep without a dream coterminous with sleep and the sleeper; flux and reflux, coil and moil; participation and concentration compounded, and then resolved again; participation and dispersal, then the subtle or violent catalysis, reorganization, the wave setting off in a new direction, the influence deflected, lapse and relapse, lapse and collapse, but out of the falling the magnificent rearising, out of the scend the pitch, out of the course of the ship the sheer, or the sheer of the ship towards stem and stern, the infinitesimal ship like a tiny luminous dream in the terrible, yes, lethal, yes, murderous, sleep of the sea—and yet not in any sense separate, ship from water, dream from sleeper, wave from wave, particle from particle, drop from drop, electron from nucleus, world from world, but all together participating and dispersing, participating and concentrating, wave-shaped and then plane-shaped, crest-shaped and then trough-shaped, revolving or

secretly still, the numbers constant for each element, limited
and finite yet part of an infinite series—[43]

In images drawn largely from chemistry and physics, this dithy-
rambic opening of *Ushant* describes the birth not of the author, as
we would expect, but of the cosmos itself. Participles and preposi-
tional phrases move in stately if violent pairs through the grammar
and the waves. There is no predication, though the pitch and roll
of nouns is held together by the caulk of conjunctions, by the "coil
and moil" of syntax. There is no "I," either, identity being submerged in sleep and dream, Wordsworth's "strange seas of
Thought."[44] But the strict cadences—the rise and fall, dispersal and
return, change and constancy—indicate that some grand principle
of form exists like mathematical laws that may, if found, guide
the mind through its, and the world's, deeps and thus avoid chaos.
Aiken's style, so self-consciously baroque, resembles elaborately
carved cartouches, but it does not here or elsewhere in *Ushant* draw
what Jean Starobinski calls the singular "contour of life,"[45] except
by indirection. We succumb at moments to the tintinnabulation of
Aiken's words, or steer through the ambiguous prose aided by the
buoys chiming their warnings, yet the sense of watching a performance by arcane abstractions never leaves the reader.

Henry James is, of course, Aiken's stylistic mentor. Aiken, who
lived for many years in Rye, England, where James had written his
late novels, salutes James's "fabulously involute symphonies . . . in
which . . . each new angle of approach revealed a different shade
or nuance of moral, or immoral, meaning."[46] The long paragraphs
through which James's consciousness winds sinuously like the four
rivers that, according to Hebrew legend, fertilize the Garden of Eden
are duplicated by Aiken in *Ushant*. The gaudy structures are large
as granaries, which he fills with "the precious golden pollen of the
past"[47] he has retrieved, sifted, and graded, and wonderful melodies
resound through them when the lumbering paraphernalia of his analytical framework does not clutter the space.[48]

But frequently in *Ushant*, Aiken's style succumbs to a disfiguring
murkiness and gets trapped in the "walled garden" of self-
consciousness. Even major people in his life fade into ghosts walking
on the battlements of his psyche or puppets manipulated by elaborate wires. He is prone to florid sermonizing and inkhorn diction,
which open cracks in his sentences from which the life drains away:

And as for language, the world of words, the books in the knapsack on his back, and the ancestral hankering to set about making one's own sibylline or hermetic onomasticon, out of which was to be architected one's own prismatic instant (if it came at last) of vision, whether of acceptance and wonder, or of denial and despair, as the logic of one's evolution might determine, this world had suddenly become as if possessed with a kind of mad erethism, exfoliating autonomously, word creating word, and meaning meaning, in an uninvoked parthenogenesis of galaxy that followed or preceded one into the dream.[49]

Like some mad lexicographer's progeny, Aiken's verbal mutants reproduce by a bizarre law of their own and speak a cosmic babble. (Mark Twain would have put a satirical arrow through this prose.) Aiken offers one half of the equation, "the world of words," but without its other half, "the [simple] words of the world," autobiography cannot breathe.

IV

"A GOOD STYLE," Paul Valéry remarks in *Aesthetics,* "implies a kind of *organization of originality,* a harmony that excludes the excesses of the imagination. Extravagance and eccentricity burst the bounds of a good style."[50] With his Gallic bias, Valéry praises an animated sobriety that keeps the howling devils of the unconscious under rational control; individuality is never domiciled too far away from types. Though he acknowledges writers' "dissimulations," Valéry pays homage to the canons of classical taste. Applied to American autobiography, his rules for "good style" seem unduly restrictive; only those whose temperament leans to moderation and balance, like Franklin and Jane Addams and Eudora Welty, would escape Valéry's censure. But in American autobiographies there seems to be a tidal pull in the direction of many "uttering tongues": styles that are by turns wild, delicate, swaggering, comic, even uncouth, corresponding to the promise of abundance, of being all things to oneself, implicit in democratic ideology. "Each life," Italo Calvino observes, "is an encyclopedia, a library, an inventory of objects, a series of styles, and everything can be constantly shuffled and reordered in every way conceivable."[51] Through such multiple subtleties and divagations the real Me—the single solid self long extolled by psychoanalysis—is nearly impossible to pin down, escaping as it does into protean shapes and postures. In perhaps the prototypical autobiographical poem, Whitman's *Song of Myself,* the poet fashioned a medley of voices that proved useful for later autobiographies because it effectively combined insides and outsides: The bravura of his verbal cakewalk, "the great psalm of the republic" (democratic religiosity at its highest pitch), a confiding erotic whisper, the "barbaric yawp," the huckster's blather, the hum of the soul's "valvèd voice," are like Charles Ives's music, encyclopedic and intimate. American autobiographies achieve their harmony by successfully organizing the "excesses of the imagination" Valéry worried about. Eccentricity, even when willed, is pursued as a blessing: the liberation of the self from the dread of banality. Style, memory's ally, strives to make whole the split between the sentient self and the observing ego. When this retrospective quest fails in a romantic autobiography, the result tends toward hysteria or prolixity; in a classicist autobiography, the failure expresses itself in tepid passion, an excess of order. But it is the chief glory of American autobiographies that, to transplant William Gass's wonderful phrase, their "pied variety of voice"[52] reverberates through history and literature, describing the grand symphony of American culture.

2

"That Insinuating Man":
The Autobiography of Benjamin Franklin

One does not dress for private Company as for a publick Ball.
—BENJAMIN FRANKLIN, Autobiography

I

No OTHER autobiographical narrative by an American projects such an air of snug self-fulfillment, of a man in joyous harmony with himself, as Benjamin Franklin's. Slippered sage, genial titan, the navigator of the "Argonauts" in a "Heroic age" that overthrew "colonial subservience,"[1] Franklin seemed to thrive on putting a confused world into workable order without disordering himself. With his genius for theater, he had a knack of making the world believe that the rise of Benjamin Franklin and the rise of America from humble beginnings to prosperous self-mastery fell jointly under an applauding Providence. Franklin's public record as benefactor to community, colony, science, country, and not least to himself was so imposing that even Thomas Jefferson, a man not given to encomiums, hailed Franklin as "the greatest man and ornament of the age and country in which he lived."[2]

Unlike most autobiographers, Franklin felt no need to scrutinize or "justify" himself. The *Autobiography* contains no intimations of neurotic behavior, no dreams or nightmares, no crises of the spirit, scarcely any inwardness. His personal disclosures lack those moments of uncertainty, terror, or anxiety that most autobiographers, from the Puritan minister Jonathan Edwards to the novelist Richard Wright, single out. Since Franklin's life is remarkable for its lack of divided self, guilt, depressions, or defeats—the humiliation before the Privy Council in 1764 was unusual and lay outside the *Autobiography*'s chronology—one is tempted to say that he appears to be the only person in American history without an unconscious.

Franklin ignored with relaxed conscience the Protestant insistence, phrased bluntly by John Wesley, that "Next to self-will and pride, the most fatal disease with which we are born is love of the world."[3] It was self-evident to Philadelphia's chief *philosophe* that God had placed man amid the world's plenty for the purpose of delighting in the chances to know it, to exploit it, and to excel in it. If Philadelphia was not quite so cosmopolitan a city as London, it nevertheless offered many more opportunities for getting ahead. Franklin parlayed his luck, his will to power, and a new country's historical momentum into an international celebrity. No wonder he took as his motto *Ça ira*—"It will all come right in the end"—and, using a printer's image, said, "that were it offer'd to my Choice, I should have no Objection to a Repetition of the same Life from its Beginning, only asking the Advantage Authors have in a second Edition to correct some Faults of the First."[4] (43) He led a charmed life, its few "sinister Accidents and Events" casting only a faint shadow across it.

Franklin's fame and self-satisfaction could not, of course, leave him immune to criticism. John Adams, ever captious about a rival, reproved Franklin's hedonism and disheveled habits of conducting diplomatic business in France, and thought him both vain and "grossly ignorant" of history.[5] Franklin's later detractors viewed him as a tinkerer who embodied the manipulative ethic of capitalist America, as if Franklin's lightning rod had ushered in the machine age of gadgets and gimmicks.

In the 1920s, William Carlos Williams and D. H. Lawrence published essays on Franklin that sought to knock his statue off its pedestal. They gibed relentlessly at his precepts. For Williams, Franklin is the mercenary advocate of a "general happy mediocrity."[6] He is "our wise prophet (profit?) of chicanery, the great buffoon, the face on the penny stamp."[7] Williams is appalled by the absence in Franklin of what Sainte-Beuve called "the fine flower of

Benjamin Franklin Drawing Electricity from the Sky,
Benjamin West, c. 1805

enthusiasm, tenderness, sacrifice—all that is the dream, and also the charm and honor of poetic natures,"[8] their place taken, Williams believes, by a suave, conniving thrift. He arraigns Franklin for a shortage of imagination, for failing to notice, for instance, the grandeur of the American landscape. The figure Kant viewed as Prometheus shrinks, in this reading, to a chained parochial dilettante: "The greatest winner of his day, he [Franklin] represents a voluptuousness of omnivorous energy brought to a dead stop by the rock of New World inopportunity. His energy never attained to a penetrant gist."[9]

For D. H. Lawrence, Franklin is a "dry, moral utilitarian little democrat,"[10] responsible for "that barbed wire moral enclosure that Poor Richard rigged up."[11] In a series of hilarious insults, Lawrence derides Franklin as a clubby trickster, a social busybody "never more than a great citizen"[12] (as though that commodity were in plentiful supply), the arch "dummy American whose God is the heavenly storekeeper."[13] The sly pleasantries of *Poor Richard's Almanac* in particular enrage Lawrence. Franklin's jocose attacks on hereditary and royal power are the sleazy underbelly of his self-reliance, just as his advice to tradesmen and farmers to be frugal and industrious were rules, promulgated by a Master of Subterfuge, for taking advantage (a key word in Franklin's vocabulary). Morality paid dividends. The *Autobiography* merely added a layer of lacquer to the cheap patented materialism of *Poor Richard's Almanac* and *The Way to Wealth*.

These charges, a mixture of the serious and the peevish, are not surprising. The image of the self-made winner especially invites defacement. Many-sided as he was, even Franklin could not be all things to all men. He was, as Williams noted, deficient in aesthetic sense, and in an age in which religious fervor often counted mightily, his spirituality was tepid. There is not a tragic bone in Franklin's body; he made no Faustian pacts in order to uncover the secrets of nature. The image of Prometheus is misleading, because far from being haughty, or engaged in godlike feuds, or suffering a lonely and heroic punishment for the gifts he bestowed on mankind, Franklin claimed only that he was an uncommon common man temperamentally suited for investigating useful knowledge, not the self. He was vain enough to enjoy his enormous popularity, but he did not grovel for it.

For men like Adams and Lawrence, given to irascible moral dogmatism and violent rhetoric, Franklin's brand of folksy tolerance
could only offend and appear self-serving. The mixed-up present did
not faze him or unbalance him, because he was not, to borrow John
Woolman's words, "single to the truth,"[14] someone who interpreted
principles strictly. "What one relishes, nourishes,"[15] Poor Richard
had said, and Franklin relished playing a repertoire of roles, aliases,
and personas, from Silent Dogood, Poor Richard, and Father Abraham to the septuagenarian ambassador landing in France dressed
like a backwoodsman and soon hobnobbing with the aristocracy
and intelligentsia. These roles were, however, tied to Franklin's central self. Miraculously, the lines never seemed to get tangled, as if
history cooperated with Franklin's will to smooth his way through
a churlish but malleable world—if not to the heavenly city, then to
a happy, successful life which proved that "Human Felicity is pro-
duc'd not so much by great Pieces of good Fortune that seldom
happen, as by little Advantages that occur every Day." (207) Franklin manages his rags-to-riches fable with the same skill, composure,
and humor with which he managed the "Scrambles of Life" and his
negotiations with the Proprietaries, the English, and the French.
The sprawl of his narrative becomes a testimonial to his busyness,
versatility, and amiable faults. It is not a serious breach of his unified self, any more than his lapses of memory are. He had to compose the memoir piecemeal because he was interrupted by the
Revolutionary War and the public affairs of the young nation, and
he apologizes for an old man's ramblings and confesses that order-
liness was the one virtue that eluded him.

In all four sections of the *Autobiography,* time is an ally that can
be enlisted on behalf of an aspiring and energetic young man or
country. Time's amplitude entrances Franklin. The lesson of the
Autobiography and of its hero's life is that man's spirited will, not
God's interfering hand, affects events. Franklin has no conception
of sacred time. Thus if the thread of narrative continuity snaps, it
can be mended as easily as a fisherman's net; if chance strews obstacles in his path, they can be removed and forward motion to his
goals resumed.

Time was, for Franklin, a natural resource, which could be frit-
tered away or used wisely and efficiently, laid out with pleasing
regularity like Philadelphia's streets. Franklin became colonial

America's greatest publicist for the habit of virtue by stressing the benefits that accrue from the proper "Disposition of [his] Time." Part II of the *Autobiography* dwells at great length on Franklin's famous plan for self-improvement. Like a gardener, he systematically sets out to uproot the faults of his unmethodical nature:

> And like him who having a Garden to weed, does not attempt to eradicate all the bad Herbs at once, which would exceed his Reach and his Strength, but works on one of the Beds at a time, and having accomplish'd the first proceeds to a Second; so I should have, (I hoped) the encouraging Pleasure of seeing on my Pages the Progress I made in Virtue, by clearing successively my Lines of their Spots, till in the End by a Number of Courses, I should be happy in viewing a clean Book after a thirteen Weeks daily Examination. (152)

The task of imposing order on the friendly clutter of his mind was harder than he anticipated, as he concedes, despite the charts, prayers, mottoes, calendars, and memoranda he employed. Weeds, following the laws of nature, always sprang up again. Moral perfection eluded him. The "Multiplicity of Affairs" prevented absolute control of his time. Typically, he settles for an indulgent appearance of virtue rather than the exacting reality: "by the Endeavor [I became] a better and a happier Man than I otherwise should have been, if I had not attempted it." (156)

Franklin compared social progress and changes in history to changes in himself: They occurred not by sudden dramatic acts but by the patient accumulation of small items. Once he had put down the flooring for his business prosperity, he could devote himself to scientific experiments and become a steward of civic welfare. Once the soil of public opinion was diligently tilled and the seed of a new idea planted, it would ripen and be harvested—a hospital opened, a university founded, fortifications built. For instance, Franklin's proposal at the Albany Conference in 1754 to unify the colonies in a common defense was undermined at the time by provincial jealousy and the British Crown's fears that its prerogatives were being infringed upon, but concerted action became both logical policy and patriotic zeal in 1774, when the colonies were united.

While Franklin pretends in the *Autobiography* that a rational, linear pattern exists in which governments topple, armies are defeated, treaties are signed, commerce expands, he knows that strict chronology is elusive; the structure of his memoir is slapdash. Like most autobiographers, he finds himself seduced by events and memories that run counter to his didactic intention to "present," as Benjamin Vaughan put it in his hortatory letter inserted between parts I and II, "a table of the internal circumstances of your country . . . the manners and situation of a rising people." (135) In the epistolary first part of the *Autobiography,* Franklin costumes himself as a picaresque hero, a Tom Jones on the make, who, before settling down into his influential role in the social order, passed through dangers to his virtue and chastened his impetuosity. The world is large, and so is his aptitude for benefiting himself and others, even as he gets in and out of scrapes with debt, infidelity, and death. Mishaps come out right, because of luck, his own initiative and adaptability, and a deep instinctive caution.

The Elder Statesman enjoys reliving the boy's brash antics and physical strength: "I carried up and down Stairs a large Form of Types in each hand when others carried but one in both Hands." (99) Even errors of judgment, like spending the money entrusted to him for safekeeping by Mr. Vernon, are mere temporary setbacks on the road to spectacular success. To the mature Franklin, the raw apprentice's mild dissipations are the lovable flaws of a privileged innocent. In hindsight, there is no rivalry between principle and inclination that can't be resolved in favor of a judicious self-regard. The young man of eighteen in London who haunted playhouses and wrote a philosophical pamphlet that sober minds construed as atheistic also improved his skills at Watts' Printing House and "acquir'd considerable Influence" over his fellow workers.

This precocious superiority is a gift of temperament, we are led to feel, not merely the manipulated myth of the self-created man overcoming handicaps of speech and writing and always computing the utility of ideas before acting. The paragon of virtue whose life is "fit to be imitated" because he is levelheaded and industrious does not seize control of the *Autobiography* until Part II. Before he acquired the habits that led him to become the well-adjusted propagandist for the prudent virtues, Franklin had to come to terms with the consequences of a playful, irreverent personality, which often got him in trouble with authority. In a highly paternalistic society, and in an era in which an ultimate rebellion against authority was waged and won, the question of why authority did not daunt Franklin is crucial and bears sustained analysis. "Any autobiographical account of a person's childhood," Erik Erikson warns us, "requires a key for the unconscious motto guiding the repression of some items and the special selection of others."[16] In the case of Franklin's *Autobiography,* the key is his artful dodging, as he alternates revolt against authority with accommodation to it, gives in to headstrong impulse and then reins himself in before losing control. The bland, comic hypocrisies that fill the pages of the *Autobiography* are the traps the clever sage set for the unwary reader. He knew what his audience wanted—a sensible strategy for getting ahead—and he gave it to them, his instructions laced with a humor as broad as his girth. His opinions about sex, women, education, Indians, and religion can be traced to the decisions he made in childhood and early manhood.

II

FROM ITS first pages, with their platitudes about God's favor, the *Autobiography* adopts a tone of disarming irony. Like a family antiquarian poring over genealogical charts, Franklin traces his bloodlines to 1555 in the village of Ecton, Northamptonshire, and discovers—presto!—kin of "decent plainness" who rose in station from relative obscurity. His uncle Thomas, in particular, "being ingenious, and encourag'd in Learning," became a "considerable man" and a "chief mover of all publick-Spirited Undertakings in his county." This ancestral blend of civic duty and talent "Transmigrated" the Atlantic and settled in his nephew Benjamin, who of course later bragged that the colonies had done away with pedigree as a test of a man's merit. This abbreviated history of his family's origins is more than an exercise in nostalgia. It indicates that even Franklin believed he did not spring full-grown from his own head.

But more striking than Franklin's closeness to his uncle is his special position in the family. By the official register at Ecton, "I perceiv'd that I was the youngest Son of the youngest Son for 5 Generations back," (46) he notes, as if he were singled out of a large family for distinction. This quirk of the order of birth meant that

Franklin would start his life under kindly auspices; he would not lose his identity in the crowd of siblings sitting down at his father's table.

It is a shame that one of New England's itinerant artisans wasn't commissioned to paint a group portrait of the Franklin family or at least of the parents, Abiah Folger and Josiah Franklin. Franklin's one extended picture of his father in the *Autobiography* is a central document, which must be quoted in full:

> He had an excellent Constitution of Body, was of middle Stature, but well set and very strong. He was ingenious, could draw prettily, was skill'd a little in Music and had a clear pleasing Voice, so that when he play'd Psalm Tunes on his Violin and sung withal as he sometimes did on an Evening after the Business of the Day was over, it was extreamly agreable to hear. He had a mechanical Genius too, and on occasion was very handy in the Use of other Tradesmen's Tools. But his great Excellence lay in a sound Understanding, and solid Judgment in prudential Matters, both in private and publick Affairs. In the latter indeed he was never employed, the numerous Family he had to educate and the straitness of his Circumstances, keeping him close to his Trade, but I remember well his being frequently visited by leading People, who consulted him for his Opinion in Affairs of the Town or of the Church he belong'd to and show'd a good deal of Respect for his Judgment and Advice. He was also much consulted by private Persons about their Affairs when any Difficulty occur'd, and frequently chosen an Arbitrator between contending Parties. At his Table he lik'd to have as often as he could, some sensible Friend or Neighbour, to converse with, and always took care to start some ingenious or useful Topic for Discourse, which might tend to improve the Minds of his Children. By this means he turn'd our Attention to what was good, just, and prudent in the Conduct of Life. (54–5)

In the matter of eighteenth-century portraiture, this conventional likeness strikes off its subject with stiff, unadorned realism relieved by a few touches of sensibility (Josiah draws prettily, sings, plays the violin). Though not as affluent as his English forebears, he wears his tradesman's virtues with an obliging sobriety, sitting at the head of his table, revered if not loved for his firm righteousness. He is not a forbidding person. He is indeed sociable. And though forced by the economic burdens of raising a large family to keep "close to his Trade," he achieves standing in the community as an unofficial magistrate. As in his son, there is no dissonance between the public and private selves. His virtues reap rewards: good health, longevity, an enviable reputation among "leading People" for "solid Judgment," a sedate conviviality, all of which Benjamin coveted and obtained. And since Josiah is a jack-of-all-trades ("ingenious," one of Franklin's favorite adjectives of praise, is used twice), his son's identification with him seems nearly complete.

It is clear that Josiah Franklin did not rule his children by fear or fiat, nor did he try to break the will of his boisterous young son. He shaped his children's characters, drew them to what was "good, just, and prudent," by affectionate guidance and reasonable discipline. He patiently refuted his son's sophistical plea that stealing a pile of stones to build a wharf for his playmates was useful work, by explaining that "nothing was useful which was not honest" (a precept Franklin adhered to his entire life); he urged his son to give up or modify his heady taste for disputes and Socratic bullying (a predilection hard to get quit of); and scanning his son's essays, he criticized their faulty logic and rhetoric (Franklin acknowledged the validity of these strictures). There is no retrospective quarrel in the *Autobiography* with his father's decisions to take him out of grammar school and not to send him to Harvard. His father did not have the money and thought that the educated gained a "mean living," and perhaps sensed that a theologically oriented curriculum and doctrinal wrangles would not suit his son's talents. But when Benjamin pushed for approval to go to sea, Josiah put his foot down and, after a tour of possible trades, apprenticed him to his brother James's printing establishment.

Even this mild authority galled Franklin. In behavior that must have alarmed and vexed his father, who was a devout "Presbyterian,"[17] Franklin evaded public worship and, worse, his "indiscrete Disputations about Religion began to make me pointed at with Horror by good People as an Infidel or Atheist." (71)

Moreover, Josiah strongly opposed Benjamin's wish to break the bonds of his indenture, which he said left him subject to beatings, verbal abuse, and bitter conflict with James. We may speculate that Franklin also resented being in a secondary or inferior position. In a footnote he bluntly remarks that his brother's "harsh and tyrannical Treatment of me, might be a means of impressing me with that Aversion to arbitrary Power that has struck to me thro' my whole Life." (69) This "Aversion" later extended to the proprietors, Parliament, and the King of England. In composing his satirical squibs against the government, under the safety of an alias, Franklin had gained an unsavory reputation as "a young Genius that had a turn for Libelling and Satyr." (69)

So he ran away from home. The old man writing at his desk dwells on this turning point in his life with undisguised pleasure. He is, for him, unusually lavish with detail. The tempo of the narrative picks up speed; there is only a cursory dissection of motive, but we can watch his character in action. The ruse Benjamin concocted to effect his escape, that he had "got a naughty girl with Child, whose Friends would compel me to marry her," (71) typifies Franklin's fancy evasive footwork. Why, he seems to be hinting, should I be punished for "my Youth, Inexperience, and the Knavery of others" (115)—note that the girl is naughty, not Franklin, and that adult authority is unpalatable (he knew that his own family would not have countenanced such sexual levity or irresponsibility).

Franklin's flight to Philadelphia shows us, then, his as yet uncommitted and immature self. Willing to risk a lasting rift with his family—he did not send news of his whereabouts for several months, until urged to do so by his brother-in-law Captain Robert Holmes; he was clearly enjoying his freedom—he set out for a strange city, "a Boy of but 17, without the least Recommendation to, or any Knowledge of any Person in the place, and with very little Money in my Pocket." (71) What he did carry with him was an enterprising spirit and the flexible self-assurance that he could live by his wits and his skills as a printer. Franklin's energy was irresistibly bold: Already, on the first journey, he rescued a drunken Dutchman from drowning, pulled an oar (spurning payment for his toil), displayed no bashfulness. He was fortune's pet and its enthusiast. Significantly, Franklin doesn't label this flight a regrettable *erratum*.

Franklin's "first Entry" into Philadelphia, a wonderful piece of storytelling, is designed, he says, to "compare such unlikely Beginnings with the Figure I have since made there." (75) By emphasizing the "awkward ridiculous Appearance" of the anonymous bumpkin-conqueror, surveying his prospects, he sharpens the contrast with the leading citizen who rides out of the city many years later, accompanied by a troop of guards in full regalia, their naked swords unsheathed, as if he were a governor. But in fact, the comical, shabby, tired, hungry Franklin, who falls asleep at a Quaker meeting (he's politely awakened after the service) and saunters down Chestnut Street eating a puffy roll, displays other traits: generosity (he gives away two rolls, not hoarding provisions for his next day's meal) and shrewd judgment in selecting a resident who can recommend a "reputable House" to lodge in.

During his early years in Philadelphia and London, "remote from the Eye and Advice of my Father," as he phrased it, Franklin prospered where other young men would have been unhinged, because he could wield his nervy will for his own gain. Although his identity was unformed, vacillating, aggressive, he cannily attached himself to a series of surrogate fathers—Mr. Denham, Andrew Hamilton—who could promote his career by extending material aid or advice that rescued him from low company, potential debt, or "barren pleasure." When governors, doctors, and rich merchants sought him out for his knowledgeable talk about books and his jocular manners, and encouraged him to set up in business as a printer, assuring him that his rival, the erratic Keimer, would surely fail, he was flattered. When Governor Keith and Colonel French invite him to drink wine at the tavern, treating him with cordial familiarity, "Keimer star'd like a pig poison'd"; the phrase has a smug malice in its sting. Similarly, returning to Boston as a dandified Croesus, he stages a "raree show" and jingles coins to impress the journeymen printers in his brother's shop and to needle his brother. Franklin's superior airs are signs of a need to be the lordly one, the man on top. (This desire to be in control is present in all parts of his life.) The autobiographer, however, concurs with Josiah's judgment that though powerful men endorsed his talents, he was not ready to be trusted with responsibility.

There was a rashness in Franklin's temperament, an impulsiveness, that he only gradually came to govern and which often led him astray in the choice of friends. Not all his friends were, like the members of the Junto, upright, literate, conscientious citizens, the cream of Philadelphia's middle-class intelligentsia, self-made men like himself. Franklin was drawn to mildly scandalous outsiders like Dr. John Brown of Burlington, who had "wickedly undertook, some years after, to travestie the Bible in doggerel verse, as Cotton had done Virgil." (74) John Collins was a sot whose drinking clouded his mind and ruined a promising career; James Ralph was a bigamist; George Webb, a dashing, improvident lad, had like Franklin run away from his people and, penniless, been transported to the colonies; Hugh Meredith, a boon companion, drank heavily. These men were, in a sense, Franklin's alter egos, what he might have become had he not put the brakes on his prankish, careless nature. Like Prince Hal consorting with Falstaff, he enjoyed their "loose behavior," their raffish unconcern with the very canons of duty and respectability Josiah Franklin had taught him. America afforded men opportunities, liberty, to create themselves, but this process was frightening: The self, once it yielded to desires, could run out of control and be smashed to pieces. Franklin always manages in the nick of time to extricate himself from situations that would permanently tarnish his budding reputation and estrange him from his father's morality. American conventional wisdom declared that one could be anything and everything, but pursuing the wrong vocation or not curbing wayward instincts led to failure: Ralph was pilloried by Pope in *The Dunciad* for his lame verses, though he became a useful writer of prose; Meredith blundered as a printer, but as a farmer in North Carolina published valuable information on that colony's agriculture; George Webb never amounted to anything, and Collins, unable to stop drinking, died a scapegrace.

Franklin also sowed wild oats, but in the *Autobiography* he brushes off as youthful peccadilloes his several visits to prostitutes (where by good luck he avoided syphilis) and his advances to his friend James Ralph's mistress in London. "Rarely use Venery but for Health or Offspring, Never to Dullness, Weakness, or the Injury of your own or another's Peace or Reputation," (150) was the twelfth of Franklin's self-injunctions, which he blithely ignored whenever it inconvenienced his pleasure. Chastity was for the next fellow. "That hard-to-be-govern'd Passion of Youth hurried me frequently into Intrigues with low Women that fell in my Way," (128) Franklin recalls. Syntax and memory meet in a roguish balance: The hyphenated adjective enacts a mock-heroic struggle to control his passion, but failing, he hurries forward to pluck the ripe if low fruit that dropped into his hands; the world conspires happily with his appetite for tarts. The fall is entirely the women's. (Imagine what Rousseau or Boswell would have made of such episodes!)

That the amorous fang bit sweetly into Franklin's flesh is one of his endearing traits. We are pleased to think of him, at seventy-nine, in love with Mme. Helvétius, grumbling at her mild reprimand of him for cancelling an engagement: "Madame I am waiting till the nights are longer." (This remark may be apocryphal.)[18] The Franklin who dandled Mme. Brillon on his knee and wooed Mme. Helvétius with gallant compliments was not shocked, as John and Abigail Adams were, by French sexual morality, which they thought dissolute. Yet in the *Autobiography* he modulated his own passion and worldly tolerance into a distant rumble, a droll inadvertence. With deadpan naïveté, he blandly urges his countrymen to practice strict continence, not to offend public notions of propriety. As hypocrisies go, Franklin's is innocent enough, even entertaining, another one of his bagatelles. But why did he advocate such devious policy when his own behavior was so markedly different?

In Philadelphia, America's most "easy, tolerant, and contented"[19] city, as Henry Adams noted, Franklin's fathering of an illegitimate son did not damage his standing and credit with the community (nor did it hurt the career of William Franklin). But since his libido was not a salable commodity and might endanger his growing business, Franklin turned a potential liability to his advantage by diverting his sexual energy into the most socially acceptable compromises: marriage and work. And if his craving for distinction became his overriding sensual hunger, his multifarious activities were the perfect feast to appease that hunger. What Melville in *Israel Potter* called Franklin's "wild slyness"[20] was thus safely tamed.

Particular women are curiously absent from Franklin's *Autobiography,* though his relations with them in life are fairly well documented. From his near silence on the subject, one might conclude that in eighteenth-century America women seldom left the hearth and rarely occupied their husbands' or lovers' consciousness. Not one scene in the *Autobiography* sparkles with the frolicsome anticipation of Samuel Sewall's courtship of the Widow Winthrop in his *Diary.* In thus relegating women to the periphery of society, Franklin is, of course, following the conventions of his historical period.

About his mother, Abiah Folger, for example, he is stingy of details. We learn from his account that she came from an illustrious family, one of "the first Settlers in New England," (51) bore ten children and suckled them all, lived respectably to eighty-five years of age; her son out of filial gratitude inscribed on her tombstone that she was a "discreet and virtuous Woman." (56) That is her entire presence in the *Autobiography*. But even if she were only a retiring, pious homebody, she would surely have exerted an important influence on her ambitious, somewhat unruly son, who describes himself as perhaps a too "saucy and provoking" (70) boy. Being one of many in the Franklin brood must, the reader suspects, have caused a jostle with his brothers and sisters for maternal attention—it is not surprising that when Franklin married he had a small family—but it also seems likely that being the youngest son and brightest child, he would also be doted upon and given the liberty to yield to his inclinations. From Franklin's enjoyment of his landlady's company on his first trip to London, his sixteen-year friendship with Mrs. Stevenson during his extended London sojourn, and his famous remark that "In all your amours you should prefer old women to young ones . . . because they have greater knowledge of the world,"[21] one infers that Franklin had a warm intimacy with his mother—or at least a longing for one. (These matrons were like chaperones, steering him away from base women.)

Franklin's account of his delayed marriage to Deborah Read is brief but telling; he imagines *her* perspective. She had mockingly watched his shabby arrival at Philadelphia. Because of her family's doubts about his financial prospects, he jilted her (he speaks cryptically of the event) and quickly forgot her in the solacing arms of London belles. He gravely rebukes himself for his rude apostasy and corrects the *erratum,* but their marriage, contracted after Franklin rejected another match because the dowry offered was too small, seems one of convenience. In treating marriage as a business transaction, Franklin was conforming to eighteenth-century custom, but an emotional blank stands where the heart should be. A slight unpleasant smell of the schemer clings to Franklin.

Marriage helped Franklin win his way in Philadelphia. He praises Deborah Read as a "good and faithful Helpmate"[22] who cuts up linen rags to make paper and tends the shop. She appears hardworking, genteel, economically functional, and seemingly satisfied with her roles of wife and mother. When she buys china and a silver spoon because she thinks his eminence deserves them, Franklin protests coyly at her extravagance, though in 1757 he shipped back from London enough handsome furniture and household wares to suit a member of the high-living Philadelphia gentry he had become. (So much for frugality!) *Poor Richard's Almanac,* written during the years of his marriage, titillated its readers with shoddy tavern jokes about the institution: "Keep your eyes wide open before marriage, half shut afterwards."[23] Poor Richard's wife, a good-natured shrew, was probably modeled on Deborah Read. She was not his intellectual equal, so that after 1750, he began a series of platonic relationships with young women, Catherine Ray being his first and Polly Stevenson his aptest pupil, which permitted him to flirt and tease and dispense avuncular advice. "Imitate Socrates," he said and did: He talked about what interested him not to Xanthippe but to Diotima. When he became Pennsylvania's and later America's ambassador abroad, he did not, as John Adams did, grieve over his long separations from his wife.[24] Literally and symbolically, Franklin was far away when Deborah Read died.

III

TWO MAJOR themes emerge from Franklin's presentation of himself in the *Autobiography:* his ability to reconcile opposing ideas and desires, both internal and external, and his manner of rebelling against authority and of then becoming the authority without inciting rebellion in others. In childhood and early manhood, as we have seen, when Franklin was improvising identities, he tended to behave in contradictory ways, sometimes asserting himself with what he called "Giddiness and Inconstancy" and sometimes practicing an iron self-control, thereby sidestepping censure or ruin. In 1728, when he formed a printing partnership with Hugh Meredith, Franklin seemed to have settled into a comfortable identity, and his dramatic rise to success accelerated. When the main chance came he seized it brilliantly; he judged his business rivals with acumen (long after the event, he gloats decorously at putting Keimer out of business). Schooling himself in patience paid off, though the struggle was harder than legend—or Franklin—has painted it. The image of an industrious Franklin pushing his wheelbarrow through the streets of Philadelphia has had a symbolic status in American folklore as the quintessential Franklin gesture, like a Norman Rockwell cover for the *Saturday Evening Post*.

But Franklin's real attitudes to power and his astute methods of increasing and consolidating it are far more interesting. They entailed a tactical suppression of the self so that he would not be accused of—or perceived as—seeking dominance. This meant dropping his habit of "abrupt Contradiction, and positive Argumentation," (64) and persuading people to adopt his proposals by not pushing forward the "I" in any enterprise, be it commercial or intellectual, and thereby rousing opposition. In a provincial society like Philadelphia's, where connections counted heavily, he curried favor and patronage among the merchants and in the Pennsylvania Assembly by impressing the leading men with his superior craftsmanship and reliability and by cultivating their goodwill through a winning deference. In the *Autobiography*, Franklin gives a classic instance of his strategy in action:

My first Promotion was being chosen in 1736 Clerk of the General Assembly. The Choice was made that Year without Opposition; but the Year following when I was again propos'd (the Choice, like that of the Members being annual) a new Member made a long Speech against me, in order to favour some other Candidate. I was however chosen; which was the more agreeable to me, as besides the Pay for immediate Service as Clerk, the Place gave me a better opportunity of keeping up an Interest among the Members, which secur'd to me the Business of Printing the Votes, Laws, Paper Money, and other occasional Jobbs for the Public, that on the whole were profitable. I therefore did not like the Opposition of this new Member, who was a Gentleman of Fortune, and Education, with Talents that were likely to give him in time great Influence in the House, which indeed afterwards happened. I did not however aim at gaining his Favour by paying any servile Respect to him, but after some time took this other Method. Having heard that he had in his Library a certain very scarce and curious Book I wrote a Note to him expressing my Desire of perusing that Book, and requesting he would do me the Favour of lending it to me for a few Days. He sent it immediately; and I return'd it in about a Week, with another Note expressing strongly my Sense of the Favour. When we next met in the House he spoke to me, (which he had never done before) and with great Civility. And he ever afterwards manifested a Readiness to serve me on all Occasions, to his Death. This is another Instance of the Truth of an old Maxim I had learnt, which says, *He that has once done you a Kindness will be more ready to do you another, than he whom you yourself have obliged.* And it shows how much more profitable it is prudently to remove, than to resent, return and continue inimical Proceedings. (172)

There is nothing venal in Franklin's shrewd campaign to disarm a potential adversary who might dry up his sources of profit. Though "servile" and "service" spring from the same root, the Latin *servus,* or slave, they are vastly different in psychological connotation: "servile" means an odious dependence, whereas "service" means an equality of footing, of mutually beneficial interests.[25] Franklin's self-esteem would not brook his being the subsidiary person in a relationship. Melville's remark that "having carefully weighed the world, Franklin could act any part in it"[26] is therefore not quite correct. Franklin's skill at gaining access to and befriending the "principal People"—Isaac Norris in the above passage—is based on a sharp psychological perception that the power to bestow favor flatters the giver's *amour propre,* where receiving it puts him in a situation of uneasy debt. Franklin's indirect approach to Norris by requesting a rare book successfully disguises his real motive and adroitly neutralizes potential conflict. He knows what he is doing and what effects he will get. Prudence is the lever to power and prestige and the retention of profit. This scene deserves to be the frontispiece to the *Autobiography.*

Not surprisingly, Franklin's suppleness and poise were sensed by merchants, governors, savants, Assembly, Continental Congress—and often tapped. They chose him as spokesman and negotiator for their interests. His assessments are seldom marred by the grumpy dogmatism of a John Adams; he could coolly separate a man from his actions or ideas, even when they were hostile to him. Keith's effusive promises to start him in the printing business were a stupid trick to play on a credulous young man, but Franklin bears him no grudge and handsomely admits that Keith was a competent governor. Power did not turn his head any more than authority daunted him. If the *Autobiography* plays down the bitterness of the quarrels with the Proprietors, it also furnishes abundant evidence of why when conciliation and rational persuasion failed to change the unjust policies of King, Proprietors, or Parliament, he was not afraid, at age seventy, to join the revolt for independence. Rebelling against his brother's "despotism" and flouting his father's will had paved the way. In the subversive affability of Poor Richard's sarcasm, the true Benjamin Franklin speaks: "The King's cheese is half wasted in parings: But no matter, 'tis made of the peoples milk."[27]

By avoiding the extremes that wrecked other men's lives, Franklin's career flourished. He owed his deliverance to keeping his eyes alert to the needs of his society; he had foresight, could grasp at once from experience the utility of lighthouses or a cleanly swept marketplace. His will "trained to power," he was never nonplussed by the unexpected. Franklin's ethic was neither unprincipled nor collusive. He prided himself on being, and his society regarded him as, an "honest man," who kept his word as scrupulously as he kept his accounts and contracts. In the absence of impersonal instruments of business, such as checks and public auditors, a man's reputation and word were very important, as the Quaker merchants with whom he dealt understood so profoundly.[28] When he took over the postmastership, he organized it efficiently, and vowing not to exploit or crowd out business novices, as Andrew Bradford had done to him, he acted accordingly.

The other side of Franklin's acquisitive nature was his inquisitive one. His scientific feats and civic projects came out of a disinterested intelligence. With its high concentration of able, prosperous men and its hospitality to Enlightenment ideas, Philadelphia was the ideal place for Franklin to pursue his diverse hobbies. Although the *Autobiography* is neither a study of his intellectual growth nor the biography of an intellectual milieu, it does make clear that Franklin viewed himself as an "idea" man, one who originated experiments while others verified them independently or took out patents to cash in on them commercially. When he invented the Franklin stove, he disdained monopolizing it or profiting by it.[29] If amateurism and an exuberant common sense stamped his efforts in the fields of natural philosophy and public works, they went along with a gift for encouraging cooperation and associated action. The Junto, a club of aspiring intellectuals, became a network to exchange information, specimens, books, to spread new ideas or propagandize for changes that would increase the welfare of the community.

Franklin never really shed his mental skin as a printer. The most ardent moments in the *Autobiography* have to do with books, for which he would skip a meal, or barter time or small possessions, with the requited love of a collector; fishing a Dutchman out of Long Island Sound, he was pleased to find a copy of Bunyan's *Pilgrim's Progress* translated into Dutch and with fine engravings. Franklin early recognized the power of print to teach, edify, and instigate political or social change. For his growing audience of subsistence farmers and workers, he published almanacs and newspapers; for the rising middle class, he designed a circulating library; and with the Peter Collinsons and John Bartrams he traded ideas, papers, and scientific paraphernalia. He stayed serenely aloof from petty scientific wrangles.

All his life Franklin balanced self-interest and altruism, leaning now this way to thrift, now that to generosity. As the *Autobiography* shows, he could not resist his own histrionic talent for trying on and discarding selves. What disconcerts one about Franklin and makes the *Autobiography* such an equivocal document is that he tried—or pretended—to "make others more moral than he ever intended to be himself."[30] *Poor Richard's Almanac* made a fortune for him because he flattered his readers' commonness. His folksy maxims made devotion to self respectable, self-denial remunerative, money a proliferating virtue: "Every little makes a nickle."[31] (One suspects that he never forgot the "straitened circumstances" in his father's house.) In the *Autobiography,* Franklin chose not to repudiate Poor Richard's slippery homespun advice. Thus on one page, as his influence and curiosity grew, he whittled himself down to the philistine size of his countrymen who had no time for art or intellectual inquiry, as if he embodied the "Divine Average," while on the facing page he enlarged his virtues and achievements with a dignified swagger: Though a common man, he sat down with kings and was elected to the Royal Society.

Franklin was the "insinuating man"[32] of John Adams's testy epithet. The autobiographies of public men are especially prone to fictional embellishment, and Franklin's *Autobiography* is no exception. His plan for moral perfection, for example, is a waggish deceit. John Adams, as ambitious as Franklin and as heedful in calculating odds, also sketched out long lists of rules of conduct for himself, and when he failed to comply with them berated himself, but this process remained private. Franklin, by contrast, published his directives for self-improvement for all the world to emulate, and with amused nonchalance forgave himself for any lapses.

Consider Franklin's sixth entry from his catalogue of thirteen virtues:

INDUSTRY

Lose no time; be always employ'd in something useful; cut off all unnecessary actions.

Franklin was not the drudge he commends others to be: He liked to loiter over a glass of sherry, to trifle, to play chess, to joke, to swim. In a similar vein, Franklin remarks that two hours after he finished dinner, he did not remember what he ate, whereas in truth he loved food and even kept a file of favorite recipes. And of course he gleefully added humility to his list when he was told that he often exhibited pride. These insincerities, like his solemn jingle "Deny self for Self's sake,"[33] are for public consumption, while he went his own merry lenient way. "One does not dress for private Company as for a Publick Ball." (56–7) Temperance may be a compelling virtue, but when Governor Clinton unbends after drinking several bumpers of wine and supplies, after an initial refusal, the needed cannon to Pennsylvania for defense against the French and Indians, Franklin looks the other way. (He stocked, Claude-Anne Lopez tells us, "five kinds of champagne" in his Paris wine cellar and "he wrote several drinking songs."[34]) When reason dictated that the end was society's or his own good, he could always skirt principle: By arranging some budgetary legerdemain, he gets the Quakers' tacit consent to appropriate moneys for armaments, thus bypassing their pacifist convictions.

Nowhere in the *Autobiography* are Franklin's equivocations more blatantly displayed than in his view of American Indians. Carl Van Doren observes:

Franklin looked upon the Indians always with the humane curiosity and natural respect which he felt for any people whose way of life was different from his own. He admired the Iroquois confederation. . . . He took a philosophical pleasure in their preference for the savage state. Nor did he foresee the conflict of cultures which would at last destroy even the powerful Six Nations. . . . As between the Indians and the white settlers, he sympathized with the Indians. It was not they who broke treaties or drove greedy bargains or presumed on superior strength.[35]

Though Franklin did, in fact, hold such enlightened opinions—they are scattered throughout his papers[36]—they disappeared in the *Autobiography* along with his sympathy and "philosophical pleasure." From the evidence of that book, he did not shed his society's mixture of fear of and contempt for Indians. He respected their ingenuity at concealing fires while keeping warm and he never underestimated their courage and tactics in war, as General Braddock did during the calamitous rout of his army in the woods before they could reach Fort Duquesne. But the Indians were a threat to the life and property of the white settlers on the vulnerable frontiers, and Franklin was active in building fortresses.

There is probably no more notorious passage in the *Autobiography* than Franklin's cool remark reflecting popular prejudices: "If it be in the Design of Providence to extirpate these Savages in order to make room for Cultivators of the Earth, it seems not improbable that Rum may be the appointed Means. It has already annihilated all the Tribes who formerly inhabited the Sea-coast." (199) This verdict follows a comic speech by the Indian elders apologizing for their people's noisy and drunken behavior after tough negotiations (Franklin likens the scene to hell, his one reference to Satan's domain), which takes Franklinesque writ so literally that it crosses over into parody: *"The Great Spirit who made all things made every thing for some Use, and whatever Use he design'd any thing for, that Use it should always be put to. Now when he made Rum, he said, LET THIS BE FOR INDIANS TO GET DRUNK WITH. And it must be so."* (199) Franklin keeps a straight face and expediently fobs off colonial policy on Providence. If the quaint savages must be sacrificed for the greater American good—expansion—he would not contest the will of Providence. The "apostolic serpent and dove"[37] that Melville satirized in *Israel Potter* speaks in the *Autobiography.*

IV

FRANKLIN'S STYLE in the *Autobiography* has often automatically been praised for its crisp, factual authority, its cheerful worldliness, and its sensible egotism. This praise is only partially deserved. There is a striking discrepancy between Franklin's account of his childhood and early manhood and his later career as a public figure. After the buoyant first part, with its escapades, impulsive acts, and cheeky humor, the "I" contracts into a public voice that seems unentranced by memory. The last three sections are written by a Franklin who is a brilliant curator of his own reputation as a prodigy of virtue. Not by accident did he insert the letter from Benjamin Vaughan, who, having read only the outline of the *Autobiography,* in a fit of hyperbole claimed that it

> will shew the use of your life as a mere piece of biography. This style of writing seems a little gone out of vogue, and yet it is a very useful one; and your specimen of it may be peculiarly serviceable, as it will make a subject of comparison with the lives of various public cutthroats and intriguers, and with absurd monastic self-tormentors, or vain literary triflers. If it encourages more writings of the same kind with your own, and induces more men to spend lives fit to be written; it will be worth all Plutarch's Lives put together. (138–9)

This fulsome passage reads like a publicity handout. Franklin, playing the role of republican grandee to the hilt, accepts the plaudits as his due.

Franklin's style, like his "fair character," was carefully constructed. From an early age, he grasped that mastering rhetoric was a key to competing successfully for the prizes the world offers: power, influence, authority. Stung by his father's telling him that his first efforts at writing fell short in "Eloquence of Expression, in Method and in Perspicuity," (61) Franklin doggedly began correcting his faults. He excerpted an essay from Addison and Steele's *Spec-*

tator and then from those short hints rewrote the sentiments in his own words:

> By comparing my work afterwards with the original, I discover'd many faults and amended them; but I sometimes had the Pleasure of Fancying that in certain Particulars of small Import, I had been lucky enough to improve the Method or the Language and this encourag'd me to think I might possibly in time come to be a tolerable English Writer, of which I was extremely Ambitious. (62)

In taking sentences apart and putting them back together again, Franklin is typically content not merely to imitate his model but to surpass it. Similarly, he scrambles poems into prose and restores them to orderly sequences so that he can inject flavor and variety into his prose (he retained a fondness for verse his entire life, and his first literary success was a doggerel ballad).

In the *Autobiography,* Franklin defined rhetoric's goals in traditional terms: "to inform, to please, and to persuade," and by dint of hard work he deployed it as skillfully as he did his fonts of type. From John Bunyan's *Pilgrim's Progress,* Franklin said, he learned to mix "narrative and dialogue," which he put to good use in this anecdote from Part I, where, miffed at himself for lending money to Collins, who then spent it on drink, he participated in the following altercation:

> Once in a Boat on the Delaware with some other young Men, he refused to row in his Turn: I will be row'd home, says he. We will not row you, says I. You must or stay all Night on the Water, says he, just as you please. The others said, Let us row; what signifies it? But my Mind being soured with his other Conduct, I continu'd to refuse. So he swore he would make me row, or throw me overboard; and coming along stepping on the Thwarts towards me, when he came up and struck at me I clapt my Hand under his Crutch, and rising pitch'd him head-foremost into the River. I knew he was a good Swimmer, and so was under little Concern about him; but before he could get round to lay hold of the Boat, we had with a few Strokes pull'd her out of his Reach. And ever

when he drew near the Boat, we ask'd if he would row, striking a few Strokes to slide her away from him. He was ready to die with Vexation, and obstinately would not promise to row; however seeing him at last beginning to tire, we lifted him in; and brought him home dripping wet in the Evening. We hardly exchang'd a civil Word afterward. (85–6)

Because the memory of Collins's overbearing insolence still rankles after nearly fifty years, the prose bristles with animosity. Franklin forgets about his high-minded purpose, recording what "Posterity may like to know," and becomes absorbed in his contest of wills with Collins. When persuasion fails, he resorts to physical action; the strong verbs "struck," "clapt," "pitch'd," and "lifted," along with the terse dialogue and vigorous rhythm, imbue Franklin's sour retribution with a vivid power. The reader sits with the rowers in the boat and fishes the soaked Collins out of the river. The autobiographer omits his usual editorial tags; the scene speaks for itself.

In another early incident, Franklin baits a wary and overmatched Keimer into abstaining from "animal Food":

I doubt, says he, my Constitution will not bear that. I assur'd him it would, and that he would be the better for it. He was usually a great Glutton, and I promis'd my self some Diversion in half-starving him. He agreed to try the Practice if I would keep him Company. I did so and we held it for three Months. We had our Victuals dress'd and brought to us regularly by a Woman in the Neighbourhood, who had from me a list of 40 Dishes to be prepar'd for us at different times, in all which there was neither Fish Flesh nor Fowl, and the whim suited me the better at this time from the Cheapness of it, not costing us above 18d. Sterling each, per Week. I have since kept several Lents most strictly, Leaving the common Diet for that, and that for the common, abruptly, without the least Inconvenience: So that I think there is little in the Advice of making those changes by easy Gradations. I went on pleasantly, but poor Keimer suffer'd grievously, tir'd of the Project, long'd for the Flesh Pots of Egypt, and order'd a roast Pig. He invited me and two Women Friends to dine with him, but it being brought too soon upon table,

53

he could not resist the Temptation, and ate it all up before
we came. (88–9)

In this caricature of "poor Keimer," Franklin again enjoys drubbing
a rival. This time he vanquishes his opponent with ridicule rather
than brawn. The prose gleams with a spiteful wit—Keimer was not
really the "Knave" or incompetent Franklin insists on portraying in
the *Autobiography*[38]—as he trifles with a person he deems his inferior. Where Keimer is gluttonous, Franklin is abstemious; where
Franklin commands his will easily, resisting the "Flesh Pots of
Egypt," Keimer succumbs to temptation, his feckless will leading
him grossly to consume an entire pig, just as he consumes his capital
and business advantages, leaving Franklin a clear field.

Part I of the *Autobiography* is entertaining because the cozy ped-
agogue writing at Twyford in 1771 dotes on the truancies of the
young boy as if he were merely bent on entertaining the young
daughters of the bishop of Asaph. Belligerence was congenial to the
aggressive tendencies of Franklin's personality. He adored disputes
and giving the "Rulers a Rub," but he recognized early that he had
to bridle himself. Being contentious was emotionally satisfying, but
it spoiled conversation and aroused both factionalism and jealousy.
So he labored to acquire a smooth demeanor that would not scuttle
his ambitions. He dropped positive words like "certainly" and "un-
doubtedly" for such polite and politic locutions as "It appears to
me" or "I should think it so or so for such and such Reasons." This
oblique approach and diffidence invariably worked, whether with
Isaac Norris or in obtaining an appropriation to build a hospital. A
wizard of honorable duplicity, Franklin was often the one chosen
to find the verbal formula that would break deadlocks.

The diplomat and arbiter did not, however, entirely abandon his
penchant for piercing hides with satirical barbs. He still loved
roughing up authority, but he did it circumspectly. His caustic
sketches of General Braddock and Lord Loudon in the *Autobiography,* as is often pointed out, reflect Franklin's hostile attitudes to
the British after the Revolutionary War. He does not challenge Braddock's blind boast that the King's troops were superior to the Indians and colonists as fighters; "I was conscious of an Impropriety in
my Disputing with a military Man in Matters of his Profession, and
said no more." (224) He then dryly records the ensuing debacle and

draws a brief cautionary lesson: "This whole Transaction gave us Americans the first Suspicion that our exalted Ideas of the Prowess of British Regulars had not been well founded." (226)

The convention Franklin used most, that he was writing an autobiography of instruction, meant that he siphoned off most of the emotional power of Part I from the remaining three parts of the *Autobiography*. Writing about the 1754 Albany Conference, he produces this:

> A Committee was then appointed one Member from each Colony, to consider the several Plans and report. Mine happen'd to be preferr'd, and with a few Amendments was accordingly reported. By this Plan, the general Government was to be administered by a President General appointed and supported by the Crown, and a Grand Council to be chosen by the Representatives of the People of the several Colonies met in their respective Assemblies. The Debates upon it went on daily hand in hand with the Indian Business. Many Objections and Difficulties were started, but at length they were all overcome, and the Plan was unanimously agreed to, and Copies ordered to be transmitted to the Board of Trade and to the Assemblies of the several Provinces. (210)

This stodgy prose sounds like the official minutes of a committee meeting, which as Clerk of the Assembly he doubtless heard often and transcribed (none of his famous doodles ornament the margins). The exposition is plodding and monotonous, mired in the passive voice. There is no rhythmic animation in the deliberations and decision of the negotiators. The facts lie inert on the page. Such material, the province of political history, has, of course, documentary value and cannot be avoided by an autobiographer who takes a leading role in such events, but Franklin is no more ingenious than other statesmen in incorporating it into the story of his life. The style is mechanically balanced.

Fortunately, Franklin's gift for metaphor never wholly deserts him in the *Autobiography*. He spices his didacticism with a well-timed joke or a pithy illustration. His journalistic savvy and his experience as a compiler of almanacs taught him the value of humor; earthy images drawn from everyday life are the bread and wine of conversation—and narrative.[39] When the Quakers have difficulty squaring their consciences with voting revenues for military defenses, Franklin contrasts them with the Dunkers, a German Baptist sect that was reluctant to codify their beliefs. He concludes:

> This modesty in a Sect is perhaps a singular Instance in the History of Mankind, every other Sect supposing itself in possession of all Truth, and that those who differ are so far in the Wrong: Like a Man travelling in foggy Weather: Those at some Distance before him on the Road he sees wrapt up in the Fog, as well as those behind him, and also the people in the Fields on each side; but near him all appears clear. Tho' in truth he is as much in the Fog as any of them. To avoid this kind of Embarrassment the Quakers have of late Years been gradually declining the public Service in the Assembly and in the Magistracy. Chusing rather to quit their Power than their Principle. (191)

Through the use of his extended simile Franklin can tactfully state his partiality for the Dunkers' reluctance to set down rules and codify their beliefs, for fear that will "bound and confine" their conduct. He turns a moral conflict into a charming homily and distances himself from sectarian dogmatism as a shortsighted policy. When principle threatens to limit freedom of action, Franklin casually disregards it. Like the Dunkers, he never published his Manual of Virtue. Franklin's style seldom gets "wrapt up in the Fog." It keeps its perspective intact.

The main defect of Franklin's style is its lack of sensibility or musical rhythm, as if he thought such qualities inappropriate in a young man or a young country, and somehow incompatible with practical tasks and ambition. He is never swept away by passion, love, or sorrow. An "Evenness of Temper" was his solution to maintaining a unity of consciousness. Franklin devotes one brief paragraph to the death of his son, Francis Folger Franklin:

> In 1736 I lost one of my Sons, a fine Boy of 4 Years old, by the Small Pox taken in the common way. I long regretted bitterly and still regret that I had not given it to him by Inoculation; This I mention for the Sake of Parents, who omit

that Operation on the Supposition that they should never forgive themselves if a Child died under it; my Example showing
that the Regret may be the same either way, and that therefore the safer should be chosen. (170)

An unspoken decorum governs Franklin's response; he will not allow any emotionally charged language: Keening in public or showing private pain would violate the protocols of his edifying memoir.
We know from a letter that the memory of his lost son could bring
tears to his eyes,[40] but here he subordinates his tenderness to the
goal of counseling parents to risk inoculating their children.[41] The
very grammatical structure inhibits the bitterness from flowing over;
each semicolon checks it. And by placing the paragraph between
one in which he tells of setting up his dead brother James's son in
business, thus erasing an *erratum* and easing his sense of loss, and
one in which he describes the popularity of clubs like the Junto,
Franklin simply ignores dramatic buildup or juxtaposition, as if he
believed that all his opinions and experiences were of the same
weight and value.

V

IN 1723, about the time Franklin was quitting his father's house
for the journey to Philadelphia and renown, Jonathan Edwards, in
startling contrast to Franklin,

made a solemn dedication of myself to God, and wrote it
down; giving myself and all that I had to God; to be for the
future, in no respect my own; to act as one who had no right
to himself in any respect. And solemnly vowed to take God
for my whole portion and felicity; looking on nothing else,
as any part of my happiness, nor acting as if it were; and his
law for the constant rule of my obedience: engaging to fight,
with all my might, against the world, the flesh, & the devil,
to the end of my life. But I have reason to be infinitely humbled, when I consider how much I have failed, of answering
my obligation.[42]

If Franklin could have read Edwards's solemn vow, he probably would have dismissed it with a shrug. No stranger to such sentiments, he was indeed running away from them in order to assert his "right to myself"; he had disobeyed his earthly father and sloughed off the sovereignty of his heavenly father with ease. What Philip Greven calls the "inner 'reprover,' "[43] that stern monitory voice of the evangelical temperament, never spoke to Franklin. Though he would become one of America's masterful technicians of humility, he did not expect to fail: "the world, the flesh, & the devil" were not foes that might block his ambitious strivings for felicity.

Franklin and Edwards represent opposing sides of the question: Who has ultimate power over the will? Franklin's gospel, whether called Arminianism or Enlightenment Humanism, was based on the premise that the will, consulting reason, is free to choose according to its own lights; human experience is a sufficient guide. Such a notion would have shocked Edwards as both blasphemous and shallow. As Perry Miller, the great historian of the New England mind, says, Edwards was "schooled in New England doctrine that man is passive in the reception of grace and that he is bound to sin if he tries to earn salvation by his own efforts or on his own terms."[44] Like most Christian doctrine, this was anathema to Franklin the self-made man, because it violated common sense and, if followed, would have foiled his wish to make his mark in the world.

Puritan autobiographies focus with unremitting intensity on this question of grace, the supreme distinction, and the subject's worthiness to receive it, its accession or absence being the cause of an "internal Armageddon."[45] Every occasion, secular or religious, personal or public, was tested by it. Afire with zeal and faith, the Puritans viewed their settlement of New England as an extraordinary moment in sacred history, in which fallen man would be lifted to his feet and made to stand upright. They compared themselves to the Israelites in the Old Testament, a chosen people with Providence on their side who accepted grave obligations to fulfill their covenant with God. Although a recently discovered corner of the New World was an unlikely site for this grand millennial drama, the Puritans acted their part with the exalted conviction that, as John Winthrop preached to the émigrés on board the *Arbella,* "the eyes of the world [were] upon us."

But in crossing the Atlantic, the Puritans also brought with them a deep mistrust of individual will and the claims of the self, which, like villains lurking in ambush, menaced the safety of the soul. They dwelt not in calm but in fear and anxiety. Their terror of the Indians might be contained by war, trade, and a God-sanctioned mission to convert the heathen to Christianity; their terror of the wilderness— dense gloomy forests, wild animals, severe winters, uncertain food supply, and makeshift shelter (decidedly not the landscape and climate of the Promised Land or of the English towns they left behind)—could be mitigated by hard work, ingenuity, and stoicism. But their terror that God in his displeasure might refuse them grace, which was tantamount to an eternal death sentence, could be dealt with only by scrutinizing their inner selves for signs that divine favor was conferred on them. And although it was necessary to regulate one's conduct scrupulously, even virtuous deeds could not affect God's decision.

This regiment of righteous idealists installed in New England a social and theological authority that was rigidly elitist and intolerant of dissent. Like all communities of the orthodox, they cared little for cultivating individuality. Although Kenneth Murdock usefully reminds us that the Puritans were not "superhuman saints" but "flesh-and-blood men, by no means sexually starved, frankly fond of rum"[46] and gossip, the testimony of their autobiographies, which ring with self-denuciations, is barren of relaxed or affable moments. No Puritan would ever dare to claim or say, as Montaigne did, "I give great authority to my desires and inclinations."[47] Power resided in an absolute God, from whose judgments no appeal could be made, and in an oligarchy of Christian militants that monitored sermons, scriptural exegesis, theological debate, and communal behavior for doctrinal conformity and sought (in vain) to silence or banish opposition. (Within a generation, harsh sectarian conflict broke out.)

Jonathan Edwards best exemplifies this anxious vigilance, these "great and violent inward struggles" that monopolize Puritan spiritual autobiographies. Describing himself as a vile sinner returning "like a dog to his vomit" and a penitent longing "after God, and holiness," he speaks in a voice of edifying passion:

My wickedness, as I am in myself, has long appeared to me perfectly ineffable, and swallowing up all thought and imagination; like an infinite deluge, or mountain over my head. I know not how to express better what my sins appear to me to be, than by heaping infinite upon infinite, and multiplying infinite by infinite. Very often, for these many years, these expressions are in my mind, and in my mouth, "Infinite upon infinite—Infinite upon infinite!" When I look into my heart, and take a view of my wickedness, it looks like an abyss, infinitely deeper.[48]

God is everything, Edwards nothing. Like a famished child dependent for sustenance on an august but forbiddingly remote father, Edwards scarcely dares to hope he will be fed, fears he will perish. In Edwards's spiritual arithmetic, everywhere he turns or gazes, his "infinite" sins multiply and engulf him. He is puny; they are gigantic. It is as though he has stolen one of God's attributes—infinitude—and is punished for this felony by being forced to repeat his sins over and over. He may grovel like a supplicant or strive for daily sanctity, but there is no exit from the hell of his consciousness, his chronic dread: Like Elijah scanning the horizon for rain, he must wait for that salvational moment when the sinner will be "brought out of darkness into marvellous light, and delivered out of a horrible pit, and from the miry clay, and set upon a rock with a new song of praise to God in [his mouth]."[49] Yet curiously, while the syntax acts out his passivity, the phrase "perfectly ineffable" applied to his wickedness, an audacious perversion of the sacred name coming from a pious clergyman, unconsciously indicates Edwards's high view of his own lowness. Paradoxically, though he is stained by sin, afflicted with a fractious will that requires superhuman efforts to keep it submissive to God, and facing annihilation, his autobiographical identity is firm, a premise like prayer and the long New England winters. Edwards's *Personal Narrative* is a superior example of the Puritan autobiography at its most introspective. Ideas of self-government, franchise, and equality—what later would become the trinity of democratic belief—were necessarily missing from the Puritans' record of their conversion experiences.[50] By the eighteenth century, America was drifting increasingly in the direction of latitudinarianism, whose chief spokesman was Benjamin Franklin, for whom all deterministic theories of the self, whatever their alleged divine origin, were to be rejected. This master of "the economy of his force"[51] erected in his life and in his *Autobiography* a monument of praise to his ego, thereby breaking the Puritan mold.

In fact, sin and punishment had no reality for Franklin. Men might be arrogant and deluded like Braddock, incompetent like Lord Loudon, obstinate like the Proprietors, autocratic like King George III. He experienced no dread: The world was hospitable to the energetic man, not unsafe, as Edwards and the Puritans felt it to be.[52] Logic prescribed that God was bound not to wish spiritual abasement. A prostrate soul could not conquer the beckoning American continent. Franklin's errands into the wilderness were of a mercantile, political, or military nature. Action was therapeutic. Even his own near death held no terrors:

> My distemper was a Pleurisy, which very nearly carried me off. I suffered a good deal, gave up the Point in my mind, and was rather disappointed when I found my Self recovering, regretting, in some degree, that I must now, some time or other, have all that disagreeable Work [earning a living] to do over again. (107)

Early death was a common affliction in colonial America—many of Franklin's friends did not survive young manhood, and his sister Jane Mecom's many children died with grim regularity—but in his facetious resignation, as if he were lazy, Franklin does not worry about the final disposal of his soul.

Although Franklin's creed grants that God exists and the soul is immortal,[53] he relegates the one to benign inactivity and denies that the other is in danger. He jettisons the entire Puritan drama of election and eternal damnation: Coercion and terror give way to persuasion. The purpose of religion becomes merely ethical; he praises the Moravian custom of coaxing children to be good. Because man is a "reasonable Creature," the best way to serve God is to do good works. Franklin salvages the practical Puritan virtues—hard work, diligence, moderation, parsimony—but rids God of his primary functions: the bestowal of grace and the power of punishment. Once again, Franklin throws off the yoke of dependence in order to become his own master, while keeping a superficial fealty to what he has overthrown.

As a young man browsing in his father's library, Franklin passed over the small stock of books on "polemical Divinity," just as he politely spurned his uncle Benjamin's offer of a vast collection of sermons in shorthand. He preferred Xenophon's *Memories,* Plutarch's *Lives,* Defoe's *Essay upon Projects;* and from Cotton Mather's *Bonifacius* he ignored Mather's argument that good works were worthless unless a person was "justified"[54] and concentrated on the "remedies and abatements"[55] for social ills. Like Mather, he asked himself every day, "What good may I do?"[56] but his answer did not require the elaborate apparatus of Mather's scholarly commentary to sanction the remedies he suggested.

Franklin also skipped public worship as a tedious obligation. In his decision to leave Boston, the center of theological controversy, for Philadelphia, a city where "religious liberty of Conscience" ruled, fortune smiled on him, for the intense fights over religious doctrine that divided Boston bored him. Philadelphia's liberal climate was more to his liking. The soul was not Franklin's concern. He had no desire to be a visible saint. Instead he would be America's Factotum, wholesome and urbane, a man of science and the future, which meant educating public opinion to recognize its collective interests and civic needs: an efficient constabulary, an increase in paper currency, a fire department, a philosophical society, street lamps that didn't blacken, the securing of houses from lightning, stoves that saved heat and wood. "Science is progressive, and talents and enterprises on the alert,"[57] Jefferson said, a sentiment Franklin shared. There was so much to do in the New World, whose provinciality was merely a temporary mishap of geography. Who had time for arid debates over metaphysical systems? Franklin, like Jefferson, had no mystical piety or awe of the transcendental. Each defined belief, in Jefferson's words, as "the assent of the mind to an intelligible proposition."[58] The "Infinite" was simply not part of Franklin's vocabulary. Reason was.[59]

Thus, on his "First Voyage from Boston," when the smell of fresh fish sizzling in the pan whetted his appetite, Frankly gave up his vegetarianism with this delicious rationale: "I recollected that, when the Fish were opened, I saw smaller Fish taken out of their Stomachs: Then thought I, if you eat one another, I don't see why we mayn't eat you. . . . So convenient a thing is it to be a *reasonable Creature,* since it enables one to find or make a Reason for every thing one has a mind to do." (87–8) He abandons his mild Deism with a similar imperturbability, because "though it might be true, it wasn't useful." These episodes read like spoofs of conversion experiences and demonstrate the flip casuistry with which Franklin could bend principle to desire.

Franklin comments with wry detachment on the drama of the conversions that affected Jonathan Edwards so deeply during the Great Awakening. Franklin is moved by the cadences of George Whitefield's evangelical oratory to empty his pockets of coin—a rare instance in the *Autobiography* when he was "out of [his] right Senses" (178)—and like an amateur acoustician marks off the distance the preacher's voice carried (incidentally proving the truth of a statement in Herodotus about the size of crowds in antiquity). But typically, while noting the atmosphere of fervid piety, "as if all the World were growing Religious," (175) and hearing psalms wafted in the air from every house, he brushes off Whitefield's efforts to convert him. He marvels, with amused contempt, at the preacher's success, "notwithstanding his common Abuse" of the populace, "by assuring them they were naturally *half Beasts and half Devils.*" (175) For Edwards, the great revivals were a sign of God's manifest wonders, though he came to doubt the permanence and to fret at the excesses of the conversions; for Franklin, they were a phenomenon of mass hysteria, to be studied, chronicled, and scoffed at. Revelation had no weight with him. Prayer was a nuisance. As Poor Richard dryly noted, "Serving God is Doing Good to Man, but Praying is thought an easier Service, and therefore more generally chosen."[60] The prayer Franklin composed, which he quotes in the *Autobiography,* was an expedient hymn, his reference to the hereafter an insincere gesture; salvation meant honors, visits to kings, archbishops, and earls, degrees from Harvard and Yale and Oxford, and a bank account multiplying like America's population. All was within reach of every man so long as he was honest, patient, and hardworking. Franklin admitted God on condition that He stir up no fuss or bother, and invoked Him when it was good for business or sound politics, like organizing a fast day to rally the community during a threat of war.

In most things, Edwards was Franklin's antithesis. Humorless, self-distrusting, though intellectually haughty, and torn by violent inner struggles, Edwards represented the spiritual authority that

Franklin so lightly cast aside. His intellect, a profounder instrument than Franklin's, could slash his theological opponents to tatters with the blade of his dialectic. Secretive by nature, a clerical Coriolanus, he engaged in polemical wars with a zeal roused by his belief that he spoke for God's truth. Franklin's warnings about disputes would have struck him as capitulation to dangerous error.

Ironically, as early as his brilliant letter on spiders, written when he was only fifteen, Edwards followed the same empirical methods that Franklin used when investigating the Gulf Stream or lightning: By careful observation and experience, he sought out "the universally acknowledged laws of nature."[61] Edwards's dilemma was how to integrate natural laws into his closed system of "man's absolute dependence on the operation of God's Holy Spirit."[62] His reason compelled him to subdue himself to God's "absolute sovereignty and justice,"[63] that is, to divine arbitrariness, in the anxious hope that he might be worthy to glimpse the remote, lovely immaculateness of God's grace. Thus, though like one of his spiders, or the "Sinners in the Hands of an Angry God," he hung by the slenderest thread over the abyss of eternal damnation, he must chastise, crucify, and empty the self, lie in the dust, on the chance that the "gently vivifying beams of the sun"[64] (God's grace) might enter and ravish his spirit.

This last phrase comes from Edwards's *Personal Narrative,* an autobiographical fragment that in its painful intimacy reveals the besieged and morbid man beneath the theologian. There are no personas in the *Personal Narrative,* just a lonely self driven by its internal conflicts facing death and God. Unlike Franklin, Edwards understands the life of the emotions. "A product of American society at its most starved and narrow," Perry Miller observes, "Edwards tried to teach it the language of affection."[65] The words "sweet," "pure," "delight," and "majesty" recur throughout the autobiographical sketch—Franklin's preferred words in the *Autobiography* are "use," "ingenious," "advantage," and "virtue"—along with weeping and ineffable joy, like the refrain of a pietistic poem, lifting him out of "the bottomless depths of secret corruption and deceit" in his heart. He is an ardent lover, verging on delirium, bashful yet unable to stem the flood of emotion at the prospect of union with his lover-God. The ecstatic chorales of spiritual beauty in the *Personal Narrative* are utterly missing from Franklin's *Autobiography.*

Consider the following paragraph:

I often used to sit and view the moon for a long time; and in the day, spent much time in viewing the clouds and sky, to behold the sweet glory of God in these things: in the meantime, singing forth, with a low voice, my contemplation of the Creator and Redeemer. And scarce anything, among all the works of nature, was so sweet to me as thunder and lightning; formerly nothing had been so terrible to me. Before [his conversion experience] I used to be uncommonly terrified with thunder, and to be struck with terror when I saw a thunder-storm rising; but now, on the contrary, it rejoiced me. I felt God, if I may so speak, at the first appearance of a thunder storm; and used to take the opportunity, at such times, to fix myself in order to view the clouds, and see the lightning play, and hear the majestic and awful voice of God's thunder, which oftentime was exceedingly entertaining, leading me to sweet contemplations of my great and glorious God. While thus engaged it always seemed natural for me to sing, or chant forth my meditations; or to speak my thoughts in soliloquies with a singing voice.[66]

In this sublime hymn, Edwards's voice and God's mingle in a sweet duet; they are each other's instrument. Edwards borrows Franklin's lightning, so to speak, and is struck by it; the bolt enters his body and spirit; he cannot but surrender to its force and beauty. He does not—and need not—ask why it operates as it does, because nature as object and nature as subject are harmonious, with God the conductor. Released from the agitations of its "vehement longings," Edwards's soul passes from terror to safety, from quiet serenity to jubilation. His song rises spontaneously and subsides, with the repetitions of words and the balance of syntax providing a logical frame for the spirit as it feels God's goodness and power. These moments of emotional fulfillment are all the more precious to Edwards because, lacking Franklin's equable nature, he soon plunges back into the dark maze of his "sinfulness and vileness," and mercilessly dissects his own and his society's faithlessness.

When in his *Autobiography* Franklin comes to the great moment when he discovers the properties of lightning, he perfunctorily refers the reader to his scientific papers. It belongs to the public record. Though Franklin's life was changed by his experiments, and his kite became a popular icon, a kind of scientific souvenir, his emotions are beside the point. The lightning did not conceal any dark and awful God.[67] What mattered was to harness its force for the common weal. In a like manner, Franklin helped engineer a far-reaching political revolution: the separation of the colonies from their political parents, George III and Parliament. America, like Benjamin Franklin, had become its own master. In its matter-of-fact style, the *Autobiography* vindicated both.

VI

IN THE POLITICS of identity Franklin was a revolutionary, virtually inventing—and publicizing—the idea that in America people did not inherit, as Europeans did, fixed historical roles. Like Walt Whitman, Franklin "contained multitudes." Just listing the occupations he crammed into his eventful career makes one marvel. V. S. Pritchett's brilliant observation that "the self-loving autobiographer is a man lost, for the moment, in the romance of his own life, who has a schizophrenic skill in splitting into self and adoring parasite,"[68] fits Franklin's *Autobiography* perfectly. Lionized in his day on two continents as the model American, the nobody who became a somebody, Franklin projects his many selves, unfazed, onto the bustling American scene as an actor slips into "changes of garment." In its sociable optimism, its discursive form, its celebration of pluralism,[69] its love of impersonation, and its belief in an unstoppable national destiny, the *Autobiography* is closer to Whitman's *Song of Myself* than to Edwards's *Personal Narrative*.

The influence of Franklin's *Autobiography* was sizable. It is not farfetched to say that, at least symbolically, the American Constitution codified many of Franklin's incentives for liberty—and his system of checks and balances. The idea of the enterprising common man as the embodiment of democratic virtue owes much to Franklin. Indeed, the dialectic of the "simple separate person" and the democratic mass, which has been the occasion of continual friction throughout most of American history, seemed for him as free of knotty contradictions as his life was clear of self-torment.

Franklin's values did not finally vanquish Puritanism so much as push it temporarily underground, and they stirred up strong opposition, especially from the Transcendentalists, who perceived his legacy as morally slippery. Emerson's essay "Prudence," for example, is a riposte against the "subaltern,"[70] materialistic virtues Franklin elevated to prominence in the well-governed self and citizenry: "the art of securing a present well-being."[71] Uneasy with the "low objects" at which Americans were aiming, Emerson exhorted his countrymen to abandon their avaricious quest for "Property," a major inducement in Franklin's scheme for American prosperity, and to find and trust the higher spiritual laws in nature and within. In place of Jehovah or the utilitarian demiurge, Emerson extolled that tutelary deity the "aboriginal Self"[72] and its courtship of nature as the sole grand paramour capable of ensuring an incomparable identity. But as his *Autobiography* shows, because Franklin is not a riddle to himself, his life is like geometry without the perpendicular. He shuns introspection, just as in the presence of nature he fails to exhibit any poetic feeling.[73] One imagines that Emerson would have agreed with D. H. Lawrence's harsh verdict that "the soul of a man is a vast forest, and all Benjamin intended was a neat back garden."[74]

While Emerson amended Franklin's gospel of opportunity, his voice is a throwback to Edwards's:

The world—this shadow of the soul, or *other me*—lies wide around. Its attractions are the keys which unlock my thoughts and make me acquainted with myself. I run eagerly into this resounding tumult. I grasp the hands of those next me, and take my place in the ring to suffer and to work, taught by an instinct, that so shall the dumb abyss be vocal with speech. I pierce its order; I dissipate its fear; I dispose of it within the circuit of my expanding life.[75]

Emerson's style, the democratic sublime, mixes the high-minded diction the Puritans favored for the soul's discourses with an aggressive syntax that is symptomatic of the untrammeled self he idealized. The "I" cleaves to verbs of action like an ax to a tree stump. The kinetic, autonomous clauses are held together by egalitarian semicolons and periods, but the paragraph and essay just barely provide a cohesive community for Emerson's thoughts, as if heralding the partition that the Civil War would bring to the nation. (Even when he is conversing with himself in his journals, Emerson is seldom intimate, forcing his sentences to shift into the imperative mode, which Franklin advised be dropped as too contentious.) Though Emerson exalts the common man's divine potential to make "the dumb abyss be vocal with speech,"[76] he cannot hide his contempt for and disappointment with average Americans, especially in the mass, because they seem lumpish and easily seduced by material objects and popular pieties from the sterner, higher claims of self-culture. He is not interested in ameliorating social abuses. Therefore, unlike Franklin, Emerson is condemned to wear the hair shirt of democratic elitism, an exceptional man isolated from the American polity yet trying through his essays, those urgent secular sermons, to strike the shackles off the supine giant, who preferred inertia and imitation. This quandary, this crisis of democratic belief in the power of the people to choose enlightened self-reliance, worried Jane Addams in *Twenty Years at Hull-House,* perplexed Louis Sullivan in *The Autobiography of an Idea,* and roused both Edward Dahlberg in *Because I Was Flesh* and Emma Goldman in her *Autobiography* to cynical invective.

Although he does not attack Franklin either in *Walden* or in his voluminous journals, Thoreau disputes every inch of the moral ground Franklin had seized.[77] To an uncompromising idealist like Thoreau, Franklin's chummy egalitarianism could only dangle the rewards of a bogus distinction, substitute commonplace ethics for lofty principle. The young America flushed with the excitement of building a nation disgusted Thoreau, who became its morose adversary, criticizing its housekeeping and architecture as fit for a race of pygmies or "mean ants," not giants. If democratic opportunity meant a mania for accumulating carpets, furniture, or a "house in the Grecian or Gothic style,"[78] then he thought his neighbors had settled for phantom liberties. It is appropriate that Thoreau should begin *Walden* with an informal treatise on economy, since he presents himself as a strict auditor of America's growing moral insolvency. When Thoreau reviles his fellow citizens as creatures of limit sunk in lethargy, cluttering their lives with superfluous goods and trivial pleasures, thus ignoring nature and pauperizing the soul, he sounds like a Puritan minister denouncing the trumpery and vanity of his congregation and exhorting them to repent and submit to higher laws. (Franklin's chastisements and corrections of vice, by contrast, are mild and humorous.)

Thoreau also notably dissents from the tradition of "Doing-good," which stretches back to Franklin and Cotton Mather and forward to Jane Addams and the Progressive reformers. His statement of opposition, though well known, bears repeating:

> If I knew for a certainty that a man was coming to my house with the conscious design of doing me good, I should run for my life, as from that dry and parching wind of the African deserts called the simoom, which fills the mouth and nose and ears and eyes with dust till you are suffocated, for fear that I should get some of his good done to me,—some of its virus mingled with my blood.[79]

This wonderful piece of prose displays Thoreau's crusty humor, his radical skepticism of the efficacy of schemes for human betterment, Franklin's specialty, but it also reveals a supercilious man fleeing from human contact for fear of contamination. One often suspects that Thoreau would have felt more at home in a Sparta of learned anchorites or perched atop a pillar like Saint Simon Stylites than living in nineteenth-century Concord, that improbable Babylon. Though nature is his god and the woods his cathedral, Thoreau is close kin to the Puritans: He burns with their icy righteousness; he recoils from what he deems "unclean"; he lacks understanding of human nature; like "a cleaver," his intellect, too, "discerns and rifts its way into the secret of things," and he does "fish in the sky, whose bottom is pebbly with stars."[80] The imagery of *Walden* veers from enclosing the self in a cramped space to letting it sail like a planet in orbit above the earth.

Such violent extremes were not in Franklin's makeup. On terms of concord with his myriad public and personal experiences, Franklin's autobiography glamorizes the liberality that America fostered in him, allowing him to escape settling into a rigidified self. That he adored travel—Emerson and Thoreau derided it as a foolish mania—relates closely to the loose, fluent self he constructed in the *Autobiography*. As Erik Erikson has pointed out: "The size and rigor of the country and the importance of the means of migration and transportation helped to create and to develop the identity of autonomy and initiative, the identity of him who is 'going places and doing things.' "[81] For Franklin, both America and the self were large continents, beckoning to be explored and offering their treasures, magical liberations. In the volatile argument about what America is and should be, Franklin's *Autobiography* offers a model of identity based on worldly tolerance, which without mutilating individuality can adjudicate their competing claims of personal desires and of the society that may deny them. In this balanced view, the needs of the self and those of America are intertwined like vines on a trellis, green, sinewy, infinitely durable.

3

Reveries of an "Incorrigible Romanticist": Louis Sullivan's *The Autobiography of an Idea*

The true architect is a poet who will someday discover in himself the presence of the tomorrow in our today.
—FRANK LLOYD WRIGHT, A Testament

I

IN 1895, when Louis Sullivan's partnership with Dankmar Adler broke up in rancor, Sullivan could not have foreseen that his architectural career would soon decline. Once the "coming man in the West,"[1] he had won the respect and envy of architects, if not their affection. "That Irish-*man* has ideas,"[2] (245) Frederick Baumann, a gruff member of the guild, had shrewdly noted of the ambitious young man come to stamp his innovative designs on booming Chicago. His buildings had presence, flair, vitality. "Be bold but prudent" his motto, he had worked out in the St. Louis Wainwright Building the most elegant solution to the challenge of the new steel-frame construction by contriving a verticality that swept upward to the sky, solid and airy in its ornamental skin, combining the most up-to-date technology with an imagination that overthrew the "tyranny of rules." The years of his partnership with Adler, 1881–95—he became a full partner at age twenty-five—

coincided with a period of accelerated capitalistic expansion; there was enough work to go around, the demand for office space creating an opportunity for unremitting effort, technological breakthroughs, and experimentation with new materials.[3] Sullivan rode the crest of this wave, the practical visionary, the man in the right place at the right time. No "cloistered monk," he was prepared for action and the testing of his powers. In a profession that was notoriously conservative, though with its share of freewheeling and eccentric men, Sullivan stood near the head, acknowledging only H. H. Richardson as his equal.

The Autobiography of an Idea, Sullivan's valedictory summation of what he stood for, devotes modest space to his personal triumphs. "Genius," he remarks, "is the highest form of play with life's forces," and while not boasting of his accomplishments, he takes great pleasure in remembering them, for that was the period in which his idealism served not "coin" or "glory" but the "beneficence of power." Even prickly geniuses, however, must go to the marketplace for clients who will hire them, and the marketplace, like fortune, is at the mercy of violent economic forces. Play and imagination and poetry, the child's most essential pastimes, are never safe from prosaic interference; giants in architecture, as in fairy tales, can have their hands and feet tied. The power of money to rule and pauperize and destroy was a lesson Sullivan had been taught but never quite learned. He had witnessed the Boston fire in 1872 and marveled at people's courage and resiliency in adversity; he had surveyed the chaos that followed the Chicago fire of 1871 and thoroughly enjoyed the equanimity of self-flattering businessmen who bragged they would turn a village into the metropolitan center of a "commercial empire." In Philadelphia, no longer a mere bystander, he saw how the 1873 panic terrorized and ruined men; he himself lost his job at Frank Furness's architectural firm.

In *The Autobiography of an Idea,* written as a third-person narrative,[4] Sullivan appraises his ignorance of economics and his innocence of evil with acute understanding: "He was too young to grasp the truth that the fair-appearing Civilization within which he lived was but a huge invisible man-trap, man-made. Of politics he knew nothing and suspected nothing. . . . In other words, Louis was absurdly, grotesquely credulous." (289) The betrayal was waiting offstage in white costume: The 1893 Columbian Exposition, with

TOP LEFT: Louis Sullivan, age sixty-four. TOP RIGHT: Louis
Sullivan, age fourteen. ABOVE: The Auditorium Building

its neoclassical "White City by the Lake," and the 1893 panic spread across America like twin plagues and after 1900 contaminated not Sullivan's ideals but his power to continue building. For in the last thirty-one years of his life, he designed only twenty-three buildings, eight of them small-town banks. His talent had not burned out, but as Frank Lloyd Wright notes, "Prejudice, provincial, quotidian, was his implacable enemy. A Genius. Well, that term damned him as it was intended to do. It will write off any man from the commercial scene we live in."[5] Commissions went to young men who were Sullivan's inferiors. Architecture had become a branch of big business. Adler had conscientiously taken care of clients while deferring to Sullivan's "superior aesthetic sense," but when he was on his own, Sullivan's hauteur alienated potential employers. With dwindling patronage, Sullivan's life caved in: In 1907, his wife, Margaret Davies Hattabough, left him; in 1908, he sold Ocean Springs, his haven in the "primeval forest" of Mississippi; in 1909, severest blow of all, he was forced to auction off much of his library, art objects, household effects, and his collection of Japanese prints. In 1918, he was evicted from the Auditorium Tower, which he had designed, because he could not pay the rent. He may even have accepted handouts from Daniel Burnham,[6] his archrival. Drinking heavily and taking bromides, Sullivan disintegrated slowly in body, brooding apart like a wounded lion, though his mind and his drawing hand were not impaired.

The Autobiography of an Idea does not include any of these mortifying events (it ends in 1893), partly because he is shy of revealing himself as down-and-out and partly because he intends the book as the history of how his idealism evolved and fared in a "democracy gone wrong."[7] When idealists write their autobiographies, they often conduct an inquiry into the reasons for the mutilation or sidetracking of their vision. Only secondarily, if at all, do they examine their own character for defects. Like crusaders enlisted in an army of saints, they dedicate themselves to combat, on behalf of the powerless, the many-headed hydra of social evils—poverty, poor health care, racial discrimination, unemployment—and they seldom renounce the self-sacrificing ideals that gave purpose to their lives.

As the son of immigrant parents, Sullivan doubtless felt the sting of prejudice, since the Irish were despised in Boston, but for most of its length, *The Autobiography of an Idea* offers a panegyric of

American democracy. Like Emerson and Whitman, he looks forward cockily to the ushering in of an age of American greatness, particularly in the arts and sciences and architecture, "the projected life of the people." Democracy, as Sullivan phrases it in *Kindergarten Chats,* is "a serene force of nature" and "a spiritual law,"[8] the symbol of the people's convenant with their unique destiny. Equality undergirds democracy, guaranteeing that all people have the opportunity to rise out of the anonymous mass and assert their perfect individuality. Democracy, "the altruistic activity of the ego," employs all man's powers for the good of all.

So ran Sullivan's theory. How he arrived at these principles, *The Autobiography of an Idea* does not make clear. The child whose development he cherishes is mostly a solitary, his head dancing with images of giants and magicians waving their wands and casting spells, usually in a constructive fashion. Most children begin with curiosity about the world and a faith in the kindliness of people, only to have both stifled by routine and dull precept. Sullivan's trust in his budding powers survives the boredom of a middling education—the old autobiographer smiles at his teachers' wrongheaded perception of the boy as a poor student—because he is fostered by love and sanely guided by parents and grandparents. And nature. Though he is a tiny figure next to the majestic ash and elm trees he adopts as his totems of lofty aspiration, nature is yet a domain over which he, a creature of vernal impulses, rules. His idealism, which lies submerged like an underground river, is sometimes interpreted by others as selfishness. In reality he feels singled out for a special destiny, unlike the children in the one-room schoolhouse "of, for, and by the people," intoning their rote lessons. Unaware of social distinctions, he talks with workmen, enjoying their explanations of their craft, and thrills to the romance of "concerted action." (Sullivan lacks Whitman's palaver about the common man.) But he never raises them to the plane of the "mighty men" he idolizes and whose ranks he expects to join someday.

Genius, exceptional in any society, is by nature elitist, hierarchical, aloof, and impelled by laws of its own internal composition. So young Louis, wrapped up in his own concerns, often overlooks signs that point to other realities—that altruism, for example, is not a universal impulse, that the behavior of societies and people often follows selfish ends. A rattan manufacturer donates a town hall to

South Reading on condition that the village change its name to his, Wakefield (it accepts the offer); on a train ride to Newburyport, Luke the brakeman cheerfully satisfies the boy's curiosity about flanges, spikes, rails, ties, and then regales him with a "get-rich romance":

> And the brakeman said the fireman expected to be an engi-neer someday but that he himself didn't expect to brake no cars all his life—it was just hell in winter; and he went on to tell of his ambition, said he'd be damned if he'd work for anybody much longer; he'd save up some money and was going to have other men work for *him,* and he'd make money out of them. He'd drive 'em, he said; he'd learn 'em what a day's work meant when they worked for him, he would; and so on, excitedly. (74)

The brakeman's ambition caricatures Louis's, but typically Louis is bored by and contemptuous of this passion for wealth and domi-nation, which, like the cutworm that destroys his nasturtium, men-aces the growth of his ideal. Other "mighty men" would appear, capture his word "power," and work their wonders: "Captains of Industry, Kings of this, Barons of that, Merchant Princes, Railroad Magnates, Wizards of Finance" (315)—feudal titles of royalty, a nomenclature that appalls Sullivan, who is helpless to stem the tide of bigness as it rushes over his democratic hopes. And sourest irony of all,

> The people rejoiced. Each individual rejoiced in envious ad-miration, and all rejoiced in the thought that these great men, these mighty men, had, with few and negligible exceptions, risen from the ranks of the common people: That this one began as a telegraph operator at a lonely way-station, and this one was boss of a section gang on such and such a rail-road; another started life as a brakeman; . . . and their hymn arose and rang shimmering as a paean to their mighty ones, and their cry went up to their God, even as a mighty anthem, lifting up its head to proclaim to all the world that this, their Country, was vastly more than the land of the free and the home of the brave; it was the noble land of equal opportunity

for all; the true democracy for which mankind has been waiting through the centuries in blood and tears, in hope deferred. This, they cried, as one voice, is the Hospitable Land,
that welcomes the stranger at its gates. This is the great Democracy where all men are equal and free. All this they sang
gladly as they moved up the runways. (315–16)

If power is sanctioned from below by the consent of the people, as
Sullivan thought, what was he to make of this momentous voluntary
collective servitude to new commercial dynasties? Like Moses, he
rails at the feckless people as a "poisonous mob" stupidly worshiping the golden calf. And when they streamed out of the Columbian
Exposition amazed by what Frank Lloyd Wright called the "florid
countenance of theoretical Beaux-Arts formalism . . . A Senseless
reversion,"[9] they were to Sullivan like the packs of rats spreading
the Black Plague in medieval Europe. All this rouses in Sullivan the
fury of an epidemiologist unable to stop a dangerous contagion because the victims in their superstition resort to quack remedies when
the cure is at hand. Burnham's cautious maxim, "It is not good
policy to go much above the general level of intelligence," (316) had
won out.[10]

Sullivan reels under the blow from this mass apostasy, as William Carlos Williams would when T. S. Eliot published *The Waste
Land:* The fulfillment of his program for change and an indigenous
art would have to be postponed fifty years, while the few visionaries
regrouped. The poet can continue scribbling poems on the backs of
prescription blanks, unlike the architect who can exercise his art
only with the assistance of moneyed powers. (The more flexible
Frank Lloyd Wright busied himself during dry spells with utopian
schemes like Broadacre City.) Having lifted the last of many veils
and discovered that given a choice, most people prefer Mammon as
their god and a "vacant, sullen materialism" as their creed, Sullivan
is outraged by this betrayal of his democratic principles: "It does
not pay to assume low origins as finalities, for it is shown that good
may come out of the sty, as out of the manger." (307) To console
himself, he tacks on a rhapsodical coda to *The Autobiography of
an Idea,* which predicts the eventual triumph of his ideas. Like other
prophets before him, he rests his hopes for the future on the new
generation. So in *Kindergarten Chats* he undertakes the education

of a bright young architect, conducting a year-long seminar in a hodgepodge of modes: the Socratic method, puns, prose poems, "heavy persiflage," rambles in nature, lectures on the ABC's of architecture, close scrutiny of the "fake" styles of buildings like Columbia University's Low Library, catechisms, and a smattering of history. Sullivan's goal in this high-flown and sometimes arch pedagogy is to wean the ephebe from the bankrupt premises of the architectural schools and to create a whole man. In his informal curriculum, the social sciences and poetry play key parts. "Every building you see is the image of a man whom you do not see,"[11] Sullivan remarks, so if he could not find work as an architect he could at least educate like Moses Woolson, his beloved teacher, and shape those unseen builders with a liberal dose of disciplined humanism.

II

SULLIVAN'S FIRST glimpse of an architect is a top-hatted Brahmin, dignified and sober. He is unimpressed by the man's dapper uniform; his imagination is stirred mainly by the fact that an "archeetect" makes plans for buildings "out of his head." That proper Bostonian came to symbolize for Sullivan the "legitimate and approved" gentility that he encountered at MIT in the amiable person of William Ware, the designer of Memorial Hall at Harvard. As *The Autobiography of an Idea* tells it, at age twelve Sullivan canvassed all the buildings of Boston and concluded that they were ugly, sordid, mediocre. Only the Masonic Temple and H. H. Richardson escaped his blanket condemnation. If buildings have faces and personalities and "builds," then the weakness of American architecture was its fear of "all but the well-behaved and docile emotions." The College of American Architectural Cardinals was a small, august body; a red hat was waiting for Louis, even though he was the arch-heretic deriding the orthodox tenets of his profession, a radical reformer like Luther or Saint Benedict, bringing the errant back to first principles that they had forgotten.

Sullivan, like Wright, invariably mentions architectural schools with contempt for running on obsolete rules, for suffocating students' nascent imaginations, and for bowing down before the monumental idols of the past. They taught by the foreign book (nearly always a term of opprobrium on Sullivan's lips), at worst reactionary and derivative, at best imparting a technical proficiency with a glaze of antique style. Sullivan acquired his own architectural education in piecemeal fashion, mostly from a series of mentors like John Hewitt, who spotted the ambition and skill of the brash young man and who taught him to be "a draftsman of the Upper Crust." Sullivan was fortunate that many architectural offices were organized in an unsystematic and unstratified way, so that a talented young man could walk off the street and talk directly to a Le Baron Jenney, a Frank Furness, or a Dankmar Adler, no gatekeeper barring the door, and be hired on the spot. Architectural offices resembled bohemian confraternities as much as businesses. Though something of a loner, Sullivan was drawn to the raffish camaraderie of men like John Edelmann, a "mercurial poseur" and a fount of ideas; they swapped anecdotes and pungent opinions, shared books, sang rousing choruses and arias from Handel's *Messiah* until the "boss" appeared. A chance word tossed out in conversation, like Edelmann's "suppressed functions," or a book like Frederick Baumann's *Theory of Isolated Pier Foundations,* kindled intellectual blazes in Sullivan.

Sullivan developed his ideas slowly, he says, "by means of incessant thought, self correction, hard work and dogged perseverance": the other side of his dreamy self. At freehand drawing he was an inspired virtuoso, but that supple pen came from hours of perfecting his technique. The romance of mathematics he felt keenly, though he regretfully jilted the grand dame of abstract thought. Throughout *The Autobiography of an Idea,* the child inquires about how things work, his curiosity for facts insatiable, his analytical intelligence exceptional. His decision to enroll at the Beaux-Arts in Paris, the Chartres of architectural schools, was logical. Like Saint Thomas, he came to Paris to sit at the feet of the masters and to test his prowess against the elite of the schools. Frank Lloyd Wright notes in *An Autobiography* that Sullivan so disparaged the educational system and training given at the Beaux-Arts that he spoiled it permanently for Wright. *The Autobiography of an Idea,* however, is more respectful. Admitted to the Atelier Vaudremer, "Louis thought the exigent condition that one held to the original sketch in its essentials, to be discipline, of an inspired sort, in that it held one firmly to a thesis." (238) The consequences of that initial sketch (*esquisse*), executed very rapidly, were considerable, since the diagram was inviolate and the student was locked into it for the rest of the year, elaborating on the scheme, developing room requirements, exits and entrances, correcting any errors in the thesis as best he could. This training in solving problems would be as valuable to Sullivan as the wash-drawing renderings, the scene depictions of mountainous terrains and trees, and the free-style decoration combining botanical and floral imagery that constituted a major part of the year's work.

Beaux-Arts theory, in Sullivan's paraphrase,

> settled down to a theory of plan, yielding results of extraordinary brilliance, . . . which, after all, was not the reality he sought but an abstraction, a method, a state of mind, that was local and specific; not universal. Intellectual and aesthetic, it beautifully set forth a sense of order, of function, of highly skilled manipulation. Yet there was for him a fatal residuum of artificiality which gave him a secret sense of misery where he wished but tenderly to be happy. And there came the hovering conviction that this Great School, in its perfect flower of technique, lacked the profound animus of a primal inspiration. He felt that beneath the law of the school lay a law which it ignored unsuspectingly or with fixed intention. (240)

The rigidity of plan prescribed symmetry. Nearly every design was arranged around a central axis, like the Paris Opera staircase, perfectly balanced. This plan governed house, museum, train station, and monastery. Moreover, for his project the Beaux-Arts student was more likely to design a temple of Athena than a church. When Louis matriculated at the Beaux-Arts, this rarefied, antiquarian, classicizing "state of mind" had become a formula that produced a kind of atrophied monumentality. Such an aesthetic could not but repel Sullivan.

Whatever their "tender" similarities as cities of "ever self-renewing youth," Paris and Chicago were worlds apart. The jewel of a polished culture, Paris gave off light and "stable motion," and like a Keatsian votary, Sullivan looked out of his casement window at buildings—Notre Dame, the Louvre—that were "perfect flowers" of a complexly layered tradition. Chicago was raw, unformed, energetic, its "state of mind" inhospitable to the aesthetic, prodigally wasteful, given to "quick turnover" and suspicious of precedent. "Highly skilled manipulation" therefore suited Baron Haussmann's Paris but not the muddy, unplanned streets of Chicago. Beaux-Arts designs would look ridiculously out of place on the prairie or at the stockyards. "Art can be no restatement,"[12] Frank Lloyd Wright's favorite quotation from Victor Hugo, was Sullivan's dogma too.

Yet part of Sullivan loved that "fatal residuum of artificiality" he rejects. His animus against tradition, sometimes shrilly expressed, was not silly chauvinism, as the one paragraph he allots to his sojourn in Florence proves:

> Louis saw Florence and does not know how he came to break the golden chains that bound him there, a too willing captive. It needed full six weeks to part a net that seemed but of gossamer; or was it the fragrance of Lotus Land? (236)

Like Odysseus, he temporarily forgot his goal, distracted by the spell that the architecture of Florence casts on all visitors. One imagines Sullivan standing for hours in front of Giotto's Campanile or the Palazzo Vecchio, measuring his ambition against such fabled achievements. Here, surely, he felt "the velvet, the down of tradition," the audacity of the masters' "constructive imagination," but he was right in deciding that the styles were not exportable, that "primal inspiration" was to be found in the power of nature so lavishly bestowed on prairie and Lake Michigan. He often claimed that the quiet solitude of the countryside was the "breeding ground" of genius.

But despite his aversion to cities, with their strife, dissipation, and "hustle," and his brash dismissal of their architecture as ugly, stale, crass, and illiterate, he settled in Chicago. He did not make Henry Adams's mistake of staying behind in the "used-up East." Chicago, he shrewdly intuited, was the architectural frontier; its "crude extravaganza" intoxicated him, and its favorite braggart word, "Big," corresponded to the big vision and ambition tucked in his head. Chicago's "prodigious expansion" in the 1870s and 1880s, as the city became the affluent center of railroads, manufac-

turing, mining, and agriculture, gave him his chance. Most of the
architects in Chicago were amateurs or engineers like Major Jenney
or old-guard dilettantes, but with prosperity, other bright talents
flocked to the city, including John Root, whom Sullivan assesses
at length:

> At once he was attracted by Root's magnetic personality. He,
> Root, was not of Burnham's type, but red-headed, large bul-
> let-headed, close-cropped, effervescent, witty, small-nosed,
> alert, debonair, a mind that sparkled, a keen sense of hu-
> mor—which Burnham lacked—solidly put together, bull-
> necked, freckled, arms of iron, light blue sensuous eyes; a
> facile draftsman, quick to grasp ideas, and quicker to appro-
> priate them; an excellent musician; well read on almost any
> subject; speaking English with easy exactitude of habit, ready
> and fluent on his feet, a man of quick-witted all-around cul-
> ture which he carried easily and jauntily; and vain to the limit
> of the skies. The vanity, however, he tactfully took pains
> should not be too obtrusive. He was a man of the world, of
> the flesh, and considerably of the devil. His temperament was
> that of the well-groomed free-lance, never taking anything
> too seriously, wherein he differed from his ponderous part-
> ner, much as dragon fly and mastiff. Nor had he one tenth
> of his partner's settled will, nor of said partner's capacity to
> go through hell to reach an end. John Root's immediate am-
> bition was to shine; to be the center of admiration, pitifully
> susceptible to flattery; hence a cluster of expensive syco-
> phants and hangers on, in whose laps it was his pleasure to
> place his feet by way of reminder, as he allowed himself to
> be called "John" by the little ones. Nevertheless, beneath all
> his superficial nonsense Louis saw the man of power, recog-
> nized him, had faith in him and took joy in him as a pro-
> spective and real stimulant in rivalry, as a mind with which
> it would be well worth while to clash wits in the promotion
> of an essentially common cause. Louis, true to his form of
> appropriating to himself and considering as a part of himself
> the things and personalities he valued—as he had done with
> Moses Woolson, Michael Angelo, Richard Wagner, *et alii*—
> immediately annexed John Root to his collection of assets;

or, if one so wills to put it—to his menagerie of personalities great and small. (286–7)

There is a friendly malice on the tip of Sullivan's pen as it inks in Root's physical features, social bonhomie, and mental agility. In sizing up Root's credentials for leadership of the new architecture, Sullivan bounces adjectives off Root's magnetism. Is he solid as his bull neck and "arms of iron," or is he just a flâneur, as the slightly envious references to Root's fluency, quickness, worldliness, and facility hint? A puritanical scowl crosses Sullivan's face as he recalls Root's skittish nature, love of flattery, fondness for the fleshpots, and, in particular, informality with subordinates, which Sullivan, who was famous for his haughty treatment of the "little ones" in his drafting room, priggishly shudders at as a breach of decorum. Though he puts Root, a "dragon fly," on his small list of major creators and men of power, the last sentence betrays Sullivan's unconscious judgment, not so much of Root as of himself: Sullivan is an impresario-connoisseur-zookeeper-emperor, adding choice territories and exotic animals (except his bête-noire, Daniel Burnham) to his collection. The clause "if one so wills to put it" barely hides Sullivan's complacent sense of his superiority; his vanity, like Root's, reaches "to the limit of the skies" (Sullivan jokes early in the book that his parents named him Louis after Louis Napoleon). Indeed, Sullivan is prone to describing men as animals and insects. Burnham is a "mastiff" and "elephantine," Root a "dragon fly," Furness a "bulldog," Woolson a "panther," Adler a "wheelhorse," and Sullivan himself the prancing "lead horse."

In *The Autobiography of an Idea,* Sullivan skims over his major architectural contributions, offering an abridged version of the steps that led to his coronation as master builder. He had followed the construction of the Eads Bridge over the Mississippi River in St. Louis and the Smith Bridge over the Ohio River in Kentucky as if they were chapters in a romantic saga, but also grasping the point that engineering advances would revolutionize the practice of architecture. Need, he asserts, generates invention. Just as one man's amputated leg set him thinking how to design a simpler and more efficient crutch, so Chicago's need for office space together with America's "passion to sell," the "impelling power of American life," produced the Bessemer steel process, the steel frame, and the Otis elevator, which tolled the last hurrah of masonry construction. Sullivan's strong utilitarian streak (and Adler's business acumen) enabled him to factor in what mattered to cost-conscious real estate speculators. He saw, for example, that masonry construction was "economically unfit" because it wasted rentable space and thus lost revenue. By exploiting the new steel frame imaginatively, he could increase the amount of usable space without sacrificing the organic beauty of the skyscraper's "vertical continuity." Sullivan's famous slogan, "Form follows function," which he says came in a flash, is a logical but obvious theorem. If the architect is called on to design an opera house, that function must ordain the form, fit special needs: Acoustics must be mellow, sight lines clear, interior space so distributed that the listener to *Tristan und Isolde,* say, will be enfolded by the music. What succeeds for an opera house will not work for a church or a warehouse or a tomb.

Unlike Frank Lloyd Wright in *An Autobiography,* Sullivan does not take the reader through the entire process from commission to blueprint to construction. Where Wright minutely chronicles the long and difficult struggle to build the Imperial Hotel in Tokyo, so that the reader puts on a hard hat and takes samples of the soil to study how much stress a building can bear in an earthquake-prone site, or sits with the architect at a meeting of the capitalists who financed the hotel, Sullivan contents himself with a few skimpy comments about the Wainwright or Auditorium building. That his office buildings do not speak with an Oxbridge or a Palladian accent *The Autobiography of an Idea* makes clear; but on the subject of their American features it falls silent: an important omission, causing a rift in the foundations.

What distinguishes Sullivan from the other architects of his time is his concern for the poet's second sight and his unorthodox view of the architect's civic responsibilities. When he listed the qualifications that characterize "a real architect," his order puzzled his colleagues: "First of all a poetic imagination; second, a broad sympathy, humane character, common sense and a thoroughly disciplined mind; third, a perfected technique; and, finally, an abundant and gracious gift of expression."[13] The architect's dexterity served the poet's uncanny imagination, for in his elation, as in childhood, "everything had something to say." The aesthetic is, for Sullivan, effete when it is severed from use, and utility, he remarked in *Kindergar-*

ten Chats, should be in harmony with the "ethical TOTALITY" of the finished building. "Ethical," however, was not part of the profession's jargon, which gravely disturbed Sullivan. "The stability and the value of democracy depend, when the last word is said, upon the fidelity of those to whom the people delegate their powers."[14] Sullivan was that faithful tribune, not pampering the privileged class, not speaking a mandarin language or stammering in a cheap vernacular, but using his gift for all the people. Sullivan never abandoned his belief that the architect and the people were allies in a grand enterprise.

With morose wit and dramatic irony, the last two chapters of *The Autobiography of an Idea,* both of them titled "Retrospect," rehearse the hero's loss of innocence; the pain throbs as if Sullivan were watching a gang of workers demolishing one of his great buildings. To his credit, Sullivan recognizes the flaws in his own character as well as the forces aligned against him, which swung giddily in the ascendancy, wounding him and the body politic. To his Antigone, Burnham is a plausibly drawn Creon, a nemesis of stature whose fascination lies in his curious resemblance to Sullivan himself, so that he might have been Louis's doppelgänger:

> Louis found Burnham a sentimentalist, a dreamer, a man of fixed determination and strong will—no doubt about that— of large, wholesome, effective presence, a shade pompous, a mystic—a Swedenborgian—a man who readily opened his heart if one were sympathetic. . . . He liked men of heart as well as brains. [He said] that there was so much loveliness in nature, so much hidden beauty in the human soul, so much of joy and uplifting in the arts that he who shut himself away from these influences and immured himself in sordid things forfeited the better half of life. It was too high a price to pay, he said. He averred that romance need not die out; that there must still be joy to the soul in doing big things in a big personal way, devoid of the sordid. (286)

Word for word, this almost spells out Sullivan's visionary program. Burnham, too, wished to be a "mighty man," and Sullivan concedes to him ownership of that scarce commodity a "dream-imagination." But in Sullivan's opinion, Burnham did forfeit "the better half of life," selling his soul—and dream—to the merchant princes, serving their interests as a courtier would his king's:

> And the while, Burnham's megalomania concerning the largest, the tallest, the most costly and sensational, moved on in its sure orbit, as he painfully learned to use the jargon of big business. He was elephantine, tactless, and blurting. He got many a humiliating knock on the nose in his quest of the big, but he faltered not—his purpose was fixed. Himself not especially susceptible to flattery except in a sentimental way, he soon learned its efficacy when plastered thick on big business men. Louis saw it done repeatedly, and at first was amazed at Burnham's effrontery, only to be more amazingly amazed at the drooling of the recipient. The method was crude but it worked. (288)

Burnham's formula for success—part P. T. Barnum showmanship, part obsequious wooing of the powerful and the moneyed—repels Sullivan, who would not stoop to such demeaning tactics. Like two meteors on a collision course,

> Thus, there came into prominence in the architectural world of Chicago two firms, Burnham & Root, and Adler & Sullivan. In each firm was a man with a fixed irrevocable purpose in life, for the sake of which he would bend or sacrifice all else. Daniel Burnham was obsessed by the feudal idea of power. Louis Sullivan was equally obsessed by the beneficent idea of Democratic power. Daniel chose the easier way, Louis the harder. Each brooded incessantly. (288)

The agon for the testing of these two polar ideas was the Columbian Exposition. Burnham was chosen administrator for this huge project, and even Sullivan praises him for his masterful executive performance in riding herd on architectural egos and getting all the buildings built on time: "He became open-minded, just, magnanimous." (321) At the same time, Sullivan castigates his rival for deferring to the conservative tastes of New York architects and thus engineering the palace revolution that introduced the reign of neoclassicism and shallow eclecticism. Although Sullivan designed the

Transportation Building at the exposition—ironically, it was the only building to win a prize bestowed by the French Beaux-Arts society—and served as secretary for the supervisory committee, he assesses the fair in *The Autobiography of an Idea* as though he were filing a report about the Apocalypse. With Euripidean invective, he heaps scorn on American architecture, drawing most of his images from pathology and pronouncing the patient dead of several diseases: "progressive cerebral-meningitis: the blanketing of the brain," "lesions significant of dementia," white microbes contaminating everything indigenous they touched. The "counterfeit form" that had unsettled him while he gazed at his grandmother's corpse had debased architecture and American society. But where once he could rush into the outdoors and under a flowering peach tree pledge himself to life, he was now helpless to counter death. An unofficial coalition of pharisaic architects, commercial giants, and apathetic masses had reinstated "feudal power," by usurping the faculty he adored lifelong, the imagination. Whether Sullivan's passionate—and tendentious—version of this vital chapter of American architectural history is correct is debatable;[15] but there is no question that Sullivan never recovered from the debacle. Rebuffed, his idealism remained intact; like Walt Whitman, he mused the rest of his life on the narrowing of the democratic vista—its landscape cluttered with old-world forms—convinced that the American people, "their shadows rummaging like a swine in the muck of cupidity," (301) had agreed to a swindle that chained their power . . . and they did not even know it. This failure, like an irritant on the nerves, runs through *The Autobiography of an Idea* and turns its vatic affirmation of democracy into a parable of disillusioned faith, the book's overarching idea a beautiful torso, like the Stock Exchange Building in Chicago (leveled in 1971 by a later generation of industrialists), whose fragments now grace a room in the Chicago Institute of Art.

III

DURING THE flush times of his partnership with Adler, Sullivan designed all the firm's commissions for private houses, but despite artful features—a light touch with materials, whimsical turrets, clever arched fenestration, charming decoration of cornices—they fall short of the dramatic power in his public buildings, whether commercial skyscraper, department store, or, late in his career, banks. The Wainwright Building, reaching boldly skyward, was an icon of the sublime, which complemented and enhanced nature's varied forms; it was an epic statement of man's dream to conquer space. Sullivan's genius for ornament luxuriated when he decorated the facades and interiors of public spaces. The lovely filigree work and floral windows over the main entrance to Carson Pirie Scott & Co. (1899–1904), along with the rounded corners, lured the prospective shopper into a magical urban bazaar. Similarly, the Golden Proscenium in the Auditorium Building sought to inspire in the music lover or theatergoer a sense of spiritual awe and beauty such as the stained-glass windows and vaulted ceilings of a Gothic cathedral roused in a thirteenth-century worshiper.

It is therefore not surprising that no house Sullivan lived in while growing up seems to have impressed him deeply. *The Autobiography of an Idea* does not belong with the handful of autobiographies, like Nabokov's, Jane Addams's, or even at times Frank Lloyd Wright's, that enshrine the family romance. Sullivan does not forage in his memory for cherished photographs, letters, books, *objets d'art,* the mementos of a shared intimacy. For long periods in his life, Sullivan boarded with other people: at his grandparents' house in South Reading, at the Tompsons' in Cambridge, at his brother Albert's in Chicago.[16] Domestic arrangements, when they did not gall, were makeshift environments to be tolerated. Whereas Frank Lloyd Wright at Oak Park, during the years he was plotting out his revolutionary designs for Prairie houses, lived in his studio, a cozy nook separate from yet attached to the tumultuous stage of his family life (he had a wife and six children), Sullivan, who did not marry until 1899 and did not have any children, had his office and spiritual home in the Tower of the Auditorium Building, an eagle's aerie where the solitary genius rested after flights of thought.

From childhood, Sullivan's favored domain was the outdoors. Most of his early revelatory experiences took place under the canopy of sky or tree or stars. He feels acute nostalgia in *The Autobiography of an Idea* for tramps through the wilderness of Brown's Tract or the unspoiled beauty of his cottage in Ocean Springs, a haven from the stresses of work and domestic strife. Schoolrooms, with two rare exceptions (those of Moses Woolson and M. Clopet), chafed him. Sentimentalist that he was, Sullivan purses his lips when talking about most houses, as if they were prisons or outposts of philistinism: He prefers being footloose and fancy free, a democratic bard fighting for his ideal and taking refuge in whatever wayside inns he stumbles upon.

Sullivan's restlessness ran in the family: like father, like son. Patrick Sullivan moved his family about from Boston to Halifax, Nova Scotia, to Chicago, as ambition, family necessity (his wife Andrienne's frail health), and his habit of wandering dictated, until he settled in Chicago in 1869. Louis remained behind in Boston, relieved to be free of parental supervision.

Sullivan's account of his "mongrel origin" in *The Autobiography of an Idea* is as casual as a person wearing a wardrobe of hand-me-downs: The ensemble doesn't match. The idealistic architect who grew out of the embryonic child dreamer refused to take his eye off his "fixed ideas" about power, democracy, choice, and the architect's duties as citizen long enough to sort out his true feelings about family ties. His sketches are hastily drawn, like preliminary architectural renderings that are not discarded from the portfolio. The composite picture of his father is a curious blend of venom and respect. At first he assigns Patrick the minor role of stereotyped father in a touring company's melodrama of the Irish immigrant in America. Patrick lurks on the fringes of the action, vaguely sinister: "unlovely in person," with "small repulsive eyes—the eyes of a pig— of nondescript color and no flash," stiff (odd in a dancing master), allegedly indifferent and self-centered, of a grim, rapacious will. Though Sullivan tries to be fair and allow that some tinge of romantic love might have colored his father's motives in marrying Andrienne, seventeen years his junior, he sarcastically calls Patrick an adventurer who realized that she would be a business asset (as piano accompanist, presumably) and trapped her in a tepid marriage.[17]

All children define themselves in relation to their parents, whether in opposition or emulation—or both. Louis Sullivan was no exception. Though reluctant to admit it, he inherited many of his father's qualities: pride, drive, probity, "virile and sensitive powers"—a combination Sullivan lauds throughout the autobiography—and above all, "a hunger for Nature's beauty." "He must have been a pagan," Sullivan remarks, "for in him Nature's beauty, particularly in its more grandiose moods, inspired an ecstasy, a sort of walking trance, a glorious mystic worship." (14)

The Autobiography of an Idea, however, shows little of Patrick's ecstasy and much of his severe disciplinary practice. Despite his love of nature, Patrick was impatient of rhapsodizing. "He would not rave for thirty minutes over a single blossom; a brief moment of appreciation sufficed." (77) Sullivan's effusions in their emotional excess often seem an unconscious protest against his father's verbal parsimony. In fact, the relationship between father and son resembles that of adept and neophyte: slightly formal, based on courtesy and a sharing of ritual activities. Patrick is like one of Sarastro's priests in *The Magic Flute,* enlightening the error-prone Tamino about mysteries whose meaning passion clouds. Patrick understood Louis's nature better than the old man writing the autobiography does. As page after page makes clear, Sullivan's habit is to be engulfed by a new experience—his first sight of the bridge over the Merrimack River, his terror at seeing his father in a rowboat bobbing on the rough seas and disappearing for a moment in the trough of the waves, listening to Handel's oratorios or Wagner's operas—and then to study the structure that underlies his sensuous pleasure or explains his confusion. Patrick saw that if Louis's extravagant fantasy life was not modified by fact, the boy would not grow out of his amorphous self-love. So he reined in his son's nature with a program of Spartan physical fitness—waking at five, cold baths, running several miles, stringent diet, which were meant to promote mental alertness—that was as strenuous as the training of a decathlon athlete. When Patrick teaches his son to swim, the boy rides his back like Arion on the dolphin, one of the few close moments between them in the autobiography. Sullivan admires his father's "lithe mastery," and more important, viewing his naked body, he identifies himself with a model of masculine sexuality:[18] "a company of naked mighty men, with power to do splendid things with their body." (79) When Louis joined the Lotos Club in Chicago, he enjoyed the fellowship of men like Bill Curtis, who, having lost a lung to consumption, had overcome the disability by a system of scientific exercise. If Sullivan disapproved of Greek classical architecture, he shared the Greek worship of the male body.

Still, Sullivan never admits his father into his exclusive pantheon of heroes, never credits Patrick's tutelage with helping him to pass the Beaux-Arts entrance exams after only six weeks of intense study "[I had] no nerves," Louis boasts), but showers all his praise on Moses Woolson for the gift of "self-discipline of self power." Further, he pettily accuses Patrick of "little human sympathy or insight," disguising the following verdict as his grandpa List's:

> "Now, I have watched you since you were a babe in arms, and I have mostly let you alone for fear of meddling with nature's work; for you were started right by my daughter, the mother who carried you and yearned for you. She is sound to the core. She alone of all my children might fittingly wear the red cap of liberty. Yet you do not know your own mother. *I* know *you*. I know your abominable selfishness—come from your father; and your generosity and courage—come from my proud daughter. You have a God-given eye and a dull heart. You are at one and the same time incredibly industrious and practical, and a dreamer of morbid dreams, of mystic dreams, sometimes clean, brilliant dreams, but these are too rare." (135–6)

The Autobiography of an Idea presents no evidence that his father was selfish. As if spitting out an old peeve, Sullivan's vanity makes him want to deny that he is the normal offshoot of his parent (and not a pure child of nature). But elsewhere in the autobiography Sullivan contradicts this mingy assessment. Patrick was, he says, "wondrous wise for his day and generation"; he opened the "world of pure knowledge" to his son. With his knack of explaining processes and phenomena—perspective, the curvature of the sea, the horizon, bridges, shipyards—in clear and concise words, Patrick reinforced the "ridiculously practical" side of the boy's unruly idealism. He did not try to break his son's will or snap off the fledgling's wings; rather, he corrected the imbalances of Louis's excitable character, guiding him, if not with sympathy, then with insight. Surely the young man who walked into Frank Furness's architectural office in Philadelphia and announced that he was going to work there showed an amazing initiative and faith in himself that owed something to his father's self-reliance. Ironically, Patrick Sullivan even had a touch of romance in him, tracing the Sullivan name past its "shanty Irish" commonness to the pirate clan O'Souleveyne, just the kind of ancestry sure to please Louis's imagination. After 1869, Patrick disappears from *The Autobiography of an Idea,* except for one brief mention as the one who grubstaked his son to roam at will along the uncertain route to identity and professional mastery. No genius is self-begotten, though Sullivan with heavy whimsy reluctantly says of himself, "He was born of woman in the usual way," and that biological law admits of no exceptions. Nevertheless, Patrick's authority was installed in Louis's mind and helped build what the self-destructive autobiographer razed.

Like most men of his generation, Sullivan divided male and female qualities along conventional lines. In *Kindergarten Chats,* he instructs the architectural tyro that the masculine is "virile, forceful, direct, clear and straightforward, that which grasps and retains in thought. The feminine: intuitive sympathy, tact, suavity and grace— the qualities that soothe, elevate, ennoble and refine."[19] An integrated art, Sullivan warns, must contain both. Nature is the fruitful mother whose care is benign and whose forms are inexhaustibly inventive. But if he acknowledges the sovereignty of Mother Earth, Sullivan is less certain about the power of his earthly mother and of women in general. In the real world, women lacked power: They did not build ships, railroads, bridges, or skyscrapers. In architecture, unlike literature and painting, women were not even arbiters of taste. But they did bestow a supreme gift that men and architects needed: By their love and sentiment, women nurtured the imagination. Alone of American architects, Sullivan was not embarrassed to speak of beauty and emotion as conscious organic parts of a building; intellect divorced from instinct, he held, led to cold and servile monumentality. One might argue that the delicate yet luxuriant curves of Sullivan's ornament are a sublimated tribute to the erotic sensibility and ennobling refinement of women, and in particular of his mother.

Yet when Sullivan writes about Andrienne List Sullivan in *The Autobiography of an Idea,* he becomes secretive. The autobiographer has inhibitions, reticences he can't overcome; he never submits his relationship with his mother to any extended analysis. Instead he bursts out at unexpected moments, in "highly emotional . . . ecstasies of speech" such as his mother was given to. A child bride, a "jewel without price," a doting mother, Andrienne is all sensibility. In a pretty scene that might have been the subject of a sentimental engraving hanging on the parlor wall, the three-year-old boy sits under the piano, listening to his mother play a languid nocturne in a style imbued with "fervor and melancholy sweetness." Obscurely moved, Louis bursts into sobs. The "flood gates open wide," and he shares with Andrienne a moment of joy and exaltation. Though not understanding the source of the artist's power to stir him, he receives a kind of sanction for the surrender to feeling.

Andrienne was not one of those robust women Whitman so fondly placed in the foreground of his celebratory poems, nor did she announce with a flourish, as Wright's mother did, that her son would be a great architect; she read no sibylline leaves. She is like the precious figure of a saint wheeled out on special occasions, shown to the congregation, addressed in gallant and devotional terms, and then carefully wrapped up and put away. The real woman seldom appears. Why she deserves Grandpa List's encomium about her courage and generosity, or how she earned the privilege of wearing "the red cap of liberty," Sullivan does not say. Unaided, the reader must accept the virtues imputed to her as fact, since Sullivan keeps his own counsel. What can we glean from this paragraph about his mother's religious creed?

> Mother had a fixed idea that existence was continuous in a series of expanded becomings, life after life, in a spiral ascending and ever ascending until perfection should be reached in a bodiless state of bliss. This ethereal belief opened to view the beauty and purity of her heart. Moreover, she read with avidity Renan's *Vie de Jesu*. (42)

As spiritual faith this aestheticism is inoffensive (it doesn't prevent Andrienne from insisting that Louis be baptized); the "expanded becomings" comport with Sullivan's idea of a gradual evolutionary curve toward a higher good, not just for the individual but for the polity. But what strikes one in this passage are the neutered or idealized terms Sullivan associates with his mother: "bodiless," "ethereal," and "purity," her philosophy, like her being, untouched by sexual longing, as if she were a Pre-Raphaelite Madonna whose one discreet avidity is for a book of mild religiosity.

Sex is curiously muted in *The Autobiography of an Idea,* tangential to the child's development or transposed into wholesome experience of art and nature:

> But the lovely elm was his infatuation—he had adopted her at first sight, and still gazed at her with a sweetness of soul he had never known. He became infiltrated, suffused, inspired with the fateful sense of beauty. He melted for an instant into a nameless dream, wherein he saw he was sufficient unto herself, that like his garden plants she lived a life of her own, apart from his life. Yet they both lived in the same big world—they both, for the moment, stood in the same green field. Was there nothing in common? Did she not know he was there? (64)

Infatuated with beauty, the young Louis has wandered into the fateful landscape of a Keats poem, with its atmosphere of swoon, dream, rapture, and painful separation. The boy's ecstasy of possession slowly yields to a quizzical search for the grounds of relation to female otherness and, covertly, through projection, to an acceptable resolution of his feelings of guilty pleasure that Andrienne loved her son more than her husband. The two questions at the end of the passage hint that he fails to establish a sexual self-sufficiency. As Albert Stone remarks, Sullivan's "complete silence about any mature relationships with women" in *The Autobiography of an Idea* suggests that "Sullivan remained throughout his life a man whose capacities for strong universal emotion masked underlying ambiguities about personal ties."[20]

In the midst of his narrative of his brief stay at MIT and a paragraph about military drills (!), Sullivan inserts a last tribute to Andrienne:

> Social strata had become visible and clear, as also the hypocrisy of caste and cant and "eminence" against which his mother, time and time again, had spoken so clearly, so vehemently in anger and contempt. Her ideal she averred was a righteous man, sound of head, clean of heart, a truthful man too natural to lie or to evade. These outbursts of his mother sank deep into the being of her son; and in looking back down the years, he has reason justly to appraise in rev-

erence and love a nature so transparent, so pure, so vehement, so sound, so filled with a yearning for the joy of life, so innocent-ecstatic in contemplation of beauty anywhere, as was that of the one who bore him forth, truly in fidelity, to be and to remain life of her life. Thus the curtain of memory ever lifts and falls and lifts again, on one to whom this prayer is addressed. If Louis is not his mother's spirit in the flesh, then words fail, and memory is vain. (183)

An "innocent-ecstatic" like his mother, Louis denounced the "caste and cant and 'eminence' " of his profession and American society in *The Autobiography of an Idea,* yet his prayer pleads that he had not betrayed her faith: I am that "righteous man," that "truthful man too natural to lie or to evade," while all around me the lie prevails. But Sullivan's words do fail, not because he is reverential but because Andrienne's portrait is a blank, a canvas of abstract perfection. The reader politely intrudes with questions: Why was she so obsessed with etiquette? Was she discriminated against because she was an immigrant or married to an Irishman? How did she preserve her purity of soul? By playing Chopin? By teaching Louis drawing? We are left with a few dim phrases about her "temperamental emotionalism" and "self flattery" that she had produced a precocious son. But the autobiography does not bring to life her crucial influence.

Though they spin the silken cocoon of emotional protection around the boy, as mentors women cannot enter his worlds of imagination and ambition, as his grandpa List can, because they lack the specialized knowledge he seeks. On the train to Newburyport, Andrienne typically does not respond to his importunate questions about how the railroad works, "why telegraph wires rose and fell and rose again"; the brakeman answers his "technical inquisition." He takes his grandmother's love for granted as a law of his young life and he appreciates it, but he soon adopts a condescending attitude to her devout Christianity and village notions of decorum, rebelling against them just as he refused to wear white pantalettes to school and ridiculed the poem "Old Ironsides" as a piece of claptrap. Women in the autobiography who stand for respectability he dismisses in a cutting phrase, as when he shies from his aunt Jenny's "dry kiss of superculture."

In *The Autobiography of an Idea,* the only women Sullivan confides in are Julia, the family's Irish maid, and Minnie Whittlesey, his cousin, whom he meets on an excursion to Lyon Falls that he takes with his grandfather. Julia's saucy and folksy affection as well as her stock of wild Irish tales endear her to him. She peoples his fantasy life with heroes and monsters and trolls, teaches him how to milk cows, and as peasant "Queen of the Orchard" interprets for her young cavalier the meaning of the procession of Irish soldiers, Civil War veterans, mustered out of the army and clung to by their women and ragged children, and even the tears that Louis shed at the spectacle. With acute perception she pronounces on his character: "Yere all sintiment, Louis, and no mercy." A surplus of feeling crossed with a lack of charity is a formula for heartless egoism: He censures Henri List's demonstrative grief at his wife's funeral as "noisy" and "mercenary," that is, unaesthetic; Louis prefers the comfort of nature's "choir of resurrection." His own feelings take precedence over the hurt of others.

About Minnie Whittlesey, Sullivan *is* all sentiment. A vivid Jamesian ingenue, part temptress, part "ordinarily affectionate sister," and part Fairy Queen to his Red Cross Knight *sans peur et sans reproche,* Minnie embodies a spirit of romance that lingers in the memory of the aged recluse like the odor of incense. He allots an exorbitant amount of space in the autobiography to their boy-girl dalliance. It is an interlude of unforced charm. The fourteen-year-old adolescent is dazzled by this belle of Utica, eighteen, "intuitive to a degree" ("intuitive" is always a complimentary word in Sullivan's vocabulary), who takes him under her wing. To his surprise, he becomes Minnie's adoring slave and protégé, and blurts out all his secret desires to her. In her sacred grove she reads Tennyson and Browning to him, plumbing his depths:

> When Minnie came, through questioning, to a full sense of the depth of Louis's ignorance of the world, of social organization both in its ephemeral and its momentous inert and stratified aspects, that he was provincial, that he was honest, frank, and unsuspecting, she became alarmed at the new danger, and determined to prepare him; and in so doing, she lifted at least a corner of a sinister and heavy veil that lay behind appearances. . . .
>
> . . . Minnie was both worldly and unworldly. With na-

ture she was dreamy [like him], but when it came to people, she became a living microscope, her sharp brain void of all illusion, for her true world was of the world of people—there she lived—as Louis's world had been a world of the wide open—of romance. Hence, with Louis she was ever gentle, even though she dangled him as though he were a toy balloon. (148)

For the only time in the autobiography, Sullivan trusts a woman and is at ease in a passive role, as Minnie alternately feeds him drops of vitriol and honey; it is a sexual awakening for him, who like an enchanted lover repeats the words *Je t'aime* without quite knowing what he's saying. Their mock-solemn betrothal under the great oaks he cherishes as a "lovely memory" of an "exquisitely human" young woman "ever thoughtful of the needs of others," mothering him with "sprightly malice and in tenderness alike."

Looking backward, Sullivan acknowledges that Minnie was one of his pivotal teachers, not merely because of her tomboy spunk or her clever civilizing of the "rough and ready" adolescent, but because she was a rebel with a satirist's eye for social details: the autocratic power of money or the stratifications of class and caste (his mother's favorite target). She declares wryly that she is "in society," which in a dreary somnolent town like Utica meant premature entombment of her hopes. Without illusion she excoriates the smug rich young men of her acquaintance who view women as their "property, their appendage, their vehicle of display," and she vows that she will not be "owned" by any man. Thus Sullivan salutes her as his peer in not compromising her dream of happiness. (He does not tell what her fate was.) Like Cassandra, she administers a warning that Sullivan does not heed: When social organization and positions of power are in the hands of men like the contemptible young bloods of Utica, "incapable of thought above the level of the sty," such negligent force and inert mind will wreck the hopes and careers of those who see deeper and aspire higher. Immediately upon leaving Minnie, he treks through the wilderness, as if enacting an episode from the Leatherstocking novels, in the company of two farm boys and a trapper, testing his male prowess and communing with "venerable immensities." The "venerable immensities" of society, however, always stymied him.

Since a good portion of his early life was spent in his grandparents' home, they were beloved surrogates, permissive and scarcely ever hindering his will. Grandparents are often loved immoderately and uncritically by their grandchildren, because the normal psychological conflicts between parent and child, which lead to friction and deadlock, are mostly absent. Grandma List, as we have seen, was "conservative of the social order of her day," (46) as cautious in her conduct as in her choice of safe horse and buggy. But Henri List, reputed to be an adventurer who married Anna List for her money, was far more complex than his wife and became in his grandson's life a companion and an affectionate tutor. A bungler at business, a freethinker, a closet idealist, he "looked upon religion as a curious and amusing human weakness—as conclusive evidence of universal stupidity." (42) Indeed, he had a long list of topics that he ridiculed cynically, and he passed on to Louis a mistrust of timid minds and conventional educators: "They are not inspired. They are victims of routine, wearied on the daily treadmill until they can no longer see into the heart of a child." (135) Louis was his prize pupil. Whenever Louis was perplexed he would appeal to his grandfather for answers, and Henri List had a gift for expounding ideas in plain yet eloquent language. Apprehensive about his grandson's future and with a grasp of the "seething" social forces that can crush the dreamer, he watched over Louis's growth with critical but generous attention. If Sullivan never figured out "what lies hidden beneath Grandpa" (137) he could speak of him in *The Autobiography of an Idea* unconstrainedly and with insight. The scoffer who "ridiculed so many things . . . never poked fun at the solar system. In this domain, and the star-laden firmament, he lived his real life. This was his grand passion. All else was trivial. The vastness awed him; the brilliance inspired him; he kept close track of the planets," even waking "in the early hours of night to make vigils with the stars, to venerate, to adore this panoply of constellations, *to be wholly lost within the splendor of the sky.*" (my italics; 44) The galaxy was Henri List's church, and he reserved his piety exclusively for worshiping in it. This spiritual proclivity, this harmony with nature, was his legacy to his grateful grandson.

IV

PROLONGING the narrative of one's childhood is not unusual in autobiography. Many authors view childhood as a privileged period and linger over it as a connoisseur sips a vintage wine or a collector examines a rare print. Memory treats the past with the courtesy one might extend to a friend not seen for twenty years: There have been dramatic changes, but familiar features and inflections can be discerned so that renewed acquaintance is a pleasure. Nabokov's *Speak, Memory* and Franklin's *Autobiography* are classics of this sort. Other autobiographers, whose childhoods were filled with trauma and humiliations, are driven to revisit the old battlegrounds, there to commune with fallen compatriots and enemies and to muse on the combination of luck and grit that let them escape extinction. So Richard Wright, Edward Dahlberg, Malcolm X, and Emma Goldman explore the menacing causes that made them controversial writers and revolutionary leaders. Only in exceptional cases, like *The Autobiography of Alice B. Toklas,* does the author refuse to establish any relations with the child; Gertrude Stein denies any gestation to her genius, as if in her cradle she assumed command of the literary vanguard by divine right.

That refusal would have baffled Louis Sullivan, for whom *The Autobiography of an Idea* was an "authentic study of child life." An architect naturally gives much thought to the foundations on which his buildings rest. Ideas and lives have similar antecedents, and Sullivan reenters the dream consciousness of the child, he says, because "It is the moving child-in-multiple of long ago that created for us the basic environment within which we now live; as ancients, we move on, unchanged from the children that we were—leaving our thoughts and deeds as a beaten trail behind us." (93) This radical determinism, as much emotional conviction as logical deduction from his own "thoughts and deeds," explains the startling excess with which Sullivan relives the boy's unfolding.

The embittered old man, the lonely demiurge, writing *The Autobiography of an Idea* in his shabby room, alienated from all but a few cronies, his dreams tarnished and his career at a standstill, gazes raptly at the shining child moving forward, innocent, impassioned, hopeful of reshaping the world by the imagination's light. The boy starting out is farthest away from death and the defeat of his ideals. The urchin's truancies, the schoolboy's scorn for virtuous routine, his hard work and growing mastery of fact, "orderly speech," and knowledge, his consecration of self to high ideals of service—all these pass before the old man's eyes, and he temporarily recovers the thread of purpose that had guided him through the maze of his contradictory nature and the adversity that beset him. He idealizes himself.

The boy Louis reaches out by natural tropism with what Sullivan calls the "wonderself" to Life, Beauty, Truth, and Goodness. (Sullivan loved the imposing look and sonority of capitalized nouns, as if they were Platonic Ideas and divinities to be invoked and idolized.) He has no desire to "plunder what he sees." Like Frank Lloyd Wright, Sullivan believed "Nature-Experience . . . the only true reading [of] the book of Creation."[21] Both insisted on the primacy of "the awakening of the child-mind to rhythmic structure in Nature," of acquiring early the "habit of seeing into and seeing from within outward."[22] When Wright's mother returned from the Philadelphia Centennial Exposition in 1876 with a box of Frederick Froebel's "gifts" (geometric blocks) to play with, she handed him a radical pedagogy, which Wright always cited with approval: "Mother learned that Frederick Froebel taught that children should not be allowed to draw from casual appearances of Nature until they had first mastered the basic forms lying hidden behind appearances. Cosmic, geometric elements were what should first be made visible to the child-mind."[23] In deifying the child and stressing this crucial embarking on a metaphysical voyage to capture the essences behind the particulars of appearance, Sullivan and Wright followed standard romantic doctrine and, in particular, Emerson's Transcendentalist preaching. It is a heroic calling to study nature's "eternal laws of change" and multitudinous forms, to lift veil after veil in an effort to find her underlying unity. As William Jordy notes, "Nature not only offered the designer an infinitude of motifs, it also permitted a range of treatment extending from near realism to near abstraction."[24] Nature, Sullivan and Wright never tired of saying, binds the self to her in holy service, supervises its development, and rewards sympathetic study with the power of efflorescence.

The young Louis lives wildly and reverently in nature, alternately abandoning himself like Caliban to the ravishing music of wind, wave, and bird surrounding him and observing closely the cyclical rhythm of soil, seed, organic growth, fruit, and decay (frequent metaphors in Wright's lexicon too). Thus, indirectly, Sullivan introduces the weaknesses in his character that contributed to his decline: He plants seeds, which put out roots, then digs them up, only to discover that the plant will die (he learns by doing and undoing); the spectacle of nature, whether sunrise or majestic ash and elm trees, as if staged for him alone, is spellbinding, and this egoism, which he never loses, is stitched together of impulsive generosity and selfishness.

In the same spirit, the nursery of Frank Lloyd Wright's idealism and egoism, according to his slanted version in *An Autobiography,* was not his father's music room and book-lined study, or his mother's classroom, but his years working as a hand on his uncle James's farm in Spring Green, Wisconsin. There the dreamy Frank sees the muck of agricultural routine, the long, exhausting toil in all kinds of weather, the rawness of procreation, the gelding and slaughtering of animals, and machines that rust or maim. A barefoot Achilles, he kills a rattlesnake in single combat (as he later, in Sullivan's architectural office, stabbed a young draftsman who taunted him for being the Master's pet). There are moonlight rambles in woods and meadows and flower-gatherings, which rouse the boy's ardor for nature; vigils, revels, and daydreams in which the "wonderself" exfoliates. But nature is not so uniformly benign as in Sullivan's account. Wright's physical conditioning in the country protects the budding genius from a reductive or effete idealization of nature and deepens his awareness of materials, labor, and the limits they invariably impose. "Keep close to the Earth, my boy,"[25] his mother had counseled him, and that axiom became the cornerstone of his architecture, especially in designing the Prairie houses.

For Wright and Sullivan, only in the renewals of nature's "Infinite Creative Spirit" were absolute liberty and self-governing authority to be found. They took it for granted that their ideas and prescriptions were intrinsically superior and altruistic, though others perceived their behavior as arrogantly elitist. In a democracy, Wright argues,

> every man born had equal right to grow from scratch by way of his own power unhindered to the highest expression of himself possible to him. This of course not antagonistic but

sympathetic to the growth of all men as brothers. Free emulation not imitation of the "bravest and the best" is to be expected of him. Uncommon he may and will and should become as inspiration to his fellows, not a reflection upon them, not to be resented but accepted—and in this lies the only condition of the common man's survival. So only is he intrinsic to democracy.[26]

This theory—and it is the gospel of Emerson, Whitman, and Charles Ives too—confers on the imagination godlike attributes and assumes that the common man would come to see the validity of the singular man's position. But the philistines did not appreciate it. And the genius of the "born soloist"[27] had to contend with vested economic interests, herd thinking, coarse social evils, and artificial distinctions, which could not be brushed aside as nuisances: They were an out-of-tune orchestral accompaniment to the Spring Song of their idealism. The "new," his most frequent adjective, was Sullivan's precious eidolon, but banks were built in the style of the Roman Capitol, mansions in the style of English Tudor or French châteaus. The infinite potentiality of the self had shrunk to debased forms of imitation.

Sullivan held to his great "idea" with the unswerving loyalty of an "incorrigible romanticist"[28] determined to make real the workings of his imagination. This fact influenced his decision to write *The Autobiography of an Idea* in the third person: He converts his subjectivity into a putative objectivity and elevates it to the status of an impersonal law like gravity or the chemistry of the blood. The omniscient author of his own life vaults into the throne of godhead, virtually viewing himself as self-created, proposing and disposing of people and ideas with an imperious righteousness. As a psychological stratagem, claiming infallible authority is brilliant. Since his main audience is his own consciousness, who can challenge the veracity of his version of events? Sullivan frees himself from wondering what others really think of him, licenses himself to invent a part real, part mythical boy, and says to the reader: If you have the courage, you can be like that. A suffering "I" is remarkably absent in *The Autobiography of an Idea;* Louis is never waylaid by temptations, crushed by defeats, prey to anguish, loneliness, and depressions; he need not take responsibility for his mistakes, repent of any choices. He is exempt from contingency. In *An Autobiography,* Wright, too, begins in the third person,[29] but when he arrives in Chicago to lead an independent life, he switches to the first person, as if he had successfully negotiated a difficult rite of passage and had earned an identity. When the "murderously actual" world invades Wright's autobiography and smites him with a vengeance— domestic problems, fires (which twice destroy Taliesin), debts, arrests, public scandal and notoriety, and a long period during which he could not obtain any commissions—his thorny sense of his genius and his worldly finesse enable him to reconstruct his life and resume his architectural practice. Wright's "I"—vain, mercurial, overbearing, resilient—prevails; the old Druid symbol his grandfather had placed on the family crest, "TRUTH AGAINST THE WORLD,"[30] sustains him, the visionary pariah, throughout his ordeal.

Third-person narrative creates for the less flexible Sullivan a distance between the self he was and admires and the "washed-up I" he has become; a cushion to avoid the frictions of remembered failure, it prohibits real intimacy between author and reader. It is also an episode in that long-playing American drama, Individuality and Its Discontents. Despite his equating ego with identity, Sullivan feels uncomfortable writing about the self, for that requires him to elevate himself above and apart from others, and so he seeks to merge with the common man in a democratic spirit as if it were somehow not noble to be unique. It seems to be an American phenomenon that in proportion as a person pursues distinction he increases his rhetorical ties to the people and to the idea of equality. The price of being that great "I" is isolation.

Third-person narrative also appeals to autobiographers with fixed ideas who are obsessed with power and like to play the sage. In *The Education of Henry Adams,* Adams's pose as the scourge of his own powerlessness and the hypothesist of theories as weightless as a helium balloon is just a transparent reversal of his aggressive certitudes. In *The Armies of the Night,* while Norman Mailer plays with multiple personas—intellectual swashbuckler, mischievous boy caught with his pants down, clown coating unpleasant truths in bawdy jokes—he smuggles the ego into the book with disarming good humor and a conspiratorial wink: We Americans aren't supposed to take ideas too seriously. And Gertrude Stein is another egoistic democrat who shuns the "I" as a loutish guest who asks prying questions. But in Sullivan's case, the desire not to eclipse the grand idea, as if its life were more durable than his own, is finally untenable because he fails to incarnate the experiences that would illustrate the idea.

An architect, Sullivan always insisted, needs heart as well as brains, poetry as well as structural clarity, or else his building will not rise above sterile professionalism or academic formalism. Sullivan uses ornament "to enliven with movement the stability of his masses," (125) and his touch, which, Wright noted admiringly, "was like the passion vine in full bloom,"[31] never deserted Sullivan. It is displayed in his late exquisite book, *A System of Architectural Ornament,* and in his designs for small-town banks in Minnesota, Iowa, and Wisconsin. When he delivered a paper before a convention of his fellow architects, Sullivan often couched his ideas in rhapsodical prose poems. Most thought him self-indulgent or mildly demented, as if he were chanting the Russian Orthodox liturgy, and they either humored him or dismissed his propaganda as harmless eccentricity (while acknowledging his formidable skills at the drawing board). A few sensed between the feverish lines a message of oracular grandeur.

There is no inconsistency between the vatic prose of 1886 and the pastiche he confected in *Kindergarten Chats* and *The Autobiography of an Idea.* Part discourse, part tirade, and part bogus poetry, Sullivan's prose, unlike his architecture, is overblown like a rococo building:

> How monstrous, how fluent, how vagrant and timorous, how alert are the living things we call words. They are the giants and the fairies, the hob-goblins and the sprites; the warrior and the priest, the lowly and the high; the watchdog and the sheep; the tyrant and the slave,—of that wonder-world we call speech.
>
> How like hammers they strike. How like aspens they quiver. How like a crystal pool, a rivulet therefrom, becomes a river moving sinuously between the hills, growing stronger, broader as its affluents pour in their tributary power; and now looms the estuary, and the Ocean of Life. (198)

This is a typical lyric effusion, its rhythm stilted, its diction fancy as a ruffled shirt and self-important as a pompous minister. A romantic enthusiast, "dramatizing himself as the Sayer or the Litera-tus,"[32] Sullivan strikes pose after pose, here the inebriate of words. From Whitman he learned the habit of setting sentences in motion and marching them in parallel pairs until they empty into the Ocean of Words. Ingenuous as a child imitating an adult, the performance is calculated to win applause but simply sounds foolishly trite.

This hammy style, with its flavor of the archaic—Sullivan often sprinkles the word "beauteous" into his paragraphs—jeopardized Sullivan's visionary enterprise because it unconsciously substituted the false Sublime. Often his literary art wavers between legitimate chaste rapture and its showy cousin, the gushing sentimentality he held in contempt yet practiced, as in this description of the six-year-old boy's first experience of a sunrise:

> Restless through the night, he arose at twilight, made ready quickly, and passed up the road leading to the great ash tree whose companionship he ever sought on high occasions. Here, under the wondrous tree—and with Cowdrey's farm-house resting silently across the way—here in stillness of on-coming dawn punctured here and there by a bird's early chirp, and chanticleer's high herald call heard near and far, raucous faint, and ever fainter far away; the few remaining stars se-rene within the dome of pale passing night, he stood, gazing wistfully over the valley toward a far away range of dark blue drowsy hills, as the pallid eastern sky, soon tremulous with a pink suffusion, gave way before a glow deepening into ra-diant crimson, like a vanguard of fire—as the top of the sun emerging from behind the hills, its slow-revealing disc reach-ing full form, ascended, fiery, imperious and passionate, to confront him. Chilled and spellbound, he in turn became im-passioned with splendor and awe, with wonder and he knew not what, as the great red orb, floating clear of the hilltops overwhelmed him, flooded the land; and in white dazzling splendor awakened the world to its work, to its hopes, to its sorrows, and to its dreams. Surely the child, sole witness be-neath his great ash tree, his wonder-guardian and firm friend sharing with him in its stately way as indeed did all the land and sky and living things of the open—the militant splendor of sunrise—the breaking of night's dam—the torrent and foam of far-spreading day—surely this child that went forth every

day became part of sunrise even as this sunrise became for-
evermore part of him. The resounding power of the voice of
the Lord of the sky and earth found in him a jubilant answer—an awakening world within, now aroused from its twi-
light dream, its lyric setting sun, its elegy of the gloaming.
The great world was alive to action. Men resumed the toil of
countless ages; the child, illumined, lost in an epic vision,
came slowly to consciousness of his own small self, and the
normal doings of his own small day. (60–1)

The roseate atmosphere of this immersion in nature, the muted ecstasy as the boy holds his breath, the revelatory power of the *mys-
terium tremendum*, are handled skillfully. Surrounded by the lights
and noises of dawn, small and lost and attentive and guarded by his
regent, the ash tree, the boy watches "the Lord of the sky and earth"
make his grand entrance in epic style. The "breaking of night's dam"
releases a torrent of feeling (and a crescendo of words), heightened
by the synesthesia, and admits him into a fellowship with nature.
Hence the jubilation. If the passage confers too much sophistication
on the boy's consciousness—what could he know of "the toil of
countless ages"?—and overstates the splendor, a word used three
times, the reader forgives these lapses into conventional language
because the symbolic meaning is so crucial: The boy sees for himself
the literal sunrise and is given as a bonus a vision such as Abraham
or Moses had when the divine voice spoke to them. The passage
winds down slowly as the boy returns home taciturn and self-
absorbed by his transfiguration.

But after a while, the reader begins to suspect that Sullivan's
sweet tooth for the Sublime has its dangers. He cannot curb his
appetite for thrilling and heroic music amplified in the manner of
Meyerbeer's stage machinery. Here is Sullivan describing the railroad journey through the Berkshires the fourteen-year-old boy took
with Grandpa List:

The day came. They departed *via* the Boston and Albany
Railway in the evening. Sleepless, restive, Louis awaited, as
best he might, the coming of the Berkshire Hills into his
growing world. He knew he would see them near dawn. The
hour came; he entered the foothills and began winding among

them, as with labored breath the engines, like heavy draft horses, began a steady pull, the train dragging reluctantly into steadiness as succeeding hills grew taller—with Louis eagerly watching. The true thrill of action began with the uprearing of imposing masses as Louis clung to the solid deep valleys below—until, amid mists and pale moons gleaming, arose the mighty Berkshires, their summits faint and far, their immensities solemn, calm, seeming eternal in the ghostly fog in the mild shimmer, clad in forests, uttering great words, runic words revealing and withholding their secret to a young soul moving as a solitary visitant, even as a wraith among them, the engines crying: "We will!" to an expanding soul listening within its own mists, its own shimmering dream, to the power without and within, amid the same echoes within and without, bereft of words to reply a bare hush of being, as though through mists of mind and shimmer of hope, SUBLIMITY, in revelation, had come to *one* wholly unprepared, had come to *one* as a knock on the door, had come to *one* who had known mountains only in books. And Louis again, in wonder, felt the power of man. The thought struck deep, that what was bearing him along was solely the power of man; the living power to wish, to will, to do. That man, in his power, with broad stride, had entered the regioned sanctity of these towering hills and like a giant of Elfinland had held them in the hollow of his hand. He had made a path, laid the rails, builded the engines that others might pass. Many saw engines and rails, and pathway, and one saw what lay behind them. In the murky mist and shimmer of moon and dawn, a veil was lifted in the solitude of the Berkshires. Louis slept, his nerves becalmed, amid the whistle's sonorous warnings, the silence of the engine, the long shrill song of the brakes, with mingling echoes, as the train, with steady pace, wound slowly downward toward the Hudson, leaving the Berkshires to their silence and their solitude—and Louis slept on, under the wand of the power of man. (130–2)

Sullivan trots out all the stock figures and props of his Fairy Tale show—giants, wands, mists, pennywhistles, mountains, valleys— and seats the "solitary visitant" as an enthralled spectator of the action on nature's stage, but the text seems stillborn and stale, the magic all tinsel and cardboard mysticism. In a vain effort to convince us that yet another veil has been lifted, Sullivan piles laborious clause on clause, as if the paragraph could not contain the power inside him pushing out and up. The climax, the revelation of the power of man, is a mechanical triumph, the message from the machine a resounding commonplace, not the "great words, runic words" so desperately needed.

These delinquencies are critical because in them Sullivan is a truant from his own ideal of an American expression untainted by "feudal" usage; his veils and giants and monsters are bookish, secondhand; he has defected from the rigorous muse of imagination and joined the party of timid and inane versifiers he lampooned. If some of the blame for Sullivan's prolixity can be laid to his years of relative obscurity, the effect is of listening to a cranky man talking to himself because he has not had human company for a long time.

Fortunately, Sullivan in the autobiography did not always wobble stylistically or confuse his gaudy fantasies with enchanted truth. As in his psychic life, so in his prose: A shower of diffuse words was followed by the clarity of fact. He could even deal straightforwardly with the boy's jumbled feelings. As the examiner in history at the Beaux-Arts examination said to Louis, "Monsieur, I see you have a certain faculty, a bit crude as yet, of making word pictures." (231) Sullivan's prose always grows alert and graphic when he presents an eyewitness report of a disaster like the Boston fire of November 9–10, 1872. Destruction excites, concentrates him:

> Louis saw this terror from its trifling beginning—a small flame curling from the wooden cornice of a building on the north side of Summer Street. There were perhaps a half dozen persons present at the time. The street was night-still. It was early. No fire engine came. Horses were sick, "epizootic" was raging. Engines must be drawn by hand. All was quiet as the small flame grew into a whorl and sparks shot upward from a glow behind; the windows became lighted from within. A few more people gathered, but no engine came. Then began a gentle purring roar. The few became a crowd but no engine came. Glass crackled and crashed, flames burst forth madly

from all windows, and the lambent dark flames behind them soared high, casting multitudes of sparks and embers abroad, as they cracked and wheezed. The roof fell, the walls collapsed. A hand-drawn engine came, but too late. The front wall tottered, swayed and crumbled to the pavement, exposing to view a roaring furnace. It was too late. The city seemed doomed. With this prelude began the great historic fire. Louis followed its ravages all night long. It was a magnificent but terrible pageant of wrathful fire before whose onslaught row after row of regimented buildings melted away. (181–2)

The fire, like Sullivan's prose, begins in an unprepossessing manner: The flames, the crowd, and the sentences are short and contained, but then they pick up speed and lengthen ("no engine came" is a refrain like an unanswered alarm), until the few stray spectators become a crowd, the sparks a conflagration, and the quiet a roar friendly as a cat and molten as a furnace. In this inferno there are no sinners being punished; the terror of the "lambent dark flames" is mainly aesthetic, luminously abstract as a Turner painting. The sound effects of the fiery onslaught are persuasive: The "crackle" and "crash" and "wheeze" of crumbling roofs and floors make all the proper musical noises in this prelude. The wrath of the fire seems directed against the "regimented" buildings in retaliation for their "stupid" ranks. Characteristically, Sullivan conveys the lessons of the cruelty and ruin wrought by the fire in vague terms—"yet a proud spirit, the eternal spirit of man rose to the height of the call of calamity. The city was rebuilt"—and the prose sags as Louis's interest wanes.

By contrast, Frank Lloyd Wright's narrative in *An Autobiography* of the "fierce brilliant blaze" that reduced Taliesin II to ashes and rubble is a curt drama of stirring combat against the elements, as if he were one of the Welsh heroes in the medieval sagas, and a rumination on "human carelessness and fallibility." Crazed, staggering, "like some dogged, foolish captain on the bridge of a sinking vessel doomed to all eyes but his," Wright stands in the midst of the fire, trying to stem the "roaring sea of devastation":

But I was up on the smoking roofs, feet burned, lungs seared, hair and eyebrows gone, thunder rolling as the lightning

flashed over the lurid scene, the hill-top long since profaned
by crowds of spectators standing silent up there—and fought.
Isaiah? [From Wright's childhood on, Isaiah symbolized the
punitive wrath of God, the great Negater.]

When the country people who answered the fire alarm urge him to
save the "priceless works of art," his household gods, Wright spurns
their advice: Only the structure, which he had built according to
almost mystical specifications, matters. At the nadir of exhaustion
and despair, human agency stretched to its limits, a *deus ex machina*
appears:

> Suddenly a tremendous pealing roll of thunder. The storm
> broke with a violent change of wind that rolled the great mass
> of flame up the valley. It recoiled upon itself but once as the
> rain fell hissing into the roaring furnace. The clouds of smoke
> and sparks as by a miracle were swept the opposite way. It
> was as though some gigantic unseen hand had awed the spec-
> tators. Super-human Providence perhaps—the thought in their
> minds was—who knows?[33]

Like Sullivan, Wright is stirred by the commotion and identifies with
the sweep and almost demented force of nature out of control. Both
men show their reluctance to be ordinary. Like a hand-held movie
camera, Wright's prose focuses on close-up images, panning from
Wright to the fire with only occasional side glances at the brigade
of weary neighbors. There is nothing merely picturesque in Wright's
account of his sacred battle against fire and wind. Though he concedes that the shift in wind direction was a "miracle," by ascribing
to the "profane" crowd the belief that an invisible Providence had
intervened, Wright does not diminish the scale or energy of his will.
Sifting through the debris for causes like a fire marshal, Wright flirts
with the idea that the "lurid crowd" personified the force (lightning)
that struck him again, but he gathers his faith, and rescuing from
the charred ruins fragments of stone and Japanese sculpture, he vows
"to weave them into the masonry fabric of Taliesin III." Unlike Sullivan, Wright places the initiative to rebuild not in "the eternal spirit
of man" but in his own volition.

When he was seventeen, Sullivan tried to think without the aid
of words, but that experiment did not last long. All his life he dis-

played an extreme susceptibility to words. A single new word or phrase, like "oakum," "poetry," "undertow," "perspective," "social order," or "suppressed functions," would send shock waves through him and rearrange his mental furniture. In Paris, he trains his ear to catch "words, locutions, intonations, and emphasis," until he achieves fluency in French. Words, of course, could be mendacious and ugly, like the Baptist church his grandfather worshiped in, or airy and romantic like the Masonic Temple in Boston, or technical like the articles in engineering journals he read so greedily. But despite their sharing a common sensibility, Sullivan's literary language, as might be expected, is not the equal of his architectural. When he enunciates his theories he chooses a kind of philosophical bombast, his explanations buckling under the weight of the big words he always judged an impediment to lucid teaching. The ineffable is notoriously hard to communicate for even the most talented poet, and Sullivan uses twelve words where five would do in an effort to convey his inspired discourse with the Unknown. Inspiration, Wright said, can sometimes be "a baying at the moon."[34]

"Without emotion nothing," Sullivan bluntly lays down as a first principle and a prophylaxis against fussy plans. In Sullivan's architecture his florid nature was purified by practical necessities: a building's site, function, materials, cost, the available technology. His ardent soul was governed by his logical intelligence. But in *The Autobiography of an Idea,* feeling seems to speak from a different part of the self, and Sullivan squanders space prodigally. His style, often mawkish, static, self-conscious, sinks into the trough of oceanic feeling that many romantics drown in. Not Sullivan's sincerity but his artistic judgment is in question. Hero worship is an unmanageable steed to ride, as when he contemplates Michelangelo's art in the Sistine Chapel:

Here he communed in the silence with a Super-Man. Here he felt and saw a great Free Spirit. Here he was filled with the awe that stills. Here he came face to face with his first great Adventurer. The first mighty man of Courage. The first man with a Great Voice. The first whose speech was Elemental. The first whose will would not be denied. The first to cry YEA! in thunder tones. The first mighty Craftsman. The man, the man of super-power, the glorified man, of whom he had dreamed in his childhood, of whom he prophesied in his childhood, as he watched his big, strong men build stone walls, hew down trees, drive huge horses—his mighty men, his heroes; his demi-gods; a powerful presentiment which he had seen and felt in the glory of the sunrise; which he had heard in the voice of spring; and which, personified through the haze of most mystical trances, he believed in, he had faith in—that faith which is far removed from fancy, that faith which is near its source and secure. (234–5)

That is more than the usual hyperbole of an adolescent in the presence of his idol; it is a hierophant chanting in a state of drugged ecstasy phrases whose banality he is oblivious of. Michelangelo is dressed in pantalettes made of fustian, the very grotesque uniform Sullivan loathed in the architecture of George Hewitt. The passage lacks all perspective, a serious error for an architect. It doesn't matter that Sullivan shuns the "I," since the author's ego seizes the stage and orates into the void. The verbless parallel sentences,[35] series, and phrases, with their abstract nouns "power," "glory," "faith," burst like a dam and spill uncontrollably over their grammatical banks, drenching the reader in the foam of sentimental affirmation. Sullivan labors to raise this edifice of words on massive piers into a poetry of praise, but it collapses into verbal rubble. It would be hard enough to accept this sycophantic prose from a young man; that a sixty-six-year-old man sanctions and writes it is embarrassing but perhaps attributable to Sullivan's addiction to the language of masculine prowess. At the same time, his style reveals a spiritual yearning that, like his architecture, did not fulfill all he hoped from it.

The child who went forth so jauntily in *The Autobiography of an Idea* ended his life in a tiny room amid strangers. The sprig had grown into a gnarled oak bowed by the buffetings of his stormy career but still standing. Among his last commissions were banks in small midwestern towns, as if life had returned him to South Reading, his starting point, and he depended on the sporadic largesse of the entrepreneurs whose mentality and materialism he abhorred. There is something fitting in this symmetry, for as Vincent Scully says, "Architecture is always based on power, and reflects it."[36] In *The Autobiography of an Idea,* Sullivan poses the central questions about power: Who wields it? For whose interest? Why is it corrupted so easily? How can we liberate its energies to benefit the greatest number of people? What is the connection between the exceptional man and his less gifted countrymen? Sullivan conducts a (losing) polemic campaign against the compromises and expediencies of "mere" social arrangements; American architecture, he contends, was hypnotized by the snobbism of imported taste, a nosegay of eclectic styles scattered in downtown office buildings and suburban residences, on college quadrangles and church plots. His dream is killed as "a steer . . . in useless protest," receives "the blow on the crown of the skull," at the stockyards. (305) But reports of the dream's demise are premature; it turns out, in fact, to be immortal: "When the golden hour tolled, all mists departed, and there shone forth as in a vision, the reality of MAN, as Free Spirit, as Creator, as Container of illimitable powers, for the joy and peace of mankind." (329) Like the Transcendentalists, Sullivan reposes trust in the benignity of the untrammeled self, which like "The democratic idea is single, integral. It holds to the good alone." (323) But as Melville showed in *Moby-Dick,* the "Container of illimitable powers" can be a monomaniac like Ahab, the good inverted and damage inflicted on an entire democratic society. The "godlike" man is unconnected to his peers, except by a kind of perverse abuse of authority. Sullivan's expansive instincts led him to glorify the shamanistic voice in the democratic afflatus. To Frank Lloyd Wright, Sullivan's one disciple whom he fails to mention in *The Autobiography of an Idea,* the legacy of "Lieber Meister" was a quixotic single-mindedness in his fight against mendacity:

> His loyalty to principle was the more remarkable as vision when all around him poisonous cultural mists hung low to obscure or blight any bright hope of finer beauty in the culture of the world.
>
> The buildings he has left with us for a brief time are the least of him. In the heart of him he was of infinite value to his country, the country that wasted him. His countrymen wasted him not because they would but because they could not know him.[37]

In Wright's eulogy Sullivan is a sun that cannot burn away the curtain of ugly vapors rising from the earth, yet in his "loyalty to principle" he refracts light of "infinite value" nonetheless.

Wright lays the major blame for Sullivan's eclipse on his countrymen, but *The Autobiography of an Idea* tells a different story: how Sullivan fell out of step with his age and, brought down by his virtues, contributed to his decline. In *A System of Architectural Ornament,* Sullivan says: "The Germ is the real thing: the seat of identity. Within its delicate mechanism lies the will to power: the function which is to seek and eventually to find its full expression in form."[38] This biological metaphor explains Sullivan's passionate identification with the child, but not what went wrong with his—and his country's—will to power. In his great buildings—the Wainwright and Guaranty Trust skyscrapers, the Getty Tomb, the Carson Pirie Scott department store—the ornament seems to emerge organically from within the blocks of stone; the inside and the outside are indivisible. But in *The Autobiography of an Idea* there is a hairline crack in the Ego, which grows more conspicuous and wide as Sullivan ages and which he repairs with nebulous effusions: The moments of efflorescence are brief. After all the ideological bluster about democracy's spiritual force, we are left to contemplate the raveled mysteries of a self that sadly failed to "find its full expression of form."

4

The Sheltering Self:
Jane Addams's
Twenty Years at Hull-House

The happiest people I have known have been those who gave themselves no concern about their own souls, but did their uttermost to mitigate the miseries of others.
—ELIZABETH CADY STANTON, Eighty Years and More

Pity, memory, faithfulness are natural ties with paramount claims.
—JANE ADDAMS, Twenty Years at Hull-House

*I*N THE LAST chapter of *The Long Road of Women's Memory,* published in 1916, Jane Addams personifies memory as "that Protean Mother, who first differentiated man from the brute."[1] The slaughter of countless millions during World War I had unnerved Jane Addams, stirring up "the constant revival of primitive and overpowering emotions which I had experienced so long ago that they had become absolutely detached from myself and seemed to belong to someone else—to a small person with whom I was no longer intimate, and who was certainly not in the least responsible for my present convictions and reflections."[2] Her ideal of a slow but steady civilizing movement among nations in shambles and her own reputation at low ebb because of her intransigent stance against United

States involvement in the war,[3] she characteristically sought to take stock, to turn "monstrous social injustice"[4] into intelligible form. She identifies her own agony and feelings of being powerless with a visible oppressed group and a social cause: the innocent victims of brutish wrong, those women and their sons whose lives were as "pitilessly rent" as the lives of women, workers, immigrants, and the poor in industrial America. Angry and perplexed, shaken by heedless forces of unreason, which corrupted the instinct to nurture into a worship of death, she found herself swept back to childhood memories disquieting as nightmares.

She cites four that mark the evolutionary stages of her social conscience:

1. At age six, her family gone to the funeral of a kinsman, Jane sits at home, "the blank wall of a stairway" her only protection against the "formless peril"[5] (death). Paralyzed by fear, she is as ethically blank as the unreliable wall and unable to climb it.

2. During a series of winter revival meetings at the village church, she anxiously worries about those who couldn't find salvation. Though tempted to mime the prescribed hallowed words and thus block out her terror at "the destruction of the visible man,"[6] she cannot pretend. It is not until her search for "magic protection from the terrors after death imperceptibly merges into a concern for the fate of the soul"[7] that she obtains some comfort. Here she begins to form her conscience, rejecting an ethic based on a conventional system of rewards and punishments (heaven and hell) in favor of one based on the widened duties of the associated life.

3. She recalls marching as a tiny child with her class to the burial of a schoolmate's mother one bleak day. Feeling "shelterless and unattended,"[8] she wanted to cry out, "Their mother is dead; whatever will the children do?"[9] This experience, closely resembling the unassimilated dread of her own mother's (and her sister Martha's) death and her grief at being left alone, goads her to take another ethical step: She demands definite action to rectify the injustice and relieve the pain of the desertion, though none is forthcoming.

4. Hearing some religious women gossiping and condemning the kind village doctor to hell on doctrinal grounds, she rebels against their theological bigotry and decides that the test of righteousness is good works, not divine election. She has reached the ethical plane on which she would stand her entire adult life. She has mastered her

Jane Addams, c. 1895

fears of self-extinction by embracing the pariah; the surety of grace comes by devotion to others, especially the fallen.

World War I had catapulted Addams backward into a condition almost as acute as the impotence she experienced in childhood; her voice, which had blazoned forth the cause of the outcast and of the oppressed, had been drowned out by the din of guns and militaristic slogans, and later by the urgent collective anguish of the war's victims. In 1916, amid the sarcophagi of the ancient pyramids, suggestive of rebirth and immortality as well as death, Addams found a route back to her lost self and regained her faith in the possibility of healing conduct. Memory serves as the integrating faculty through which the child and the woman become reunited, and it fulfills two functions: "first, its important role in interpreting and appeasing life for the individual, and second its activity as a selective agency in social reorganization."[10] Where others might have immured themselves in self-pity or continued a technique already proved futile, Addams rose above the self precisely by working through it. Her unusual flexibility of character—she candidly admitted errors—permitted her to find exits in apparent culs-de-sac. As an advocate of action, she refused to stay on the sidelines of life's struggles but sought always to engage them, even when they threatened failure or humiliation.

This magnanimity toward others and stringency toward herself governs Jane Addams's memories of her childhood in *Twenty Years at Hull-House,* the lines connecting the woman of fifty to the shy child as complex as perspective in painting. She once remarked that the past is "part mystery, part music."[11] In her life, her mother, who died when Jane was two and a half years old, was the mystery and her father the inspiring music. There is no reason to doubt Addams's assertion that her father was the dominant influence of her life. Her early impressions of him recorded in *Twenty Years at Hull-House* are colored by an adoration time never blurred. Though austere, scrupulous, imposing (a word she uses often to describe him), and something of a demigod, John Addams, unlike Elizabeth Cady Stanton's forbidding father, loomed as a figure of dependable affection.[12] He inculcated both a love of learning (he paid Jane a nickel for each volume of Plutarch's *Lives* she read in his well-stocked library)[13] and a strict conscience, but he also fostered self-esteem in difficult circumstances. Upon the death of his wife, he took on the added role of mother for several years and, to judge from his daughter's ardent account, performed it well. As a child, Jane Addams imagined herself to be a grotesque outsider: "I prayed with all my heart that the ugly, pigeon-toed little girl, whose crooked back obliged her to walk with her head held very much upon one side, would never be pointed out to the visitors as the daughter of this fine man."[14] (23) The tender gallantry of Mr. Addams bowing to his little girl and tipping his "high and shining silk hat" in public recognition, a charming fairy-tale picture the older autobiographer remembers with abiding gratitude, prevents a morbid self-hatred from festering in her mind. She could, at least inwardly, hold her head high. Nonetheless, it is likely that her spinal deformity made Jane Addams feel that fate had excluded her from marriage and children and led her to identify with those suffering from social deformities. As confidant, John Addams listens to her girlish confessions of sin with a solicitude that dispels her anxiety of permanent isolation. That all her life Jane Addams believed in the curative power of fellowship to break down "the persistent and secretive purpose" that solitary misfits like Leon Czolgosz, the assassin of President William McKinley, harbored in their half-crazed minds owes much to her father's sensitivity. The sharing of grievances that she considered necessary for social amity was grounded in her emotional relations with her father.

In John Addams's personal behavior, business affairs, and political judgments, no rift between conscience and conduct appeared. He embodied many Quaker traits: a mistrust of sectarianism, a balancing of business enterprise and public service (Jane inherited her practical intelligence from him), and a plain morality, "always be honest with yourself inside," (27) which his daughter clung to as the backbone of her dealings with all classes. Like Susan B. Anthony, she was "taught simply that she must enter into the holy of holies of her own self, meet herself, and be true to the revelation."[15] An aura of invincible probity surrounds her father, like the angel Abdiel in *Paradise Lost,* but he is not without a certain stiff charm and dry humor as she remembers him:

> Although I constantly confided my sins and perplexities to my father, there are only a few occasions on which I remember having received direct advice or admonition; it may easily be true, however, that I have forgotten the latter, in the man-

ner of many seekers after advice who enjoyably set forth their situation but do not really listen to the advice itself. I can remember an admonition on one occasion, however, when, as a little girl of eight years, arrayed in a new cloak, gorgeous beyond anything I had ever worn before, I stood before my father for his approval. I was much chagrined by his remark that it was a pretty cloak—in fact so much prettier than any cloak the other little girls in the Sunday School had that he would advise me to wear my old cloak, which would keep me quite as warm, with the added advantage of not making the other little girls feel bad. I complied with the request but I fear without inner consent, and I certainly was without the joy of self-sacrifice as I walked soberly through the village street by the side of my counselor. My mind was busy, however, with the old question eternally suggested by the inequalities of the human lot. Only as we neared the church door did I venture to ask what could be done about it, receiving the reply that it might never be righted so far as clothes went, but that people might be equal in things that mattered much more than clothes, the affairs of education and religion, for instance, which we attended to when we went to school and church, and that it was very stupid to wear the sort of clothes that made it harder to have equality even there. (26–7)

Mr. Addams does not talk down to his daughter; he talks to her. When he rebukes her about the vanity of wearing an expensive cloak poor girls cannot afford, he furnishes an explanation that does not deny the little girl's difficulty in complying with his advice—Jane at first withholds "inner consent" and the "joy of self-sacrifice," both powerful motives with her, as though her intellect agreed with her father's argument but her feelings required time to get aligned with it. This was a lesson in family values: Don't puff yourself up at the cost of giving pain to a less fortunate person;[16] sometimes personal satisfaction must be sacrificed to larger social needs. Mr. Addams is careful in his guide to the perplexed not to preach an impossible ideal of complete equality. His voice has a patriarchal gravity, but his opinions are not delivered from a lofty throne; he walks by her side. The very syntax of this memory, with its three "howevers," strikes the balance that Jane Addams sought whenever she stood before the tribunal of her conscience for approval.

Balance is as natural to her style of reflection as the rhythm of her heartbeat.

Jane Addams's "careful imitation" of her father extended beyond her girlish wish to wear the honorable stigmata of a miller's thumb and to bake an honest loaf, to an adoption of his forthright maxim "mental integrity above everything else" (28) and his faith in law as, ultimately, the only secure guarantee of cooperative human endeavor. Like many self-made men of the pioneer generation, Mr. Addams acquired wealth through hard work (in his youth he got up at 3 A.M. to start up his flour mill) and foresight (he carried with him to Illinois seeds of Norwegian pine, which he planted to beautify the land and which like him took root). "Politically," Allen F. Davis notes in his biography of Jane Addams, John Addams "was a conservative, small-town Republican, though he did take a special interest in improving the prisons, the insane asylums, and the state industrial and normal schools."[17] (This concern was lacking in the self-made manufacturers in Chicago in the 1890s.) He taught Jane the duties of the "superior class" to those less fortunate, yet frowned on social ostentation: "The early pioneer life had made social distinctions impossible," (42) she says in her autobiography.

Probably we should ascribe to John Addams's mental toughness and moral sentiments his daughter's conception that "somewhere in Church or State are a body of authoritative people who will put things to rights as soon as they know what is wrong." (70) *Twenty Years at Hull-House* traces with evident fascination on Jane Addams's part the winding, brambly pathway she takes to fashion herself into the authoritative person upon whose sibylline utterances her society will come to depend. The glimpses of her childhood help us understand why she fervently believed, like Benjamin Franklin, that social change comes about by the "slow process of structural modification," (25) not by convulsive upheavals. (By nature she was not a rebel. When her father refused permission for her to attend Smith College, she bowed to his will.) John Addams was not parochial, as his admiration for Mazzini demonstrates, and though craggy in demeanor, he was not one of those cerebral men who are cut off from their feelings: He was not ashamed to cry at the death of Lincoln. Two lines from an Elizabeth Barrett Browning poem Jane Addams quotes sum up her profound attachment to her father: "He wrapt me in his large / Man's doublet, careless did it fit or no." (32)

The emotional weather of Jane Addams's childhood, as described in *Twenty Years at Hull-House,* is often unsettled, with the light of cheerful "free-ranging" country games occasionally breaking up the overcast. Except for a passing reference to her stepbrother and a "large family," one might think that Jane Addams was an only child (in fact, she had three older sisters). A considerable body of evidence points to the early untimely death of her mother, which threatened Jane's psychic security, as the plausible motive for this curious omission. She recounts a dream that haunted her night after night:

> everyone in the world was dead excepting myself, and . . .
> upon me rested the responsibility of making a wagon wheel.
> The village street remained, as usual, the village blacksmith
> shop was "all there," even a glowing fire upon the forge and
> the anvil in its customary place near the door, but no human
> being was within sight. They had all gone round the edge of
> the hill to the village cemetery, and I alone remained alive in
> the deserted world. I always stood in the same spot in the
> blacksmith shop darkly pondering as how to begin, and never
> once did I know how, although I fully realized that the affairs
> of the world could not be resumed until at least one wheel
> should be made and something started. Every victim of night-
> mare is, I imagine, overwhelmed by an excessive sense of
> responsibility and the consciousness of a fearful handicap in
> the effort to perform what is required; but perhaps never were
> the odds more heavily against "a warder of the world" than
> in these reiterated dreams of mine, doubtless compounded in
> equal parts of a childish version of Robinson Crusoe and of
> the end-of-the-world predictions of the Second Adventists, a
> few of whom were found in the village. (22)

This tense dream suggests the deep strain, anger, and dread that a child feels following the inexplicable death of a close relative. The world is deserted, as she possibly felt she was by her mother, and the fact that she has the power to destroy the world may mean that she guiltily blamed herself for her mother's death, or in her rage wished to retaliate, though typically the destructive impulses are channeled into constructive acts. The cozy, familiar landmarks of the village take on an eerie emptiness, as the bereft, mourning child, like an orphaned survivor of a gang of vicious marauders or a Crusoe saved from shipwreck and a watery death, "darkly ponders" her task. She is numbed by the immense responsibility—the word's six syllables, repeated twice, emphasize the burden of asking a child to do an adult's work—of making a wheel, that earliest of implements which pulled mankind out of primitive want and ignorance. She cannot bear the thought that she might be accused of being a "warder" who left her post. The dream reflects the conflict that warred in Jane Addams for over thirty years: an almost grandiose desire to be heroic and self-reliant and a fear that she may not be adequately equipped to tend the sacred fire (the word "handicap" implies both physical and moral impediment).

At fifteen, Jane Addams encounters death again, this time not in a nightmare but in "direct contact." She narrates the episode as though it had happened the previous evening, not thirty years before. Once more the death is associated with her mother. Driven through a "blinding snowstorm" to stand vigil at the deathbed of her mother's and her own nurse, Polly, Jane exchanges her "lamplit, warm house" for the lonely and cold farmhouse:

> Suddenly the great change came. I heard a feeble call of "Sarah," my mother's name, as the dying eyes were turned upon me, followed by a curious breathing and in place of the face familiar from earliest childhood and associated with homely household cares, there lay upon the pillow strange, august features, stern and withdrawn from all the small affairs of life. That sense of solitude, of being unsheltered in a wide world of relentless and elemental forces which is at the basis of childhood's timidity and which is far from outgrown at fifteen, seized me irresistibly before I could reach the narrow stairs and summon the family from below.
>
> As I was driven home in the winter storm, the wind through the trees seemed laden with a passing soul and the riddle of life and death pressed hard; once to be young, to grow old and die, everything came to that, and then a mysterious journey into the Unknown. Did she mind faring forth alone? Would the journey perhaps end in something as familiar and natural to the aged and dying as life is to the young

and living? Through all the drive and indeed throughout the night these thoughts were pierced by sharp worry, a sense of faithlessness because I had forgotten the text Polly had confided to me long before as the one from which she wished her funeral sermon to be preached. My comfort as usual finally came from my father, who pointed out what was essential and what was of little avail even in such a moment as this, and while he was much too wise to grow dogmatic upon the great theme of death, I felt a new fellowship with him because we had discussed it together. (31)

In the above excerpt, Jane Addams leaves the moral safety of her house, riding through a snowstorm, which obliterates all signposts and leaves her vulnerable and isolated. As in her dream, the familiar is transformed into a weighty mystery; the "dying eyes" that transfix her, the death rattle, and finally the retreat of Polly's soul, imagined as a face unraveling into its component parts, assail her. (Such vigils became commonplace when she was summoned from Hull-House to care for a dying child or the aged.) Jane reacts with a panic of being, like King Lear, "unsheltered in a wide world of relentless and elemental forces"; the claustrophobia is replaced by homelessness. It is probable that when Polly called out for Sarah, Jane's mother's name roused buried feelings of resentment and caused Jane to forget the confided text, a breach of trust. On the drive home, her stormy mind swirls with questions as she strives to regain her self-control. It is typical of Jane Addams that by an intuitive empathy she hears, like a pagan or a hallucinator, the passing soul in the wind, the trees "laden" as her soul was; that she seeks a solution to "the riddle of life and death" by asking questions from another's point of view; and that discussion quells her fears (it does not give final or absolute explanation), communion with her father bringing the mercy of self-forgiveness.

The eloquence of this sequence casts light on Jane Addams's mature character and mental processes. She always begins by concentrating on physical detail rather than on abstractions. Experience was almost a fetish with her, so that any discourse on ideas never strays far from the people whose sufferings or frettings (about a ne'er-do-well husband or where the next meal will come from) set the train of thought in motion, as Polly's "feeble call" initiated tumultuous emotions. The "I" is appropriately present. Jane Addams is not embarrassed by her adolescent self's terror; she neither belittles nor deifies her. The interior drama is acted out on a stage uncluttered with objects but not so sparse that the external world is cropped out as by an arty photographer: The normal is downstairs. at supper. The pillow, narrow stairs, trees, and wind belong to the scenes because Jane Addams respects the dailiness that is so important to most people: Polly's "homely household cares," "the small affairs of life," which loom large to workers, a mother staying home to nurse her sick child but worried by the loss of meager pay. By entering intimately into the unglamorous parts of other people's lives, Jane Addams can render them with novelistic inclusiveness. (A revolutionary like Emma Goldman, often on the run and forced to adopt aliases, is not drawn much to that dailiness, except at moments of exhaustion, as a refuge, deriding it as dull and ungrand and bourgeois.)

All of Jane Addams's writings are permeated by a special sensitivity to, even an awe of, death, the "great Experience," as if the integrity of her self were contingent on mastering its terror—and not just for herself. Death, in particular premature death, rides through the pages of *Twenty Years at Hull-House* like the Four Horsemen of the Apocalypse: A family of five sons is mowed down, four in the Civil War, the last in a gun accident; children fall out of windows; a young man with tuberculosis expires in a scarifying alcoholic delirium; a thirteen-year-old girl swallows carbolic acid because she spent the week's wages, her family's food money, on a frippery and in despair cannot believe she will be forgiven; a man who was a goldsmith in Europe shovels coal in America and kills himself. Each case solicits Jane Addams's compassion. Because the mortality rate in the Nineteenth Ward, where Hull-House was situated, was one of the highest in Chicago, owing to poor sanitation, she undertook a municipal campaign for better public health services and education of the immigrants.

At Hull-House, Addams comforted the thousands laden with sorrows, as her father had comforted her, by entering into fellowship with them. She even laid out the dead and eulogized them at funerals (she published a volume of these graceful addresses, *The Excellent Becomes the Permanent*). But if she knew from John Addams what comfort was, she had never had it from her own mother, and so she fashioned herself into a surrogate for a community of children, protecting them from abuses their own mothers and fathers were helpless to prevent, interpreting a hostile, devious world to baffled ethnic groups. In factories, machines chewed up hands and feet because the owners refused to invest the small sums needed for safeguards, and parents, unwittingly, often signed a paper exempting the owner from responsibility for on-the-job mishaps. Addams's faith in democracy as "the great mother breasts of our common humanity," (93) nurturing the "submerged tenth," surely sprang from an unconscious motive to compensate for the absent mother. Being allied with her father, a figure of kind authority, mitigated but did not eliminate her deprivation. Hull-House stood on "the Via Dolorosa of the poor"[18] of Chicago's Nineteenth Ward; its squalid tenements were a travesty of decent shelter. Jane Addams always took pride that Hull-House was not a monument to officious philanthropy but a shelter, planted in the mud, that helped the dispossessed to withstand the buffeting seas of strangeness and misery around them.

To run a house was, of course, woman's traditional role. It could and often did, for middle-class women, mean confinement to marriage, child rearing, and a limited domestic circle; churchgoing, charity work, and dinner parties; homeopathic doses of culture, like a visit to a performance of *Tristan und Isolde* or an edifying lecture, or some stolen minutes of leisure to read a book.[19] Like many of the brilliant women who broke down barriers and entered the professions or pioneered new social institutions—Alice Hamilton, Grace and Edith Abbott, Elizabeth Blackwell, Julia Lathrop, Ellen Starr—Jane Addams created an alternative model of female identity, decidedly not passive, which could live serenely the life of the mind, dispense with marriage altogether, or substitute a "Boston marriage" (a close relationship between two women, such as Jane Addams enjoyed with Mary Rozet Smith). Often financially self-sufficient, these women were not stunted spinsters or like Dr. Prance, that nasty caricature of an "unfeminine" or unnatural intellectual Henry James drew in *The Bostonians*. The solidarity of women committed to political reform and social innovation was an enormous resource, both intellectual and emotional. They exchanged ideas and information, trained and found jobs for gifted college graduates, read and criticized drafts of each other's speeches and legislation, championed the cause and health of children at a congressional hearing rather than in the nursery, lobbied for reforms in the workplace: higher wages and fewer weekly hours on the job, some form of health insurance, workmen's compensation. They were all, as Carroll Smith-Rosenberg says, "effective manipulators of public opinion,"[20] adept at forging coalitions and not afraid of visibly wielding political power. The mutual respect that guided their personal relations was projected onto the public sphere as an ideal, which a fractured American democracy might come to emulate. "The settlement house represented their [the New Women's] home, their fellow women residents, their family."[21] Thus Hull-House was an extension of Jane Addams's Cedarville home, but it quickly expanded to become a refuge for the emotionally destitute, a social center for all immigrant groups, adolescents, and the old, a post office, a library, a day care facility for the children of working mothers, a theater, and a museum, but most of all, a forum for the discussion of divisive issues (and not in genteel terms), where a Prince Kropotkin, a socialist carpenter, or a shy Greek grandmother might debate and quarrel and propose utopian or practical solutions. Jane Addams administered this complex organism with great skill: the single woman as head of the family.

Logically, then, in her closest approach to bitter polemics in *Twenty Years at Hull-House,* Addams protested against the sheltered life, which corrupted the sheltering self by corseting it in cultural dilettantism. The important goal for the daughters of the wealthy middle class, she argued vehemently, was not to slip into the exclusivity and well-bred sloth that parents encouraged (the "family claim"). The life of music and drawing lessons, of trips to Europe, of refined leisure, she saw as a trap of selfish respectability—"fatuous security," in her cutting phrase—and she associated it with her stepmother, Anna Haldeman, a woman of taste and sensibility.[22] Anna Haldeman is mentioned only once or twice in the autobiography, and in an offhand manner. Jane Addams rationalized this usage by pleading that the relationship was a "complicated thing," but one feels that she was repaying her stepmother for being a successful rival for John Addams's love when Jane was eight years old. Though hardly a page of *Twenty Years at Hull-House* goes by without references to culture—a performance of a Sophoclean tragedy in the original Greek, concerts, lithography lessons, lectures, murals—Jane Addams insists that culture can distract from the more pressing obligation to treat the social maladjustment so endemic in America.

This spirit of earnest devotion to others and a singular embrace of pluralism were fostered and strengthened, at times indirectly, by her years of "higher education" at Rockford Seminary. Jane Addams was disappointed at being forced to enroll at this "humdrum" parochial academy for girls. Its curriculum was old-fashioned, its tone intensely propagandistic. The chapter in *Twenty Years at Hull-House* about this critical period is curiously subdued, the middle-aged woman faintly ironic toward her adolescent self. She sketches a young woman inclined to priggishness, grandiloquence of style, and erratic will, with "the intolerable habit of dropping my voice at the end of a sentence in the most feminine, apologetic and even deprecatory manner." (53) The imbalance between ardent idealism and paucity of experience, not surprising at a fairly sequestered boarding school in northern Illinois, bemuses Jane Addams as she relives the strenuous soul-searching or leafs through the stilted diaries she had kept. A kind of bookish cult of experience animates her: She takes opium so as to understand De Quincey's *Dreams,* or cleans the dirt off Bronson Alcott's boots with "ecstatic energy" when he visits Rockford. Her libido seems to be hunting for outlets of expression; she fears it will be blighted by "the perils of self-tradition." (59) Yet she imagines herself somewhat floridly performing heroic deeds: "The oration upon Bellerophon and his successful fight with the Chimera contended that social evils could only be overcome by him who soared above them into idealism, as Bellerophon, mounted upon the winged horse Pegasus, had slain the earthy dragon." (48)

But the chimera was not so easily to be slain at Rockford (or later in Chicago). Seductive voices tried to claim her for evangelical missionary work in Turkey by solemnly dangling the allure of self-sacrifice. She was tempted. After all, it corresponded to her father's teaching that the moral person set his own wants aside for a worthy cause, and some graduates of Rockford had led distinguished careers, as, for example, an innovative teacher of the blind and a librarian who pioneered in bringing books to the working classes. In addition, as one of the few "unconverted" girls in a highly charged religious atmosphere, she was the target of appeals from teachers and fellow students alike who wished to save her soul by getting her to agree to their doctrine. Jane Addams's response was mixed: She felt spiritually infirm, yet she cultivated a passive resistance to theological dogma, "a clinging to individual conviction," which she credits as "the best moral training I received at Rockford Seminary." (54)

The quest for vocation that preoccupies Jane Addams at Rockford—like Gertrude Stein and Emma Goldman, she contemplated a medical career—is inseparable from her stumbling efforts to put together Christian principles she can live by that do not demand a uniformity of creed. This tenet runs through every discussion of Christianity in *Twenty Years at Hull-House*. She does not like the "disputatious" Saint Paul, preferring the Christianity of the Gospels, especially the Sermon on the Mount, and she extols early Christianity before the erection of a hierarchical church inhibited the direct expression of Jesus' teachings. "The impulse to share the lives of the poor," she said in the lecture "The Subjective Necessity for Social Settlements," which she reprints entire in *Twenty Years at Hull-House,* "the desire to make social service, irrespective of propaganda, express the spirit of Christ, is as old as Christianity itself." (95) Action as the holy imperative of the Truthful and Loving Word was implicit in Addams's Rockford ideal that "mingled learning, piety, and physical labor" (51) and in her favorable allusion to the Jansenist Port Royalist experiment, where Christianity was based on experience, not theology.[23] ("Fiery Hell was never mentioned at home."[24] [20]) Indeed, one of Jane Addams's early formulations echoes Benjamin Franklin's view of Christianity: "the actual Justice must come by trained intelligence, or by broadened sympathies toward the individual man or woman who crosses our path; one item added to another is the only method by which to build a conception lofty enough to be of use in the world." (55) (Franklin would have dispensed with the word "lofty"; he took for granted that he would be of use in the world.)

In a sophisticated and rapturous paragraph in "The Subjective Necessity for Social Settlements," Jane Addams comments:

> That Christianity has to be revealed and embodied in the line of social progress is a corollary to the simple proposition that man's action is found in his social relationships in the way in which he connects with his fellows. By this simple process

was created a deep enthusiasm for humanity, which regarded man as at once the organ and the object of revelation; and by this process came about the wonderful fellowship, the true democracy of the early Church, that so captivates the imagination. The early Christians were pre-eminently nonresistant. They believed in love as a cosmic force. There was no iconoclasm during the minor peace of the Church. They did not yet denounce nor tear down temples, nor preach the end of the world. They grew to a mighty number but it never occurred to them, either in their weakness or in their strength, to regard other men for an instant as their foes or as aliens. The spectacle of the Christians loving all men was the most astounding Rome had ever seen. They were eager to sacrifice themselves for the weak, for children, and for the aged; they identified themselves with slaves and did not avoid the plague; they longed to share the common lot that they might receive the constant revelation. It was new treasure which the Christians added to the sum of all treasures, a joy hitherto unknown in the world—the joy of finding the Christ which lieth in each man but which no man can unfold save in fellowship. (96–7)

Part lay sermon, part history lesson, part visionary program, this passage is remarkable for what Jane Addams leaves out: God, heaven, ecclesiastical structures and laws, ritual worship and prayer. For a brief spell she and the residents at Hull-House tried evening prayer, but they abandoned the practice because it interfered with the nondenominational activities of a settlement house. Her vocabulary of emotions—"deep enthusiasm," "love," "eager," "joy"—buoyantly envelops her as she unfolds her revelation paralleling that of the early Christians. Finding "the Christ which lieth in each man" is not Emersonian writ, sanction for the ego to embark on a quest for self-fulfillment, but an unwritten social covenant that connects one man to another: She caresses the word "fellowship" as if it were an icon of the "true democracy." Sacrifice is not linked here to the crucifixion, to the glamour of martyrdom.[25] The early Christians did not deny painful realities, launch crusades against nonbelievers, stand aloof from the slave, or fear contamination from the plague. Love as "a cosmic force" (96) is no insipid otherworldly formula to cloak widespread suffering by offering the promise of happiness and equality after death.

Jane Addams seized on the Primitive Christians, mostly poor fishermen and slaves who "had been boldly opposed to the accepted moral belief that the well-being of a privileged few ought justly to be built upon the ignorance and sacrifice of the many," (69) as the model for an ideal democratic community. They pointed the way to breaking out of the effete prison of self-regard, with its mildewed will, and to breathing the heady air of social obligation. In a curious parable in *Twenty Years at Hull-House,* Addams wryly explains how in losing a self the committed reformer can gain a new one. A leading member of the Chicago Women's Club said that

> when she was a little girl playing in her mother's garden, she one day discovered a small toad who seemed to her very forlorn and lonely, although she did not in the least know how to comfort him, she reluctantly left him to his fate; later in the day, quite at the other end of the garden, she found a large toad, also apparently without family and friends. With heart full of tender sympathy, she took a stick and by exercising infinite patience and some skill, she finally pushed the little toad through the entire length of the garden into the company of the big toad, when, to her surprise, the toad opened his mouth and swallowed the little one. The moral of the tale was clearly applied to people who lived "where they did not naturally belong," although I protested that was exactly what we wanted—to be swallowed and digested, to disappear into the bulk of the people.
>
> Twenty years later I am willing to testify that something of the sort does take place after years of identification with an industrial community. (217–18)

What begins as a cautionary lesson about the foolish innocence of do-gooders who attempt to alleviate the isolation of the unfortunate turns into a hymn to caring for those in need. Because in the brutal world the strong do swallow the weak, and predatory social and economic acts are not rare, the club member concludes that she was meddling, that her "tender sympathy" was ineffectual and damaging, but Addams rebuts this view. Identification, as with the early

Christians, does not erase identity. The disappearing self is compensated for by the enhanced sense of community and a "constant revelation." The glib commonplace of social Darwinism is upended: The strong, in a form of communion, feed the weak.

Jane Addams's style, too, derives from the simple homilies and parables of the Gospels and, like the early Christians, refuses to engage in tirades. Her narratives teach without condescension to the downtrodden, and they apply to the struggles of her own strict conscience, which she patrols like a sentinel so that no evasions of Christian duty slip by:

> In one of the intervening summers between these European journeys I visited a western state where I had formerly invested a sum of money in mortgages. I was much horrified by the wretched conditions among the farmers, which had resulted from a long period of drought, and one forlorn picture was fairly burned into my mind. A number of starved hogs—collateral for a promissory note—were huddled into an open pen. Their backs were humped in a curious camel-like fashion, and they were devouring one of their own number, the latest victim of absolute starvation or possibly the one least able to defend himself against their voracious hunger. The farmer's wife looked on indifferently, a picture of despair as she stood in the door of the bare, crude house, and the two children behind her, whom she vainly tried to keep out of sight, continually thrust forward their faces almost covered by masses of coarse, sunburned hair, and their little bare feet so black, so hard, the great cracks so filled with dust that they looked like flattened hoofs. The children could not be compared to anything so joyous as satyrs, although they appeared but half-human. It seemed to me quite impossible to receive interest from mortgages placed upon farms which might at any season be reduced to such conditions, and with great inconvenience to my agent and doubtless with hardship to the farmers, as speedily as possible I withdrew all my investment. But something had to be done with the money, and in my reaction against unseen horrors I bought a farm near my native village and also a flock of innocent-looking sheep. My partner in the enterprise had not

chosen the shepherd's lot as a permanent occupation, but hoped to speedily finish his college course upon half the proceeds of our venture. This pastoral enterprise still seems to me to have been essentially sound, both economically and morally, but perhaps one partner depended too much upon the impeccability of her motives and the other found himself too preoccupied with study to know that it is not a kindness to bed a sheepfold with straw, for certainly the venture ended in a spectacle scarcely less harrowing than the memory it was designed to obliterate. At least the sight of two hundred sheep with four rotting hoofs each, was not reassuring to one whose conscience craved economic peace. A fortunate series of sales of mutton, wool, and farm enabled the partners to end the enterprise without loss, and they passed on, one to college and the other to Europe, certainly sadder for the experience. (69–70)

As in one of Walker Evans's photographs of Alabama sharecroppers in *Let Us Now Praise Famous Men*, Jane Addams depicts poverty's toll unblinkingly. The reader's eye travels from the grotesquely humped hogs cannibalizing one of their weak fellows to the farmer's wife, a figure of immobile despair huddling in the doorway of a hovel, and finally to the two children stunned by hunger, their faces matted with "coarse hair" and their bare feet like the hogs' "flattened hoofs." Here Jane Addams confronts the unbearable suffering of the poor and flees in moral discomfort; she cannot condone earning money off such hardship, but during this unfocused period of her life, she cannot devise another plan, which might address the plight of the farmer's family directly and solve it. As the rest of the paragraph makes clear, she does not carry her Christianity to the extreme of renouncing her wealth. At this stage she is an economic naïf, not a prudent or knowledgeable investor or faithful shepherd (the rotting hoofs are symbols of poor animal husbandry and of the inept amateurism of half-cocked measures, which she came to despise at Hull-House), but where she can cut her losses and escape to Europe, the farmer cannot ward off natural or man-made disasters. Addams's prose lingers pityingly on the monstrous deformations of hunger, which can turn hogs into camels and children into sick barnyard animals, on the defenseless mother and children framed in the doorway in mute reproach (the objective problem), and then examines her own motives (subjective necessity). Throughout *Twenty Years at Hull-House* Jane Addams rushes to disburden herself of a moral conflict that places her in a bad light to herself. Shortly after, the sufferings of others become a cue to purposeful action.

Like all autobiographers, Jane Addams projects covert passions and mixed motives onto the world. In her method of self-presentation, she teaches us what she expected for herself and her society, and which ideas of a humane community compelled her. How Addams dealt with change in her life—her edgy fear of enervating gentility, for example—dictated how she imagined change for an unruly polity; how she regulated her own emotions affected her prescriptions for the social ills that afflicted juvenile delinquents or a household in which the father had deserted; how she challenged authority and organized people to join in a program that would reduce the strife generated by industrial disputes testified to her ways of adjudicating the claims of the striving self and a recalcitrant world. *Twenty Years at Hull-House* is an important document because it displays and illuminates the character of the social reformer.

Addams's autobiography is a masterpiece of balance—a trait that seldom inspires rapture. The balanced man or woman, we say in insincere tribute, is mature and self-controlled, as unflustered in crises as a general directing his troops in a crossfire. Yet we secretly scorn balance as a dilution of feeling, a kind of static neutrality that lacks the thrill of adventure at the extreme—not the golden mean but the tinny average security of the bourgeoisie. Etymologically, "balance" comes from the Latin *bilancia,* a pair of scales, "an apparatus for weighing, consisting of a beam poised so as to move freely on a central pivot, with a scale pan at each end."[26] Addams's conception of her function as that central pivot with its latitude of movement includes the word's traditional connotation of the scale in which justice is weighed and measured. Stylistically, Addams is neither timid nor abrasive. The spinal column of logic sheathed, after all, the heart; people could not live with only one and not the other.

This balance did not come to her simply as a genetic endowment, a prudent social law, or a political rule. Although drawn early to sacrificial effort, during the eight years between her father's death in 1881 and the opening of Hull-House's doors in 1889, Jane Addams was marooned on an island of study and culture, her personal odyssey "to learn life from life itself" stalled. What, borrowing Tolstoy's phrase, she calls "the snare of preparation" was an emotional imbalance exacerbated and prolonged by her grief for John Addams's death. Self-government, the ideal she cherished for herself and later for a polyglot democracy, eluded her. She could not shed a sense of uselessness. To combat it she went on binges of self-improvement: two long tours of Europe, a program of reading, visits to museums, enchanted evenings at the opera. But immersing herself in culture was only a partial cure for her "nervous depression and sense of maladjustment." (67)

Twenty Years at Hull-House affords a faithful self-accounting of these years of painful stumbling and procrastination. In retrospect it becomes clear to Addams that she was trying to juggle two sometimes contradictory needs: an assertion of individuality and a quest for "unity of spirit." She views herself derisively as one of the many "sheltered and pampered" young women "smothered and sickened with advantages," which she likens to "eating a sweet dessert the first thing in the morning." But images of "hideous human need and suffering" break into the fortress of taste and awaken Addams's conscience:

I recall one sunny morning in Saxe-Coburg, looking from the window of our little hotel upon the town square, that we saw crossing and recrossing it a single file of women with semicircular, heavy wooden tanks fastened upon their backs. They were carrying in this primitive fashion to a remote cooling room these tanks filled with a hot brew incident to one stage of beer making. The women were bent forward, not only under the weight which they were bearing, but because the tanks were so high that it would have been impossible for them to have lifted their heads. Their faces and hands, reddened in the cold morning air, showed clearly the white scars where they had previously been scalded by the hot stuff which splashed if they stumbled ever so little on their way. Stung into action by one of those sudden indignations against cruel conditions which at times fill the young with unexpected energy, I found myself across the square, in company with mine host, interviewing the phlegmatic owner of the brewery who received us with exasperating indifference, or rather received me, for the innkeeper mysteriously slunk away as soon as the great magnate of the town began to speak. (65–6)

This brilliant passage, a scene Dürer might have sketched, begins with the American girl a spectator, idle and warm in her hotel room, while outside in the cold the women, like beasts of burden, carry the heavy wooden tanks of beer, their bodies stooped in their heart-rending yoke (this image may also have moved Addams because it reminded her of her own body, bent by a spinal defect). The red of the women's hands and faces contrasts with the white of their scars, the stigmata of economic exploitation, and the sequence of past participles—"scalded," "splashed," "stumbled"—like drops of acid on the engraver's plate, bite into her mind and the reader's. The "I" moves shyly in this passage, as if surprised by a force from the outside ("I found myself"), and merges into a larger group ("the young"), which seems to comfort her. Though her protest is futile— the phlegmatic magnate is the first of many pharisaical manufacturers whose indifference she would try to overcome—she identifies with the file of silent women, interceding in a world of complicated wrongs and class distinctions.

That Addams writes *Twenty Years at Hull-House* from a secure identity, neither self-effacing nor brassily self-absorbed (her forum, unlike Emma Goldman's, was the conference, not the street rally), can be clearly seen in her style of presenting memories:

We had been to a bullfight rendered in the most magnificent Spanish style, where greatly to my surprise and horror, I found that I had seen, with comparative indifference, five bulls and many more horses killed. The sense that this was the last survival of all the glories of the amphitheater, the illusion that the riders of the caparisoned horses might have been knights of a tournament or the matador a slightly armed gladiator facing his martyrdom, and all the rest of the obscure yet vivid associations of an historical survival, had carried me beyond the endurance of any of the rest of the party. I finally met them in the foyer, stern and pale with disapproval of my brutal endurance, and but partially recovered from the faint-ness and disgust which the spectacle itself had produced upon them. I had no defenses to offer to their reproaches save that I had not thought about the bloodshed; but in the evening the natural and inevitable reaction came, and in deep chagrin I felt myself tried and condemned, not only by this disgusting experience but by the entire moral situation which it revealed. It was suddenly made quite clear to me that I was lulling my conscience by a dreamer's scheme, that a mere paper reform had become a defense for continued idleness, and that I was making it a *raison d'être* for going on indefinitely with study and travel. It is easy to become the dupe of a deferred purpose, of the promise the future can never keep, and I had fallen into the meanest type of self-deception in making myself believe that all this was in preparation for great things to come. Nothing less than the moral reaction following the experience of a bullfight had been able to reveal to me that so far from following in the wake of a chariot of philanthropic fire, I had been tied to the tail of the veriest ox-cart of self-seeking. (73)

Addams treats her younger self as a pilgrim in a maze, the bullfight being the last treacherous detour before she confided her dream of starting a settlement house to her friend and traveling companion, Ellen Starr. This passage, an arraignment of her restless confusion and of the temporizing literary self that falls under the spell of romantic idealization, shows Jane Addams's unsparing yet serene introspection. She conveys the allure of the bullfight's pageantry and exotic ritual, and the imagination's powers of weaving false analogies from them, but she does not fully explain her "brutal endurance." Thrilling vicariously to the dangers and deaths that the knights, matadors, and gladiators face in the arena, she can sup on real life and be the decisive heroine she wished to be. The appeal of the bloodshed was perhaps the appeal of the extreme, of the barbaric person within, which she normally repressed but which fascinated her more than she cared to admit. Perhaps her lack of disgust enabled her to draw close to those who lived on the margins of society, including prostitutes and criminals. This underside of her self checked any finicky righteousness when she dealt with social outcasts.

As the trance wears off and self-revulsion sets in, the prose picks up in tempo. Addams enjoys the gentle mockery of exposing herself as a dupe of her "lulled conscience," her clever psychic defense against commitment. The final image convincingly gores her dawdling self. The "I" is natural, poised, of an energetic gravity but not showy, just as the syntax is neither staccato nor prone to Jamesian convolutions. If the crisis as told is a trifle contrived, the passage nonetheless illustrates the compulsive way Addams's memory reshapes experience so as to bring her past into harmony with her developed self.

Jane Addams could not have chosen a more propitious moment to establish Hull-House. In the aftermath of the Haymarket Affair, Chicago was a jittery, polarized city. The unprecedented conditions produced by industrial expansion, including periodic economic hemorrhages, caused "the overaccumulation at one end of society and the destitution at the other" (98) that in turn erupted into strikes by workers and their often violent suppression by the new huge corporations. Anarchist and socialist agitation led in times of stress (after an assassination, for example) to phobic attacks on civil liberties. The premises of American democracy were rocked and strained by these pressures, as if the country, lacking a center, was hurtling forward into a concussive future. "The decade between 1890–1900," Jane Addams remarks in *Twenty Years at Hull-House,* "was, in Chicago, a period of propaganda as over against constructive social effort; the moment for marching and carrying banners, for stating general principles and making a demonstration, rather than the time for uncovering the situation and for providing the legal measures and the civic organization through which new social hopes might make themselves felt." (133)

Despite her impatience with this turbulence, which resembled her own decade of waffling inner debate, Addams understood that legitimate questions were being posed. Where did authority reside? Who should wield it and for what purposes? If pluralism and reciprocity were not to be shams, how was American democracy to settle the question of power and overcome the deepening class division that so distressed Jane Addams? As Jackson Lears notes in *No Place of Grace:*

For centuries, the internal dynamic of bourgeois individualism had been undermining all the older, external forms of moral authority—the authority of king over subject, priest over communicant, master over slave. Freed from older constraints, each masterless man needed a moral gyroscope to keep him on course or else market society might dissolve into a chaos of self-seeking individuals. The destruction of old oppressive forms created new problems of social control; in order to preserve any semblance of public order, oppression had to yield to repression.[27]

To social reformers like Jane Addams, the process of dissolution into self-interested egos scrambling for advantage, leaving human wreckage in its wake, was far advanced; old social brakes, like philanthropy, failed to cope with the new scale of human misery. An army of the disinherited bivouacked on the streets or inside the hovels of most big American cities. Factory workers were not "masterless"; they were indentured to the machines and to the owners who paid them subsistence wages and whose ideas of social control were dominant, though by no means unchallenged. The moral gyroscope was damaged, and a noisy fracas broke out over how to repair it. It was into this volatile situation that Jane Addams, no longer tied to the oxcart, stepped, tentatively at first and then with more and more confidence, fashioning herself into a kind of bold mediator —active, impartial, fact-finding, balanced—who could influence the conduct and actions of both the populace crowded into the slums around Halsted Street and those who held economic and political power in their hands. Jane Addams's balance was a genius for form, a gift she could exercise in the "formless and subdued city," which might reconcile social extremes and renew a depleted moral authority.

Because "political passion easily submits all other values to its purposes,"[28] as the Marxist historian C.L.R. James remarks in *Beyond a Boundary,* only an acrobatic and a mature mind will be trusted by people divided by ideology and personal dislike. Hull-House did not occupy middle ground, nor did it operate exclusively as a social service organization offering parish relief. It branched out into investigations that trod on the toes of special interests and politicians; it lobbied for bills in city hall, in the state legislature and in congressional hearings; it shamed callous manufacturers into installing safety devices on dangerous machines. A resident might be vilified for advocating child labor laws or see her speech distorted in the press. When Jane Addams vigorously and publicly defended the radicals' rights to the protection of the law, opprobrium was heaped on Hull-House. "He who feeds and shelters the heretic is upon *prima facie* evidence considered a heretic himself," (284) she muses, but she did not tack with the expedient winds: She continued to succor pariahs. Describing these quandaries, Addams never sounds shrill, paranoid, or self-pitying, but rather seeks to restore equilibrium by framing social problems in an ethical context. In the face of stubborn cleavages, her instinct, like Benjamin Franklin's, was for conciliation and a pragmatic recognition of mutual duties and obligations.

This was a tricky challenge in a raucous city not far removed from its days of frontier volatility. "Americans," Czeslaw Milosz remarks in *The Captive Mind,* "aware of their law, compare democracy to an awkward raft on which everyone paddles in a different direction. There is much hubbub and mutual abuse, and it is difficult to get everyone to pull together."[29] This centrifugal state of affairs alarmed Jane Addams because it subverted the very self-government that democracy was meant to ensure. Classes railed at each other, wielding paddles as weapons to settle disputes; inequality was rife. And "because our very democracy so long presupposed that each citizen could care for himself," she explained defensively to English critics about the slow pace of municipal reform in America, "we are slow to develop a sense of social obligation." (255) The law did not safeguard the young and the careless, the old and the helpless, and often seemed as remote from the daily needs of the poor, especially the bewildered immigrants, as the planet Saturn.

Yet Addams conceived of the law as a majestic garment that should protect citizens from autocratic and capricious acts, as the hand that could steady the raft and prevent it from capsizing. Practically, the law could modify noisome conditions by abolishing sunless rear tenements or forbidding four-year-olds to work at tasks beyond their strength, and law enforcement could be tempered with clemency so that a judge might know the mitigating circumstances that explained why the German immigrant's daughter shoplifted a piece of silk or a son pilfered coal. Through hard work and statistical studies, Addams and the Hull-House residents were able to get a special court set up for juvenile offenders. In such ways the law could be more than a punitive father. But observing constitutional procedures, seeking by education, persuasion, example, and statute to obtain the consent of mutually suspicious groups to needed changes, demanded patience and tact. For if the law and its strict administration afforded the best hope for effecting the lasting changes she labored for, it still moved glacially, representing the interests of moneyed powers more often than those of the powerless petitioning for relief. Since the poor whose sufferings she strove to ameliorate were her main constituency, and since she strongly believed that "when the sense of justice seeks to express itself outside the regular channels of established government, it has set forth on a dangerous journey inevitably ending in disaster, and . . . this is true in spite of the fact that the adventure may have been inspired by noble motives," (289–90) there was for her no easy route out of this dilemma.

With philosophical realism, Jane Addams accepted the limits on what a social settlement worker or reformer could achieve. From years of struggle she reluctantly concluded that it is "hard to value highly enough the imperfect good so painfully acquired and, at the best, so mixed with evil."[30] She envied but rejected the militant absolutism of partisans who "would never tolerate the use of stepping-stones. They are much too impatient to look on while their beloved scheme is unstably balanced, and they would rather see it tumble into the stream at once than to have it brought to dry land in any half-hearted fashion." (233) In ministering to social need and in changing deeply ingrained evils, she believed that the unstable balance was preferable to an acrimonious impasse: Intransigence negated change. Yet the alternative left her uneasy: "The man who insists upon consent, who moves with the people, is bound to consult the 'feasible right,' as well as the 'absolute right.' He is often obligated to obtain only Mr. Lincoln's 'only possible,' and then has the sickening sense of compromise with his best convictions."[31]

Jane Addams's greatest strength as a social reformer, apart from her acute common sense, was her disinterested moral intelligence. As Charlotte Perkins Gilman observed, Jane Addams's "mind had more 'floor space' in it than any other I have known. She could set a subject down, unprejudiced, and walk all around it, allowing for everyone's point of view."[32] She shied away from the polemics so dear to the socialists and anarchists of her period, resisting the "uniformity of creed" pressed by religious and social ideologues. Like

Benjamin Franklin, she didn't have a single millennial bone in her body. She habitually submitted controversial ideas to reflection and debate, to hypothesis and generality, only after she had gathered facts in the field (she was a pioneer urban anthropologist) and tested them by *experience*. Any tendency she might have had to impose elitist solutions on her neighbors' problems, whether nutritional or economic, she curbed by the sensible precaution of frequently taking along to meetings a victim of the abuse she was investigating. "No one so poignantly realizes the failures in the social structure as the man at the bottom, who has been most directly in contact with those failures and has suffered most." (137) William James's extravagant compliment that she "inhabited reality"[33] is justified because she respected the reality of others, learned from it, and modified her views because of it.

This empiricism stamps Jane Addams's style in *Twenty Years at Hull-House* and in all her sociological books.[34] Lucid, seldom sentimental, careful not to interpose any bureaucratic layers between her and her subjects, she writes about the tragic waste and distress of the poor with a pensive yet assured concreteness. She sears into our minds not just the grim statistics of disease, unemployment, juvenile delinquency, and suicide, but the mangled bodies and worn faces of social castaways. She listens to their talk and reports it with its inflections intact. Like Goya and Dickens, she had a gift of making us see the grotesque and touching detail, the exemplary image, which is meant to rouse the dormant conscience of the middle class: the woman scrubbing floors late at night in a downtown Chicago building, her breast milk mingling with the water splashing from her bucket; the woman boarding a trolley on a rainy night, clutching a wet sack filled with provisions for her family, the flour and beans leaking out onto the floor while in extreme despair she curses poverty itself; the "pale, listless working girls" like Chloe, "little bunches of human misery," who take to prostitution in order to buy a few trinkets and escape the unending monotony of their jobs; the Neapolitan immigrant evicted from his house for carving ornaments on the doorposts of his tenement in an effort to beautify his and the community's life; the child manacled to a bedpost because his mother had nobody to watch him while she toiled in a sweatshop; the emaciated man in London's East End who tore apart a filthy cabbage and devoured it unwashed and uncooked.

These images are not just emblems of Jane Addams's literary

skill; they are intrinsic to her methods of social diagnosis and intro-spection and ultimately to her sense of the kinds of politics practi-cable within the framework of faulty democratic institutions. Her analyses of social evils begin with the appeal and goading presence of a particular suffering human being, proceed to a contemplation of remedies, and then conclude in a plan of action. One old German woman, about to be evicted from her home by county authorities and transferred to the County Infirmary (poorhouse),

> had thrown herself bodily upon a small and battered chest of drawers and clung there, clutching it so firmly that it would have been impossible to remove her without also taking the piece of furniture. She did not weep nor moan nor indeed make any human sound, but between her broken gasps for breath she squealed shrilly like a frightened animal caught in a trap. The little group of women and children gathered at the door stood aghast at the realization of the black dread which always clouds the lives of the very poor when work is slack, but which constantly grows more imminent and threatening as old age approaches. . . . To take away from an old woman whose life has been spent in household cares all the foolish little belongings to which her affections cling and to which her very fingers have become accustomed is to take away her last incentive to activity, almost to life itself. To give an old woman only a chair and a bed, to leave her no cupboard in which her treasures may be stowed, not only that she may take them out when she desires occupa-tion, but that her mind may dwell upon them in moments of revery, is to reduce living almost beyond the limit of human endurance. (119)

The defenseless old lady, as battered as the chest she clings to for safety, is a figure of ineffable sorrow, reduced by poverty to the broken gasps and squeals of a cornered animal. The short physical verbs—"thrown," "clung," "clutching," "moan," "squealed," "caught"—convey the ferocity of a frail creature trapped in the vise of poverty. "The little group of women and children" stand in the doorway like a Greek chorus eloquent in their mute, impotent de-spair, bearing witness to the pathetic drama unfolding before them. What makes the "black dread" menacing is the word "always," a cloud permanently eclipsing the lives of the poor. Jane Addams does not stand aloof; she is a participant in the scene, the one who can speak up for these forlorn victims in the spirit of *caritas*. Typically, she broadens the perspective of the anecdote to include other old women whose lives are harried and reduced by the callous literalism of official social policy to a few bleak appurtenances doled out. To the old people's material woes is added a more awful spiritual blow as they are deprived of the social space for the few possessions ("treasures") that their memories and affections might cling to; the recurrence of the verb "cling" fixes the reader's attention on the aged's bodily and emotional needs to live out their last years in dignity, which cannot be measured by a merely rational calculus, and to be protected from the assaults of a system that heartlessly discards or isolates them. This vignette thus constitutes a stinging rebuttal to those who claimed there was no poverty in Chicago and that local charities were adequate to alleviate the vast suffering. Head and heart in balance, Jane Addams acts as a trustee for the neglected and shelters them.

But a trustee is a member of the very society that has caused the neglect. Jane Addams refused to disqualify her own reforms on this ground. *Twenty Years at Hull-House* contains a tacit running argument with what Addams viewed as the doctrinaire radical creeds that would have discredited her efforts. Though admiring the radicals' habit in discussion of getting at the root of matters, she disliked their insistence on violent confrontation and on the immutable fact of class warfare and economic determinism—their tendency to view the masses, monolithically, as a redemptive force. The child laboring in a dank copper mine and seldom seeing the light of day, and the woman driven to prostitution, were to radicals symptoms of a degrading and collapsing system. The individual was in thrall to larger, more dangerous powers: the state, the church, the heads of steelworks and railroads, the banks. Because they dreamed of the ideal system in which all inequities would disappear, radicals sometimes ignored the immediate plight of those whose sufferings fueled their righteous anger. To the social reformer like Jane Addams, "grandiose movements for rebuilding the foundations of human life impressed"[35] little. The absence of bellicosity in *Twenty Years at Hull-House* is striking. Addams avoids three errors radicals often commit: She does not talk about people, her neighbors or her adversaries, in reifying abstractions like "the masses" or "the bosses" (them and us); she never invokes history as a force inevitably taking her side; and she does not allow her compassion for the injuries of children or for pinched and desperate breadwinners to romanticize the poor.

> If the underdog were always right, one might quite easily try to defend him. The trouble is that very often he is but obscurely right, sometimes only partially right, and often quite wrong; but perhaps he is never so altogether wrong and pigheaded and utterly reprehensible as he is represented to be by those who add the possession of prejudices to the other almost insuperable difficulties of understanding him [the immigrant worker].(291)

This frankness could only rile both sides: The underdog was not as clearly right as his champions claimed, but neither was he the seditious and foolish hothead the business classes inveighed against.

Jane Addams was sensitive not only to these sources of friction but also to those grievances and recriminations that crossed the generations and made the process of Americanization at times an internecine struggle. She had none of the xenophobic fears of and repugnance toward the immigrants that many other Americans felt. Like a pilot, she steered the overwhelmed and scared newcomers past the treacherous reefs of American mores into relatively safe harbors (many of course foundered anyway). At Hull-House, she tried to abate the ethnic strife that made maladjustment so painful, stressing what united Sicilian peasant and Austrian shopkeeper, Russian sweatshop laborer and Greek artisan, rather than what divided them. The Nineteenth Ward sometimes seemed, to Jane Addams, to resemble a collection of insular villages through which ran a breach between the parents' "quaint" traditional customs and their children's impatient desire to adopt American ways of dress, socializing, and morality.[36] Addams mulls over this spiky problem in the following passage:

> An overmastering desire to reveal the humbler immigrant parents to their own children lay at the base of what has come to be called the Hull-House Labor Museum. This was first suggested to my mind early one spring day when I saw an old Italian woman, her distaff against her homesick face,

patiently spinning a thread by the simple stick spindle so reminiscent of all southern Europe. I was walking down Polk Street, perturbed in spirit, because it seemed so difficult to come into genuine relations with the Italian women and because they themselves so often lost their hold on their Americanized children. It seemed to me that Hull-House ought to be able to devise some educational enterprise which should build a bridge between European and American experiences in such wise as to give them both more meaning and a sense of relation. I meditated that perhaps the power to see life whole is more needed in the immigrant quarter of a large city than anywhere else, and that the lack of this power is the most fruitful source of misunderstanding between European immigrants and their children, as it is between them and their American neighbors; and why should that chasm between fathers and sons, yawning at the feet of each generation, be made so unnecessarily cruel and impassable to these bewildered immigrants? Suddenly I looked up and saw the old woman with her distaff, sitting in the sun on the steps of a tenement house. She might have served as a model for one of Michelangelo's Fates, but her face brightened as I passed and, holding up her spindle for me to see, she called out that when she had spun a little more yarn, she would knit a pair of stockings for her goddaughter. The occupation of the old woman gave me the clue that was needed. Could we not interest the young people working in the neighborhood factories in these older forms of industry, so that, through their own parents and grandparents, they would find a dramatic representation of the inherited resources of their daily occupation. If these young people could actually see that the complicated machinery of the factory had been evolved from simple tools, they might at least make a beginning toward that education which Dr. Dewey defines as "a continuing reconstruction of experience." They might also lay a foundation for reverence of the past which Goethe declares to be the basis of all sound progress. (171–72)

The old Italian woman in the window is not sketched in detail. Instead Jane Addams cleverly uses the distaff, an obsolete form of weaving in an age of textile factories, as a homely prop to present a difficult issue. The human appeal of the "simple stick spindle" against the old displaced peasant's homesick face is memorable, and she does not ignore its historical provenance. Though she and the woman sitting on the steps are strangers, there is a solidarity between them, if not yet a "genuine relation." A second glance at the woman raises her to a symbolic role: By likening her to one of Michelangelo's Fates, Addams transforms the woman from a passive bystander to a force actively deciding the lives of others. That analogy passes like a flash of insight, and the woman is again seen in her domestic, familial role. In that brief contact the idea of a labor museum at Hull-House is born and Addams's "perturbed spirit" is soothed. Her style reveals her easy friendly relation to the immigrant woman and her cultivated relation to the reader. She feels no self-consciousness citing Michelangelo, John Dewey, and Goethe, her respect for tradition being an essential part of her faith in "sound progress." The labor museum was not proposed as a placebo. Addams was aware that mounting an exhibit of evolutionary sequences in labor might be construed as sentimental education—it did not replace efforts by the Hull-House residents to obtain legislation protecting men, women, and children in the workplace—but the spindle, like the blacksmith's tool of her early dream, stood for a beginning in reshaping the world and providing warmth (a pair of stockings here), which could serve two valuable purposes: to bring the battered cogs of society into some enlightened relation with the machinery that ruled them, and to help some of the young see their parents in a new, more lenient light (in this the exhibit succeeded). The skein of generational continuity snapped often in America, Addams observed, and could be mended only by the "reconstruction of experience."[37]

To the impatient revolutionary, reformers like Jane Addams were naive children whose timid policies could achieve at most "a surface modification of the old society,"[38] "the rose water for the plague,"[39] cures that Addams herself scoffed at. Perhaps the classic formulation of this criticism is Rosa Luxemburg's:

The principle of justice is the old war horse on which the reformers of the earth have rocked for ages, for the lack of surer transportation. We return to that lamentable Rosinante on which the Don Quixotes of history have galloped toward the great reform of the earth, always to come home with their eyes blackened.[40]

Democratic methods and institutions are, in this view, anachronistic, slow, and rickety vehicles of "historical transportation" because they are owned by the "ruling class," not the people. For the radical, the "feasible right" is merely a palliative, a minor concession wrung from the capitalist, leaving his economic domination, and therefore his power, untouched. Jane Addams herself had pangs of nausea at compromises that fell far short of an ideal agreement, but revolutions, she thought, gave too fast and bumpy a ride, with the vehicle likely to career off the road or injure all the passengers (and drivers) when it crashes into the barricades. Clearly her upbringing in a small town and her father's moral training and leadership, as well as her conviction that the working classes were often conservative, acted as interior restraints in her assessment of revolution and class conflict. She harked back to the model of simple cooperative enterprises in rural Illinois[41] in much the same way Jacob Riis retained an image of the sunny pastoral Danish town he was born in as an alternative to the airless, fetid slums of urban ghettos.

About capitalists Jane Addams was of two opinions. Men of "ruthless will," strivers driven "almost without their volition" to become "mere slaves of possession," these self-made factory owners are inflexible negotiators ruled by a narrow creed, certain that industrial growth "would be curtailed if the welfare of its employees were guarded by the state."[42] They chant a monotonous litany that any able man can find work, and only reluctantly concede during the 1893 panic that their optimism is misguided. Any form of social control, except perhaps the paternalistic benevolence of a George Pullman,[43] is anathema to them, and socialism especially revolting. Jane Addams analyzed their mentality brilliantly in *Twenty Years at Hull-House*:

A Settlement is above all a place for enthusiasm, a spot to which those who have a passion for the equalization of human joys and opportunities are early attracted. It is this type of mind which is in itself obnoxious to the man of conquering business faculty, to whom the practical world of affairs seems so supremely rational that he would never vote to change the type of it even if he could. The man of social enthusiasm is to him an annoyance and an affront. He does not like to hear him talk and considers him *per se* "unsafe." Such a business-man would admit, as an abstract proposition, that society is susceptible of modification and would even agree that all human institutions imply progressive development, but at the same time he deeply distrusts those who seek to reform existing conditions. There is a certain common-sense foundation for this distrust, for too often the reformer is the one who defies things as they are, because of the restraints which they impose upon his individual desires rather than because of the general defects of the system. When such a rebel poses for a reformer, his shortcomings are heralded to the world, and his downfall cherished as an awful warning to those who refuse to worship "the god of things as they are." (137–8)

From varied dealings with businessmen, Jane Addams could write about them in a rounded way. She had tried to fathom the ethics of a man who underpaid his employees or used "unscrupulous business methods" to make his money and yet worried about the "irreligious" nature of a settlement house. She can get underneath the skin and inside the mind of the businessman; she incorporates him as a part of herself that is undesirable perhaps but not alien, thus not isolating him on the other side of the class barrier. She also understands the weakness of his position and its psychological origins. Despite his faith in a "supremely rational" world,[44] the businessman is an idolator, the status quo his divinity. His mind moves slowly when faced with ideas that don't consort with his limited stock of cautious precepts. The man who has conquered by a series of well-executed computations is loath to entertain even a tinkering with "existing conditions"; he is a prisoner of his ideology, able to take two paces in his cell, who cannot see fairly or even in a spirit of play what somebody else thinks: The socialist, by fiat, is a ruffian. That leap Jane Addams can take, condemning one type of reformer the businessman would condemn. But she is not trapped in his generalities illogically drawn from a few deviant samples, nor does she gloat unbecomingly as he does. She has a finer sense of the spotted composition of good and evil. Reason, unirrigated by enthusiasm, is a dry channel for change; it misses the small details that alter the picture. Addams clearly favors the enthusiasts who grasped that "pliable human nature is relentlessly pressed upon by its physical environment." (139)

A more caustic analysis of the capitalist appears in allegorical form late in the autobiography, in a beautiful passage about—and interpretation of—the Oberammergau Passion Play:

> [The peasants] made clear that the opposition to the young Teacher [Jesus] sprang from the merchants whose traffic in the temple He had disturbed and from the Pharisees who were dependent upon them for support. Their query was curiously familiar, as they demanded the antecedents of the Radical who dared to touch vested interests, who presumed to dictate the morality of trade, and who insulted the marts of honest merchants by calling them "a den of thieves." As the play developed, it became clear that this powerful opposition had friends in Church and State, that they controlled influences which ramified in all directions. They obviously believed in their statement of the case and their very wealth and position in the community gave their words such weight that finally all of their hearers were convinced that the young Agitator must be done away with in order that the highest interests of society might be conserved. These simple peasants made it clear that it was the money power which induced one of the Agitator's closest friends to betray him, and the villain of the piece, Judas himself, was only a man who was so dazzled by money, so under the domination of all it represented, that he was perpetually blind to the spiritual vision unrolling before him. (270–1)

A dozen years had elapsed since Jane Addams sat enthralled by the bullfight, sorting out what events meant, groping for self-direction. In the "magic space" that the old play creates, she again loses herself, but this time her mind floats free to wonder at and examine the meaning of Christ's life and message. The peasants impersonating the New Testament figures were this one day lifted out of their destitution and permitted to speak out, through the words of a hallowed text, their protest against oppressive authority. These simple folk became bearers of a profound revelation, as the word "clear" chimes three times, marking the stages of the mounting conflict between Jesus and the merchants. Jesus' teachings earn him the epithets Radical and Agitator, as the conservatives, their complacent power challenged, react with haughty anger, the pitch rising as each verb—"dared," "presumed," "insulted"—slashes through the air at the insolent stranger. How without censure, by contrast, is Jane Addams's use of the word "radical," as if it was perfectly natural that the Teacher, meeting total incomprehension, should change to a Radical, since the "vested interests" falsely equated their own selfish interests with "the highest interests of society." Money dominates completely, its influence penetrating into every corner of church and state so that it could in its arrogance put the radical to death with apparent impunity.

Jane Addams's oneness with the young Agitator is as active as the emotional verbs she chooses. Doubtless the familiar tale stirred her deep religious feelings and reminded her how germane the opposition of "spiritual vision" and money was to Chicago.[45] In this passage, the "I" hides in the background or in the personas of others. Addams's missionary humility, her fervor to see into souls, into conditions, are what feeds her ego, and imbues her style with a luminous presence.

If one stripped this subtle homily of its Christian trappings and concentrated on its theme, there would be little difference between Jane Addams's revulsion from the entrepreneur and any radical's. They would, however, quarrel over tactics for reducing or ending the immense power of the merchants. For despite her indictment, Addams decided after a fractious decade of debate and rigid ideological poses that reformers should work with the businessmen. A barrage of fact and moral persuasion would teach them their duty to the less fortunate, and society would harness their practical acumen and experience for the common good: "the dependence of classes on each other was reciprocal." (76) Jane Addams had close friends among the wealthy: her companion Mary Rozet Smith, for instance, and Mrs. Louise DeKoven Bowen. These upper-class benefactors enlisted in her causes, donating large sums of money, pulling strings behind the scenes, and, perhaps of inestimable value, lending the power of their social standing and influence to Hull-House, particularly in crises when fickle public opinion lashed Jane Addams for heterodoxy. These capitalists contradicted the conventional wisdom that the rich were indifferent to the lot of the poor, though Addams would admit they were exceptional women and men.[46] To a radical like Alexander Berkman, Addams's position would be logically absurd, applying cosmetics to a corpse, because the businessmen *were* the problem, the chronic thorn in the workers' side, the enemy, as she had seen at Oberammergau but backed away from in her policy. Economic exploitation, "the real despotism of republican institutions," Berkman argued, rested and throve on "the popular delusion of self-government and independence," "the source of democratic tyranny."[47] These phrases, painfully contemptuous of Addams's values, underscore the nearly absolute incompatibility between the anarchist and the liberal.

Extreme public crises, like the McKinley assassination and the mass hysteria, the cries for vengeance it unleashed, tested Addams's sheltering self to the utmost. When the Chicago police, rounding up anarchists suspected of abetting Leon Czolgosz (in the event, no conspiracy was found), netted the editor of an anarchist newspaper and held him incommunicado, Jane Addams persuaded the mayor to let her visit the man so that she could calm the fears of his family and of the terrified Russian community that reprisals ("official aggression"), such as occurred regularly in czarist Russia, would not happen in America. But solace was not enough. Larger educational ideas needed to be pressed:

> It seemed to me at the time that mere words would not avail. I had felt that the protection of the law itself extended to the most unpopular citizen was the only reply to the anarchistic argument, to the effect that this moment of panic revealed the truth of their theory of government; that the custodians of law and order have become the government itself quite as the armed men hired by the medieval guilds to protect them in the peaceful pursuit of their avocations through sheer possession of arms finally made themselves rulers of the city. At that moment I was convinced firmly that the public could only be convicted of the blindness of its course, when a body of people with a hundredfold of the moral energy possessed by a Settlement group should make clear that there is no method by which any community can be guarded against spo-

radic efforts on the part of half-crazed, discouraged men, save by a sense of mutual rights and securities which will include the veriest outcast. (281)

Here are the customary Jane Addams themes and methods, though for once written in a tortured prose, as if the conflict was extremely strenuous to analyze: the cheapness of talk divorced from sensible action; the faith in law as the barrier against tyranny by the majority; the comfort of historical perspective; the effort to take into account the grievances of all sides, and the generosity of vision that folds in the "veriest outcast"—embittered, unformed, uncared for, a cipher to himself—under the shelter of "mutual rights and securities."[48] Addams does not permit herself to pander to the eagerness for glib solutions; she throws no political sops to the community. Nor does she sentimentalize Leon Czolgosz: His assassination of the President wasn't a political act; he did not have the knowledge, will, or calculation of consequences to perform such a deed. His search for "passwords" was the cryptic cry of a confused soul for fellowship. Though the "I" is firm, she perceives that even virtuous individual action is as futile as the clan's blind response to the morose boy's bullet, and she rebukes "public-spirited citizens" and "the forces for social betterment," including herself, for their failure to practice the preventive social medicine that would not have let Czolgosz stand outside the community. Alice Hamilton described Jane Addams in 1897 as "having looked upon the misery and sin of the world and having accepted them as an inevitable burden which she must bear with no hope of ever reforming them."[49] But this melancholy resignation to the tenacity of evil did not paralyze her will, and she never recanted her belief that "antagonism [was] a foolish and unwarrantable expenditure of energy." (195)

The legitimacy of authority, which troubled Jane Addams in the Czolgosz case, is a major preoccupation of *Twenty Years at Hull-House.* Her choice of a topical structure for the autobiography after she had followed standard chronology (childhood, girlhood, adolescence, young womanhood) is the sign of a confidence that the flounderings, the spiritual invalidism, of her twenties had given way to a fluent, stable, autonomous person. The narrative voice, the "I," which seems to vanish into the miscellaneous topics she takes up in orderly fashion—labor strife, schemes for civic cooperation, investigations into abuses from truancy to poor sanitation, social clubs, the arts—actually stays as visible and solid as the settlement house itself. Precisely because she has become an authoritative public figure whose ideas count and who can make a sphere of action graspable to professionals and laity alike, she can put forward her analysis and not linger on her accomplishments. The chapter on Tolstoyism in the autobiography seems at first a curious digression, a kind of bogus crisis of self-distrust. But the pilgrimage to Yasnaya Polyana, where Tolstoy, embodying the "sermon of the deed," made "the one supreme personal effort, one might almost say the one frantic personal effort, to put himself into right relations with the humblest people," (193) is a crucial turning point of self-validation. If Jane Addams starts out with the expectation that Tolstoy will offer guidance to a mind perhaps feeling guilty at her class privileges and perplexed by the "divergence between our democratic theory on the one hand, that working people have a right to the intellectual resources of society, and the actual fact on the other hand that thousands of them are so overwhelmed with toil that there is no leisure nor energy left for the cultivation of the mind," (193) she ends by rejecting his saintliness. Instead of undertaking discipleship, she becomes her own master. Like her father, Tolstoy "the great authority" (195) reproaches Jane Addams for wearing an inappropriately voluminous dress, which separates her from the working girls; and he urges her to bake bread, to resume a sacramental manual labor she had performed for her father. But Tolstoy, like his followers who set up a utopian colony in Arkansas, is "more logical than life warrants," a fanatic martyr to impossibly lofty principles. When Addams consults her conscience and chooses her own form of action, she realizes that she has become a figure of authority herself, and the thought does not disorient her. Though she might confide in Canon Barham or Canon Ingram, on one of her trips to England, as she had in her father, nearly every meeting was conducted on a footing of intellectual equality. She did not defer shyly to the men. What she had wanted for herself she had obtained: a chance to be useful and change the world (how Franklinesque that sounds!).

The one fleck of egoism in *Twenty Years at Hull-House* is Jane Addams's conscious lapse in not sketching in full detail the many brilliant women, like Alice Hamilton, Florence Kelley, Julia Lathrop, and Ellen Starr, who led Hull-House's investigations, as if their distinction was self-evident and the significant point was the collective effort. The settlement, Jane Addams said, "receives in exchange for the music of isolated voices the volume and strength of the chorus." (97) She was not rigging her portrait as the Saint of Halsted Street, as both Christopher Lasch and Allen F. Davis suggest.[50] Significantly, none of the women, considerable personages in their own right, raised this charge;[51] indeed, Jane Addams inspired extraordinary loyalty in her neighbors, who called her "Kind Heart," and in the residents, three quarters of whom were women. Alice Hamilton's first letter about Hull-House is humorously emblematic:

> Miss Addams still rattles me, indeed more so all the time, and I am at my very worst with her. I really am quite school-girly in my relations with her; it is a remnant of youth which surprises me. I know when she comes into the room. I have pangs of idiotic jealousy toward the residents whom she is intimate with. She is—well she is quite perfect and I don't in the least mind raving over her to you.[52]

The style of *Twenty Years at Hull-House,* tuned to the sufferings of others, is richly communicative. Theater, Addams believed, reduced propaganda to conversation, and her own favored style blended dramatic vignettes with a kind of sparkling intellectual conversation with her readers as shaded and direct as her talks with her neighbors. When she upbraids herself or an obstinate adversary, she is neither shrill nor euphemistic. Most impressive of all, she can introduce the voices of a beleaguered Polish immigrant or a rebellious child without jarring the continuity of her thoughts. Over the ostinato of her immaculate grammar in *Twenty Years at Hull-House* she sings soloistically and in unison with the workers, her refinement of culture no obstacle to the genuine relations she sought to cultivate with the poor around her. That the door of Hull-House always remained open, as the door of her father's house had in Cedarville, is a symbol of Jane Addams's hospitality to experience, her trust in the integrity of even the most desperate of her neighbors, and her sheltering self.

TOP LEFT: Ben L. Reitman, c. 1912. TOP RIGHT: Emma Goldman, 1906.
ABOVE: Emma Goldman and Alexander Berkman, 1917

5

The Shelterless Life:
Emma Goldman's *Living My Life*

I

W HEN ROBERT HENRI wanted to paint her portrait,[1] to depict the "real Emma Goldman," she asked, "But which is the real one? I have never been able to unearth her." (529) This was not arch evasion but honest bafflement, which the thousand pages of *Living My Life* confirm. Her autobiography sprawls and meanders through time, crammed with adventures and romances that would have exhausted the knights in Ariosto, but despite her belief in eternal change, "new currents flowing from the dried-up springs of the old," (522) the overall impression is of a woman trapped in repetitions. Inside the Queen of the Anarchists (so dubbed by her anarchist "knight," Robert Reitzel) hid a Jamesian ingenue who yearned for and acted out a heroic life. Goldman was aware of the discrepancy between the public personality and the private woman.[2] In a letter to Ben Reitman, she wrote: "If ever our correspondence should be published, the world would stand aghast that I, Emma Goldman, the strong revolutionist, the daredevil, the one who has defied laws and convention, should have been as helpless [in love] as a shipwrecked crew on a foaming ocean."[3]

   Sitting down to compose her autobiography in St. Tropez, Emma
Goldman, like Benjamin Franklin, did not have on hand many of
the key books, papers, and memorabilia of her life—they had been
confiscated by the United States government and never returned to
her.[4] What fazed her was not a paucity of materials or a fear that
her memory was unreliable but, as she noted in her introduction to
Living My Life, the task of "reliving my long-forgotten past, the
resurrection of memories I did not wish to dig out from the deeps
of my consciousness. It meant doubts in my creative ability, depression, and disheartenings."[5] (vi–vii) Writing in exile, she could not
summon the humorous detachment that Franklin brought to his autobiography. Franklin's disheveled narrative mirrors the busy public
servant's cheerful duplicities and lapses from order; he would never
dream of asking which is the real Benjamin Franklin. Emma Goldman by contrast is never the sage. Her narrative plunges her immediately into a maelstrom of emotion, from which she emerges at
the end no closer to her "real" self. Near sixty, she still felt "adoles-
cently young," and it is in the voice of the adolescent that Goldman
often speaks, despite the fact that on her vast canvas every disorder
that convulsed her age touched her directly: labor unrest, class strife,
assassinations, revolutions, prison, deportation, and statelessness.
Her sexually emancipated views and her blunt political statements,
which often ruffled public officials, made her a figure of notoriety,
feared, admired, lampooned, and denounced as a menace to the
American way of life. Like Jane Addams, she felt a kinship with the
"derelicts on the social dung heap," (137) but her life veered constantly between violent extremes, as if she had been born into the
Karamazov family.

   Living My Life is a garrulous, exhausting autobiography. Goldman could not let go of a single experience, and therefore could not
boil down the blubber in a stylistic tryworks in order to extract
cruets of pure oil.[6] Reading *Living My Life,* one feels like a spectator
who has stumbled on the fringes of a parade, a sea of abstract faces
passing by in stupefying numbers, with every now and then a recognizable person emerging with clear features. Goldman's shapeless
and repetitive narrative is a mirror of the eternal recurrence of human misery and our puny attempts to relieve it; her windiness is a
touching unconscious testament to the failure of propaganda—and
self-glorification. Her voice always seems too exhibitionistic, too
stentorian, as if still aimed at the crowd in the back of the hall.

The fact is that Goldman was a brilliant platform speaker,[7] a master of repartee, poised in emergencies and able to calm hecklers who baited her in the hopes of breaking up meetings. She throve on the atmosphere of confrontation, buoyed by the danger, like an unwelcome missionary amid indifferent or hostile tribes. The political lecture was a form of theater, and Emma an oratorical diva who knew how to spellbind an audience. In America, she remarks at the end of *Living My Life,* "I had lectured before the most diversified crowds—longshoremen and millionaires, poor working and professional women, in halls behind saloons and in drawing rooms, in mines hundreds of feet below the ground, from pulpit and soapboxes." (972) Large audiences stimulated her to a high level of performance. Her rhetoric was bearish and direct, employing questions and answers which conveyed information and roused the crowds that turned out to hear her to a pitch of emotion.

Throughout *Living My Life* Goldman displays an extraordinary susceptibility to the human voice, falling into a near trance, her nervous system vibrating to the timbres of the speaker, as he or she modulated from invective to satire to tender celebration. When she first heard the German anarchist leader and journalist Johann Most speak, his language "seemed lava shooting forth flames of ridicule, scorn, and defiance." (7) "The storm of his eloquence . . . was thunder interspersed with flashes of lightning." (43) These elemental images equate the human voice with forces of nature, dangerous and erotic, a thrilling music in which reason and logical presentation, though important, were secondary. The voice was a weapon in a sustained battle against entrenched power, and an index of character strength or weakness.[8]

For Emma Goldman, who was not listened to during her childhood, public speaking offered special gratifications. Alone on the rostrum, transported out of herself, she felt a surge of power and purpose and seized the initiative. Everybody paid attention to her. During her first talk, she recalls,

> I began to speak. Words I had never heard myself utter before came pouring forth, faster and faster. They came with passionate intensity; they painted images of the heroic men on the gallows, their glowing vision of an ideal life, rich with comfort and beauty; men and women radiant in freedom, children transformed by joy and affection. The audience had

vanished, the hall itself had disappeared; I was conscious only
of my own words, of my ecstatic song. (51)

Goldman had the knack of establishing a rapport with audiences,
stirring them by her own passionate delivery, what she called her
"ordinary determined and aggressive manner." (254) As a novice
speaker, she learned that a merely factual presentation left both
the audience and herself dissatisfied; heart must address heart across
the chasm of ideology or different perspectives. She often prepared
for a public address carefully but then discarded her notes, improvising on the spur of the moment, trusting that the spirit of the occasion would inspire the right words. At a public meeting in Union
Square during a period of severe mass unemployment, she got up
resolved to make up for the "apologetic oratory" that preceded her:
"I heard my name shouted from a thousand throats as I stepped
forward. I saw a dense mass before me, their pale, pinched faces
upturned to me. My heart beat, my temples throbbed, and my
knees shook." (122) Like an actress, she overcame the attack of
nerves as soon as she uttered her first words, and she held the
crowd enthralled:

> "Men and women," I began amidst sudden silence, "do you
> not realize that the State is the worst enemy you have? It is a
> machine that crushes you in order to sustain the ruling class,
> your masters. Like naive children you put your trust in polit-
> ical leaders. You make it possible for them to creep into your
> confidence, only to have them betray you to the first bidder.
> But even where there is no direct betrayal, the labour politi-
> cians make common cause with your enemies to keep you in
> leash, to prevent your direct action. The State is the pillar of
> capitalism, and it is ridiculous to expect any redress from it.
> Do you not see the stupidity of asking for relief from Albany
> with immense wealth within a stone's throw from here? Fifth
> Avenue is laid in gold, every mansion is a citadel of money
> and power. Yet there you stand, a giant starved and fettered,
> shorn of his strength. Cardinal Manning long ago proclaimed
> that 'necessity knows no law' and that 'the starving man has
> a right to a share of his neighbour's bread.' Cardinal Man-
> ning was an ecclesiastic steeped in the traditions of the

Church, which has always been on the side of the rich against the poor. But he had some humanity, and he knew that hunger is a compelling force. You, too, will have to learn that you have a right to share your neighbour's bread. Your neighbours—they have not only stolen your bread, but they are sapping your blood. They will go on robbing you, your children, and your children's children, unless you wake up, unless you become daring enough to demand your rights. Well, then, demonstrate before the palaces of the rich; demand work. If they do not give you work, demand bread. If they deny you both, take bread. It is your sacred right."

Uproarious applause, wild and deafening, broke from the stillness like a sudden storm. The sea of hands eagerly stretching out towards me seemed like the wings of white birds fluttering. (122–3)

This is a shrewd piece of rhetoric: a call to action, if not a call to arms. Goldman teaches the crowd some elementary lessons about its own rights and class strife. She makes no effort to ingratiate herself; indeed, she lashes out at her listeners' credulous natures, not hesitating to use words like "stupidity" and "ridiculous," as if to shame them awake. As their unillusioned surrogate, she leads them on to consider their collective interest. As if conceding to their awe of ecclesiastical authority, she broadens the ethical sanction of her proposition that "you have a right to share your neighbour's bread" by invoking Cardinal Manning; by cleverly calling the ruling classes the workers' neighbors and then stating as an irrefutable fact that those neighbors have violated the spirit and letter of the Bible ("they have not only stolen your bread, but they are sapping your blood"), she has brought her audience to the verge of action. The climax, a sequence of imperatives—"demonstrate," "demand," "demand," "take"—incites the assembly to tumultuous applause. From her vantage point above them, Goldman sees not people but a "sea of hands," a force as yet untapped, a flock of birds poised to take flight.

The army of the unemployed who cheered Emma Goldman's speech did not in fact demonstrate in front of the palaces of the rich, though she was once indicted for "inciting to riot" and sent to jail for one year. Judging her speech soberly as a piece of rhetoric, one cannot help noticing the emphatic but hackneyed language she employs. The state is an "enemy," a "machine," "the pillar of capitalism"; the ruling classes are masters who live in mansions that are citadels of money and power, and the poor are both slaves and "a giant starved and fettered, shorn of his strength," like Samson. These stock antitheses might fan an apathetic crowd into a bonfire, since the words do not have to register with precision so long as the rhythm, the crescendo, and the diminuendo are crisp. But on the page they crumble like scorched paper. As Thoreau said, "What is called eloquence in the forum is commonly found to be rhetoric in the study."[9]

In *Living My Life*, Goldman habitually projects her ardor in the vague, general terms and hammering rhythms of platform oratory. She lapses often into the jargon of leftist polemics: "wild beasts," "herculean tasks," "wage slaves." Military images, not inapt for an embattled anarchist and believer in class warfare, rattle the page. Invariably the paragraphs rise and fall as her manic energy flattens into romantic despondency. The grandiosity of Goldman's language verges on the ludicrous: She is either being engulfed by "tidal waves" or being consumed by fires blazing out of control; either scaling the heights or toppling into the depths. Even in its most intimate moments, *Living My Life* cannot escape this strident public manner. When she talks about her love life, she musters "primitive calls" and "ecstatic songs" or attaches the adjective "infinite" to "tenderness" and "sympathy," like a magical lock that will ensure their not escaping; the emotional weather turns from clichéd turbulence to balminess:

> In the arms of Ed [Brady] I learned for the first time the meaning of the great life-giving force [sex]. I understood its full beauty, and I eagerly drank its intoxicating joy and bliss. It was an ecstatic song, profoundly soothing by its music and perfume. My little flat in the building known as the "Bohemian Republic," to which I had moved lately, became a temple of love. Often the thought would come to me that so much peace and beauty could not last; it was too wonderful, too perfect. Then I would cling to Ed with a trembling heart. He would hold me close and his unfailing cheer and humour would dispel my dark thoughts. "You are overworked," he

would say. "The machine and your constant anxiety about Sasha [Berkman] are killing you." (120)

This effusion might have been lifted from the pages of a pulp magazine like *True Confessions*. The champion of Ibsen and Strindberg and the New Woman is unaware of her banalities.[10] Here and elsewhere in *Living My Life* she associates the love of a man with a father's protection of his child from dark, foreboding thoughts; the very rhythms of the prose, static and predictable, evoke a desire for the conventional security she avowed was false. And indeed, three paragraphs later, her mistrust has returned, the bliss become a handicap, because the man tries to own her: "Did he consider me his property, a dependent or a cripple who had to be taken care of by a man?" (121) As soon as her lovers hoisted their sexist colors, she had to run from "emotional bondage."[11]

Goldman's portraits of famous people, from the heroine of the Paris Commune Louise Michel to the anarchists Kropotkin, Reitzel, and Voltairine de Cleyre, are similarly mediocre, like a Sunday painter's work. She cannot get outside herself. Her prose sounds mincing, combining the name-dropping of a social climber with the mawkish idolatry of a teenage fan:

I had never seen a woman so utterly oblivious of anything that concerned herself. Her dress was shabby, her bonnet ancient. Everything she wore was ill-fitting. But her whole being was illumined by an inner light. One quickly succumbed to the spell of her radiant personality, so compelling in its strength, so moving in its childlike simplicity. That afternoon with Louise was an experience unlike anything that had happened till then in my life. Her hand in mine, its tender pressure on my head, her words of endearment and close comradeship, made my soul expand, reach out towards the spheres of beauty where she dwelt. (168)

These corny phrases are so pervasive they must signify more than just aesthetic blemishes. "Speech is the twin of my vision,"[12] Whitman correctly observed, and style is the unfailing clue that drives "selves in hiding"[13] into the open. In Goldman's case, it is the uncontrollable self-inflation and "self-display,"[14] as Patricia Meyer

Spacks notes, that tarnishes her professions of love for those immortals who dwell in "spheres of beauty" and of concern for the masses. In Goldman's vapid idealization of Louise Michel, the hero of the Paris Commune, the affected votary and the child hungering to be loved are joined together like Siamese twins. Goldman's style is a strained effort to attract notice.

But in the moments of *Living My Life* when Emma forgets herself—for example, in describing the troubles of poor women bringing unwanted children into the world—she can poignantly evoke the plight of others scarred by their powerlessness.[15] If she never achieved the earthy directness of Mother Jones's style—"A sewer rat never changes,"[16] "The military has no regard for human life. They were sanctified cannibals"[17]—and of her relations with copper miners and their families, Emma's struggles on behalf of the shelterless, including herself, were bighearted.

II

EMMA GOLDMAN claimed, at age twenty, to have cast off her "meaningless past" like a "worn-out garment," (3) but such bravado is misleading. The past was, for Goldman, a tyrant that tortured the weak and the innocent, and she spent her entire life striking back at it, often with blind impulse. Indeed, her own childhood was so painful to her that she could tell about it in *Living My Life* only by flashbacks, which seem to strike suddenly, like electrical storms that do not clear the air. Though Goldman listened to Freud lecture in Vienna, few autobiographies are as barren of self-knowledge as hers. When Johann Most explains to her that "early environment and conditions are powerful factors in moulding one's life," that her "awakening to social problems" was not due exclusively to the Haymarket tragedy but "was the flowering of what had its roots in myself, in the past and in the conditions of my childhood," (66) she neither agrees with nor refutes his point.[18] Nevertheless, *Living My Life* contains enough material about early traumas, conflicts with her parents, and uprootings—she was an expert on violence—to permit us to draw some conclusions about the personal sources of her anarchistic ideas.

Emma Goldman, born a Jew, grew up in an atmosphere of profound insecurity. Wherever her family had settled—in Popelnya, Königsberg, or St. Petersburg—they were vulnerable to countless humiliations and constraints. Pogroms do not respect national borders; Jewish families were not safe from rapists, looters, murderers, and mobs often egged on by priests and czarist agents. Irrational behavior and brute force were routine. Nor, of course, were the Russian peasants immune to cruel treatment. Goldman recounts in her autobiography one harrowing scene in which a peasant was flogged and left bleeding.[19] Such incidents stirred in her a wish to avenge injustice.

Emma Goldman's family life was also unstable and unsheltered: She was an emotionally battered child, the victim of her parents' tense, loveless marriage. Abraham Goldman demanded absolute obedience and was prone to uncontrollable rages; he generated "an atmosphere charged with antagonism and harshness." He whipped his daughter and abused her verbally, and once, in a frenzy when the fifteen-year-old Emma refused to marry his choice of husband, he threw her French book into the fire and pounded her on the head, instructing her in her future role: "Girls do not have to learn much! All a Jewish daughter needs to know is how to prepare gefüllte fish, cut noodles fine and give the man plenty of children." (12) At rare intervals Abraham did become jolly and loving—on the holiday of Sukkoth he lavished gifts and affection on her, even kissing her—and he once shielded her from an episode of brutalization. Emma hoarded these memories in the vain hope that they would signal a permanent change of heart. In *Living My Life*, she recalls that despite herself, she was drawn to his dashing, virile ways—indeed, he became a prototype of the "handsome brutes" she was attracted to in adult life—and even dreamed that "if I was stricken with some consuming disease! It would surely soften Father's heart." (59) But as if gripped by a folk superstition because she was not a boy, he saw Emma as the devil's baby. In one of the autobiography's most dramatic scenes, Emma Goldman scathingly reproaches her father for his assaults on her, as she bangs her scrubbing brush on the floor. Then he fades from the autobiography. Emma declares that when she finally saw him as a victim like the masses, she forgave him—he was no longer a threat—but her tone belies her words: He symbolized the coercive authority against which she hurled her dark indictments.[20]

Little comfort was to be obtained from her mother. A bitter, aloof woman, disappointed in her second marriage and engrossed by petty bickerings with her husband, Taube Goldman treated her daughter as an unwanted burden. Like her husband, Taube was punitive, slapping Emma when she masturbated and when she menstruated for the first time. (This last blow was an old-country superstition, a "remedy" to ward off disgrace; in *Bronx Primitive* Kate Simon recalls her own mother, an enlightened woman, doing likewise.[21]) But Taube was not simply a passive wife and mother. When her brother Yeger was jailed as a nihilist conspirator, she pleaded successfully before the governor-general of St. Petersburg to have him released. In her account of this incident, Emma Goldman envisions her mother "before the stern" official, "her beautiful face, framed by her massive hair, bathed in tears." (27–8) What she most remembers about this episode is her mother's denunciation of the nihilists, with whom Emma identifies because she "felt that they could not witness without protest the sufferings of the people and that they had sacrificed their lives for them." (28) She seems not to have noticed her mother's assertive bravery, which should have been a crucial model for the daughter to emulate.

The absence of maternal affection left a hole in Emma's life that was only partially filled by the women who fussed over her in childhood, like the two sisters in Königsberg who fed her chocolates or the consumptive German teacher who took her to the opera. Her favorite sister, Helena, often interceded on Emma's behalf, taking the blows her father aimed at the younger child, but although Emma was grateful for these expressions of love, she viewed Helena's "feminine" nature with faint contempt because it acquiesced in suffering; such timidity and selflessness were construed as unacceptable passivity. Years later, when Helena was devastated by the death of her son in World War I, Emma would give no comfort because, she said, she disapproved of her nephew's enlistment in the army.

Throughout her life, Goldman worries the question of how a woman aspiring to leadership in political agitation can avoid being "treated as a mere female." (53) Several pages in the autobiography are devoted to a prolonged crisis of Goldman's young womanhood: Should she undergo an operation that would permit her to bear a child? Prostrated by severe menstrual cramps, brought on in girlhood when she was immersed in an icy river during a nighttime escape across the German-Russian border and aggravated by emotional distress, she falls into reveries and remembers herself at age seven, giving her brother her breast:

> I picked him up in my arms and pressed his little mouth close to me, rocking and cooing and urging him to drink. Instead he began to choke, turned blue in his face, and gasped for breath. Mother came running in and demanded to know what I had done to Baby. I explained. She broke out into laughter, then slapped and scolded me. I wept, not from pain, but because my breast had no milk for Leibale. (58)

The desire to suckle, to nurture, a pervasive impulse in Emma's life, is met by adult ridicule and violence; she is made to feel that she has a "bad" breast and her femaleness is inadequate. As if by a logic of the unconscious, there erupts a series of memories of her "ghastly childhood," her mother seldom returning the child's "hunger for affection" and her father beating her or abusing her verbally. Being unloved is an injury so deep it breeds a lifelong ambivalence toward nurturing: On the one hand, Emma studied in Vienna to be a nurse and midwife and mothered two generations of anarchist men;[22] on the other hand, she sometimes dismisses her sister Helena as a mere domestic drudge. When Emma decides against motherhood, she adduces these reasons:

> I had learned since then that my tragic childhood had been no exception, that there were thousands of children born unwanted, marred and maimed by poverty and still more by ignorant misunderstanding. No child of mine should ever be added to those unfortunate victims.
>
> There was also another reason: my growing absorption in my new-found ideal. I had determined to serve it completely. To fulfill that mission I must remain unhampered and untied. Years of pain and suppressed longing for a child—what were they compared with the price many martyrs had already paid? I, too, would pay that price, I would endure the suffering, I would find an outlet for my mother-need in the love of all children. The operation did not take place. (61)

In identifying herself with the thousands of victimized children (and victimizers), Goldman seems sure she cannot overcome the unreliable legacy of her parents' child rearing[23]: the pattern of internalized violence, the absence of trust. Like Sergio Davide, the anarchist hero of Elsa Morante's novel *History*, she believes that "In the face of the obvious impossibility of certain human damnations, you have to dedicate yourself more than ever to the IDEAL, which, alone, acting mysteriously, like miracles, can free the earth from the monsters of the absurd."[24] It is incontestable that Goldman lived by the noble creed that in order to liberate yourself you have to liberate others. She enacted what most women hadn't been able to do. But the "IDEAL," like miracles, implies the intervention of a force outside human will, which in fact seldom arrives. In rejecting motherhood, Goldman places herself in a visionary company of martyrs, for whom suffering, persecution, ostracism, and even death gave an exalted sense of self. But this state of grace often waned and vanished, replaced by a disillusionment that seared the spirit. Remaining "unhampered and untied" was too much of an affliction even for the austere Berkman, as he learned from years in prison; for Emma Goldman, it meant an emptiness which, in spite of her many admirers and friends, she carried to her grave (she often used the word "void" to describe her mood when the ideal no longer sustained her). The vocation of revolutionary forced her to confront officially sanctioned violence—hooligans, vigilantes, militia, Pinkertons—again and again, and she did so courageously. But the etymological root of the word "revolutionary" suggests the disappointment built into her commitment: a turning back to old ways and self-destructive acts. Revolutions usually cannibalize their own children. How a society cared for its children, its workers, its shelterless, its sick, and its old was, to social reformers from Jacob Riis to Lillian Wald, the touchstone of its ethical authority. That authority, so the Progressive argument ran, had to be reconstructed from within so that economic and social relations that were indifferent, cruel, or wasteful would be replaced by compassion and justice, as if society were a wise parent. Emma Goldman could not trust in a kindly authority, except in a millennial future. Yet the surge of optimism that accompanies her pledge to sacrifice her life for the ideal is grounded in a quasi-religious faith: "The days and weeks . . . were illumined by the glorious new light in us." (62) That light is extinguished and rekindled in a cycle that dominates her life and her autobiography.[25]

III

AMERICA WAS the object of some of Emma Goldman's most complicated feelings. It incarnated a "beautiful Ideal," to which she turned as a child seeks its mother for solace and reassurance. Like many immigrants, she was ill-prepared for America's stark contrasts of materialism and squalor, its great mansions and fetid tenements stacked with large families like cords of wood. Commercialism seemed to swarm not only in the marketplace but in every alley and thoroughfare, trampling everything in its path to success. New York was no different from the Manchester that Engels had studied or the St. Petersburg of palaces and dark workshops. The factories of Rochester, Goldman complained, were more airless and the supervisors more inhuman than in Russia; the distance between a manufacturer like Mr. Garson, whose desk sported a vase filled daily with fresh roses, and an impoverished employee like Emma was immense. The streets noisy with the shouts of peddlers and a babel of tongues stimulated and bewildered her, but this discovery that America was two countries disappointed her like unrequited—or half-requited—love. Her "beautiful Ideal" was now deformed, another casualty of capitalism.

The mass exodus of Russian Jews that followed a virulent outbreak of pogroms brought many who "transported from Russia the banner of idealism, scarred and bloodstained in the Russian revolutionary movement."[26] It was difficult for them to adjust to their new homeland, and they tended to look at American life, especially its flaws, through the distorting lens of their Russian experience. Because America was to them a "capitalistic prison," the struggles of the labor movement to organize unions, to raise wages, and to better working conditions were considered palliatives, as if instead of burning down the prison, labor leaders wanted to repaint it. Loose talk abounded that "there was no more freedom in America than in Russia."[27] In his autobiography, Abraham Cahan, the socialist journalist who moved in radical circles, explained the Russian emigré view this way:

> In Russia politics meant a challenge to tyranny; it meant students risking their lives for freedom; it meant martyrdom.
> But to the young American, politics was a game, a sport,

a means for making money directly or indirectly, a way of acquiring power and influence. So it is in republics or in monarchies with parliaments.[28]

Contact between these exiles and Americans of an idealistic and cultural bent was extremely limited; language was a barrier to communication. Common ground on which immigrant radicals and American social activists might meet for the mapping out of a social and economic program was blocked by mutual suspicion.

Emma Goldman, whose unformed political ideas were colored by the arrests, imprisonments, exile, and violence of czarist autocracy, arrived in America in 1886, her psychological bruises unhealed.[29] Her dilemma was this: Her romantic nature, acutely sensitive to injustice, and her pent-up fury ardently sought an outlet. Should she nurture the needy, thus accepting a slow and possibly "surface modification of the old society,"[30] or strike directly at the abusive system which protected the privileged few and made life hellish for the many? (*Living My Life* shows that even when she was sixty, this conflict was unresolved.) Along with other anarchists and some socialists, she rejected an evolutionary model of social change; American politics seemed superficial, and reform a patchwork of expedient solutions that left the power of business interests, abetted by the state, intact.

Goldman's disenchantment with America began, she claimed in her autobiography, as soon as she reached Castle Garden, where the rude handling of confused immigrants by surly, overworked officials persuaded her, in a rush of indignation, that American liberty was a fraud: She equated America with Russia as heartless despotisms. Psychologically adrift,[31] she consented—in a last gesture of docility to her family and to a life of dull respectability—to marry Jacob Kersner. The regimen of the sweatshop, in which she eked out a living, imperiled her health; she was trapped in the workers' daily plight. When her marriage failed (Kersner was an impotent and lethargic husband), she sought relief in radical meetings. Listening to Johanna Greie describe the arrest of the Haymarket anarchists and their trial for "judicial murder," as Greie put it, roused in Emma a tumult of emotions, though she understood as little about them as she did about anarchism itself. After the talk, Greie predicts to her that "you will make their cause your own." (9)

This talk did not precipitate Goldman's decisions to leave parochial Rochester and the family nest in order to test her wings; conversion experiences, we know, have a long gestation period. But
when she entered a sweltering New York City, carrying her sewing
machine with her (a palpable symbol of her ability to earn a subsistence wage and of her servitude to industrial masters), and with no
more prospects than Benjamin Franklin had on his arrival in Philadelphia, she felt as though she had broken out of a cramped cell.
She was immediately gripped by the intellectual passions, the unin-
hibited talk and debates, that marked the active circles of anarchists
and socialists on the Lower East Side, despite police surveillance: at
public meetings, at the *Freiheit's* offices, and until late in the night
at Sachs' Café and Justus Schwab's Tavern. Alexander Berkman was
her Virgil. In anarchism she found an inspired faith; in public speaking, a métier; in political Bohemia, an education and sexual freedom; in her friends, a temporary shelter.

The Haymarket bombings of May 4, 1886, at a mass meeting
protesting an attack on workers who were striking against the Mc-
Cormick Harvester Company and the subsequent hanging of the
"martyrs," sent a series of tremors through the radical community
in New York and elsewhere.[32] Certainly for Emma Goldman, Haymarket was a turning point. For one thing, it settled in her mind
any doubts that America tolerated dissent, and sent her into nearly
permanent opposition against most American institutions. Second,
it led her to endorse the legitimacy of political violence as a means
of overthrowing imperious authority. Again and again she returns
to a consideration of "The Psychology of Political Violence,"[33] as if
it were part of an inner dispute between love and power that she
could never mediate. She invokes Haymarket in *Living My Life* any-
time her faith in the sacrificial ideal wavers, as though that historical
tragedy were an icon she carried around in a portable reliquary from
refuge to battlefield.

Two historical events eight years apart absorb Emma Goldman's
memory in *Living My Life*, shedding light on American forms of
violence and Emma's complex reactions to them: Berkman's attempted assassination of Henry Clay Frick and Leon Czolgosz's assassination of President William McKinley. During the Homestead
Strike of 1893, Frick acted with haughty inflexibility, refusing to
negotiate and then calling in armed guards to break the strike (even

the conservative press chastised him for his blunderbuss tactics).[34] Indignant, Goldman and Berkman decided that the time was ripe for an *attentat,* a terrorist weapon practiced by one wing of the European anarchist movement.[35] "A blow aimed at Frick," she argued in her autobiography, "would re-echo in the poorest hovel, would call the attention of the whole world to the real cause behind the Homestead struggle. It would also strike terror in the enemy's ranks and make them realize that the proletariat of America had avengers." (87) The flaw in Goldman's reasoning, as she later admitted, came from the delusion that Berkman's planned assassination of Frick would incite "the dull, inert workers to overthrow capitalism's yoke." Part of this grandiose self-deception, shared by Berkman, can be blamed on their political naïveté: They confused American workers with their European, or Russian, peers. The very word "proletariat" showed the triumph of theory over reality, since American workers' class consciousness was funneled into practical advancements within the system and greater autonomy in the workplace, not into the overthrow of capitalism.[36] The consequences of the *attentat* were disastrous: The workers actually helped to pinion Berkman's arms; sympathy for the workers was transferred to the wounded Frick; the radical movement, given to factionalism at the best of times, was hopelessly splintered, thus destroying any chance for cooperation among radicals, liberals, and trade unionists. Worst of all, the workers were puzzled by Berkman's act, interpreting it as a personal grudge rather than a measured political blow aimed at the industrialists.[37]

In choosing what was best for the workers, Goldman and Berkman acted out of a tacit elitism, for unlike Mother Jones or Eugene Debs, they did not know much about the workers and their dreams. Only in prison, when he came closer to some of the loyalties and limitations of the "proletariat," and only after her devastation at Berkman's long incarceration in "the house of the living dead,"[38] her experiences as a midwife and nurse, and her contact with the prostitutes, shoplifters, drug addicts, and hard criminals in Blackwells Island prison, did Berkman and Goldman abandon their simplistic theories and assess the American working class more soberly.

But Goldman's impetuous nature, at least in the early years of her career, was not comfortable with the disinterested analysis of ideas and issues. The key word in her argument above is "avengers."

The legacy of her father's violence and of all the wanton cruelty she had seen was to legitimize retaliation in kind. That authority could be moved only by exceptional force was not an ideological conviction of hers so much as an emotional truth, as determined as her own genes. When Johann Most ridiculed the usefulness of Berkman's *attentat*, a position he adopted partly out of principle and partly out of sexual rivalry, Emma felt betrayed, and she horsewhipped Most in public. This violent reaction was not an isolated incident: She had earlier pummeled a woman in Rochester for saying that the Haymarket anarchists deserved to hang. In retrospect, Goldman fails to notice this pattern. Even after she concluded that *attentats* failed to correct the conditions that actuated the bomb thrower or political assassin, she still insisted that

> behind every political deed of that nature was an impressionable, highly sensitized personality and a gentle spirit. Such beings cannot go on living complacently in the sight of great human misery and wrong. Their reactions to the cruelty and injustice of the world must inevitably express themselves in some violent act, in supreme rending of their tortured soul. (190)

Some assassins—like Berkman and Angiolillo[39]—did act out of a noble motive, to avenge what they felt were profound injustices. But in the folds of Goldman's rationale lurks an unwitting glorification of violence as a heroic act welling up out of an exceptional soul. Idealists "must inevitably express themselves in some violent act, in some supreme rending of their tortured soul." Goldman's choice of words—"must," "inevitably," "supreme"—suggests that the champion of the downtrodden, driven by an internal moral fiat, is not a pathological criminal (as the popular view of the anarchist had it) but an instrument of justice who, in the extremity of his moral suffering, can see no alternative but to strike a blow at repressive authority. The anarchist disdained the law because it not only failed to protect the weak but cloaked the brutal deeds of self-serving government leaders in euphemism and made them respectable.

Goldman's position, however shaky in logic, was emotionally consistent. Leon Czolgosz's assassination of the President put it to an extreme test, for she was almost alone in defending not his act but his ostensible motive, in viewing him as a timid, "supersensitive" boy distressed by an intolerable evil system and forced to violate his nature by recourse to murder. "Unlike your idealless and brainless American brothers," she apostrophizes Czolgosz in "The Psychology of Political Violence," "your ideals soared above the belly and the bank account."[40] Though the government tried to implicate her in Czolgosz's act and held her incommunicado for weeks in a Chicago jail, the evidence exonerated her. But as with Berkman's *attentat,* she felt herself complicit in the deed, since Czolgosz had twice heard her lecture (slender grounds for a causal link). Of her physical and moral courage there can be no doubt. At no time in her career did she receive such a barrage of abusive, even hysterical criticism. Clearly her defense of Czolgosz touched a raw nerve in America's sense of itself. The consequences were, by her own admission, devastating. The radical community almost unanimously condemned the act, leaving her isolated (she deplored her comrades' "abject fear"), and Berkman from his cell praised her maternal offer to nurse McKinley and to aid "the poor boy, condemned and deserted by all," (322) but bluntly declared the assassination was futile, lacking the "background of social necessity." (323) She was once again shelterless—"no landlord willing to lodge me" (318)—and forced to assume an alias, Miss E. G. Smith, the most common and innocuous name she could invent.

Characteristically, Goldman's account of this prolonged and shattering "St. Bartholomew of the Anarchists"[41] in *Living My Life* is diffuse and unsatisfactory. Twenty-five years after the events, she still cannot allow that those who argued that her position was irresponsible might have had some truth on their side. They, too, shared her belief that "the degrading, soul-destroying economic struggle [could] furnish the spark that kindles the dynamic force in the overwrought, outraged souls of men like Czolgosz and Averbuch."[42] But they did not see any sign that Czolgosz had any political consciousness. Why, then, did she feel so guilty and identify so deeply with Czolgosz? "In the pathetic Leon Czolgosz," Alice Wexler writes, "Goldman seemed to see a terrifying image of her own deepest fears of rejection and abandonment, as well as—less consciously, perhaps—her own anger and violent fantasies."[43]

Emma so sympathized with the odd pariah that she visited his parents in Cleveland in 1902:

I had hunted up his parents, they were dark people, the father hardened by toil, the stepmother with a dull, vacant look. His own mother had died when he was a baby; at the age of six he had been forced into the street to shine shoes and sell papers; if he did not bring enough money home, he was punished and deprived of meals. His wretched childhood had made him timid and shy. At the age of twelve he began his factory life. He grew into a silent youth, absorbed in books and aloof. At home he was called "daft"; in the shop he was looked upon as queer and "stuck-up." The only one to be kind to him was his sister, a timid, hard-working drudge. When I saw her, she told me that she had been once to Buffalo to see Leon in jail, but he had asked her not to come again. "He knew I was poor," she said; "our family was pestered by the neighbors and father was fired from his job. So I didn't go again," she repeated, weeping. (354–5)

This is the portrait of a stunted lumpenproletariat life, bleak in its massive deprivations. Leon is not the streetwise Dickensian urchin or the spirited and spunky lad of American legend, who would climb to the top of the ladder; he is preternaturally shy and prematurely defeated. As Jane Addams notes frequently about immigrant families routinely pinched by poverty and visited by tragedy, they seldom came to the attention of settlement houses or parish relief organizations.[44] The Czolgoszes were an American commonplace. Yet Goldman insists that Czolgosz was not "ordinary," that the "poor creature" may have been one of "the sanest in a crazy world." (355) How should we explain her zeal in sticking to this idealized reading of Leon's character? This loveless family is not a replica of Goldman's, though hunger and neglect and punishment shadow the son, and a favorite sister furnishes a crust of solace. They are victims of a particularly listless sort, and Emma's sense of kinship with Leon, as if he were the hurt and misunderstood child she was, resembles, in its elevation of an inappropriate figure to sainthood, other infatuations in her life she cannot lay to rest.

IV

The way of even the most justifiable revolutions is pre-
pared by personal impulses disguised into creeds.
                    —JOSEPH CONRAD, The Secret Agent

GOLDMAN'S RELATIONSHIP with Alexander Berkman dominates
Living My Life.[45] Despite the gulfs between them, Berkman was her
most important friend and colleague, an apparition that paced the
battlements of her mind, a dialectical opponent of subtle skills, a
graph that plotted the wayward storms and steadfast allegiances of
her inner life and political commitments. Activists of any stripe do
not hatch from a public egg and then go pecking in the barnyard of
history. Trotsky's portraits of Stalin and Lenin in *My Life* are not
musical interludes while the actors withdraw behind the scenes to
confer or to change costume and policies.

From her first meeting with him, Goldman looked up to Berkman as the embodiment of austere revolutionary single-mindedness.
A hypersensitive, romantic young man with a trenchant intellect and
precocious poise, he seemed to her a gallant candidate for sainthood, who in the Middle Ages might have gone on the Children's
Crusade to the Holy Land; he was also a fanatic ideologue willing
to suppress everything—family obligations, sexual attachments,
friendship, aesthetic passions, even his own life—to the anarchist
cause;[46] and a worldly prig so intolerant of those who swerved an
inch from the revolutionary goal that he judged anybody who pursued beauty, love, art, and nature—expendable luxuries, he
claimed—as dangerously weak. "Ideologies," Erik Erikson notes in
Young Man Luther, "serve to channel youth's forceful earnestness
and sincere asceticism, as well as its search for excitement and its
eager indignation, toward the social frontier where the struggle between conservatism and radicalism is most alive. On that frontier,
fanatic ideologists do their busy work and psychopathic leaders their
dirty work; but there, also, true leaders create significant solidari-
ties."[47] This profile fits the extremely self-conscious Berkman.

In *Living My Life,* Goldman looks back on her younger self's
thrall to Berkman with a mixture of affection and edgy disapproval.
His power over her came from an unbending, effective will allied to
an acute analytical mind—he was abreast of advanced ideas in po-

litical philosophy that detonated in socialist and anarchist circles—
in control of his appetites. By tacit agreement, this avenging angel
and populist transplanted to the Lower East Side became her tutor,
though not her exclusive one, his classroom the city and the anarchist saloons and halls where he fired off volleys of opinions on
personalities from the anarchist orator Johann Most to Terence
Powderly, the labor leader. His creed was a demanding one for a
young woman just freed from an unhappy marriage and not versed
in revolutionary texts and history:

> He told me about the famous Russian revolutionary cate-
> chism that demanded of the true revolutionist that he give up
> home, parents, sweetheart, children, everything dear to one's
> being. He agreed with it absolutely and he was determined
> to allow nothing to stand in his way. "But I do love you," he
> repeated. His intensity, his uncompromising fervor, irritated
> and yet drew me like a magnet. Whatever longing I had ex-
> perienced when near Fedya was silent now. Sasha, my own
> wonderful, dedicated, obsessed Sasha, was calling. I felt en-
> tirely his. (46)

Despite Goldman's avowal of yielding herself to Berkman mind and
body, she in fact held back an essential part of herself from the
absolute renunciation his revolutionary ethic demanded. Though an
apt pupil, Goldman rebelled against his catechism because it reduced love to an afterthought—a condition against which she fought
all her life—and thwarted her romantic craving for release and
beauty in sensuality, flowers, and soft words.[48] Although Berkman,
like Johann Most, concealed beneath his hard demeanor a child's
need for affection, he treated play as a serious transgression against
the duties of redressing social wrongs or postponed it to an indefinite utopian future; and since Goldman remembered her own
"ghastly childhood" (59) as dominated by her father's harshness,
Sasha's dogmatism, like her father's, infringed on her liberty to act
according to her impulses, however contradictory:

> Yet I knew the personal would always play a dominant part
> in my life. I was not hewn of one piece, like Sasha or other
> heroic figures. I had long realized that I was woven of many

skeins conflicting in shade and texture. To the end of my days
I should be torn between the yearning for a personal life and
the need of giving all to my ideal. (152–53)

For Goldman, Sasha is a man of stature, a figure of marble, like the
statue of a general on horseback in a public park. He appears un-
divided, an impersonal force of nature, like rock "hewn of one
piece," a masculine participle that also suggests stubbornness and
lack of feeling, while Emma is "woven of many skeins," a participle
that implies a woman's greater subtlety, range, and fragility. Though
enamored of heroism, she cannot give up fantasies of love and fulfillment, so in this crucial period of her life, she refuses to make any
permanent attachments: She takes pleasure in Fedya's artistic sensibility, courtly and spendthrift (the antithesis of Berkman's), because
"He never expected me to live up to the Cause. I felt release with
him." (45) And she is flattered and enticed by Most's offer to groom
her for public speaking.

It is quite remarkable that in a period when women were trained
to serve, Goldman refused to accept the stereotyped role of the
household female whose main function was to oil the armor of the
Warriors for the Good and soothe their wounds when they returned
from the fray. (Radicals and anarchists were seldom more enlightened than their conservative breathren on this point.[49]) Yet Goldman never entirely resisted the seductive offer of a temporary
emotional shelter, though being taken care of was often contingent
on her obeying male prescriptions of acceptable and proper behavior. When a cousin of Sasha's rebukes her, saying "it did not be-
hoove an agitator to dance," especially with "reckless abandon," (56)
she reacts with asperity, as if rebutting Sasha:

> I was tired of having the Cause constantly thrown into my
> face. I did not believe that a Cause which stood for a beau-
> tiful ideal, for anarchism, for release and freedom from con-
> ventions and prejudice, should demand the denial of life and
> joy. I insisted that our Cause could not expect me to become
> a nun and that the movement should not be turned into a
> cloister. If it meant that, I did not want it. "I want freedom,
> the right to self-expression, everybody's right to beautiful,
> radiant things." Anarchism meant that to me, and I would

live it in spite of the whole world—prisons, persecutions, everything. Yes, even in spite of the condemnation of my own closest comrades I would live in my beautiful Ideal. (56)

There is a touching inexperience in Goldman's defiance, since she had not yet tasted the thrill of principled opposition or the bitter bread of prisons, persecutions, and condemnation. Three times the polysyllable "beautiful" tries to fend off the blunt capitalized monosyllable "Cause," like a velvet glove on a callused hand. But the exhilaration of this public pledge to the ideal collapses when Sasha accuses her of "narrow egotism": She "danced no more that evening." In this brief scene are braided the major themes of *Living My Life:* Goldman's gravitation to spectacular gestures; her romantic hopelessness; her oscillation, as she goes from rebellion to rebellion, between narcissism and altruism as a means of affirming her self. The very rhythm and periodicity of her sentences follow a habitual gyrating pattern from frenetic energy to exhaustion, from establishing connections with others to retreating into agonized isolation.

Such immediacy always marked Goldman's prose; she placed no literary distance between emotion and its expression. When Berkman was released from prison after a fourteen-year sentence, both he and Goldman wrote about their first meeting. Here is her version:

Tense I stood at the railroad station, leaning against a post. Carl and his friend were near, talking. Their voices sounded afar, their bodies were blurred and faint. Out of my depths suddenly rose the past. It was July 10, 1892, and I saw myself at the Baltimore and Ohio Station in New York, standing on the steps of a moving train, clinging to Sasha. The train began moving faster; I jumped off and ran after it with outstretched hands, crying frantically: "Sasha! Sasha!"

Someone was tugging at my sleeve, voices were calling: "Emma! Emma! The train is in. Quick—to the gate!" Carl and his girl ran ahead, and I too wanted to run, but my legs felt numb. I remained riveted to the ground, clutching at the post, my heart throbbing violently.

My friends returned, a stranger walking between them, with swaying step. "Here is Sasha!" Carl cried. That strange-looking man—was that Sasha, I wondered. His face deathly white, eyes covered with large, ungainly glasses; his hat too big for him, too deep over his head—he looked pathetic, forlorn. I felt his gaze upon me and saw his outstretched hand. I was seized by terror and pity, an irresistible desire upon me to strain him to my heart. I put the roses I had brought into his hand, threw my arms around him, and pressed my lips to his. Words of love and longing burned in my brain and remained unsaid. I clung to his arm as we walked in silence. (383–4)

It is psychologically convincing that anticipating and dreading their reunion, Goldman should dwell on the past, for when the law sentenced Berkman to a long prison term for his role in the attempted assassination of Frick, she felt intense guilt at having escaped his cruel fate. She always remembered the day of Berkman's departure for Homestead, as she did the anniversary of the Haymarket hangings, in a spirit of mourning and rededication to the cause. Being a more conventional autobiography than Berkman's, *Living My Life* is narrated entirely in the past tense, in which Goldman feels trapped. She wants to render the anguish and dislocation she felt (the repetition of Sasha's name blends into the urgent doubling of her own) and to track them to their lairs in the heart and brain, but because of her addiction to a hackneyed vocabulary—"my heart throbbing violently," "an irresistible desire . . . to strain him to my heart," "Words of love and longing burned in my brain"—the effect is of a maudlin pantomime in a popular Yiddish melodrama; she cannot transcend the stagy formulas of nineteenth-century naturalism.

Berkman's description, a measured and natural expression of his own more reserved personality, resembles the frames of a slow-motion silent movie:

With an effort I descend the platform, and sway from side to side, as I cross the station at Detroit. A man and a girl hasten toward me, and grasp me by the hand. I recognize Carl. The dear boy, he was a most faithful and cheering correspondent all these years since he left the penitentiary. But who is the girl with him, I wonder, when my gaze falls on a woman leaning against a pillar. She looks intently at me. The wave of her hair, the familiar eyes—why, it's the Girl! How little she has changed! I take a few steps forward, somewhat surprised that she did not rush up to me like the others. I feel pleased at her self-possession: the excited voices, the quick motions, disturb me. I walk slowly toward her, but she does not move. She seems rooted to the spot, her hand grasping the pillar, a look of awe and terror in her face. Suddenly she throws her arms around me. Her lips move, but no sound reaches my ear.

We walk in silence. The Girl presses a bouquet into my hand. My heart is full, but I cannot talk. I hold the flowers to my face, and mechanically bite the petals.[50]

Outside the gates of hell, Berkman wanders shaky and unnerved by normal voices (he had spent his last year in the workhouse, observing a kind of enforced silence), yet his prose is lucid and inward, with the strenuous simplicity of a stroke victim learning to speak again. By writing in the present tense, he achieves a painful immediacy, ensuring that events do not fade into the limbo of history. The short, mostly declarative sentences wrung from his consciousness are a means of controlling his emotions and are suited to the unhurried gait of his perceptions: He trusts himself to take in only small increments of detail and make sense of them. A small public space becomes a chasm across which Emma Goldman stands, immobile and silently terrified. The familiar is transmogrified into the poignant images of figures in a frieze: Goldman grasping the pillar for security, Berkman biting the petals of her welcoming bouquet like Chaplin's Little Tramp. Berkman's tense style does more than reenact the first tentative steps he takes toward rejoining the community he lost fourteen years before: It is a mirror of his chastened arrogance.[51] Prison taught Berkman empathy, and he is now the intellectual whose outlook is tempered by self-doubt. But his adjustment to change was problematic, as the prose tells us, and posed a continuing difficulty in the dynamics of their relationship. He resented Emma's becoming "a woman of the world," with a mind of her own.[52] By referring to her as the "girl," he unconsciously tries to render her harmless and subservient. Like the head of a monastic order rooting out slack observance, Berkman accused Goldman and her friends of false consciousness, as if Emma presided over an anarchist salon at 210 East 13th Street, where dilettantes promiscuously embraced the latest intellectual fashions, cut off from the Great Cause. Berkman temporarily flees the sophisticated woman in stifled rebellion.

V

EMMA GOLDMAN'S most effective work in America took place between 1905 and 1919, the year of her deportation for having protested against World War I conscription laws. She crisscrossed the country frequently as a sort of free-lance itinerant propagandist for unpopular or advanced ideas like birth control and progressive education, raising money for strikers, publishing *Mother Earth* (a much-loved child),[53] opposing Comstockery and assaults on free speech everywhere, defending homosexuals. "You can't squelch that kid," a newspaperman's tribute, fits the mature woman too. Although she preferred remaining unaffiliated to any group, she increasingly spoke to audiences of American-born liberals and socialists, thus modifying her opinion that American idealism was "mummified."[54] In *Living My Life,* Goldman complains about the drudgery of long train rides, the loneliness of nights in cramped hotel rooms, the hurried meals, the harassment and spying by officials, the endless speeches and planning, the worries about money. But her expenditure of sacrificial effort was adventuresome, proving that a woman's place was not in a doll's house but in public forums and at the bottom of mines, excoriating military buildups and battling vigilantes in San Diego.

After a tiring speaking tour, Goldman would gladly come home to her apartment, which doubled as the publishing office for *Mother Earth;* it was a hearth at which those who adhered to the arts and politics of revolt could warm themselves, swap information, plan strategy, or issue manifestos. But most important, it provided a sanctuary for Emma from the instability of her relationship with Ben Reitman. Indeed, all the anomalies of her love-hate affair with America, and all the contradictions of her character, were mirrored in her ten years with Reitman, a rocky journey from hell to paradise, with long stopovers in purgatory.

Ben was the grand passion of Emma Goldman's life. In photo-

graphs he looks like a cross between a "drummer," a dandified sales-
man, and the Whitman of the open-road period. Brash, boyish,
energetic, promiscuous, exceptionally filial toward his mother, he
had seen much of the world from the age of eleven as an apprentice
hobo, yet was unworldly. He might have been lifted from the pages
of Mark Twain: a Mississippi River gambler, a roustabout in a
circus, a stuntman, or a prospector at a Nevada silver mine. He was
in fact a doctor, a womanizer, a boon companion, an unthinking
liar, and the chum of Captain Schuettler—the policeman "who had
almost strangled Louis Lingg," one of the Haymarket anarchists,
and "who had threatened and bullied me in 1901." (421) These traits
were as removed from the severe intellectuality of Berkman and the
immigrant anarchists and socialists as St. Petersburg from Chicago.
"Ben had the American swagger, which he would display with particular gusto at our meetings and in the homes of comrades," (433)
Goldman remembers in *Living My Life*. Emma drank in the picturesque tales of his tramps across American and Europe as Desde-
mona had listened to Othello. His swashbuckling manner and dress
impressed her. Ben was an American type she had not often run
across. At their first meeting, he wore "a large black cowboy hat,
flowing silk tie," and carried a "huge cane. . . . His voice was deep,
soft, and ingratiating."

> My visitor was a tall man with a finely shaped head, covered
> with a mass of black curly hair, which evidently had not been
> washed for some time. His eyes were brown, large, and
> dreamy. His lips, disclosing beautiful teeth when he smiled,
> were full and passionate. He looked like a handsome brute.
> His hands, narrow and white, exerted a peculiar fascination.
> His finger-nails, like his hair, seemed to be on strike against
> soap and brush. I could not take my eyes off his hands. A
> strange charm seemed to emanate from them, caressing and
> stirring. (415–16)

This is a stock description of a Lothario from the lower depths, and
"like a schoolgirl in love for the first time" (her phrase), she succumbs against the judgment of her reason and becomes a "lovesick
fool," "blinded by passion." In *Living My Life,* Goldman struggles
valiantly again and again to extricate herself from an infatuation

that leaves her deadlocked; she repeatedly ponders their incompatibility of tastes and intellect, adds up his assets and debits in her emotional ledger: "He had profound sympathy for society's derelicts, he understood them, and he was their generous friend, but he had no real social consciousness or grasp of the great human struggle. Like many liberal Americans, he was a reformer of social evils, without any idea of the sources from which they spring." (432) This criticism was irrelevant; it was his eyes and hands that captivated her, not his mind. What Candace Falk calls "the artifacts of her weakness"[55]—an erotic dependency in whose toils Goldman is hopelessly caught and which makes her feel like a traitor to her principled advocacy of the free love of equals—is evident in Goldman's overheated style:

> That night at Yampolsky's I was caught in the torrent of an elemental passion I had never dreamed any man could rouse in me. I responded shamelessly to its primitive call, its naked beauty, its ecstatic joy. (420)

The threadbare euphemisms, the conventional Victorian decorum, of Goldman's sexual vocabulary—"torrent," "elemental," "shamelessly," "primitive," "naked," "ecstatic"—are demure compared to the steamy, explicit eroticism of her letters to Reitman, with their code words "treasure box," "mountains," and "Willie," and their greedy anticipation of sexual pleasure, which at moments shocked her.[56] She was one of the first women of her generation who asserted that women desire sexual gratification as much as men. In bed, her "inner barrier" (420) fell and she had no obligation to apologize for Ben.

But despite her initial hope that Ben would fulfill "my great hunger for someone who would love the woman in me and yet would also be able to share my work," (433) she was soon disillusioned. Although Ben did not regard women mainly as domestic creatures marked by biology to be mothers and by culture to cater to their men's needs—the showman and vagabond in Ben enjoyed Emma's notoriety too much—the main problem, as Goldman was forced to admit, was that he was an incorrigible philanderer.[57] When she slipped into erotic reveries, she thought she could change him, help him discipline his "childlike nature, unspoiled, untrained, and utterly lacking in artifice," (433) so unlike the sardonic, analytical temperament of Berkman.[58] In the light of day, reason argued cogently that Ben would always flee commitment. Goldman fumbled, in *Living My Life,* for a formula that would excuse Ben's lies and betrayals, but she could not "harmonize the conflicting elements that were warring in my soul." (441) As his "blue-eyed Mommy," she was called on to forgive his infidelities, which wounded her to the quick (against her own stated principles, she could not help being jealous), and to grant his piteous petitions to be restored to her favor.

An undeniable masochism in Goldman permitted this pattern to continue for ten years. A woman of extremes, she herself frequently attached the adjective "mad" to her desire for Ben. When passion overrules principle, it is common for a person to feel guilty and to seek punishment as an act of atonement. A dream Goldman retells shows this frustrating conflict and her effort to resolve it:

> I dreamed that Ben was bending over me, his face close to mine, his hands on my chest. Flames were shooting from his finger-tips and slowly enveloping my body. I made no attempt to escape him. I strained towards them, craving to be consumed by their fire. When I awoke, my heart kept whispering to my rebellious brain that a great passion often inspired high thoughts and fine deeds. Why should I not be able to inspire Ben, to carry him with me to the world of my social ideas? (422)

In the dream Goldman is incinerated by sexual passion. At first she is passive, and then, with an eager unconscious movement, she seeks to be absorbed by a force greater than herself (here it is fire associated with Ben; elsewhere, her ideal), but when she wakes up she does not feel whole. Needing to justify herself and Ben, and to fit passion into her ethical scheme, she subtly reverses herself. No longer does the "handsome brute" dominate her; she takes charge and becomes the active one. Her diction grows elevated: she will inspire Ben to noble goals ("high thoughts and fine deeds") and carry him with her as a few moments before she was carried to him. But the tentative interrogative sentence dilutes the force of her hopeful fantasy, the heart's argument not persuading the "rebellious brain" but trying to cajole it into consent. Addicted to change, she could not bring it about; she could only continue to divide the men in her life into the two parts of her self. The two worlds were, tragically, never integrated.[59]

The burden of this conflict, with its "daily denial of my pride" (527) and its occasional sensuous feast for a famished self, shadowed her work and dragged on for years. Searching for relief, Goldman's narrative keeps looking away from the intrusive Ben to the duties and dramas of her public career. She tries to restore balance to her autobiography as she does to her life, but perhaps because the habit of reflection is weak, she cannot; outsides and insides remain strangers to each other:

> Always on the side of the underdog, I resented my sex's plac-
> ing every evil at the door of the male. I pointed out that if he
> were really as great a sinner as he was being painted by the
> ladies, women shared the responsibility with him. The mother
> is the first influence in his life, the first to cultivate his conceit
> and self-importance. Sisters and wives follow in the mother's
> footsteps, not to mention mistresses, who complete the work
> begun by the mother. Woman is naturally perverse, I argued;
> from the very birth of her male child until he reaches a ripe
> age, the mother leaves nothing undone to keep him tied to
> her. Yet she hates to see him weak and she craves the manly
> man. She idolizes in him the very traits that help to enslave
> her—his strength, his egotism, and his exaggerated vanity.
> The inconsistencies of my sex keep the poor male dangling
> between the idol and the brute, the darling and the beast, the
> helpless child and the conqueror of worlds. It is really wom-
> an's inhumanity to man that makes him what he is. When
> she has learned to be as self-centered and determined as he,
> when she gains the courage to delve into life as he does and
> pay the price for it, she will achieve her liberation, and inci-
> dentally also help him become free. Whereupon my women
> hearers would rise up against me and cry: "You're a man's
> woman and not one of us." (556–7)

There is a half-truth in Goldman's analysis. In the early years of the twentieth century, after seventy years of feminist striving for equality, power still rested in the hands of men. Not surprisingly, Emma took men as her model. She gained her successes in fields previously considered male preserves; she practiced none of the wiles traditionally labeled womanly. Allowing Goldman's fondness for the provocative statement, it is still ironical that she should view men as the "underdog" and refuse to apply her analysis to herself. For Ben is the textbook example of the pampered male ruined by a doting mother, and Emma the mistress who half-consciously idolized the man who enslaved her. But why was Ben a "poor male"? Why were women responsible for his being a lady-killer, and not the man himself or his father? Were not men partially to blame for the paradox that Emma Goldman, who did have "the courage to delve into life" as men did and "pay the price for it," achieved only a partial liberation? Saying that "it is really woman's inhumanity to man that makes him what he is," she falls into the radical's intemperate error of attacking liberals as the enemy instead of those who really wield power. Goldman clearly relished her position as a dissenter from feminist tenets; by including their charge in her autobiography, she concedes that she was a "man's woman."

Most of her closest friends in and out of the movement were men. It is striking that in the wake of Reitman's reckless behavior, Goldman warded off despair without the sympathy of women friends. Her friendships with women in the movement, like Voltairine de Cleyre,[60] often began warmly, then cooled into a distant formality, and finally foundered, as if destroyed by an unconscious competition.[61] A woman who has not been mothered, or who has been badly mothered, may choose one of two reactions: be cold and seek out a succession of surrogate mothers, or become the mother of a movement and give others what she never got herself. Emma Goldman obviously chose the second alternative but with a bitter reservation, as the needling of feminists ("ladies") and the asperity of her attack on motherhood testify. Perhaps the subject recalled her mother's favoritism toward the sons in the Goldman family, or Ben's mother, who idolized her son and disliked Emma as a rival and temptress who embroiled Ben in anarchist dangers.

VI

The scrupulous and the just, the noble, humane, and devoted natures; the unselfish and intelligent may begin a movement—but it passes away from them. They are not the leaders of a revolution. They are its victims: the victims of disgust, of disenchantment—often of remorse. Hopes grotesquely betrayed, ideals caricatured—that is the definition of revolutionary success.

—JOSEPH CONRAD, Under Western Eyes

"THE LIFE of a revolutionary would be quite impossible without a certain amount of 'fatalism,' "[62] Leon Trotsky remarks in his autobiography, *My Life*. This political maxim is plausible only if, like Lenin and Trotsky, you claimed that "personal considerations" never played a part in your decisions and that your "steps [were] merging with those of history."[63] Such revolutionary leaders, serving not God or king or even the proletariat but History, and hardened "under the fire of danger," dismissed political morality as an anachronism like parliamentary deliberations. No absolute value could be allowed human personality. Although Trotsky uses the startling image of the masses as "infants clinging with their dry lips to the nipples of the revolution,"[64] implying that the dictators of the proletariat *were* Mother Russia, revolutionary doctrine excluded the appeal of the individual case. Angelica Balabanoff, for example, was rebuked for worrying about finding milk to feed nursing babies. The revolution, in Trotsky's words, was "breaking up the resistance of the old rocks with the help of steel and dynamite"; its true parturition was mechanical: "We were moving in jerks, as if that iron womb [a torpedo boat] were giving birth to shells in grinding pain."[65]

When Emma Goldman stepped on Russian soil early in 1920, after an absence of thirty years, she was elated by the workers' and peasants' welcome, that of a family clasping its long-lost child to its heart. She felt she had entered the pages of a Russian folk epic of vast suffering and heroic fortitude, and she begins her account of her two-year stay, which occupies two hundred pages of *Living My Life* (she does not pause even for conventional chapter breaks), with a romantic apostrophe:

Soviet Russia! Sacred ground! Magic people! You have come
to symbolize humanity's hope, you alone are destined to redeem mankind. I have come to serve you, beloved matushka.
Take me to your bosom, let me pour myself into you, mingle
my blood with yours, find my place in your heroic struggles,
and give to the uttermost to your needs! (726)

Goldman offers herself to Mother Russia in an ecstasy of self-
surrender, like a vestal virgin or a patriot. The maudlin language of
this public supplication is identical with her erotic effusions. Since
she had expressed misgivings in America about the Bolsheviks' direction of the 1917 revolution, one might expect her to preserve a
modicum of caution before embracing so extravagantly another glorious savior. Some compulsion drives her to repeat past mistakes,
to set herself up for a colossal defeat. By the fourth paragraph,
evidence of Russian duplicity troubles her, and soon the sacred
ground is stained with the blood of the anarchists, the magic fades,
and hope, "the Thing with feathers," as Emily Dickinson called it,
is plucked clean.

The Russian Revolution, the worst betrayal of Goldman's search
for a just society, tested her courage and political intelligence. For
when the magnitude of Lenin's policy to liquidate all real and imagined foes of the Soviet state dawned on her, she felt dazed and
"paralyzed" (a word she repeats with unconscious frequency). All
around her, violence was bureaucratized, party privilege entrenched, free speech ruthlessly disallowed (during these two years
Goldman was tongue-tied, and not because her Russian was faulty),
anarchists and supporters of the revolution imprisoned and shot.
The staccato bursts of the Cheka's rifles haunted her, as did the
official catchwords justifying the wholesale executions in the name
of "revolutionary necessity," a cynical phrase guaranteed to wound
an anarchist who had sacrificed much of her life to pursuing a visionary community based on voluntary association; the Soviets castigated all dissent to this policy as "bourgeois sentimentality." The
list of official rationales for the country's ills and the party's draconian methods of curing them was long and shuffled into different
combinations depending on which visiting dignitary or labor group
needed to be cosseted and enlisted: "The blockade, the intervention,
the counterrevolutionary plotters"; civil war, an exhausted army,

dilapidated railroads, shortages of food and medicine, inefficient factories; and later on, the limitations of the people themselves, jeered at by most commissars as boorish illiterates, superstitious barbarians. Goldman did not underestimate the adversity facing the young revolution, or the enormous task of bringing an economy largely feudal into the modern industrial age, but its coarse apologetics and slogans mocked her revolutionary ethics.[66]

Goldman had little of the fatalist in her nature. As a veteran of many propaganda campaigns, she could see when facts were twisted to fit the party line. Her will to believe that her beloved ideal was being fulfilled in Russia could not survive exposure to hundreds of despotic acts. (Goldman's intellectual honesty was unassailable.) When her anarchist comrades hooted at her for defending Zinoviev and Shatoff, her first guides, she had to scream to be heard, calling the accusers liars, but the chorus of clandestine voices rising in dirges from the overcrowded Soviet prisons soon forced her to acknowledge the truth of the "monster indictment":

> Nothing was of moment compared with the supreme need of giving one's all to safeguard the Revolution and its gains. The faith and fervour of our comrade swept me along to ecstatic heights. Yet I could not entirely free myself from the undercurrent of uneasiness one feels when left alone in the dark. Resolutely I strove to drive it back, moving like a sleepwalker through enchanted space. Sometimes I would stumble back to earth only half-aroused by a harsh voice or an ugly sight. (731)

Like a terrified child, Goldman tries to push back the spectral images rising from her unconscious, but fails. Sleepwalking is a symptom of nervous insecurity. "Enchanted space" turns into disenchanted time. Characteristically, Goldman seeks relief from her disappointments in the anodyne of work. All her proposals, however, from improving hospital care to organizing a network of cafeterias in Petrograd to alleviate mass hunger, were ignored or watered down, either by incompetence, by petty envy, or by bureaucratic dawdling. When she and Berkman were sent out to gather documents of the revolution for a projected archive, they performed their duties skillfully. But although Goldman valued the chance to serve, to travel and talk to peasants, party members, and fellow anarchists persecuted by the Soviet government, thus blocking out the din of propaganda and judging conditions for herself, she felt frustrated: She who had modeled herself on the great heroic Russian women of the past chafed at being reduced to a kind of powerless mother figure on the fringes of Russian society, cooking chicken soup for sick friends and sheltering fugitives and anarchists on the run.

"Like a rabbit in a trap," Goldman writes, "I dashed about in my cage, beating against the bars of these fearful contradictions. Blindly I reached out for someone to ward off the mortal blow." (738) She appealed for guidance to the mentors she most admired— Kropotkin, Balabanoff, and Gorky. But they could not help her. Kropotkin lived in isolation, a figurehead hypocritically venerated by the Soviet leaders, who manipulated his saintly reputation for their own ends. He despised and denounced the corruption of the revolution's noble goals, but he was too old and gentle to pose a threat to the government. Balabanoff, excluded from the inner circle of power and thus from policy-making, merely escorted visitors to model farms and receptions. And Gorky, whose "clarion voice had thundered against every wrong and . . . had castigated the crimes against childhood in words of fire," (738) now defended the Terror as unavoidably imposed on the Bolsheviks by external circum- stances. Goldman's response was curt: "But I had grown weary of the same rosary about the causes of Russia's ills." (752)

As a student of theater, Goldman knew that Lenin was the star of the revolutionary drama unfolding before her, so she jumped when she and Berkman were summoned to Lenin's office. It was as if the two Americans were auditioning for a place in the revolution- ary troupe. Here is her sketch:

His slanting eyes were fixed upon us with piercing penetra- tion. Their owner sat behind a huge desk, everything on it arranged with the strictest precision, the rest of the room giving the impression of the same exactitude. A board with numerous telephone switches and a map of the world covered the entire wall behind the man; glass cases filled with heavy tomes lined the sides. A large oblong table hung with red; twelve straight-backed chairs and several arm-chairs at the windows. Nothing else to relieve the orderly monotony, except the bit of flaming red. (764)

Lenin is disembodied and faceless, with only his eyes prominent, as in a surrealist portrait ("piercing penetration" is a typical Goldman redundancy). He is sterile and cold, like the room and its stiff furnishings, a sort of monumental cell for a Grand Inquisitor methodical and dangerous to cross. "Severe," "strictest," "orderly monotony"—these words conjure up a formidable concentration of will and "flint-like brain" that has banished compassion as an irrelevancy.[67] Even his laugh lacks humor, resembling the cackle of an animal about to swallow its prey: "Especially if he could put one at a disadvantage, the great Lenin would shake with laughter so as to compel one to laugh with him." (764)

Lenin keeps the pair on the defensive with a mixture of queries, flattery, and opinions, which never seem tinged with self-doubt. When Berkman asks him why anarchists who aided the revolution languish in Soviet jails, Lenin parries the question with dismissive bluster: " 'Anarchists?' Illich interrupted; 'nonsense! who told you such yarns, and how could you believe them? We do have bandits in prison, and Makhnovtsky, but no *ideiny*[68] anarchists.' " (765) Lenin's autocratic views fit his unyielding self-control like skin pulled tight over bone, and Goldman quotes some of his declamatory lines as illustrations: "Free speech is a bourgeois prejudice, a soothing plaster for social ills"; Russia "was igniting the world revolution, and here I was lamenting over a little blood-letting"; concern for persecuted anarchists is "bourgeois sentimentality," the cant phrase applied like rouge to conceal tyrannical acts.

Leaving Lenin's office as if by an invisible cue, Goldman muses over the interview with this godlike creature: "I was certain now that he knew everything that was going on in Russia. Nothing escaped his searching eye, nothing could take place without first having been weighed in his scale and approved by his authoritative seal. An indomitable will easily bending everyone to its own curve and just as easily breaking men if they failed to yield. Would he also bend and break us?" (767) The answer was no, because although one strand of Goldman's self subscribed to the creed "Who is not with me is against me,"[69] she could not submit to Lenin's demand for absolute obedience to his authority without extinguishing her identity. Lenin, Gorky had told her, "was the real parent of the October Revolution. It had been conceived by his genius, nurtured by his vision and faith, and brought to maturity by his far-sighted and patient care." (744) But for Goldman, the health of the "lusty child" was jeopardized by Lenin's systematic assault on all those who opposed him. Although he contained his violence behind an impassive facade, he ran over whatever got in his way. (Trotsky noted that "the words 'irreconcilable' and 'relentless' [were] among Lenin's favorites."[70]) For a short period Goldman might make excuses for abusive authority or pretend to herself that an appeal to conscience would effect a dramatic conversion. She does not equate Lenin with her father, but again and again in this section of *Living My Life* she returns to the revolution's decimation of its best and most precious children—the Kronstadt sailors, Fanya Baron, Nestor Makhno—whose deaths she mourns as though they were her own sons and daughters. The Soviet state was another coercive family in whose midst a child could not find safety.

To symbolize the betrayal of her ideals by the Soviet leaders, Goldman adopts imagery largely drawn from Christianity. Lenin, once the steely wizard with a "magic wand," is now "pope of the Kremlin," a false messiah; revolutionary Eden has become purgatory; the "luminous star" of high purpose has been first dimmed, then snuffed out, leaving the masses "nailed to the cross." Goldman's borrowing of images from a system she abhorred is not a conscious irony; it signifies a literary defect and perhaps an incomplete rebellion against the forces she sought to uproot from herself and from society. Nevertheless, it is emotionally logical: Revolution was Emma Goldman's religion. Her life was ruled by a faith in the ideal and in anarchism, a sect without a church, which exalted sacrifice and accepted persecution, jail, ostracism, and personal unhappiness as the martyr's lot for adhering to an unpopular idea. That communism with its hierarchical organization and calcified orthodoxies should remind her of the ecclesiastical authority of Catholicism should not surprise us; she was a connoisseur of intolerant institutions. Hers was the anarchists' dilemma whenever they joined a revolution—or made a pact with the Communists—be it in Russia or Spain, whose drive was to set up a highly centralized state: The anarchists would always be destroyed by men with a will to power, which the anarchists had renounced.[71] It was foolish to expect Lenin to behave ethically, to curb the revolution's excesses. As James Joll points out, "anarchists and communists are temperamentally far apart; all they have in common is their view of property and their rejection of private ownership."[72]

Goldman's disillusionment with the Russian Revolution altered her political beliefs. Watching Thermidor and the Reign of Terror close up, as Nemesis exterminated the innocent, taught her that desirable ends could never be reached by amoral means. Ideological pilgrims flocked to the "Socialist Lourdes" from America and Western Europe, to witness the miraculous cures of a society's crippling ailments. Old comrades in arms like Big Bill Haywood extolled the revolution, parroting the party line and glossing over atrocities; radicals snubbed or reviled Goldman for apostasy to the faith; even liberals like Lincoln Steffens twitted her (and Eugene Debs) for being squeamish, like genteel parlor insurrectionists, about "violence, bloodshed, tyranny." "As I told Emma Goldman once, to her indignation, she was a Methodist sent to a Presbyterian heaven, and naturally she thought it was hell."[73] For a time, Goldman and Berkman remonstrated and argued with such romantic enthusiasts, but they eventually gave up. "Caught in a trap," John Reed's dying words, summed up her verdict.

Emma Goldman's private life was not vexed in this period by romantic liaisons. She spent much of her time with Berkman, their friendship growing deeper as they became alienated from their former colleagues and sickened by all that they saw. Sasha represented "a safe anchor in the roaring sea of Russia." (781) As she concerned herself with the suffering and misery of men and women in the present, not in a utopian future, she rejected the radicals' contention that curtailing liberties and killing people were intermediate stages in the building of an uncoercive state. It is an irony Emma Goldman savors in *Living My Life* that her position moves her close not to Mother Russia but to her own mother, who, "always strong and self-assertive," "had, since Father's death, become a veritable *autocrat* [my italics]. No statesman excelled her in wit, shrewdness, and force of character," (696) Emma says with affectionate pride. After the loss of her husband, Taube Goldman flourished. She broke up an exploitive and highly profitable monopoly run by the undertakers of Rochester and built an orphanage. She takes her wayward daughter to her bosom and lectures her mildly. "I had once told her that my aim was to enable the workers to reap the fruit of their labours, and every child to enjoy our social wealth. A mischievous twinkle had come into her still sparkling eyes as she replied: 'Yes, my daughter, that is all very good for the future; but what is to become of our orphans now, and the old and the decrepit who are alone in the world? Tell me that.' And I had no answer to give." (696) Emma's silence is a confession of self-doubt (not a repudiation of anarchism). The pragmatist's loving lesson is telling because Taube does not disparage her daughter's ideals (and Emma reports it); she just urges a modification of them. In memory, Goldman cherishes this moment of quiet harmony, of identification with her mother. In Russia, however, depressed by the triumph of tyranny and facing possible arrest, she decides to leave. Like the Wandering Jew, like Trotsky eight years later, in 1929, Emma Goldman is deported, stateless and unsheltered, into the void.

VII

THE EPITAPH on Emma Goldman's gravestone in Waldheim Cemetery—she is buried near the Haymarket martyrs, whom she always beatified[74]—sums up with laconic force her lifelong brave resistance to passivity and determinism: "Liberty will not descend to a people. A people must raise themselves to liberty." She lent her prodigious energy to helping those unbefriended and lost souls who had no "social consciousness of themselves as victims of injustice and inequality," despite her frequent annoyance at "the unattackable stolidity"[75] of the masses. Most moving of all, she was a relentless enemy of the spirit of cruel domination. For rejecting all authority except her inner one, for being loyal to her ideals, for espousing unpopular causes, Goldman paid a high personal price: She became a symbol of the twentieth-century refugee, what I have called the "shelterless life," persecuted, imprisoned, "repudiated and shunned," (329) driven underground or into a crushing spiritual loneliness that felled her like a nervous seizure and temporarily stifled her voice. Invariably, she rallied and returned to battle her own demons and the world's injustices, crying out for change and liberty and yet not often able to obtain them for herself.

The raw vitality and sheer eventfulness of Goldman's life is impressive and well served by the thousand pages of *Living My Life:* She and Berkman built a bomb in a tenement and operated a candy store in Worcester, Massachusetts; she ran through dozens of occupations, from midwife, hairdresser, masseuse, and theatrical impresario to cook and mother hen; she waltzed, in a nun's habit, at a benefit ball for *Mother Earth;* she even once tried to impersonate a prostitute in order to raise money for Berkman's *attentat.* (The ruse was a fiasco.)

Like many of the Russian socialists and anarchists of her generation, she was stirred by Chernyshevsky's novel *What Is To Be Done?,* the narodnik bible, which preached service to the people and revolt against czarist oppression. Her taste in literature ran to the naturalist writers—Hauptmann, Gorky, Ibsen, Strindberg, Dreiser—and she lectured extensively on their works.[76] Indeed, it is possible to imagine Goldman as the literary heroine of a novel, a bohemian Joan of Arc. Yet the very qualities that made her such a notable force in revolutionary agitation and scandalized the bourgeoisie often weaken *Living My Life* as literature and wreck it as autobiography. To be a successful political activist, it is essential that one think in extremes, in black-and-white terms, rather than hesitate over fine points. The object of political activism is to invoke the grand sweep and treacherous tides of history and to carry the audience away in them. Rabble-rousers like Goldman needed, above all, a huge appetite for people and experience, a tolerance for defeat and the unhealable rift between private self and public actor. Self-knowledge in such figures might even be viewed as a liability, since people who understand themselves, or the impact of family patterns on their actions, are usually too well-adjusted to go running around the country, acting out their childhood abandonment by haranguing the ungrateful masses. Despite *Living My Life*'s verbose banalities and conventional rhythms, a passionate vision of justice based on love, rather than violence, somehow emerges.[77] But one ruefully agrees with Goldman's admission in the last sentence of the book that she had not found a form for her massive autobiographical narrative: "Would I had the gift to paint the life I had lived!" (993)[78]

6

"Principled Hedonism":
Gertrude Stein's
The Autobiography of Alice B. Toklas

*I*N HIS AUTOBIOGRAPHY, *Speak, Memory,* Vladimir Nabokov interpolates this remark: "I witness with pleasure the supreme achievement of memory, which is the masterly use it makes of innate harmonies when gathering to its fold the suspended and wandering tonalities of the past."[1] By the delicate maneuverings of his lexical net, Nabokov draws near to his prey—his experiences—and captures them, then carefully examines and reports their unique tracery and color in glamorous prose. Translating moods, rooms, people (peasants, tutors, government personages), family life, and schooling in prerevolutionary Russia, or even the simplest figure, a fat woman sitting in a chair, his is a luminous commemoration. Memory does not hound him, because he can summon fugitive moments from their diaspora in the unconscious; chords that have strayed return to their home key. With patrician assurance, Nabokov believes that he will find the "coincidence of pattern [that] is one of the wonders of nature."[2] So exquisite are the patternings of his "innate harmonies," so naturally does his style seem to grow out of an imperishable center, that the reader falls under a spell and marvels at the plenitude and imaginative accuracy, the elegant diagrams of his life.

Although *The Autobiography of Alice B. Toklas* conveys a similar air of vivacious confidence and settled character, Gertrude Stein mistrusted the "retrospective faculty."[3] The prospect of digging up her past rattled her. Like a No Trespassing sign hung on a tree, she warned that she would not tolerate revealing the private self she had so sedulously protected. Psychoanalytic method was the domain of her brother Leo, one of the twentieth century's most prodigious neurotics. As the exponent of a "continuous present" in narrative, on principled grounds she believed that rummaging in memory was a boring and futile exercise. In her writings, as in her driving, "she [went] forward admirably, she [did] not go backwards successfully."[4] (173) It is not that Stein was a hermetic person—the gay sociability of the autobiography is not feigned—but that throughout her life she puzzled over "the phenomenon of a multiple self. Sometimes identity seemed to her bewilderingly unstable, likely at any moment to fall to pieces. . . . She found it difficult and yet imperative to reconcile the sundered parts."[5]

If for years Stein fended off all requests that she write her autobiography by replying bluntly, "not possibly," nevertheless the autobiographical impulse showed up strongly in nearly all her work from *Q.E.D.* (1903) on. Her early interest in character and her naturalistic observations of lower-class life among the German immigrants and Negroes in Baltimore when she was a medical student at Johns Hopkins University led to the psychological portraiture of *Three Lives* (1905–6). While investigating the interior lives of three average victimized women and their domestic tribulations, Stein conveys some of her own agitated and suppressed erotic consciousness. Anna, Melanctha, and Lena live for long stretches in emotional deadlock, loyal, unformed, self-sacrificing, their own desires channeled into narrow duties or household drudgery. Each suffers her doom with a quiet dignity, worn down by her struggles with unconscious forces she cannot identify or overcome. Isolated and self-divided, conditioned to docility, these women dwindle to death. Melanctha in particular, who "had not found it easy with herself to

Gertrude Stein and Alice B. Toklas on a 1934 U.S. visit

make her wants and what she had, agree,"[6] wanders on the edge of sexual knowledge, but it constantly eludes her, and her yearning for safety and love collapses into confusion and mute distress.

The style of *Three Lives* is uneven. When it falters, Stein is self-consciously lyrical, given to awkward inversions of syntax and a factitious simplicity; when it succeeds, it tunnels slowly in hypnotic rhythms toward a character's center:

> Melanctha Herbert was always losing what she had in wanting all the things she saw. Melanctha was always being left when she was not leaving others.
>
> Melanctha Herbert always loved too hard and much too often. She was always full of mystery and subtle movements and denials and vague distrusts and complicated disillusions. Then Melanctha would be sudden and impulsive and un-bounded in some faith, and then she would suffer and be strong in her repression.
>
> Melanctha Herbert was always seeking rest and quiet, and always she could only find new ways to be in trouble.
>
> Melanctha wondered often how it was she did not kill herself when she was so blue. Often she thought this would be really the best way for her to do.[7]

The narrator has the droning authority of minimalist music. Stein keeps returning to the invocation of Melanctha's name, and the prose flows with a melodious vagueness. All of the substantives are abstract, and already grammatical particles, like the adverbs "always" and "then" and the conjunction "and," usurp space normally allotted to verbs and concrete words. We don't learn what the content of Melanctha's denials and disillusions is, yet a subtle movement from unfulfilled love to the verge of suicide takes place in four summary paragraphs. There is not a trace of raw experience, Stein's interest in types washing it out. Her impersonal style, which she never entirely relinquished, appears to work for short segments, but like driving an interstate highway, it induces tedium over long stretches.

In Stein's next experiment, the labyrinthine *The Making of Americans* (1902–11), the bulk of which she wrote at the beginning of her relationship with Alice Toklas, she tried to come to fictional terms with her past, her "family feeling," especially her anger at her father's irksome authoritarianism ("He had come to be a dead one"[8]). Outwardly an American *Forsyte Saga* tracing the history of the immigrant Hersland family, *The Making of Americans* is really an epic of language that substitutes humorless monumentality for Homeric pithiness. The book is an epistemological puzzle, a classifying system that reads much of the time like a logarithmic table. The earnest literalism and (to use Paul Rosenfeld's phrase) "rich sloth"[9] of her prose is eminently democratic in admitting all words or rather the same words on an equal basis, but in its pursuit of that phantom Universal Man, it confirms Tocqueville's judgment that for American writers, "An abstract word is like a box with a false bottom; you may put in it what ideas you please and take them out again unobserved."[10]

The Making of Americans is an example of the disembodiedness Gertrude Stein asserted was the primary trait of the American mind. She ruthlessly sacrifices individual being to the generic: the qualities and categories of fathers, wives, adversaries, the poor; dependent independents and independent dependents; women who resist reality and those who attack it. Religion, sex, work, character—all are huge forces flattened out into sentences that march across the page in ranks like Xerxes' army. "The marvelous meadows of her monotone,"[11] as John Malcolm Brinnin calls them, are imposing, and the sheer scale of the book—Stein quotes a Frenchman's count of 565,000 words—is a tribute to her ambition. For nine years she labored in this stylistic laboratory, experimenting, tinkering, discarding, accumulating words, shifting ideas. In her essay "The Gradual Making of *The Making of Americans,*" Stein offers a rationale for the form of her investigation:

> I then began again to think about the bottom nature in people, I began to get enormously interested in hearing how everybody said the same thing over and over again with infinite variations but over and over again until finally if you listened with great intensity you could hear it rise and fall and tell all that there was inside them, not so much by the actual words they said or the thoughts they had but the movement of their thoughts and words endlessly the same and endlessly different.[12]

Even if we grant Stein's premise that a "bottom nature" can be reached by a method that relies on sheer quantity and the tracking down and recording of "minutest variation," the aesthetic effect, despite Stein's faith that "Repeating is a wonderful thing,"[13] is cumbersome; it is precisely the "movement," the rhythm, of her sentences that is static.

> Every one is one inside them, every one reminds some one of some other one who is or was or will be living. Every one has it to say of each one he is like such a one I see it in him, every one has it to say of each one she is like some one else I can tell by remembering. So it goes on always in living, every one is always remembering some one who is resembling to the one at whom they are then looking. So they go on repeating, every one is themselves inside them and every one is resembling to others and that is always interesting. . . . [14]

Stein's fascination with types here becomes canonical law, but where types were tied to the unfolding of individual consciousness and specific characters in *Three Lives,* this link is severed in *The Making of Americans.* As Donald Sutherland notes, repetition is, for Stein, "the constantly new assertion and realization of the same simple thing, an existence with its typical qualities, not an event."[15] The formula is infinitely extensible—sentences and paragraphs go on and on—and annuls "reminiscent emotion." Whatever the reader's final judgment of *The Making of Americans* is, the book's additive and monolithically regular style is a heavy taxonomy.

"Sentences, not only words but sentences and always sentences have been Gertrude Stein's life long passion," (41) Alice Toklas remarks aptly in the *Autobiography.* Whether she worked in the grandiose style of *The Making of Americans* or the jaunty divertissements of such portraits as "A Valentine for Sherwood Anderson" (1922) and "An Elucidation" (1923), sentences were hewn out of the quarry of her mental processes and built into edifices of sound and meaning. Often, as in the repetitions of the Matisse portrait of 1909, she would explore one gamut of sound, one corner of her mind, diligently weaving her composition:

> There were very many wanting to be doing what he was doing that is to be one clearly expressing something. He was

certainly a great man, any one could be really certain of this thing, every one could be certain of this thing. There were very many who were wanting to be ones doing what he was doing that is to be ones clearly expressing something and then very many of them were not wanting to be being ones doing that thing, that is clearly expressing something, they wanted to be ones expressing something being struggling, something going to be some other thing, something being going to be something some one sometime would be carelessly expressing and that would be something that would be a thing then that would then be greatly expressing some other thing then that that, certainly very many were then not wanting to be doing what this one was doing clearly expressing something and some of them had been ones wanting to be ones clearly expressing something. . . .[16]

The subject of this verbal fugue is Matisse's reputation, which at first attracts followers wishing to emulate him, who subsequently abandon their discipleship. Like an oracle's priest, Stein sits unseen behind the dense thickets of sentences rendering her capsule judgment: Matisse is "certainly a great man," but a subtle flaw taints his art. The sumptuous elegance, the Fauvist color, the pictorial rhythm of Matisse's canvases are too smooth, too transparent; "clearly expressing something," in Stein's view, limits one aesthetically (it will be recalled that *La Femme au Chapeau* did not shock her, as Cézanne's and Picasso's nudes did). "Something being struggling," a feature missing from Matisse's work, is what made her and Picasso's genius so special. In *The Autobiography of Alice B. Toklas,* Stein furnishes a gloss of this opaque text:

> Matisse intimated that Gertrude Stein had lost interest in his work. She answered him, there is nothing within you that fights itself and hitherto you have had the instinct to produce antagonism in others which stimulated you to attack. But now they follow. (65)

In the absence of concrete words, almost puritanically excluded from the passage, revelation comes by way of abstract patterns, carefully calibrated tiny increments or subtractions—the word "really," for example—or the clangorous chimings of participles ("wanting," "doing," "expressing," "being"), adjectives, and adverbs ("very many," "then," "sometime"). A thematic motif, like a grammatical fragment, is introduced in the first sentence, slowly conjugated, minutely altered, until, like an inverted pyramid, it comes to a rest. Although the rhythmic accents fall ever so slightly on different words, and the passage rises to the key word "struggling," the eye and the mind rather than the ear are the parsing agents. In *The Autobiography of Alice B. Toklas,* such sentences are compared to "the symmetry of the musical fugue of Bach" in "exactitude, austerity, absence of variety in light and shade, by refusal of the subconscious." (50) This hyperbole is mostly harmless self-flattery. The inert momentum of Stein's syntax and her sparse vocabulary in no way share the contrapuntal expressivity and harmonic variety of Bach's fugues.

The relation of insides to outsides, the hinge of Stein's work, is also problematical. "She always was, she always is, tormented by the problem of the external and the internal," (119) Alice declares flatly in the *Autobiography.* Nowhere is this struggle so manifest as in *Two* (1910–12), and it affects Stein's style profoundly. In a kind of furtive self-excavation, Stein combs every inch of the reasons for her split with her brother Leo. In a photograph of 1904–5, Leo Stein looks like the shady villain of a wide-open Arizona town in a Western, but he exerted an incalculable influence on his sister as intellectual mentor and protector. Voluble, cantankerous, overbearing, brilliant, Leo led, as James Mellow notes, "a life of perennial self-analysis in the pursuit of self-esteem."[17] As Gertrude Stein became absorbed in her love with Alice, a more truly symbiotic relationship than had obtained with her brother, and in her writing, she and Leo drifted apart. The obsessional consciousness of *Two* explores these permutations of identity and difference. Both couples are unconventional pairs, first brother and sister and then two women. Living in the shadows of her brother's cultivated assurance, a kind of hectoring tutelage, as if he were conducting a seminar on aesthetics, Stein felt a shaky identity. When Leo overtly despised her writing, the two began dissolving into irreconcilable halves. The solitude of her single self entailed an extended crisis, from which she emerged by a plumbing of herself and a reassessment of Leo. By subtle, microscopic changes, she exorcises Leo's influence and becomes secure in her own authority: "She did not die. She said it was the time to grow. . . . She was not pretending."[18] Alice then replaces Leo as the second unit of the refurbished two.[19]

Like a nucleus dividing and subdividing, Stein's incantatory and exhaustive sentences seem to push out from inside and, taking on a demonically logical life, act out their impasse:

> Sound coming out of him is completely that thing is completely the sound coming out of him. Sound coming out of her is completely that thing, is completely the sound coming out of her.
>
> Sound coming out of him is something that coming very often is that thing is the sound coming out of him. Sound coming out of her and coming very often is that thing is the sound coming out of her.[20]

Sound is the measure of each one's voice in this nearly strophic agon, of Leo's obdurate refusal to hear her or acknowledge the artistic merit of her prose experiments, and of her steady loosening of dependency on his judgments. In contrast to Leo's insulting deafness is Alice's rapt attention to Gertrude, as the final paragraph of "Ada" (1909) makes clear in a rush of elation:

> . . . She was telling some one, who was loving every story that was charming. . . . Some one who was living was almost always listening. Some one who was loving was almost always listening. That one who was loving was almost always listening. That one who was loving was telling about being one then listening. That one being loving was then telling stories having a beginning and a middle and an ending. That one was then one always completely listening. . . .[21]

One holds no terror any longer. The word "completely" reappears, transfigured by the unifying power of love.

So severe are its repetitions and parallelisms that *Two* reads like grammar without a lexicon. Stein strips her language so that only the feeling of pure sound comes through; she refuses to let any adjectives or descriptive words cloud her meditation with associations. The He and She resemble numbers in a mathematical series. "Style," Donald Sutherland remarks, "is the whole behavior of the artist's mind conducting the composition, choosing, insisting, interrupting, reverting, and so on."[22] In the style of *Two,* one feels an intransigent self in absolute control, afraid of yielding control, moving in each sentence (and with astonishing stamina and concentration) like a binary star. One can scarcely penetrate the armor of Stein's meditation, but one hears in the prose an exalted voice floating above the walls of its cloistered mind.

When Gertrude and Alice were in Spain in 1912, Stein inaugurated a strenuous period of stylistic changes: "She says hitherto she had been interested only in the insides of people, their character and what went on inside them, it was during that summer that she felt a desire to express the rhythm of the visible world." (119) As *Tender Buttons* (1912) breaks out of its stylistic enclosures, the concrete world floods in with a dazzling copiousness. While her style still retains its mystifying features, a joyous sense of play is released, as if Stein was relieved to put away her classifying zeal. "A sentence is a subterfuge refuge refuse for an admirable record of their being . . . ,"[23] Stein said in a 1928 portrait of the painter Christian Bérard. This piquant triad—subterfuge, refuge, refuse—registers Stein's new stylistic timbres perfectly. A sentence is a construct that permits the writer to evade rules and to hide feelings in abstract spaces; it is a haven, a sacred space; and it is where the unrelated objects of our daily and domestic life ("tea rose," "snuff box," "horse," "butter," "willow," "telegram") find a valuable dumping place. Concrete objects, in the Bérard sketch, reduce the buzz of grammatical particles and record being with the charm of a friendly sphinx.

This stratagem, this sense of well-being and sexual satisfaction, permeates *Tender Buttons* too, as Stein revels in the sensuous qualities of diverse objects, food, and even rooms (interior space):

A BOX

Out of kindness comes redness and out of rudeness comes rapid same question, out of an eye comes research, out of selection comes painful cattle. So then the order is that a white way of being round is something suggesting a pin and is it disappointing, it is not, it is so rudimentary to be analysed and see a fine substance strangely, it is so earnest to have a green point not to red but to point again.[24]

A TABLE

A table means does it not my dear it means a whole steadiness. Is it likely that a change.

A table means more than a glass even a looking glass is tall. A table means necessary places and a revision a revision of a little thing it means it does mean that there has been a stand, a stand where it did shake.[25]

In these passages—grammatical arabesques, one might call them—randomness and order, change and steadiness, engage in a *pas de deux:* Questions trail off or are answered gnomically; analogies and definitions are proposed in a tone of casual gravity, then modified. Cause and effect seem to govern the statements, for as one opens these Chinese boxes, "Out of kindness comes redness and out of rudeness comes rapid same question, out of an eye comes research, out of selection comes painful cattle." One sound, "redness," suggests "rudeness," and, later, "rudimentary," as in a conjuring spell. An arch and indulgent teacher, Stein instructs her pupil in the art of seeing ordinary objects "strangely," coaxing reasonable meaning out of quiddities ("A table means does it not my dear it means a whole steadiness"). Juxtaposition presides over this pleasurable feast of words like an amiable host.

To break down the dominance of stale convention—"What is the custom, the custom is in the centre"[26]—the eye and the mind must travel along peripheral routes; any point on the circumference is a temporary shelter for the self. Suddenness and change, which Stein disliked in her life, are here in charge. Thus, in rendering the familiar objects of daily life—food (so important in the Stein-Toklas household and to the artists of her sodality), clothes, furniture, bodies—Stein composes poems savored for their hazardous improvisations with tautology, circularity, dotty verbal gestures, caprices:[27]

A PETTICOAT

A light white, a disgrace, an ink spot, a rosy charm.

A WAIST

A star glide, a single frantic sullenness, a single financial grass greediness.[28]

APPLE

Apple plum, carpet steak, seed clam, colored wine, calm seen, cold cream, best shake, potato, potato and no no gold work with pet, a green seen is called bake and change sweet is bready, a little piece a little piece please.

A little piece please. Cane again to the presupposed and ready eucalyptus tree, count out sherry and ripe plates and little corners of a kind of ham. This is use.[29]

The surface of these sentences is beguiling, a Galérie Lafayette of prismatic items. The poems are unexpectedly social, with exchanges of endearments, bits of conversation, directions for preparing for a party, polite requests. The wordplay bordering on nonsense, the alliterations ("grass greediness"), reversals of words ("seed clam," "calm seen" [calm scene], and internal rhymes ("light white"), are the province of the child's counting games and riddles, of the genius and the schizophrenic. In Gertrude Stein's linguistic kitchen, the chef whips up recipes from whatever ingredients are at hand; precise measurements are omitted and creative accidents—successes and failures—occur. The product itself is an exotic relish, a special taste perhaps, but stylistically, "This is use." As Stein herself explained her method, "A sentence of a vagueness that is violence is authority and a mission and stumbling and also certainly also a prison."[30] Codes and disguises are needed on missions, and the missionary's new tidings often elicit ridicule or quick dismissal. She confesses disarmingly that her sentences do violence to conventional demands for order, that she stumbles on the road, that her manipulation of words is a prison, but the style of *Tender Buttons* is not a cramped cell. The irony is that only a small congregation of true believers has ever been willing to heed her gospel.

The style of *The Autobiography of Alice B. Toklas* is often taken to be a relaxed tangent from Stein's more exigent work. But its low-keyed, inflected plain idiom is as much the product of the aesthetic concentration with which Stein pursued her radical theories about language as are the portraits and *Tender Buttons*. Though the *Autobiography* necessarily makes concessions to popular taste by emphasizing the anecdotal, the amiable fluency of her style, its discursive informality, is well suited, as was Benjamin Franklin's, to show off her eminence and her adventures as the pioneer of that rare thing: a successful revolution.

Before the curtain rises in *The Autobiography of Alice B. Toklas* on Alice's arrival in Paris, the bars of the skittishly charming overture invite the reader settling into his seat to sample and enjoy the insouciance of Stein's style. Here are the first three paragraphs:

> I was born in San Francisco, California. I have in consequence always preferred living in a temperate climate but it is difficult, on the continent of Europe or even in America, to find a temperate climate and live in it. My mother's father was a pioneer, he came to California in '49, he married my grandmother who was very fond of music. She was a pupil of Clara Schumann's father. My mother was a quiet charming woman named Emilie.
>
> My father came of polish patriotic stock. His grand-uncle raised a regiment for Napoleon and was its colonel. His father left his mother just after their marriage, to fight at the barricades in Paris, but his wife having cut off his supplies, he soon returned and led the life of a conservative well to do land owner.
>
> I myself have had no liking for violence and have always enjoyed the pleasures of needlework and gardening. I am fond of paintings, furniture, tapestry, houses and flowers and even vegetable and fruit-trees. I like a view but I like to sit with my back turned to it. (1–2)

The playful choreography of these sentences is deliberately simple: Except for Alice, only minor actors, like a straggly corps de ballet, enter, execute a few steps, and exit. The texture is spit-and-polish clean, Stein favoring declarative and compound sentences as the vehicles of personal preferences and quirky opinions; basic facts of birth and ancestry are disposed of with an offhand humor. Alice's mother, Emilie, is whisked on and off stage so fast that all we catch is her first name (incorrectly given). Alice's grandmother, at least, has an artistic link to Clara Schumann's father: Even in the frenzy of the gold rush, panning for the nuggets of art is what matters most. This family history, abridged as it is, suggests a mingling of pioneer spirit with bourgeois habit, the fortuitous confluence of California and Paris, the type and powerful name (Napoleon). Heredity, the past, is a genial oddity.

At the outset, the narrator establishes her credentials as a temperate if eccentric voice, ticking off an amateur's long list of hobbies, none of which she seems passionate about. Into this genteel routine, Alice confides, "no unconquerable sadness" and no ardor intrude ("pleasant" is the bland adjective she uses); her intellectual adventures are quiet and timid (writing a letter to Henry James to suggest he turn *The Awkward Age* into a play). But, the reader wonders, what sort of woman likes a view but then sits with her back to it? Is Alice waiting for fate to tap her on her shoulder and bring about "complete change"? It comes, as always, unforeseen, like the San Francisco earthquake and fire:

> I was at this time living with my father and brother. My father was a quiet man who took things quietly, although he felt them deeply. The first terrible morning of the San Francisco fire, I woke him and told him the city has been rocked by an earthquake and is now on fire. That will give us a black eye in the East, he replied, turning and going to sleep again. I remember that once when my brother and a comrade had gone horse-back riding, one of the horses returned riderless to the hotel, the mother of the other boy began to make a terrible scene. Be calm madam, said my father, perhaps it is my son who has been killed. (4–5)

The laconic wit and equanimity with which Alice's father reacts to natural disaster foreshadows Alice's and Gertrude's reaction to the man-made artistic earthquake in Paris, which permanently changed the modern practice of art—and its perception. Deep feelings are controlled, distanced, veiled with irony.

In the Stein-Toklas ménage, style was the identifying sign of distinction. One of the pleasures of artifice, whether a hat that elicits whistles from a carpenter or a knotty prose that incites catcalls or applause, is that people notice and react to it. Stein's long residency in Paris put her in a milieu in which the art of living well was inseparable from the art of putting things together in unusual forms. The aesthetic was not an extraneous trait but as natural as the Cubists' incorporation of scraps of newspaper and other mundane objects into their paintings. Thus, in *The Autobiography of Alice B. Toklas,* Stein practices the serial portraiture at which she excelled, building Picasso's character out of countless small details, observations of his gestures, speech, contentious or rueful *bons mots:* "a good-looking bootblack" dressed in a *singe* or monkey suit, he grabs a piece of bread from Gertrude's hand, pouts, dances, reads the Katzenjammer Kids comic strips with the same avidity with which he looks at Mathew Brady Civil War photographs or Francis Rose's paintings, moves around with an entourage like a bullfighter with his squadron or "Napoleon followed by his four enormous grenadiers." We hear his "high, whinnying spanish giggle" (141) and his frank responses to everything from callow American young men to skyscrapers: "He had a characteristic reaction when he saw the first photograph of a skyscraper. Good God, he said, imagine the pangs of jealousy a lover would have while his beloved came up all those flights of stairs to his top story studio." (50)

Stein's sophisticated European sense of style and form went hand in hand with an American artlessness. The writing in *The Autobiography of Alice B. Toklas* has a suspicion of the polished and the framed, a distrust of literary niceties as fussy and antiquated. Narrative time often floats free, its momentum speeding up or slowing down or abruptly terminating when Stein's attention flags and the punch line has been delivered (hence the numerous short paragraphs):

> Mrs. Lathrop was waiting for one of the cars to take her to Montmartre. I immediately offered the service of our car and went out and told Gertrude Stein. She quoted Edwin Dodge to me. Once Mabel Dodge's little boy said he would like to fly from the terrace to the lower garden. Do said Mabel. It is easy, said Edwin Dodge, to be a spartan mother. (173)

Whether the narrative meanders with a purpose or destination—Picasso's ramshackle studio in Montmartre, say—or serendipitously, like Stein's walks around Paris with their distractions, detours, window shoppings, and social encounters—she talked to policemen and concierges and neighbors—there is no time for reflection or the complications of style. Stein handles transitions with a careless efficiency: "As I was saying"; "Speaking of Matisse"; "But I am once more running far ahead of those early Paris days"; "But before I tell this, I must tell that." The virtue of this untethered narrative is that we feel the random dailiness and immediacy of the author, a central consciousness engrossed with the retelling of an anecdote, then suddenly dismissing the moment as she would a guest overstaying his time at the atelier.

Stein's description of Leo's and her first visit to Vollard in 1904 in quest of Cézanne paintings, which opens Chapter 3, epitomizes Stein's narrative and stylistic habit:

> Vollard was a huge dark man who lisped a little. His shop was on the rue Laffitte not far from the boulevard. Further along this short street was Durand-Ruel and still further on almost at the church of the Martyrs was Sagot the ex-clown. Higher up on Montmartre on the rue Victor-Masse was Mademoiselle Weill who sold a mixture of pictures, books and bric-a-brac and in an entirely other part of Paris on the rue Faubourg-Saint-Honoré was the ex-café keeper and photographer Druet. Also on the rue Laffitte was the confectioner Fouquet where one could console oneself with delicious honey cakes and nut candies and once in a while instead of a picture buy oneself strawberry jam in a glass bowl. (29–30)

Vollard, as he heads the paragraph, heads this list of art dealers, whose shops, except for Druet's, are in an unfashionable quarter of Paris, and who seem almost to have stumbled into selling "pictures" after failing in other professions or just growing restless. Stein's precise street map does not explain that behind the unprepossessing facades of these establishments, cluttered and plebeian in the mélange of objects to sell, stand the dealers of unofficial art. These are the only places where struggling artists—the Impressionists for Durand-Ruel, Whistler for Druet, Cézanne for Vollard, Picasso for Sagot and Weill—could find champions for whom art had nothing to do with commerce or respectability. Typically, Stein sketches in two of Vollard's physical features, then drops the portrait. Fouquet the confectioner is allotted the most space, food being a sensuous treat that nearly always accompanies talk and the celebration of art in the *Autobiography*. The style is as simple as the glass bowl, commonplace and folksy without trying to be ingratiating. Stein makes no effort to vary word order or to substitute pungent verbs for the utilitarian "was." Hers is the language of the newspaper.

The next paragraph focuses on Vollard in his shop as the two questers cross the threshold:

> The first visit to Vollard has left an indelible impression on Gertrude Stein. It was an incredible place. It did not look like a picture gallery. Inside there were a couple of canvases turned to the wall, on one corner was a small pile of big and little canvases thrown pell mell on top of one another, in the centre of the room stood a huge dark man glooming. This was Vollard cheerful. When he was really cheerless he put his huge frame against the glass door that led to the street, his arms above his hands on each upper corner of the portal and gloomed darkly into the street. Nobody thought then of trying to come in. (30)

The shop is mildly disorienting because it does not resemble an art gallery. The paintings are not hung in gilt frames; in fact, the proprietor's attitude seems curiously negligent, as if he wished to discourage buyers and cared little for the treasures heaped in the dark cave. When Stein finally locates Vollard, he is a hulking dragon watching over his hoard, dangerous to approach. The image of Vollard spread-eagled against the doorframe and gazing into the street is memorable. The mystery of his eccentricity is respected and heightened by the repetition of key words—"huge," "dark," "gloom"—as was Stein's practice in more recondite work. What matters is to record the image accurately: The syntax falls approximately into a subject-verb-object pattern.

When the Steins ask to see the Cézannes, Vollard "looked less gloomy and became quite polite. As they found out afterwards Cézanne was the great romance of Vollard's life. The name Cézanne was to him a magic word." (30) Art is romance, adventure, magic, not a branch of merchandising. Before proceeding further, as we expect, Stein backtracks and explains that it was Pissarro who had discovered Cézanne and tipped off others (in an aside, we learn that Cézanne was "living gloomy and embittered at Aix-en-Provence," the word "gloomy" making him kin to Vollard).

The fourth paragraph interrupts the narrative flow even more deliberately, jumping into the future, when Stein's poem "Vollard and Cézanne" and a review of Vollard's book on Cézanne were both printed by Henry McBride in the New York *Sun*. Vollard "was deeply moved and unspeakably content." Stein treats her generosity matter-of-factly and then returns to that first incredible visit:

> They told Monsieur Vollard they wanted to see some Cézanne landscapes, they had been sent to him by Mr. Loeser of Florence. Oh yes, said Vollard looking cheerful and he began moving about the room finally he disappeared behind a partition in the back and was heard heavily mounting the steps. After a quite long wait, he came down again and had in his hand a tiny picture of an apple with most of the canvas unpainted. They all looked at this thoroughly, then they said, yes but you see what we wanted to see was a landscape. Ah yes, sighed Vollard and he looked even more cheerful, after a moment he again disappeared and this time came back with a painting of a back, it was a beautiful painting there is no doubt about that but the brother and sister were not yet up to a full appreciation of Cézanne nudes and so they returned to the attack. They wanted to see a landscape. This time after even a longer wait he came back with a very large canvas and a very little fragment of a landscape painted on it. Yes that was it, they said, a landscape but what they wanted was a smaller canvas but one all covered. They said, they thought they would like to see one like that. By this time the early winter evening of Paris was closing in and just at that moment a very aged charwoman came down the same back stairs, mumbled, bon soir monsieur et madame, and quietly went out of the door, after a moment another old charwoman came down the same stairs, murmured, bon soir messieurs et mesdames and went quietly out of the door. Gertrude Stein began to laugh and said to her brother, it is all nonsense, there is no Cézanne. Vollard goes upstairs and tells

these old women what to paint and he does not understand us and they do not understand him and they paint something and he brings it down and it is a Cézanne. They both began to laugh uncontrollably. Then they recovered and once more explained about the landscape. They said what they wanted was one of those marvellously sunny Aix landscapes of which Loeser had several examples. Once more Vollard went off and this time he came back with a wonderful small green landscape. It was lovely, it covered all the canvas, it did not cost much and they bought it. Later on Vollard explained to every one that he had been visited by two crazy Americans and they laughed and he had been much annoyed but gradually he found out that when they laughed most they usually bought something so of course he waited for them to laugh. (30–32)

This long comic episode shows off Stein's style at its best: the conversational ease, the timing of a raconteur, the cautious relish with which both parties play their moves in a game without rules, the unhurried politeness of Vollard's whimsical behavior, as though he was testing these new customers, and the Steins' tenacity in waiting for him to bring what they want. The back-and-forth builds until the charwomen wander onstage and the mood becomes farcical, the pitch raised a few degrees higher, as if Leo and Gertrude and Vollard were acting out a charade and Cézanne was a hoax. The uncontrollable laughter breaks the tension, and when Vollard brings "a wonderful small green landscape," the purchase is quickly made. Since this is not a financial transaction and a painter's talent can't be calculated by price, only in a passing phrase does Stein say "it did not cost much." For the sake of symmetry, Vollard's version of this rich ceremony resolves the drama of cultural misunderstanding: The Steins' laughter was the signal that they were ready to buy.

The language of this passage contains not a single unusual word (it comes close to being reportage), yet its unvarnished neatness and carpentry proclaim it an example of New World design. Stein's fondness for the grammatical series permits a rapid covering of ground; the conjunction "and" bolts the sentences together; the wealth of detail is gossipy or informational, like silhouettes on a screen. The reader has a sense of being in the scene, hearing what

Stein heard, seeing what she saw, but not often feeling what she felt.

The stripped, neutral style Stein chooses for most of the *Autobiography* loses its sparkle whenever the art of selection has been corrupted into lazy chitchat or snap judgments about people she approves of or detests:

> There was another german whom I must admit we both liked. This was much later, about nineteen twelve. He too was a dark tall german. He talked english, he was a friend of Marsden Hartley whom we liked very much, and we liked his german friend, I cannot say that we did not. (100)

This paragraph is like a blank image in a kaleidoscope, a court diarist's fatigued entry. The nondescript "dark tall german" turns out to be Rönnebeck, a sculptor who translated some of Stein's portraits into German and so helped to foster her "international reputation," but as he grows officious and loudly patriotic, the friendship sours. Only after two pages of stories does the reader understand that Stein is apologizing to herself and trying to be fair to Rönnebeck. But the paragraph nonetheless illustrates the dangers of empty repetition into which a descriptive style can fall. In like fashion, vaguely honorific terms, the middlebrow critic's sentimental appreciations, seep into the prose: "very absorbing," "very attractive and interesting," "very wonderful," "very splendid," and "very happy" are applied equally to Apollinaire and to an obscure pilgrim to the shrine at 27 rue de Fleurus. Although the visitors come voluntarily to gaze at the famous paintings and to pay homage, as at a papal audience, the effect of this and other stories is of a search for those who might amuse the queen. When Stein deals in a sustained narrative with events like the legendary banquet for the Douanier Rousseau, her style gleams and frolics, sings and solemnly declaims, a kind of "materialism of action." As in the first Cézanne painting the Steins bought, every inch of the canvas is covered with vivid detail. "The world is a theatre to you," Matisse said to Gertrude Stein, and he was right—her stage bustles with activity, queer props, moments of pageantry, fantastic scenery, parlor humor, her breezy language whirling reality purposefully around. But when, as in the passage quoted above, her subject is minor, her style succumbs to an impoverished preciosity, and gritting her teeth, she says after losing the way, "wrong or right, we are going on." (173) That style exhausts itself quickly, and the reader impatiently wishes to hitch a ride in a different autobiographical vehicle.

II

GERTRUDE STEIN'S literary methods, her "impulse toward an elemental abstraction," did not promise the flexible conceptual model every autobiographer consciously or unconsciously chooses. Composing an autobiography thus posed a fascinating literary problem to her. Straightforward narrative was bankrupt, a fossilized form. Confession was equally anathema. She solved this dilemma and stepped around all obstacles by a brilliant theatrical ruse: The setting down of the ordeals and beatitudes of creation would be assigned to the sorcerer's apprentice, Alice Toklas, her companion, lover, and acolyte. By transposing consciousnesses, Stein boldly allowed herself the latitude to present the drama of her transformation from daughter of a decent bourgeois family to Athena setting to right the foolish judgments of Paris; to neutralize the threat of the past to her vulnerable identity; to avoid the directly revelatory, especially of her adolescence, "those bad years"; to remake (not compromise) her style by pretending it was Alice's,[31] and to settle in her own mind once and for all whether she was a success or a failure. Since Alice was Gertrude's confidante, her *ficelle,* she would possess the privileged facts of Stein's past, but remain limited in her knowledge and bound by an unspoken decorum to stay on the outside and regale her readers with what Gertrude said or did ("what happened" or "what was happening"). Affectionately twitting the tyro author, Stein proposes titles that remind one of those pulp books a devoted nanny or maid might publish about the famous actress or politician she served: My Life with the Great, Wives of Geniuses I Have Sat With, My Twenty-five Years With. These titles give a whiff of the inside dope, but Alice must still take her cues from Gertrude.

In the *Autobiography,* Stein impishly characterized Alice as lady-in-waiting to Queen Gertrude, sometime cook, loyal amanuensis who deciphered the illegible handwriting and typed and proofread the manuscripts, guardian of privacy, bouncer of bores, a minor artist in needlepoint, and an indispensable majordomo who constantly quoted the oracle: "Gertrude said." (Alice did not resent the way she was portrayed.) The cozy domesticity and teasing familiarity of their life together, as recounted in the *Autobiography,* is a tribute to Alice's importance as the provider of the emotional equilibrium that released Stein's creativity. Just as in dreams the figures who represent you embody aspects of the personality the waking self never fully acknowledges, so in *The Autobiography of Alice B. Toklas* Alice serves as a trusted surrogate for those reactions and feelings, tested over time, that had troubled Gertrude. There is little doubt that her long love for Alice, a close marriage, conferred a wholeness of identity on Gertrude. It had come to her at first as a gift exotic as Alice's gypsy looks and then gradually deepened into a dependable fulfillment, which steadied her even as her literary irregularity situated her in a frustrating limbo. Alice was a mirror in which Gertrude Stein could see her own image reflected as the known instead of as the psychic outsider. It is perhaps safe to speculate that Stein's new arrangements of sentences stemmed as much from her intimacy with Alice as from staring repeatedly at Cézanne's *Portrait of a Woman.*

Although it was easier to be a lesbian in Paris than in America, the *Autobiography* is silent about the sexual relationship between the two women, intentionally distorting it into a refined companionship. Why? In the joyous verbal disguises of "Susie Asado," "Lifting Belly," and *Tender Buttons,* among other works, Stein had celebrated her sexual contentment ("Toasted Susie is my ice cream"). Gossip and sexual freedom have always been staples of artistic bohemias, sexual liaisons shifting almost as often as artistic ones, and the *Autobiography* offers a panorama of infidelities, misalliances, marriages, casual affairs. Knowing that Picasso had a new mistress because he had painted "ma jolie" into a corner of a painting was prized as highly as knowing about the heated debates and rivalries ignited by a shocking new style like Fauvism: It confirmed one's status as an insider. Clairvoyant comments and quips were passed around like news of a sale or the discovery of African sculpture. The *Autobiography* is studded with them—for example, Max Jacob's witty remark about Alice Princet's marriage to a government bureaucrat after seven years of living together: "It is wonderful to

long for a woman for seven years and to possess her at last." (24)
The penumbra in which Stein encloses her lesbianism is in keeping
with the bourgeois reticence of her life; perhaps probing it would
have seemed a phallic intrusion on a shy self, the reopening of an
emotional wound that had pained her for so long. Stein's high spirits
in the *Autobiography,* like an elusive but powerful fragrance in the
air, is her form of expressing gratitude to Alice.

The *Autobiography of Alice B. Toklas* is a cagy performance.
With showmanship and verve, Gertrude Stein describes the making
of the artist. The result is part hagiography, part social and art
history: an insider's recital of the slow, agonizing birth of a new
creative idea and "a very dominating creative power" seen from the
outside. Written in a droll, plain style, as we have seen, the autobiography shows little of Stein's reflective mind but much of the
charm of the artistic life in Paris during "the heroic age of cubism"
and afterward. It is an adventure story of how, in Leo Stein's phrase,
"a Columbus setting sail for a world beyond the world"[32] came to
write the aesthetic laws by which it would be ruled. Her account,
like Columbus's voyage, follows two axioms: "If you begin one place
you always end at another,"[33] and "there is moving is in any and
any various direction."[34]

These makeshift steering devices did not disturb Gertrude Stein's
readers in 1933. *The Autobiography of Alice B. Toklas* was an immediate best-seller; even the conservative *Atlantic Monthly,* which
had repeatedly rejected her manuscripts, serialized the book. Alice,
"the bonne," had pulled off a gratifying coup. Everybody was reading Gertrude Stein. No more was she the literary Jove with an
intense private reputation and public celebrity as an eccentric,
the sport of newspaper wags. Like Picasso and Matisse, she was
certified—or certified herself—as a founding mother of Literary
Modernism.

It isn't hard to see why the book had such widespread acceptance. For if Alice Toklas talked with the wives of genius, she also
had time to eavesdrop on her friend's conversations and preserve the
witty pronouncements, peeves, maxims, and amusing tattle. It was
as if Friday were recounting below stairs Robinson Crusoe's adventures in survival as drawing room comedy. Readers might still be
mystified by Cubist paintings or Stein's most arcane works, but they
could thrill vicariously to the glimpses of bohemian life, the free

manners and frank sexuality, the grim, seedy poverty yet rough camaraderie of Montmartre, the intrigues and scandals.

With wry equability, Gertrude Stein took extreme pleasure in
being friend, sponsor, and arbiter of the arts in her informal salon
and "ministry of propaganda"[35] at 27 rue de Fleurus. The inexpert
public had finally, as it were, asked "this Mother Goose with a
mind"[36] (as F. W. Dupee had called her) to instruct them, as she
had her many literary godchildren, in all that she and her circle
valued—friendship, food, flowers, style, conversation. *Expliquez-
moi cela,* echoing Picasso.

The curiosity seekers and art lovers of all nationalities who
flocked to the Saturday evenings to look at the legendary paintings
often left more impressed by the stout California Jewess who sat as
a lounging goddess receiving homage or speaking in her "gay con-
tralto." She radiated the invincible authority of genius. "You felt
there," Lincoln Steffens noted, "her self-contentment and shared
composure. But best of all, the prophetess gave you glimpses of
what a Buddha can see by sitting still and quietly looking."[37]

A remarkable sameness runs through the tributes of friends and
guests. She was a sibyl, a Roman emperor, "a wise woman," or, as
Alice teased, "a Civil War general in retirement"—given her inertia,
Ulysses S. Grant. Americans in particular felt that she had what
other American geniuses often lacked, what she later confided, in
Paris France, was the secret of being civilized: "to possess yourself
as you are."[38] Being her own Boswell, Gertrude Stein could fill out
her portrait with Johnsonian abundance and sententiousness. The
timidity and fear that underlay the robust animation of her autobiographical persona could be kept out of sight, like the unpublished
manuscripts stored in her armoire.

Though one of the Thrones, Principalities, and Powers, Gertrude
Stein delighted in stressing her innate sense of equality. It was the
reason, she explained to her friend Mrs. Lathrop, that everybody
volunteered to repair her car when it broke down during the war.
She and Alice were California democrats. They had not succumbed
to the sour corruptions of the expatriate. No social privileges governed entrance to the Saturday evenings. All races, nationalities, and
classes mingled together; royalty came to the door with as much
trepidation as a Hungarian peasant. All stood on equal footing before the illustrious paintings. The password that visitors had to

whisper was only a game, a concession to the formulas of Parisian social life.

The history of the paintings told a different story, however, as did Gertrude Stein's quest for serious recognition. The world of art, from creators to hangers-on, functions by a network of discriminations, inferences, and superiorities: "There is the sensitiveness of the hysteric which has all the appearance of creation, but actual creation [by the saint] has an individual force which is an entirely different thing."(228) There is official art, with its slick academic imagination and flattery of the buyer, and there is unofficial art, which by breaking new ground rouses the public to aggressive contempt or indifference. The crowds at the Salon d'Automne were so incensed by Matisse's Fauve painting *La Femme au Chapeau* that "they tried to scratch off the paint." (By contrast, a five-year-old boy crowed, "Ooh, la, la, what a beautiful body of a woman"; connoisseurship in France is intuitive and begins at a tender age.) Picasso was fond of saying that the exceptional "ugly" pioneering canvas, which offends the public, paves the way for the prettifiers and vulgarizers like Delaunay (Stein's verdict too). Even the sophisticated Gertrude was confused and discomforted by her first encounters with Cézannes and Picassos. Art involves a necessary elitism. As Daniel-Henry Kahnweiler, the great art dealer, says, "The capacity to appreciate painting is not given to everyone."[39]

The passage from outlaw to *cher maître* is thus a precarious one. Without romanticizing poverty or neglect, Stein chronicles the suffering and hard work, the boisterous humor and intense competition, that marked the art world. Indeed, this consecration of art is the most moving feature of the autobiography. Financial security and reputation arrive and are greeted with equivocal satisfaction; after he left Montmartre for good, Picasso pined for his shabby studio in rue Ravignan, where Juan Gris, still unbought, lived in deplorable conditions. The story ends happily: Almost all the painters, Braque joked, could afford a cook who makes soufflés.

After the war, at Juan Gris's funeral, Gertrude Stein petulantly asks Braque, "Who are all these people?" He replies, "They are all the people you used to see at the vernissage of the independent and the autumn salon and you saw their faces twice a year, year after year, and that is the reason they are all so familiar."(20) They are not bumptious supernumeraries placed for a spot of color in the background or standing officiously in the middle distance while the star actors play the compelling roles. They are indispensable members of a hierarchy. To classify as Gertrude Stein might, there are the enthusiasts and propagandists for the new art, with their uncanny taste and keen eye, like Apollinaire, and the philistines who derided it; the go-betweens like H.-P. Roché, the author of *Jules et Jim,* who knew everybody in Paris and introduced the Steins to Picasso; the numerous satellites swinging in orbit around the powerful geniuses, tolerated for their usefulness and *rigolo* (Montmartre slang for "joking amusement"); the faithful disciples and changelings; the troubled believers, Mildred Aldrich, for example, who meekly asked if maybe all this avant-garde painting wasn't just *fumisterie* (a practical joke) but bowed to her friend's assurance it wasn't. And above all, there were the few art dealers—Vollard, Sagot, and Kahnweiler—for whom money or prestige was incidental to the joy of participating in a radical refashioning of art and consciousness. "The afternoons with the [Cubist] group coming in and out of his shop were for Kahnweiler really afternoons with Vasari." (108) So Kahnweiler nurtured Juan Gris through a period of struggle.

If *The Autobiography of Alice B. Toklas* is a genial firsthand report of the triumph of the twentieth-century revolution in painting, its verdict on Gertrude Stein's innovations is ambiguous. For despite depicting herself as the "onlie begetter" of modern literature ("I am the only one"), barely acknowledging any peer or forerunner, except, grudgingly, Henry James, Gertrude Stein had to endure the humiliating fact that though she insisted that her writing was "clear and natural," she had become, perversely, the favorite of a cult, "the few who understand." The public at large and even other writers found her writing private and impenetrable, and she was a stylistic expatriate. To her credit, although hungering for a taste of *la gloire* as deeply as one of Shakespeare's kings, she refused to compromise her artistic goals for the desired popularity.

Her defiant response "I write for myself and strangers" was a show of courage, for the strangers' jocular mocking of her work got under her skin as her verbal play got under theirs. Being underapplauded provokes the nasty gibes and unpleasant self-promotion that mar the autobiography: She sanctions Picasso's haughty dismissal of Braque and Joyce as "the incomprehensibles whom anybody can understand." (212) And, surely, Ezra Pound was expelled from her house not because in falling out of a chair he violated decorum—Stein was as nonchalant about such things as she was about the breakage of *objets d'art*—but because as a village explainer he was a competing cultural doyen . . . and widely published. Her brother Leo, nettled by her fame, lambasted her "massive self-admiration" and "stupid brag."[40] His envy forces him to miss her pathetic defensiveness. How grateful she is for any words of praise! How starved for recognition, so that she takes such touching pleasure in walking all over Paris to look at her book displayed in shop windows! Her ire was correctly directed not against the public's whimsical neglect so much as against the unwillingness of any publisher to risk losing money during a period of educating and cultivating an audience to appreciate the importance of her art. Even John Lane, her cautious English publisher, who went through circuitous and comic hesitations before agreeing to print *Three Lives* in 1914, was no Kahnweiler. It was not until the twenties, when Hemingway, Ford Madox Ford, Robert McAlmon, and Elliot Paul, the editor of *transition,* came to Paris and championed her work, printing it in substantial formats, not in snippets, that she reached out to a somewhat larger readership. Ironically, the publication of *The Autobiography of Alice B. Toklas* brought her the long-desired vindication and quelled some of her worst torment.

III

GERTRUDE STEIN fled from "machine-making" America, like Henry James before her and many of the young sitting at her feet, because America feared the value of singularity, an accusation that Louis Sullivan and Frank Lloyd Wright also leveled against their country. Stein settled in Paris for simple reasons. Her brother Leo was already living there. It was a beautiful city which provided the artist with the bourgeois stability ("unchanging human nature," Stein called it) needed to pursue experimental work. A woman of "full habit" ("if you are way ahead with your head, you naturally are old-fashioned and regular in your daily life"[246]), she blossomed slowly but irreversibly, especially after the split with Leo and Alice's moving in. *Allez doucement* was her motto and her method. She possessed anything with dogged patience and usually after viewing it from a distance, as she came to purchase the summer house in Bilignin.

By coming to Paris, Gertrude Stein averted the catastrophe of Olive Chancellor, the tragic lesbian heroine of James's *The Bostonians*. Her moral idealism ran high and found its consummated form in her writing, her métier, which she liked to contrast with the pragmatic venality of a career. *The Autobiography of Alice B. Toklas* may plausibly be thought of as a Jamesian novel with a skimpy plot, for its theme, and the secret superiority it endorses, is the ability to see well.* When Alice arrives from San Francisco, she displays naive wonder at the raffish, complicated activities, the bitter factionalism, of the art world. She sees that at the *vernissages* men outnumber women three to one (the reverse held true in America). When she accidentally sits down in front of the painting that declares that Braque and Derain have gone over to the camp of Picasso (a momentous change), as an outsider she cannot interpret the signals flashing before her. Is Fernande Olivier, Picasso's mistress, wearing an earring? If so, they will be reconciling. Is she wearing a ring? If so, they are planning to separate. Alice can't answer either question, so Gertrude Stein good-humoredly needles her: "Well, notice." Like a mother superior, Stein leads Alice into the School of Perception and undertakes the eager neophyte's education. Alice does notice, and passing all the guild's perceptual tests, she becomes an adept, an insider. The charm in learning to notice is sensuous, festive, ritualistic. She now knows how to value a witty put-down or a compliment, to discriminate exactly the flaw in a painter's vision, to cook, knit, entertain the bores. Presumably, like Picasso, she could sense through three rooms that Stein has cut her hair short. In the kingdom of art, the eye is moral sovereign. Even Stein's style relies on sight: ". . . you see, I feel with my eyes and it does not make any difference to me what language I hear, I hear tones of voices and rhythms, but with my eyes I see sentences."(70)

Too many important things, however, are excluded when one feels with the eyes. Exasperated, the reader may feel trapped in a world of surfaces in which Stein fondles *her* little ways, *her* edicts and impressions and sentiments. The root of the problem is Ger-

*When the parade to celebrate the Allies' victory in World War I passed under the Arc de Triomphe, Stein complacently observes: "And we ourselves were admirably placed and we saw perfectly." (191)

trude Stein's unswerving commitment to the external. The defects of her vision are illustrated by her treatment of World War I as sensibility. One would scarcely know from her descriptions in *The Autobiography of Alice B. Toklas* that World War I was an enormous tragedy, wasting young life with appalling monotony. She screens out the horror. The trenches resemble a Cubist canvas, or are merely absorbing landscape, as strange as a new work of art. Seeing camouflaged artillery for the first time, Picasso, fascinated, exclaims, "We invented that." The battle of the Marne is viewed by Mildred Aldrich from her hilltop aerie, the proper aesthetic distance needed to follow the action, though in fairness the ivory tower has its uses: It rallies American support for the Allied war effort. Nellie Jacot hears of the impending battle by an annoying inconvenience—the taxis can't leave the city limits of Boulogne-sur-Seine. And Alfy Maurer knows something dire is afoot when he sees the nation's gold being trundled away for safekeeping. World War I comes close to being nothing more than an episode in counterfeit style, an international bloodletting less significant than the tremors that struck the world of art. The war disrupts the normal, to Stein's dismay, the barbarians' invasion of Paris bringing the golden age to a neat if ignominious end: "The old life is over."

Yet Gertrude Stein was not an egomaniac insensitive to the human misery and devastation that the "Great War" inflicted on Europe. Her desolation when Paris is threatened by the German armies is not due to selfish worries about the safety of the paintings or her manuscripts. Eventually she and Alice did relief work for the American Fund for French Wounded, and with democratic maternal solicitude adopted soldiers just as they had writers and painters in peacetime, and (like Walt Whitman) tenderly nursed the wounded. As always with Gertrude Stein, one must read between the lines to sense how unnerved she was by these irrational events. *The Autobiography of Alice B. Toklas* fails to mix the outside with the inside. Her psychological premises—she says with pride that she "never had subconscious reactions" (79)—inhibit any deep analysis of a disaster such as World War I. She vehemently expresses her loathing of the unconscious, of pathology; only the simple complications of the normal interest her, she avows. But if war is the ultimate pathology, her refusal to acknowledge abnormal emotion, that collective psychosis rising out of the subconscious, then her psychology, however consistent, is shallow, incomplete, and suspect. Carrying the nuances of the salon into the war is a feeble expedient. How vital is it to discern the different national color schemes in camouflage? The chapters on the war are as poignantly banal as "The Trail of the Lonesome Pine," the doughboys' favorite book and ditty.

IV

IF GERTRUDE STEIN was, as Virgil Thomson says, an essentially solitary and introspective woman,[41] there is little evidence of it in *The Autobiography of Alice B. Toklas.* Several pivotal episodes are either truncated or omitted altogether. The most obvious, Leo Stein's contribution to her artistic development, is spitefully razed from the record. Her crucial break with him, an event of decisive psychological repercussions, is allotted one curt paragraph in the autobiography, though as we have seen, it is explored with obliquity in *Two.* Stung by the book's popularity, Leo reacted with hauteur and sarcasm: The book "maintains very well the tone of sprightly gossip rising at times to a rather nice comedy level. But God what a liar she is."[42] Many years later, he warned against taking the book as an authoritative document. This was sound advice, not personal pique. Braque, Matisse, and Tristan Tzara angrily complained that Stein had mischievously or, they darkly hinted, maliciously distorted the historical truth, that she was a peripheral force in the Cubist movement, not the commanding figure she drew, but their disgruntled voices were drowned out in the chorus of praise that swelled everywhere. She could not miss the irony that for the first time in her career it was not the cognoscenti who were hailing her but *vox populi,* and it couldn't care less whether the comedy was fiction or truth.

The Autobiography of Alice B. Toklas is a romance, and as American writers from Hawthorne to James and Faulkner have argued, romance allows them to take imaginative liberties with events and forms. Autobiography is supple enough to accommodate protean structures, deliberate insincerities, inaccurate dates, multiple selves. It collapses from the willful denial of complexity. "Inside and outside and identity is a great bother,"[43] Stein grumbles in *Everybody's Autobiography.* (Anybody can write an autobiography, she adds. Alas, that is another superficial opinion.) By leaving out much of her past (and Alice's), Gertrude Stein sheared away causality, the form of her life and, therefore, of her book existing solely as externality, as a rarefied phenomenon. We are given the *femme decoratif* and *femme intrigante,* but only tantalizing clues to the inner woman, which the reader must construe as an astronomer might reconstruct the force and motion of a meteorite from a fragment come to rest in his backyard. After finishing *The Autobiography of Alice B. Toklas,* the reader is tempted to turn on her the clucking remark she loved to repeat about Hemingway: "If only she had told about the real Gertrude Stein, what a book that would be!"

Throughout *The Autobiography of Alice B. Toklas,* passion, pain, anxiety, separation are eclipsed by the journalistic transcribing of "what happened." But Gertrude Stein can't keep up the act. One notices the erosion of confidence, the cracks in the facade. After the war, she was "restless and disturbed," even quarreling with Picasso. The dynamic genius of the Cubists and the Fauvists dwindled into the more minor arts of Dadaism and Surrealism, which she surveyed with waning interest. Like an irritable shopper, she picks up and discards the new painters, but Tchelitchew and Bérard are not in Picasso's class; Cocteau, though clever and amusing, is no Apollinaire. The bloom is off. Despite all the glittering names (the majority writers), the last third of the book is diffuse, the cast of characters shuffling on and off the stage at the caprice of the director, who has become bored and fatigued by the impersonation. After a sojourn in the south of France, triumphs at Oxford and Cambridge, and more frequent publication, she resumes the prewar rhythm of normal living and recovers her poise. But by then the damage has been done.

The Autobiography of Alice B. Toklas is an anomaly in Gertrude Stein's vast literary output. Written in six weeks in 1932, it is obviously her most accessible work, a valentine to the artistic calling. She shares with us the excitement of a brilliant art movement at its apogee. The flow of anecdotes and aperçus, like a cruise of the archipelagoes of the surface with a delightful companion, is diverting: "Irene a very lovely woman who came from the mountains and wanted to be free"; (169) the "brutal thumbs" and "madonna face" (23) of Alice Princet; the "tall maids who were like annunciation angels"; (127) Manolo, Picasso's friend, who "was like a sweet crazy religiously uplifted spanish beggar." (97) *The Autobiography of Alice B. Toklas* is held together by the sheer galvanizing presence of Gertrude Stein, who steps forward in the last paragraph and admits authorship. "If you must do a thing do it graciously," (5) Miss Toklas's father had counseled her, a precept conformed to in the Stein-Toklas household and in the autobiography.

"Of course I rank Gertrude with Wittgenstein," Guy Davenport once wrote me, "—a genius working by compulsion and with atomic integrity. There was no trace of vulgarity in her, no posture, no dependence on a damned thing except her stubborn resolution to be free to be herself."[44] This tribute *The Autobiography of Alice B. Toklas* bears out. Genius also has its quirks: Stein liked improvising at the piano on the white keys alone—Virgil Thomson composed a piano sonata to satisfy that whim—because she thought the black keys were too harmonious and chords too emotional. This side of her character is also ably served by the *Autobiography*. It is the prerogative of genius to contradict its own theories, and Stein blithely ignored some of the directives she most doted on, not banishing "associational emotion" to some linguistic Siberia. "Our moods do not believe in each other,"[45] Emerson shrewdly noted in "Circles," a truth that bothers some autobiographers but not Stein. It is finally the authority of style, not self-revelation, that Stein endorses and fulfills in *The Autobiography of Alice B. Toklas*.

7

"You Can't Beat Innocence":
The Autobiography of
William Carlos Williams

*What asses we are to be crushed when we fail by mere lack
of mental agility! We fix ourselves in orders of being and think
that is the end of us. The wise French are more labile.*
— WILLIAM CARLOS WILLIAMS, Autobiography

I

THERE IS PROBABLY no American autobiography more skittish than William Carlos Williams's. The idea of composing an autobiography first occurred to him in 1934, though he immediately dismissed it.[1] In 1938, he returned to the idea with a more friendly attitude, but decided the project could not be hurried.[2] After meditating on the subject for several years, he jotted down some *Notes Toward an Autobiography* in 1947 and drafted a few early chapters, which were eventually published.[3] Several personal crises intervened before Williams could resume the book. For one thing, he had been felled by a heart attack, which threw him into a depression. Accustomed to a life of restless motion, he found being an invalid during his convalescence an ordeal; the senses had for so long been household gods at 9 Ridge Road, his home in Rutherford, New Jersey, that he could not resign himself to their breakdown. Besides that, after nearly forty-five years' labor as a general practitioner and pediatrician, he had been forced to curtail his medical activities drastically. And he had strong fears that he had bungled *Paterson,* the long poem in which he had invested so much imaginative energy.

To conquer despair and prove to himself that these blows had not impaired his mind, Williams undertook to follow memory as it beckoned him to descend, like Orpheus, into hell, without any guide accompanying him. The prizes he retrieved from the "fertile darkness" (to use Sherman Paul's phrase) were the *Autobiography* and two poems, "The Descent" and "The Desert Music." Memory's excursions through space and time, without fixed itinerary, opened for Williams "new places/inhabited by hordes/heretofore unrealized,/of new kinds" ("The Descent").[4] He had not lost his power to hear "the protecting music" and his "skill sometimes to record it" ("The Desert Music").[5] From late 1950 until early March 1951, when he suffered a cerebral stroke[6] which injured his speech and ability to write, Williams piled up an astonishing 1,200 pages of manuscript.[7]

It is thus not surprising that Williams confessed in *I Wanted to Write a Poem* (1959) that the *Autobiography* was written with "speed, inaccuracy, gusto." He then added: "I trusted to memory about too many things. I didn't make up any of it but I didn't edit—where in some cases I should have. There are some inaccuracies about dates, places. The book made a lot of people mad. But it was good therapy for me. It got me back to the typewriter in high spirits."[8] Williams's nonchalance about unedited errors is not unusual but part of the genre's pedigree. Inaccuracies are a hazard for any autobiographer—even Nabokov, the most fastidious of authors, could not escape them—because memory is unreliable. The lens of perception easily scratches. Moods and events blur, facts are forgotten, misremembered, distorted. Faced with these handicaps, the autobiographer substitutes surmises, daydreams, idealizations, enthusiasms, thematic designs. Through the potent magic of style, the solitary confinement of time and consciousness may be transcended, and autobiography becomes what Edwin Muir called a fable.

With due allowance for Williams's infirmities, haste, and pleasure in writing it, the *Autobiography* is still a baffling performance. It seems to proceed by fits and starts, as if Williams kept losing interest or the pathway as he recreated his past. The *Autobiography*

William Carlos Williams, 1956

lacks the rich nostalgia of Nabokov's *Speak, Memory* or the raging psychodrama of Dahlberg's *Because I Was Flesh*. Williams's narrative rambles along, stopping to admire the intense blue of monkshood here, the facade of Rheims Cathedral there, to retail a piece of gossip or a childhood escapade, or to insert excerpts from Charles Olson's essay on projective verse, a document he approved because it validated his own experiments with rescuing the poetic line from stodginess. Like young Bill in the swing, he rocks back and forth, back and forth, the captive of no single mood, indifferent to longueurs, appearing to admit all memories on equal footing and trusting to some invisible principle of coherence, or the reader's indulgence.

"It can't all be told" or "That's not it, either," Williams will say with a shrug of his shoulders and pass abruptly to a new, unrelated point. After a number of these snappish exclamations, the reader begins to suspect that Williams is engaged in subtle self-censorship. If his wife, Floss, was the rock on which he built his life, as he says, why is she assigned only a cameo role in the *Autobiography*? If his brother, Ed, was the model for all of Williams's friendships with men, why does he disappear from the book after sharing in a few family crises and boyish games, and after touring Rome with his brother as an architectural cicerone? Why are Williams's two sons scarcely mentioned? And why, at the place most autobiographers find abundant material to occupy their mature reflections—namely, their relations with mother and father—does Williams grow incommunicative? Pop and his mother, Elena, are nearly ciphers. "Pop was a good storyteller but too abstemious and modest a man for his own happiness,"[9] (281) Williams tosses out, and then lapses into a provoking silence. For someone who staked so much of his poetic career on "the open, free assertion,"[10] Williams suppressed a central part of himself, and in resisting the disclosure of the most basic influences on him, he ironically slipped into the piecemeal evasions he elsewhere warns against.

Anyone seeking answers to the above questions soon finds the *Autobiography* a map of tricky equivocations and culs-de-sac, as if put together by a whimsical or careless cartographer. Carelessness indeed was for Williams an attitude toward living that immunized him from lethal rigidities. One of Williams's aphorisms in *Kora in Hell* runs: "Carelessness of heart is a virtue akin to the small lights of the stars."[11] His exploratory books of the twenties—*Kora in Hell, Spring and All, The Great American Novel, A Novelette, The Descent of Winter*—purposely shed fixed forms, sometimes petulantly and sometimes with a surrealistic gaiety, with the goal of a cleansing anarchy that would liberate the senses. From *Kora in Hell* through *Paterson,* Williams attacked the arbitrary and false clarities of dialectical reasoning[12] because, he contended, they led to closed systems.

Williams's mistrust of pattern was lifelong and had both artistic and psychological roots. In an often-quoted letter to his friend John Riordan, in 1926, Williams explained:

> But my failure to work inside a pattern—a positive sin—is the cause of my virtues. I cannot work inside a pattern because I can't find a pattern that will have me. My whole effort . . . is to find a pattern, large enough, modern enough, flexible enough to include my desires. And if I could find it I'd wither and die.[13]

Because he conceived of pattern as a deadly poison starving his imagination of oxygen, Williams would avoid committing himself to one poetic or another, would take his chances with the play of process. By temperament he loved beginnings. As Mike Weaver notes, "Williams was strenuously opposed to completion, and to perfection as 'composition.' He was equally opposed to the incompletion of the broken object."[14]

Here was a dilemma to tax the most ingenious logician and poet, and Williams neatly solved it simply by accepting its insolubility and by blithely turning sin into virtue. The circular reasoning of Williams's letter to Riordan also contains a curious equation: The fulfillment of his desires will bring death. Yet in the book that is his masterpiece, *In the American Grain,* which was published a short time before he described his scruples about pattern to Riordan, Williams had devised a polyphonic structure capacious and capricious enough to include intimate portraiture, historical text and commentary, chronicle, harangue, dialogue, rhapsody, and social autopsy and to find words for his multiple desires. And he had not withered and died. It is possible that he regarded *In the American Grain* as a windfall, a lucky break not to be repeated, but surely the book's perfections as "composition" should have given him the confidence to judge himself and pattern more charitably. It is also possible to interpret Williams's letter as a kind of Whitmanesque brag: "I'm too large and multifaceted to be enclosed or contained by a pattern. My self is limitless. Definitions do not apply to me." This harmless egotism is the other side of Williams's gruff self-deprecation.

If aberrant forms fitted the topography of Williams's mind, in none of his books are they so manifest as in the *Autobiography*. Readers looking for a magisterial summing up of his careers as doctor and poet are invariably disappointed by the slapdash style of the book. It is as though, afraid of being nailed as an *homme serieux,* Williams decided to present himself as a man of normal sensuality with a proclivity for playful enthusiasms, peevish or racy opinions, and humorous anecdotes. The very look of the short paragraphs on the page testifies to a breathless running style (Williams's favorite sport as a boy was running, and he developed adolescent heart strain from overdoing it one day) that betokens a refusal and terror of being pinned down. "ONE PERCEPTION MUST IMMEDIATELY AND DIRECTLY LEAD TO A FURTHER PERCEPTION," (330) Edward Dahlberg's loud slogan quoted by Olson in his essay on projective verse, is embraced as a workable method for the *Autobiography*. Williams did believe that so long as he conveyed the tug and vibration of feelings, objects, ideas, as the boy holding the taut kite senses the energy passing through his hands, the form would take care of itself. The perfect pitch of his random perceptions would serve immediate experience better than the fraudulent tonality of polished sequence that he tended to associate with the English poets.[15] Thus Williams does not apologize when Part III of the *Autobiography* unexpectedly deserts chronology and returns once more to the poet's childhood in Rutherford, though transposed to a minor key and marked by a slightly slower tempo. Whether Williams grew aware that the skeletal structure of the book was defective, or he simply needed the stimulus of a new beginning, he fell back on an old bit of involuntary guile: He would charm and improvise his way out of an awkward spot by playing the role of innocent.

II

"Beati innocenti."

—WILLIAMS, *Autobiography*

"BUT INNOCENCE is hard to beat," Williams begins Chapter 15, which launches a series of droll anecdotes about his internships at French Hospital and Nursery and Child's Hospital. The young raw-boned recruit to medical ranks in 1908 is recalled as a homespun, unworldly, chaste fellow who didn't know what masturbation was, "hardly knew women and felt tender to them all." (81) Patient, wide-eyed—"I guess I looked easy and they all tried to break me down," (100) he says—he relishes his encounters, in the rough, notorious Hell's Kitchen neighborhood of New York, with "the dregs of the city, a fine crew," (94) never patronizing them; he catches glimpses of the secret underside of city life, a transvestite construction worker, for example, and is fascinated (a favorite Williams word); he delivers babies and witnesses patients dying. Resigning his head residency at Nursery and Child's Hospital rather than sign a report falsifying statistics and thereby condoning graft, Williams is amiably virtuous, and his innocence seems appropriate to a period of initiation and probation.

Williams's idealistic action is only the mildest of turning points. His innocence does not disappear. It is a favorite prop in his literary trunk. So we must interpret his sly motto "innocence is hard to beat" (76) in two ways: Innocence is hard to top because it is the royal road to approval and reward, as in childhood; and innocence is hard to overcome because it is a second skin that shields a person from attack. Williams exploits both meanings of "beat" in order to deceive both the reader and himself. For he is never so foxy as when he is "sincerely" confessing his weaknesses as a poet, his preferences and immoralities, or striking his brow at some gauche slip of the tongue or embarrassing ignorance—as when he mocks himself for not knowing that "venereal" and Venus are etymologically related, this by a sixty-five-year-old physician and poet!—or presenting himself, especially in the Paris chapters, as Doc Williams from Rutherford, a suburban yokel cutting a sorry figure in the modish world of art and wealth. Williams struts and jokes about culture like the most madcap of Mark Twain's philistines abroad, while caring deeply for its fate. Indeed, he carries his innocence in his pocket, so to speak, as Dr. Dev Evans, in *Voyage to Pagany,* carried an arrowhead in his excursions to the great cultural capitals of Europe: an amulet of his Americanism.

Psychologically, innocence functions as a delaying of maturity while Williams accumulates experiences to be stowed away for future use. So he stands for hours before the Venus Andromeda in Rome, listens to Richard Strauss's *Elektra* in Leipzig, or debates with himself whether to go with a whore in Seville: "Had I the nerve or the insanity to follow the little whore who waved her buttocks at me near the plaza that evening, I don't know where I might not have landed in this world or out of it. But I didn't, and so I am a writer." (122) This fantasy of nocturnal adventure—and there are many passages like it in the *Autobiography*—with its tacked-on naive conjecture as to what might have been had his practical self not intervened, is Williams impersonating the artless provincial rogue and grinning over the memory. (He was engaged to Floss at the time.) We know that Williams would have been a writer whether or not he had accepted the whore's invitation. But the style carries the joke: the double negatives enacting his circular reasoning, the phrase "the nerve or the insanity" leaving his motive of refusal ambiguous, and the schoolboy's non sequitur ending the skit.

Williams's naïveté, allied to his peculiar vulnerability and durable sense of wonder, is a ruse that enables him to get literary business done. *"Beati innocenti,"* the benediction he bestows on the past and on himself, is a formula Williams fashioned for survival, like his suburban practice in pediatrics and his stable marriage. It was most of all a cover for his slow and circuitous development as a poet, from the ornate maunderings of his early poems, the crystalline images of his transitional period, to his efforts in the twenties to imbue his poems with the "tactile qualities of words." (380) Walking the hospital wards gradually weaned him from romantic insipidities, as did Pound's stinging criticisms from London, but despite winning the Dial and Guarantor prizes in the twenties, Williams felt insecure, as if he were consigned to the fringes of modernism. Hence his preternatural sensitivity to insults and to intimations that he was only a minor composer of fragments.

One sketch in the *Autobiography,* of a brief run-in with Marcel Duchamp, throws light on Williams's manipulation of his bumptious innocence. At a party at Walter Arensberg's studio, Williams spots Duchamp's painting *The Sister* hanging on the wall. Wishing to compliment the painter, he says to him, "I like your picture." Duchamp's retort, "Do you?" so completely unhinges Williams that, remembering the incident forty years later, he gives this account:

> He had me beat all right, if that was his objective. I could have sunk through the floor, ground my teeth, turned my back on him and spat. I don't think I ever gave him that chance again. I realized then and there that there wasn't a possibility of my ever saying anything to anyone in that gang from that moment to eternity—but one of them, by God, would come to me and give me the same chance one day and that I should not fail then to lay him cold—if I could. Meanwhile, work. (137)

How does Williams intend us to take his violent reaction? That innocence *can* be beat? In the aftermath of the 1913 Armory Show, Duchamp was indisputably a sensation, the leader of what Williams a paragraph later calls that "fabulous moment" which gave the poet a chance to find a "local assertion," freeing him from colonial servitude to English models. As the Prince of the Avant-Garde, Duchamp was used to receiving deference, but did he wish to mortify Williams? One doubts it. Williams had met the "great Marcel" before in cordial circumstances and had enjoyed the brouhaha Duchamp's famous urinal had raised, thinking it a liberating artistic gesture.

Nor was Williams's gregarious side underdeveloped. He crossed the Hudson River two or three times a week, browsing at Stieglitz's gallery and talking with him about Braque and Marin and Marsden Hartley; he acted at the Provincetown Playhouse; he invested cash and energy in various short-lived literary magazines, like *Broom* and *Others*. (He was one of the "gang.") Far from being isolated, Williams had allies, friends, and critics like Paul Rosenfeld,[16] who fostered his at times inchoate aspirations to mine the materials of his art in his own backyard. And he was nurtured by good talk: Kenneth Burke may have lived simply on a farm in western New Jersey without modern plumbing and electricity, but he had a sophisticated and learned mind which he willingly put at Williams's disposal. Even without Pound's bulletins, exhortations, and mentorship, Williams kept an eye cocked on the doings of the international avant-garde.

The truth is that Williams had a shrewd and complex mind. The dance of intellect that he cherished pirouettes throughout the *Autobiography*. We should not therefore misread, or be conned by, his seemingly ingenuous nature as he blurts out feelings, opinions, secrets. Though Williams left a briefcase full of recent work in a taxicab soon after his terse exchange with Duchamp, which suggests an unconscious dissatisfaction with that work, he was not easily intimidated—by Duchamp or Eliot or Joyce—or emotionally capsized. Pretending to be a country hick is a convenient stratagem for Williams: an ingrained psychological defense against his own ambitions, captious moods, and the possibility of failure. The point of the anecdote is the older man's savoring not his revenge—there is no incident in which Duchamp or a member off his clique is laid cold—but his pleasure that starting later than the literary hares, his tortoise self won the race, fulfilling his "long-range objectives." Williams's innocence enabled him always to land on his feet.

In Williams's life and art, the desire for intimacy and a need for distance fought long, exhausting skirmishes. This major rhythm, a key to understanding Williams's *Autobiography*, is the source of the book's appeal. It governs the repertoire of voices at his command, by turns sassy and earnest, confiding and aloof, flaunting the pugnacity of the tough guy and, more rarely, the surprised tenderness of the lover. Intimacy means to him contact, empathy, touch, sexual abandon, the temptation of infidelity, and the dread of being carried away and losing his identity; distance means perspective, detachment, and correction of error, a kind of cosmopolitan knowingness and the ignominy of safety—the husband. Williams approves of both but can bear neither exclusively for more than a short time. His obsession with measure throughout his adult life had its roots in his psyche as well as in his prosody.

Williams's writings abound, in all periods, with an ardor for intimacy. "Advice to a Young Poet" is typical: "The art is to get through to the fact and make it eloquent. We have to make a direct contact, from the sense to the object [within us] so that what we disclose is peeled, acute, virulent."[17] Thus, in the *Autobiography*, he thoroughly approves Hemingway's getting off a bus in Spain, in the middle of a hot afternoon, and taking out his notebook to sketch, close-up, the carcass of a dog. The writer must not flinch or avert his eyes from the contours of any object. Yet looking too close at an object can harm the eye, as when Williams once squinted into a jammed firecracker, which suddenly ignited and almost blinded him. Distance is protective: When he absentmindedly forgets to give fictional names to characters in a story based on real events, he is sued and nearly ruined financially.

But in the *Autobiography,* intimacy is too often theoretical; the circuit between the sense and "the object [within us]" fails to give off its electrical charge because it is not completed; the facts are not made eloquent. Williams's accounts of the deaths of his father, his mother, Grandmother Wellcome, and Pa Herman, Floss's father, are icily curt. His blunder at Pop's deathbed, pronouncing him dead ("He's gone"), only to notice Pop's faint refuting nod, leads to no paroxysm of self-accusation such as the bedeviled Edward Dahlberg would have yielded to. How his mind adjusted to this loss of a parent is a secret that only stray comments later in the book illuminate. In the *Autobiography*'s only dream, Pop appears to Williams and, as if in retaliation for his son's disastrous slip, says, "You know all that poetry you're writing. Well, it's no good." (14) (Pop had annotated and corrected some of Williams's early poems.) Williams characteristically does not interpret this devastating judgment and never reports dreaming of Pop again. When Pa Herman is accidentally killed by his own gun, as his son Paul was twenty years before, Williams reports the facts in the dry language of a coroner. There is no moralizing about the grim symmetry of the deaths and only the barest hint of Floss's agony: Memory goes cloudy and numb.

Doubtless Williams's scientific training inculcated this habit of clinical reticence: Detachment was necessary to keep the emotional shocks of patients dying, especially members of one's own family, from unnerving him. The stoical side of Williams's character, the exertion of his will to control threatening forces, came by way of his father's rationalism and liberal Unitarian ethic. Even though Pop was absent for long periods on business trips, he instilled in his son a respect for competence and a humane practicality. If Pop was like an "old Chinese philosopher," the figure suggests a sober guide of wise remoteness and cautious sanity. Pop, Williams notes, was "a stickler for fundamentals, I'll say that, and when he took hold of a thing insisted on going through with it to the bitter end to find out what it amounted to. If he couldn't understand a thing at last, he'd reject it, which was not Mother's saving way of facing the world." (91) Williams shared this mental tenacity, but his "saving way of facing the world" he took from his mother, the parent with whom he was more intimate.

Though Williams claims in the *Autobiography* that Elena Williams was foreign to him, the evidence, sparse as it may be, suggests that she was the formative influence on her son. Because her beloved brother Carlos had been a doctor, she wished her son to choose that profession, and because she had studied at the Beaux-Arts in Paris, a romantic interlude she never forgot and a paradise from which she was expelled owing to family circumstances, she encouraged her son's artistic career and lived vicariously through it.[18] That she was a difficult, thwarted woman most witnesses agree; Williams considered her both stern and frivolous. Of Latin extraction, mercurial and dreamy, she never adapted to life in suburban New Jersey. There was something of the noble tragedienne and hotheaded diva in her: She liked to declaim a speech from Corneille or trill an aria from *La Traviata*. But her discontent came out most prominently during séances, at which she would fall into a trance to summon and talk to spirits from the dead. For hours she would literally be out of her mind, and Williams describes one session in which she did not recognize her own children. To the impressionable and dependent young boy, these visitations were frightening and "horribly embarrassed" (17) him: He was, for the moment, disowned.[19] It is a plausible guess that Williams came to associate intimacy with a perilous letting go, and thus while fascinated by the performance of the occult drama, he resolved not to lose control of himself. There was also the lesson of his uncle Godwin, "a grand rouser of the imagination," (4) who went insane. As Williams put it in the poem "To Daphne and Virginia," "In our family we stammer unless,/half mad,/we come to speech at last." Williams's alternation between cheerful accessibility and a shy, almost panicky retreat into solitude very likely had its origin in his experience of maternal instability. The deeper strata of the self were emblems of secret pathology to be approached with the utmost circumspection, lest his identity crumble.

"We always try to hide the secret of our lives from the general stare," Williams remarks in the foreword to the *Autobiography.* "What I believe to be the hidden core of my life will not easily be deciphered, even when I tell, as here, the outer circumstances." (xi-xii) Williams issues here both warning and challenge to the reader who looks to follow him into his past and understand his development as poet and man: "Keep your distance. Don't expect intimacy to spring up between us quickly. Don't trust the outer circumstances: The real me, the sources of my moral and emotional being, are hidden from view." The *Autobiography* is strewn with false clues, dark passageways, dissembling signposts. Williams wears an armor hard to shed; indeed, he is uncertain whether it can or should be shed. Yet the dangerous secret also contains, like an oyster a pearl, a "perfection." In the chapter "Of Medicine and Poetry," one of the few sustained meditations in the *Autobiography,* Williams observes:

This immediacy, the thing, as I went on writing, living as I could, thinking a secret life I wanted to tell openly—if only I could—how it lives, secretly about us as much now as ever. It is the history, the anatomy of this, not subject to surgery, plumbing or cures, that I wanted to tell. I don't know why. Why tell that which no one wants to hear? But I saw that when I was successful in portraying something, by accident, of that secret world of perfection, that they did want to listen. Definitely. And my "medicine" was the thing which gained me entrance to these secret gardens of the self. It lay there, another world, in the self. I was permitted by my medical badge to follow the poor, defeated body into those gulfs and grottos. And the astonishing thing is that at such times and in such places—foul as they may be with the stinking ischiorectal abscesses of our comings and goings—just there, the thing, in all its greatest beauty, may for a moment be freed to fly for a moment guiltily about the room. In illness, in the permission I as a physician have had to be present at deaths and births, at the tormented battles between daughter and diabolic mother, shattered by a gone brain—just there—for a split second—from one side or the other, it has fluttered before me for a moment, a phrase which I quickly wrote down on anything at hand, any piece of paper I can grab.

It is an identifiable thing, and its characteristic, its chief character is that it is sure, all of a piece and, as I have said, instant and perfect: it comes, it is there, and it vanishes. But I have seen it, clearly. I have seen it. I know it because there it is. (288)

At the bedside of a patient, the poet-doctor becomes an explorer, like Christopher Columbus in *In the American Grain,* sailing the winds of chance and purpose toward the discovery of a "secret world of perfection," calm, concentrated, beset by a mutinous crew (the body and the brain) and treacherous vortices. The news of the long-awaited but doubted discovery is hurriedly written down on a scrap of paper, a fragile vessel for such glad tidings, to instruct a skeptical or indifferent audience.

What Williams is describing is not the art of medical diagnosis, not even the dissection of "the stinking ischio-rectal abscesses of our comings and goings," but the agony of poetic creation. Williams's first venture in pursuit of the "Beautiful Thing,"[20] his "three-pound"[21] (54) Keatsian poem, had been thrown into the fire because it was a tedious imitation of "Endymion": a papier-mâché prince wandering aimlessly through an unreal landscape and meeting up with silly obstacles. No metamorphosis took place. Subsequently, however, Williams tracked the "Beautiful Thing" as it fluttered like a butterfly, nameless and slippery, from within himself to the world outside, and came to rest, "for a moment," in the ruined gardens, gulfs, and grottos of the "poor, defeated body." The process and the iconography are romantic standards: With luck, intense observation, and inspiration, beauty can be wrested from the maimed, a perfect word or phrase salvaged from decay. Normally Williams shied away from "perfection," suspecting it was a chimera. But in this passage, though poetic creation is as elusive as godhead, a spirit of exaltation haunts him. His attempt to unriddle the oracle can only be tentative and vague, like the syntax doubling back on itself, the liturgical into-nation of the word "thing," and the pronouns floating free of exact references. When he falls back into the public world, he proclaims twice, as though stunned by what has happened, "But I have seen it, clearly. I have seen it."

One word, however, leaps out of the nervous rhythms of Wil-liams's anatomy of poetic birth: "guiltily." Though privileged by his professional badge as medicine man of the tribe to enter the sanctum of the "Beautiful Thing," he feels uneasy, an interloper. Freedom born of intimacy seems to induce guilt. The "Beautiful Thing" itself, like a tabooed object, disturbs him, as if creation simulated one of his mother's séances, which "horribly embarrassed" him as a boy. Something, hard to identify, interferes with vision.

Dissatisfied with his first effort to formulate the link between medicine and poetry, Williams returns to the subject in a later chapter, "The Practice." Two passages deserve close scrutiny:

> I lost myself in the very property of their [his patients'] minds: for the moment at least I actually became *them,* whoever they should be, so that when I detached myself from them at the end of a half-hour of intense concentration over some illness that was affecting them, it was as though I were reawakening from a sleep. For the moment I myself did not exist, nothing of myself affected me. As a consequence I came back to myself, as from any other sleep, rested. (356)

In "coming to grips with the intimate conditions" (356) of his patients' lives, Williams crosses the threshold to enter the golden doors of perception, surrenders himself entirely to the object of his contemplation, indeed identifies with it, and returns to himself "rested." Intimacy does not threaten Williams's identity this time but enhances it. Contact with this "elementary world" (357) brings confidence and survives incidents when his patients reject him. Poetically and medically, Williams describes the operation of negative capability.

Williams then goes on to observe:

> every sort of individual that it is possible to imagine in some phase of his development, from the highest to the lowest, at some time exhibited himself to me. I am sure I have seen them all. And all have contributed to my pie. Let the successful carry off their blue ribbons; I have known the unsuccessful, far better than their more lucky brothers. One can laugh at them both, whatever the costume they adopt. And when one is able to reveal them to themselves, high or low, they are always grateful as they are surprised that one can so have revealed the inner secrets of another's motive. To do this is

what makes a writer worth heeding: that somehow or other, whatever the source may be, he has gone to the base of the matter to lay it bare before us in terms which, try as we may, we cannot in the end escape. There is no choice then but to accept him and make him a hero. (358)

This hymn to his dual professions is simple in utterance but complex in theme. The doctor and the poet, though each is sometimes deemed a spy, perform the essential, almost religious office of revelation (both disdain the journalistic as trivial, "lying dialectics" [360]). There is a quiet exhilaration such as a chemist might feel who discovers a new and rare element or as a poet who attains "a new, a more profound language." (361) Craftsmanship is a means of naming the disease, of identifying the "private motives," (358) but technique does not suffice unless to it is added the scientist's humility before great laws of nature and the poet's mystical obstetrics of the spirit.

Williams is, for the moment, unabashed before the "Beautiful Thing." His syntax no longer hesitant, he has triumphed over his inarticulateness. He has become a healer of division and a hero of faith that the "underground current can be tapped and the secret spring of all our lives will send up its pure water." The poet is a servant of people's need for wholeness. Williams grasps the paradox that this "rare presence" is "jealous of exposure" and "shy and revengeful. . . . Its face is a particular face, it is likely to appear under the most unlikely disguises." (362) (Williams's description bears an uncanny resemblance to his own character!) But, ironically, despite his optimism, in the *Autobiography* Williams only intermittently goes "to the base of the matter." In the end, he is a flawed hero because he draws back from the "inner secrets" of his own private motives. It is easier for him to expose others.

III

IN 1927, Williams, like hundreds of artists before him, made his pilgrimage to 27 rue de Fleurus to look at the famous paintings, "one of the sights of Paris," (254) and to talk with Gertrude Stein, whose pioneering work "tackling the fracture of stupidities bound in our thoughtless phrases, in our calcified grammatical constructions and in the subtle brainlessness of our meter and favorite prose rhythms," as he put it in a later essay ("A 1 Pound Stein") should have made her a natural ally. But instead of producing shoptalk and mutual commendation, the meeting ended rancorously because of a cruel gibe Williams aimed at his hostess. Unlocking her armoire, Miss Stein asked her guest what he would do if, like her, he had a stack of unpublished manuscripts (indeed, he was an expert on the topic). Here is what Williams in the *Autobiography* remembers happening:

> It must have been that I was in one of my more candid moods or that the cynical opinion of Pound and other of my friends about Miss Stein's work was uppermost in my mind, for my reply was, "If they were mine, having so many, I should probably select what I thought were the best and throw the rest in the fire."
>
> The result of my remark was instantaneous. There was a shocked silence out of which I heard Miss Stein say, "No doubt. But then writing is not, of course, your métier."
>
> That closed the subject and we left soon after. (254)

Williams's boorish behavior may not have been calculated to wound Miss Stein—he later on, in a different mood, paid handsome amends by praising her work publicly and in print—but it is typical of the way an aggressive caprice often seized him in the company of or while writing about fellow artists. He enjoys the role of upstart democratic crow railing at his rivals; Miss Stein's salon, so like a Temple of Art, aroused his instinct to blaspheme. The positive side of this prickly self, as Pound saw, prevented Williams from "grabbing ready-made conclusions and from taking too much for granted."[22] Williams thought slowly and laboriously, but his emotions were often mercurial. Extremely competitive,[23] when his insecurity was in the ascendancy he lashed out at his enemies with a nasty hysteria. He needed enemies, and the *Autobiography* contains many military images; he felt continually embattled. (His generosity toward young writers was, of course, legendary.) His favorite villain or scapegoat was T. S. Eliot, to whose Caesar he cast himself as Vercingetorix, the famous Gallic hero who was "betrayed in the end by his tribesmates, as we all are in the end." (210) As though it were a personal attack, *The Waste Land* felled Williams like a "sardonic bullet." "It wiped out our world as if an atomic bomb had dropped upon it and our brave sallies into the unknown were turned to dust." (174) Williams's feud with and contempt for Eliot were in earnest over real poetic issues: Eliot, he believed, had blighted the seed of a new poetic form rooted in the local. *The Waste Land* had given poetry back to the academics—a word synonymous in Williams's vocabulary of abuse with timidity and sterile orthodoxy—and had reinstated a genteel and false literary language. Williams stammers his rage at Eliot's blackguardism. Derailed, he must pick himself up from the ditch and start over. Eliot appears once in person in the *Autobiography,* entering the Dôme in Paris dressed "in top hat, cutaway, and striped trousers," (217) the uniform of a priggish dandy lording it over the habitués, in sharp contrast to Williams's country manners and dull clothes. Williams relishes his malice toward Eliot: It made him vow to resume the struggle and uphold his "rebellious" experiments. He would count on final vindication.

And vindication and success finally did arrive. Part III of the *Autobiography* is bathed in a mellow light. Perhaps because Williams had completed and published the first four books of *Paterson,* according to his original design, perhaps because his physical ailments had chastened him, perhaps most of all because he was no longer afflicted with sexual tension, he seems reconciled with himself. He can recollect the past in tranquillity, as the epigraph he affixed to Part III hints: "Old though I am, for lady's love unfit,/the power of the beauty I remember yet." At the end of Chapter 48, Williams recited the roster of friends and foes, illustrious and minor figures, who had fought in the literary wars. Many had died, some had given up, others had fallen silent. A few, like himself, were "alive and working." He had stayed the distance.

One charming scene crystallizes Williams's satisfaction at having become a literary Caesar in his own right. In the summer of 1949, in the garden of his friends the Gratwicks, he is crowned Poet Laureate of the Tree Peonies. He enters into the spirit of this ceremony of investiture with witty solemnity and proper levity. A "garland of Siberian Olive" wreathing his brow, he recites part of Paul Valéry's speech before the French Academy on the occasion of his admission into that august body (even Williams's old enemies have a place in his coronation): "I threw out my chest and frowning, like a Caesar, let fly," the children in the audience rapt, "as if it had indeed been a demigod come to earth." (327) This scene of familial intimacy launches a grand barnstorming tour of American colleges (another citadel captured), on which he is courted, feted, acclaimed, loved. His public lectures, as he outlines them, have the ripe, carefree wisdom of a sage who can laugh at himself—and his audience—and invent fables *ex tempore*. Williams was even more popular, he jokes, than Dylan Thomas, the reigning matinee idol of the poetry circuit.

But one shadow hovers over the valedictory glow of the *Autobiography*: Ezra Pound, Williams's old friend and sometime rival, incarcerated after World War II in St. Elizabeths Hospital for the Insane in Washington, D.C. Pound's presence was impossible to banish. For over forty years, from their first meeting at the University of Pennsylvania in 1906, where both were students, to Williams's visits to St. Elizabeths, they engaged in a knockabout fight in private, through the mails, and in the public lists. Williams championed the poetics of the local: bread, the "raw new," the loam; Pound, the poetics of tradition: caviar, "the graciousness of an imposed cultural design,"24 the polished artifact. Williams was captivated by Pound. Who wouldn't be? Daft, gifted, gabby, bossy, an erudite dervish, a "crow with a cleft palate,"25 Pound took his friend's literary education in hand, sending reading lists from London, Paris, or Rapallo, bawling him out for a mulish inattention to the past and an immoderate passion for immediacy, yet generously arranging for English publication of *The Tempers* in 1913. Though Williams was generally, as Marianne Moore astutely pointed out, "restive under advice,"26 he listened to Pound and learned, accepting some tenets of the Poundian gospel while rejecting others. He liked fencing with Pound (they took lessons in the art from rival schools— Williams the French, Pound the Italian). But one bout, when Pound, taking unfair advantage, "came plunging wildly in without restraint, and hit me with the point of the cane above my right eye to fairly lay me out," leads Williams to decide, "You can't trust a guy like that!" (65) He didn't. Pound is another person whom Williams loves—at a distance.

The seriocomic portrait of Pound in the *Autobiography* is a study in multiple perspective of a subject who won't sit still. In the early years of their friendship, Williams is a passive accomplice, sidekick to the clown; he is eager to acquire the tricks of the trade, but also suspicious that there may be sham in the master's act. (Williams loved the theater, thought for a time that he might choose it as a profession, acted at the Provincetown Playhouse, constructed a stage in the backyard of 9 Ridge Road, and wrote plays, some of which were staged professionally.) Pound had a bent for impersonation that shaded into imposture. Williams recalls Pound's performance in Euripides' *Iphigenia in Aulis,* in which he had a minor role as "one of the women of the chorus": "He was dressed in a Grecian robe, as I remember it, a toga-like ensemble topped by a great blond wig at which he tore as he waved his arms about and heaved his massive breasts in ecstasies of extreme emotion." (57)

These "ecstasies of extreme emotion," almost an augury of Pound's future obsessiveness, held Williams spellbound—and repelled him. Pound would, apparently, try anything: Like an amateur daredevil, he would leap on Pegasus and ride off in all directions. The spectacle was thrilling, the value problematic. Pound even composed an opera, *Villon,* in 1925. Although Williams did not hear any performance, he reports, secondhand, Brancusi's outrage and the more amused comments of Yves Tinayre, who sang the title role, as his own. Blessed with a keen ear for verse time, Pound had no gift for tonality and so could not write well for the human voice. The result was, except for musical serendipity, ludicrous. Williams shakes his head and with affectionate sarcasm says, "It must infuriate Ezra to know that there is *something* in the world of which he is not the supreme master." (225) Part cultural busybody, part polymath, Pound was a phenomenon. "Ezra has always paid homage to old distinctions: it is one of his handsomest traits," Williams concedes.[27]

Williams's prose bounces along with a queer comical tipsiness when judging Pound, as the following sample will show:

I could never take him as a steady diet. Never. He was often brilliant but an ass. But I never (so long as I kept away) tired of him, or, for a fact, ceased to love him. He had to be loved, even if he kicked you in the teeth for it (but that he never did); he looked as if he might, but he was, at heart, much too gentle, much too good a friend for that. And he had, at bottom, an inexhaustible patience, an infinite depth of human imagination and sympathy. Vicious, catty at times, neglectful, if he trusted you not to mind, but warm and devoted—funny, too, as I have said. We hunted, to some extent at least, together, and not each other. (58)

From this contradictory evidence,[28] "sweet Ezra" (58) emerges as a cautionary figure. Setting up in life as a high priest of art, especially in foreign cathedrals, despite the noble ideals and service of the calling, did not appeal to the bluntly practical Williams. Visiting Pound in London in 1910, he was taken to hear Yeats read to a small group of reverent acolytes in a "darkened room," but the atmosphere of incense and worship, so like a throwback to some Pre-Raphaelite cult of beauty, was not Williams's "dish." (Lionel Johnson, Dowson, and Pater were never as important to Williams as they were to Pound.) To be sure, there is an element of self-protection in Williams's curt dismissal, since he had only recently abandoned his own long hymn to beauty, and he felt like an anonymous apprentice compared to the "great man" Yeats and the more advanced Pound. Williams's scientific training, he says, warned him away from "arty posturings."[29] Pound had to scrounge for a living in Grub Street, but Williams "didn't intend to die for art nor to be bedbug food, nor to ask anyone else for help." (49)

By the 1930s, Williams had achieved a kind of psychological parity with Pound. Their friendship temporarily cooled over politics. When Pound defended Mussolini's aid to Franco, brushing aside as negligible Franco's suppression of the Spanish Republic as "no more than a gesture toward cleaning out a mosquito swamp in darkest Africa," Williams reacted with a "furious blast."[30] (316) In a letter to James Laughlin, Williams poured out his bitter feelings:

Ezra is an important poet, we must forgive him his stupidities. I do, no matter how much he riles me. But I prefer not to have to do with him in any way. He wants to patronize me. Don't tell me this isn't so, for I know better. His letters are insults, the mewings of an 8th-grade teacher. That's where he thinks I exist in relation to his catastrophic knowledge of affairs, his binding judgments of contemporary values. In one sense, he is quite right to protect himself as he does. But my perceptions overtook him twenty years ago—not however my accomplishments. When I have finished, if I can go to the finish, there'll be another measuring.[31]

World War II intervened, and the two friends parted company until Pound broke the silence by mentioning "ol Doc Williams of Rutherford, New Jersey," in a propaganda broadcast overheard by a local bank teller. Williams sets down this brief colloquy with Floss:

> "What the hell right has he to drag me into his dirty messes?"
> "I'm just reporting what I heard," said Floss. "You're always getting mixed up in something through your 'friends,' " she said. (316)

Floss's tart comment is one of the few signs in the *Autobiography* that her forbearance could be frayed by Williams's literary friends, but his reaction was mild, even though the FBI came investigating twice.

Though in prison and among the certifiably insane, Pound held state like a deposed monarch whose habit of command remains while his kingdom has shrunk. As Williams describes him, Pound had changed very little; he was uncontrite; the old prophetic fury still blazed in his denunciations of the economic perfidy and stupidity practiced by governments, Franklin Roosevelt foremost among the "criminal" leaders. Williams had been comfortable in what he called the city of the hospital because he considered it a normal place. The city of St. Elizabeths Hospital was, undeniably, *not* normal, and Williams admits that "the disturbed mind has always been a territory from which I shrank instinctively as before the unknown." (335) The idea of Pound's "close confinement" had upset Williams; he was fearful of what he would find. Here is his portrait of Pound at their first meeting:

> He looked much as I had always found him, the same beard and restless twitching of the hands, shifting his shoulders about as he lay back in the chair studying me, the same bantering smile, screwing up his eyes, the half-coughing laugh and short, swift words, no sentence structure worth mentioning. I was of course happy to find him looking so well. (336)

Williams captures Pound's physical gestures with a harrowing accuracy, but he seems unsure how to interpret them. Is Pound a disturbed intellectual centaur whose frightening exterior is a mirror of an inner breakdown, or is he simply a slightly grotesque and affected literary eccentric martyred to his own opinions?[32] Williams does not say. He keeps a personal and professional distance and reserves judgment. Like a court stenographer, he takes down Pound's ideas, the most astonishing of which is a conviction that if "Stalin would have given him a five-minute interview, he [Pound] could have shown the man the error in his thinking, made him see, comprehend, and act on it, and all the subsequent confusion and disaster [of America's relations with Russia] could have been avoided." (337)

After the jagged intensities of this first visit, which molested his peace of mind, Williams is relieved to chat with the black taxi driver who will return him to the community of the normal. Williams labels the taxi driver an "important messenger," the voice of the common man, to whom he listens attentively. Like Pound, the driver was "interested mostly in himself" and had "important convictions" about the "present world situation," including Stalin. The relaxed humor of the conversation—the driver asks for medical advice—releases some of Williams's tension. When told Pound's views, the driver, a surrogate for Williams, declares: "He ain't crazy. He just talk too much." (340) Pound is not mad, just opinionated like any average citizen.

On another visit, however, Williams stumbles upon an image so shocking he cannot avert his eyes:

> I saw this man, naked, full-on and immobile, his arms up as though climbing a wall, plastered against one of the high windows on the old building like a great sea slug against the inside of a glass aquarium, his belly as though stuck to the glass that looked dull or splattered from the bad weather. I didn't stop, but kept looking up from time to time. I glanced around to see if there were any women about. There was no one on the grounds at that point but myself. The man's genitals were hard against the cold (it must have been cold) glass, plastered there in that posture of despair. When would they come and take him down? After all it was glass, window glass, bars though there were beyond it. The white flesh like

a slug's white belly separated from the outside world, without
frenzy, stuck silent on the glass. (342)

Familiarity with the hospital had subdued some of Williams's initial
terror, but he was not prepared for the utterly numbing helplessness
of the naked inmate. This, surely, was one of those rare moments
when the "Beautiful Thing" exposed itself and its jealously guarded
secret; the very transparency of the glass magnifies the picture of a
permanently wrecked mind. Williams does not stop, but as though
mesmerized, his eyes keep returning to the silhouetted figure, just as
his syntax keeps circling back to its point of origin and his mind
repeats the image of the sea slug and the words "belly," "stuck,"
"glass," "cold," "plastered," "white." Madness is viewed as a primordial, inert creature rising from the depths of the mind and
adhering to the surface by some interior suction, its white belly repulsive, in its silence the terror of the shattered will abandoned by
the world. What embarrasses Williams is that the inmate's genitals
are on public display; he furtively looks around to see if any women
are present, which is an odd reversion to Victorian prudery in a
modern doctor and writer. But "embarrassment" is Williams's code
word in the *Autobiography* for emotional confusion and the dread
of dealing with irrationality. Faced with the effigy of madness, Williams is singularly barren of reflections.

Williams does not mean us to associate the sea slug with Pound,
who is mentally active, even frenzied—in bondage to his abstract
system, perhaps, but capable of continuing the tasks of a man of
letters. Williams represses his consternation by rationalizing that
Pound's confinement, like that of such writers as Aesop, Sappho,
Bunyan, and Cervantes before him, brought his "mind to harvest."
(343)

Williams follows this consoling thought with one of his loveliest
definitions of the poem:

> The poem is a capsule where we wrap up our punishable
> secrets. And as they confine in themselves the only "life," the
> ability to sprout at a more favorable time, to come true in
> their secret structure to the very minutest details of our
> thoughts, so they get their specific virtue.
>
> We write for this, that the seed come true, and it appears

to be this which makes the poem the toughest certainty of
continued life that experience acknowledges. . . . (343)

Like a seed planted in the dark earth or the genes carried by the
fetus in the womb, the poem has its origin in our "punishable secrets." What is hidden will come to term (terms) in the organic
structure of flower, child, or poem. The poem is an act of atonement
and thus a way of avoiding punishment. "That the seed come true":
Williams knew how hazardous this process could be—he tells us of
hydrocephalic babies—that much his experience acknowledges. But
neither his definition, elegant as it is, nor his pragmatic intelligence
could incorporate the madman or his friend Pound, as his autobiographical art cannot integrate or interpret a mind laid waste.
Throughout the *Autobiography* Williams disclaims any interest in,
even jeers at, pathology. He is not being duplicitous so much as
failing to confront the evidence he is unearthing before our eyes. He
was, as we shall see, fascinated by sexual deviance, by anybody who
when stripped to his naked self is not what he appears to be, by
excess of emotion, as with Pound,[33] or by yielding to transport and
ecstasy. His heroes in *In the American Grain* were Daniel Boone
and Aaron Burr, men who let themselves go, not the prudent, like
Benjamin Franklin. But in the *Autobiography,* Williams joins Franklin's party: He presents himself as a plain "literary guy," a poet of
surfaces, but he pays a heavy price in recoiling from what lies beneath the skin.

IV

TOWARD THE romance of the artistic life so glamorously portrayed
in *The Autobiography of Alice B. Toklas* and so fondly remembered
by his mother from her youth, Williams adopted a curious combat-
iveness that bordered at times on puritanical animosity but which
came from his own awkward efforts to conceal from the reader—
and himself—just how tempted he was by the promiscuities of the
bohemian world of New York and the demimonde of Paris. With
his amorous disposition, Williams found the heedless or showy or
languorous sexuality of women who seemed to be ladies-in-waiting
to Venus, looking for adventure, a troubling pleasure. Williams led

a double life. At home he had a comfortable middle-class marriage, a devoted wife, children, a thriving medical practice; in New York he had stimulating talk, the lively commotion of literary groups in ferment, and the possibilities of sexual liaisons.

Williams's comments on how he managed this arrangement are so contradictory, so full of a rascally frankness and a coy make-believe, that the reader soon suspects him of playing the diplomat's deep games. To one interviewer he will say, "I was very sexually successful, as a young man, but I did not go so far that I lost my head. I wanted always to be conscious. I didn't want to indulge in sex so much that I lost my head."[34] To another person, he will declare that he and Pound "talked frankly about sex and the desire for women which we were both agonizing over. We were both too refined to enjoy a woman if we could get her. Which was impossible. We were too timid to dare. We were in agony most of the time. Anyhow we survived with the loss of everything but our heads."[35] Which version should we believe? Both have Williams's usual racy patois about sex, and both are evasive. In the *Autobiography,* he depicts himself as so tense and wary and fumbling with nurses and literary women that Huck Finn by comparison was a Don Juan. What matters, as Williams says in the foreword, is not how many women he took to bed but how sex and women influenced his art and why he was afraid of losing his head.

As obstetrician and poet, Williams had the best seat in the house to observe sex as an elemental force. The topic obsessed him, but his contact with women elicited from him spontaneous eruption of thought. Like Aaron Burr, he saw women as serious and generous, not decorous or weak. He was especially sensitive to their plight. Society afforded few outlets for their talents and energies beyond domestic drudgery. Women were "neglected in the arts" or, like the nurses in hospitals, possessed of a close knowledge of the body yet tragically stymied. Williams does not belittle marriage and the raising of children as vocations—he admires Nora Barnacle and Dorothy Shakespeare for their selfless devotion to James Joyce and Ezra Pound—but he is aware how dreary and passive domesticity can be. The *Autobiography* is like a dossier crammed with case histories of women who sought space to escape conventional roles, some succeeding and some failing: Katherine Johns, the restless Vassar graduate eager to type Williams's manuscript so that she can exercise her intellect; poets like Marianne Moore, Mina Loy, and H.D.; painters, nuns, singers, like Sally Bird and Clotilde Vail, book people like Sylvia Beach and Adrienne Monnier; the neighbor who committed suicide because she could not bear the prospect of a life solely given over to the care of her retarded brother; and aimless pilgrims like Nancy Cunard and Iris Tree, who embody in their "passionate inconstancy" (202) a "depraved saintliness," (221) experiencing everything and feeling little. It is a remarkable gallery of women.

Even when they are sexually profligate, women, Williams muses, are centered in a way that men, "the technical morons of the tribe," (224) seldom are. The promiscuity of Nancy Cunard and Iris Tree in Paris intrigued him because they "denied sin by making it hackneyed in their bodies, shucking it away to come out not dirtied but pure." (222) They were "completely empty" (220) yet paradoxically whole. Like an anthropologist, Williams collects stories about women, impressions, customs, oddities of behavior, but he has no theory that explains them coherently. He cannot make up his mind about woman's nature. In some moods, she appears to have the knack of fearlessly acting on her desires, of being able to say, as did Red Eric, one of the heroes of *In the American Grain,* "I am I, and remain so." Williams believed that life was truncated unless one fully surrendered to emotional experience. In much of his work, Williams ardently embraced sensual delight and spiritual discovery, but in his life some inner qualm "braked the great liberalities."[36] In other moods, he could not quite trust women. "What do I look for in a woman?" he asks in the *Autobiography,* and answers, "Death, I suppose, since it's all I see in those various perfections." (222) To possess woman is to be possessed by her, and that, despite the intoxicating scent of danger, brings the threat of self-extinction. He personifies the New World as Helen of Troy, exquisite and promising sexual bounty, but sowing discord, greed, treachery, and death among her suitors.

Williams's tactic is to withdraw to the high ground of cultural analysis, where he can safely study the influence of sex as implacable (and deranging) force. But when he vilifies the Puritans for retreating from the plenitude of the American continent unfolding before them and burrowing into their narrow theocratic shells—it is a major theme of *In the American Grain*—he is also rebuking himself for timidity. Because Williams is so often seen as a passionate foe of puritanism, we miss the fact that his acute understanding of its *pré-dicateur* mentality, pinched morality, and hidden fear of the "hungry animal" springs from a deep puritanical place in his own psyche. Part II of the *Autobiography* ends appropriately with the compelling sentence: "It is strange to bathe alone in an Arctic sea." (276) The icy shock of this immersion is a sensual experience that verges on mortification of the flesh, like some monastic cure for sexual fever.

Williams's entanglement with the Baroness Elsa Von Freytag Loringhoven is symptomatic of how, in the *Autobiography,* he handles romantic imbroglios as comic mishaps. "I was really crazy about the woman," (169) Williams exclaims, but in reliving the episodes he makes their relationship seem like a bourgeois's foray into the "sexual slums"37 or an adolescent's infatuation with an older woman. Theirs was an unlikely attachment. Sculptor, model, shoplifter, friend of the *Little Review* coterie, and protégé of Duchamp, the baroness was a flamboyant woman of fifty who, Williams reports, once "advised me that what I needed to make me great was to contract syphilis from her and so free my mind for serious art." (165) While Williams in *Kora in Hell* observed that "pathology literally speaking is a flower garden. Syphilis covers the body with salmon-red petals," he found the baroness's ideas about sexual horticulture extreme.38

From an unpublished essay, "The Baroness Elsa Von Freytag Loringhoven," we learn that Williams considered the baroness a "clandestine fake" who like Cortez needed to shed blood for the sake of some imagined "clarity and delight" and who scoffed at his suburban "pretensions." In spite of her "insanity," he found her "a great field of cultured bounty" and drank "pure water from her spirit. . . . I could not go to bed with her. Disease has no attraction for me."39 Williams offers little evidence of the baroness's "cultured bounty," but this tormented misalliance with a demonic muse was clearly a form of intellectual and emotional philandering as necessary to him as an office to see patients in or the poetic faculty itself.

When the baroness pursues him to Rutherford, he is flattered but annoyed; ungallantly, he flattens her with "a stiff punch to the mouth" (169) and has her arrested. Williams might be moved by the baroness's quirky talk and sultry manner and, appalled by the squalor in which she lived, might give her money—there is a definite whiff of paying her off to get rid of her—but once she intruded into his domestic sanctuary, thereby jeopardizing his conjugal peace, he discarded her. The baroness's vagabondage eventually ends in France, where she is murdered by a "French jokester" (169)—a sordid climax to a bedroom farce. A trifle sheepish and discomposed, Williams comes through intact.

Williams's assemblage of memories in this chapter makes a bizarre sequence. For he interrupts his story of the baroness to narrate the deaths of Pop and Grandmother Wellcome, the birth of his first son, and the arrival of Wallace Gould, a rustic innocent from Maine who falls into the clutches of a predatory New York literary admirer much like the baroness and must be rescued by Williams. But there is an inner logic to offhand juxtapositions. His deepest loyalties, he seems to be saying, are to his family; it is the strong, unbroken thread of his life; the solemn and joyous family events are intimacies not to be compared to his dalliance with the baroness. Rutherford would always triumph over the fleshpots of Egypt.

But not without a harsh struggle. The essay on the baroness explains philosophically Williams's mature view of the link between sex and mind. Sex and its fevers, however pleasurable, he waits impatiently to pass:

> The mind afterward is my field. Coming to that with the satisfaction of performance ensanguined in me the mind is lit, serene, the eyes as if released from cages, the breath comes unobstructed and the mind rushes to its inventions.
>
> The odors, the light, the fillamentous [sic] stimulae of the sexual contact, the languorous delights are known to me. I know the building up of shock to the fainter, refused parries. I see that it is a country. I too have lived there. Nevertheless it is not my country. The serenity of morning and the people who inherit that Urania I love best. I desire them continuously even through the sexual tropic.
>
> This is the thing that gives me difficulty.[40]

Tempting as the "languorous delights" of Venus were, they left his mind besieged by rebellious instincts, his will in the grip of a powerful compulsion. Williams did not—and could not—repudiate the "sexual tropic," that bewitching gilded cage somewhat like expatriate Paris, but it is to him finally a lesser thing than citizenship in

Urania's kingdom, where desire was free of stress and poetic invention could flourish.

Surely Floss was "one of the people who inherit that Urania I love best." What she thought of the baroness, Williams does not say.[41] In the *Autobiography,* Floss is almost a silent partner in their marriage, coming in and out of focus, her role like Alice B. Toklas's in the Stein ménage: so important she can be taken for granted, unobtrusively staying in the background, her rule unacknowledged but uncontested. Floss was no "Venus de Milo, surely," (130) Williams mocks with cruel candor in the *Autobiography;* rather, she resembled Patient Griselda, dependable, long-suffering, forgiving, courageous, and poised in crisis, as when she acts to save her son's life when he catches diphtheria in Switzerland.[42] After "a rough breaking in for both of us," (131) Williams says, the marriage was successful. "Hard as nails," (130) Floss became the anchor of Williams's emotional life, but how that occurred the *Autobiography* is reluctant to divulge.[43]

Their marriage, as Reed Whittemore has pointed out, incited in Williams a mixture of "penitence and belligerence";[44] he wryly included a "full confessional" as one of the rooms in his blueprint for the space a marriage needs to thrive.[45] Yet in providing a lawful enclosure in which he could work and conserve family values, marriage kept Williams's fear of losing control within manageable bounds. When the "tortured constancy"[46] oppressed him, the impulse to escape stirred in him. But as the *Autobiography* indicates, his pagan self had first to thrash and master its sibling puritan self, and that was never easy. The two fought to a standstill.

In this predicament, Williams's next step was to project his conflict onto the larger stage of culture:

> Frustrated, the measure of a culture is its depth, its thickness, its opportunities for employment of the faculties. The end of life may be to penetrate the female or to be completed in the reverse of that. Right. But what females? There are females of too many coverings and wishes to explore them all. By finding only one pocket for relief we bore our women to the point of frustration, indeed, our own. (376)

Monogamy is frustrating to both men and women because it produces mental and sexual boredom,[47] but the prospect of too many pockets, too many possibilities, is equally frustrating, because the mind diffuses its energies. A culture, if versatile enough, "allows us to beat our enemy, the husband" (376) and employ all our faculties. (Williams concedes elsewhere that women—including Floss?—have been restricted by cultures from releasing *their* inventive powers.) For Williams, the poem is the supreme harnessing of sexual instinct and cultural play. The poet's quest, which he came to understand in old age, "the advancing season of pity,"[48] when his conscience could accept the role of elder statesman and relax its punitive zeal, is to set free the erotic imagination and "to find one phrase that will/lie married beside another for delight."[49] The pleasure of this hunt for style, whatever the setbacks along the way, never diminished for Williams. In the *Autobiography,* style, with its beneficent vanities, is the battleground for another difficult marriage.

V

*I must find my meaning and lay it, white, beside the slid-
ing water: myself—comb out the language—or succumb*

*—whatever the complexion. Let me out! (Well, go!) this
rhetoric is real!*

—PATERSON, Book III

IT IS NOT FARFETCHED to view the swarm of memories in the autobiographer's mind as (to borrow a phrase from *Paterson*) "the whole din of fracturing thought," which somehow must be subdued into a healing music. Who but a doctor-poet, an expert in two kinds of anatomy, is best equipped to set the broken bones? Medicine provided Williams, as did the poem, "the excitement of the chase, the opportunity for exercise of precise talents, the occasion for batting down a rival to supersede him." (292) These aspects are ably served by the anecdotal humor of the *Autobiography.* Whether recording the tribulations of his working-class patients, the rowdy, seamy, and inspiring routines of a hospital, or the professional politics and "untrustworthy self-seekers," (291) the clinician and raconteur are blended in a humane, supple prose. Who can forget the three-hundred-pound woman who gives birth to twins while her policeman husband holds a gun over Williams and another doctor? or the "case of placenta previa with every joint in her body infected

259

(I drained them one after the other over a period of at least three months while she lay there) and she got well"? (160) or the "woman shrieking in a room over a candy store from an inoperable cancer of the uterus while her bemused husband, overwhelmed by doctrinaire convictions, looked at her with stony eyes"? (160) In the exercise of his medical talents, Williams felt unalloyed enjoyment—work stimulated him as whiskey did his Parisian friends like Robert McAlmon—which carries over into the prose. Spinning yarns about his patients, Williams grows alert, as if he were matching wits with death, and vagueness would lose the game. His style takes on a colorful specificity and warmth.

Though Williams announces in the last section of the *Autobiography* that "the practice of letters concerns the whole man no matter what the stylistic variants," (291) does he follow his own good counsel? Apparently he believes that he does and that the study of medicine enabled him "to know what goes on in myself as well as others." (291) He aligns himself with Gertrude Stein in this matter. "She began with the psychic factors under William James" ("from the top down") and then went on to "Johns Hopkins for the somatic factor . . . to make her knowledge whole." (291) Williams's metaphor implies that he and Stein both plumb the depths of the mind and are concerned equally with insides and outsides.

If he is not being disingenuous, Williams is the one most gulled by illusion, for despite (or because of) the ebullience of his style, which skims lightly over events and is based on quick glimpses of objects and people, the psyche scarcely exists. The *Autobiography* contains only the most meager introspection; thinking, as in Stein, comes perilously close at times to mere scribbling. Perceptions bounce off each other like scattered particles of meaning. It is as though Williams, in the *Autobiography,* took Olson's exhortation literally to "get on with it, keep moving, keep in, speed, the nerves, their speed, the perceptions, theirs, the acts, the split-second acts, the whole business, keep it moving as fast as you can, citizen." (330) (Olson sounds like a literary cop directing poetic traffic at a busy intersection.) Such a plan, depending as it does on fleeting contacts, leaves little time to reflect, to "comb out the language." Meaning recedes with the ebb of memory into "the sliding water." The *Autobiography,* only lightly edited, thus resembles the clumsy montage of a home movie.

Invoking Gertrude Stein as Williams does is misleading. The fluent structure of *The Autobiography of Alice B. Toklas* is built, like a Cubist painting, on the principle of two-dimensional planes: The surface is all. Stein rejected the unconscious more drastically, in theory and in practice, than Williams. By choosing Alice B. Toklas as narrator, she escaped the need of essaying introspection; her fiction allowed her to pretend she knew all worth knowing; self-knowledge and its acquisition was a Freudian sport or sham that simply bored her. Williams may emulate Stein in elevating perception to the leading role of his *Autobiography* (he was less dismissive of Freud), but he lacked her handy narrative ploy and self-assurance. Williams is more humble in claiming what he knows, and though he only raggedly seems to sense what goes on in himself, he pretends to care about depths as well as surfaces. Finally, the structure of the *Autobiography* is built on continuity-in-discontinuity, its form choppy, indefinite, spontaneous.

Williams's strategy is to knock the reader off balance. Sense impressions, ideas,[50] lyrical moments of discovery, especially of trees, flowers, and animals, the rough-and-tumble of boyhood games, caper across the page in rapid discursive sequences, much like Frank O'Hara's "I do this, I do that" method. Williams mistrusted the formality of the high style almost as much as he mistrusted ideological systems. His folksy idiom is therefore a prophylaxis against aesthetic preciosity. That is why to an interviewer questioning where he got his language, Williams quipped, "from the mouths of Polish mothers," (311) even though he was aware that Polish mothers, like poets, could fall into "the lying habits of everyday speech." (359) By casting his linguistic net wide and in popular streams, the poet may haul in unusual specimens along with much debris. "One uses what one finds," Williams argues in the *Autobiography,* whether that be a cigar stub to catch a trout (Paul Herman's angling trick), a solitary Christmas Day spent at the Bronx Zoo, or the "hunted news" (360) he gets from a sick patient's eyes and inarticulate speech.

Williams's faith in the vitality of an American vernacular is particularly noticeable in his chapters on childhood and growing up. He portrays himself as a Penrod or Tom Sawyer type getting into and out of scrapes, "squirting around" (6) in the fields like a colt—normal and not vicious. The older man recreates the boy's formative years with an amused geniality that he tinctures with just enough vitriol to keep the vignettes from slipping into sentimentality, and to show who and what roused his imagination, from Uncle Godwin's mostly harmless riddles, pranks, and poems to a hunter skinning a rabbit. The tone is percussive: Bam! Bam! like his very early memory of banging a drum in syncopation with his uncle Irving's beat. The colloquialisms that sprinkle Williams's style—"Wow," "bang out," "sound off," "Wham," "that's that," "no use"—are employed in the early chapters as examples of his playful assimilation of American slang,[51] and in the later chapters for the sudden closing of a story or speculation that generates more tension than he can bear, as though some inner warning system has been tripped off.

The *Autobiography* strings together hundreds of experiences and facts. Memories jump through the hoop at the wave of a baton. Williams is, by turns, self-interested, selfless, cantankerous, likable, wily, direct, infantile, mature. But the parts do not add up to the whole man, just a blurred facsimile. The problem is that while Williams's breezy style suits his fickle moods and the romance of casual perception, it cannot pull them together to achieve depth. What works for the relatively simple cellular structure of his imagistic poems and modest lyrics is inadequate for the complex physiology of an autobiography (or epic poem). "Invention," the imagination's transforming power, is for long stretches on holiday in the *Autobiography*. The Paris section, for example, has wonderful details that illuminate the expatriate crowd in Paris, but it relies too much on diary entries. Too impatient to recreate the past, Williams settles for eavesdropping on himself and scrawling a few comments in the margins of a sightseer's faded album. He makes only a cursory stab at getting behind the facts and understanding how and why he felt, acted, or thought as he did.

Williams's artifice of choosing copiously from the outside in order to complement a thin inside is mirrored in his syntax. Attuned to "the inevitable flux of the seeing eye," as he put it in *Spring and All,* he deliberately keeps his sentences and paragraphs short, briskly declarative, commonsensical. Few subordinate clauses put in an appearance to enter demurrers or qualifications; ideas are modified or contradicted after an interval of several sentences or in a later paragraph. However heterogeneous the autobiographical material, Williams's syntax frequently forecloses complexity. The upshot is not concision but prosiness.

The limits and strengths of Williams's anecdotal style may be seen in two distinct passages from the *Autobiography*. The first occurs in the chapter "Sour Grapes." Having just published a book by that title, Williams gives a sampling of readers' reactions:

> *"Sour Grapes!* Do you know what that means?" they said.
> "No. What does it mean?"
> "It means that you are frustrated. That you are bitter and disappointed. You are too . . . too . . . You don't really let yourself go. You think you are like the beautiful god, Pan. Ha, ha, ha, ha! The young Frenchmen, yes, they really let go. But you, you are an American. You are afraid" (this from the women and the men also) "you are afraid. You live in the suburbs, you even *like* it. What are you anyway? And you pretend to be a poet, a POET! Ha, ha, ha, ha! A poet! You!"
> I got it from all quarters: *"Sour Grapes*—that's what you are and that's what you amount to."
> But all I meant was that sour grapes are just the same shape as sweet ones.
>
> Ha, ha, ha, ha! (157–8)

This sketch builds skillfully to the comic timing of the last line. In short, staccato sentences—Williams's favorite stylistic device—the chorus of derision swells from fatuous psychiatrists to unnamed women and men, until it is heard from all quarters, like a universal judgment. The smug mob of critics, city slickers all, pounces viciously on the innocent poet, accusing him of pretentiousness, fear, and frustration. Each barbed exclamation point pierces his thin skin. The repetition of phrases and words turns the critics into a pack of children taunting an unlucky victim. Williams then turns on the bullies and gives himself the last, if slightly hysterical, laugh.

There is a malicious edge to Williams's laugh, as there is a core of truth in his clever retort that his uncomprehending critics miss. But Williams is on the defensive. The hollow peal of mirthless laughter, like that of a juvenile Mephistopheles, is still painful and raw to the reminiscing poet. The indictments leveled against him are those he leveled against himself. As the context for this story makes clear, Rutherford's ostracism of Pa Herman for pro-German sentiments during World War I, the publication of *The Waste Land,* and the death of Paul Herman in a gun accident all meant that "my year, my self was being slaughtered." Williams had solid reasons for feeling sour grapes, but his style characteristically distills the bitter anecdote and disguises it as a placebo whose medicinal qualities he has fully justified—then he hurries on to the next anecdote.[52]

The second passage is a long tirade:

> A first-rate show, for some charity or other, many distinguished people of all nationalities, the *haut monde* on all sides. The orchestra had struck! But after a long pause, things went on. The ballet *"Salade"** I liked well, but it might have been the girl who tried to dislocate her knees and elbows assuming the angular poses assigned to her. When I told H.D. I had enjoyed that one, she merely laughed in her cryptic and irritating way so much as to say "you would." "Gigue" also and the "Blue Danube" were excellent.
>
> I felt out of place, self-conscious and alone in that mob. My clothes were dull, my manners worse. The drink, as always, meant nothing, to me. Among the whole crowd of talents about me not a face was open, even among my own group. I saw women who seemed to want to open up, but the only one I felt anything for was that young girl taking the solo part in the ballet *"Salade."* Everyone else was closed, closed tight, with eyes like something under a submerged rock, waiting covertly to feed. From what I knew of even those in my own group, painfully in detail, the cupidity, the bitchery, the half-screaming hysteria, I wasn't attracted. It was a gelatinous mass, squatting over a treasure; a *Rheingold-musik*. Calculating bitches that they were, not only toward me, but toward each other, they were biding their time while the cash was worth their attention. By what I knew of their moves, the cheapness, the grimaces, even their manner of standing or sitting on a chair, I hated them. They revealed all too brilliantly (if one could read) how the hand was offered and food put to the mouth, foully enough among my own intimates; how then should one interpret the whole mass of dancing, laughing figures? They were completely indifferent, you might say, to the performance onstage as to me.

*"Salade" is doubtless a satirical send-up of the ballet *Parade*.

Their own lives and movements were (naturally) far more complex than the dancing and the music. Strain as she would, the little ballerina, break her bones even though she might in the grotesque routines, she could never equal what lay before her.

So that, in a sense, if I had known it, the indifference to both dance and music in this straining crowd of social automatons was justified. They looked and revealed nothing that I, at least, could see, though I judged (from what I did know in detail, accurately) that it was for sale to the highest bidder, as usual. At least they were here, they had come and it was worth it to them. The show on the stage was not serious: the success of the work presented depended on its ability to put that indifferent crowd in its place—art vs. society. This evening society was in the ascendant. No score for art.

Could these works be rescued, or something of them be rescued for use against a lesser intelligence? That's what the contest between new works of art and an alert *haut monde* means: The fight that goes on between the stage and the audience. For it is certain that though the onlookers appear indifferent, talk, turn their backs, they have eyes there too.

It is the cruel battle of wits that goes on in all cities and as between city and city. I was a rustic in my own eyes, completely uninitiated, but it is certain that though I was in no way affected by the well-dressed crowd, and it was the alert best of Paris, I ground my teeth out of resentment, though I acknowledged their privilege to step on my face if they could. Anyhow I was having a rotten time and I liked the little dancer. (215–6)

This scene would fit perfectly into any nineteenth-century novel that chronicles the efforts of an ambitious young man from the provinces to penetrate the world of high society, wealth, and art. Williams, the rank outsider, acutely aware of his social deficiencies, shabby dress, and plebeian manners, measures himself against the established order with its easy air of superiority and corrupt selfishness. He hates yet craves their insouciant sense of their own distinction. Once again in Williams's fantasy the rustic hero from New Jersey marches into battle, under the banner of democratic art, against the elite corps of European society. It is a war of perceptions, Williams's against the fabled Argus's, and the "uninitiated" soldier goes down to defeat.

What is remarkable about this passage, besides its prolixity, is how the myth of his own inferiority still rankles in Williams twenty-five years after the event. He nurses each alleged snub and insult, as if he were "squatting over a treasure." The style unconsciously abets his insecurity. The mostly short uncouth sentences crackle with immediacy as Williams strikes alternately at the "mob" of sophisticates, including his friends, and at himself. Provoked by H.D.'s sneer at his bad taste and by his inconspicuous presence, he reacts with the vituperative excess of a maddened satirist: The Paris avant-garde is reptilian, venal, decadent. Art is a commodity to them, like their bodies, that they coolly buy and sell, their morals as despicable as those of the dwarfs and giants in Wagner's opera seeking the *Rheingold* and its magical power of dominance. Where Williams is open, they are closed; where he vents his envy and hatred, they bury theirs behind impassive exteriors. Soon after, he certifies them all "dead, dead, dead."

But Williams lacks the satirist's style of absolute righteousness (he has misplaced his sense of humor too). The more he uses such locutions as "it is certain" and "from what I did know," only to contradict himself in the next clause or paragraph, the more he undermines his credibility. The surly anger of Williams's account of the spectacle would alone suffice to make the reader doubt him when he says, "I wasn't attracted" or "I was in no way affected by the well-dressed crowd." Why then grind your teeth in resentment? Why look uneasily over your shoulder at this hypocritical world's opinion of you? Why fear they will step on you? The awkward rhythms of his sentences belong to a distracted, not a confident, commentator. Moreover, elsewhere in his Paris diary, Williams harps on the point that he was constantly attracted to and affected by these very same women and men, who, far from treating him with contempt or indifference, admitted him to their charmed, snobbish circle.

Notwithstanding the comic deflation of Williams's curtain line, in which he bravely reasserts his fondness for "the little dancer," the panache of the entire passage suggests that he did not have "a rotten time." Why does this cryptic hostility crop up again and again in the *Autobiography?* If these Parisians are indeed moral monsters, a "gelatinous mass," why are they his friends? And most important of all, how aware is Williams of his many inconsistencies?

These questions are hard to answer, but we can draw some strong inferences from Williams's style and customary modes of judging himself and others. That he was no bumbling innocent, his shrewd citation of Wagner's *Rheingold* shows; he was a reasonably cultured, tolerably frustrated, highly competitive man. His nervous, darting style, like his innocence, served an invaluable psychic purpose: He could avoid fixed commitments and disclose his "punishable secrets" in an indirect fashion. Like a boxer, he bobs and weaves and jabs at a truth, takes a punch and backs away, then advances again.

Williams was also exorbitantly enamored of deception, of people who are not as they seem to be, like the beggar in Spain he sees nonchalantly changing from rags to a decent business suit. Early in the *Autobiography,* Williams warns the reader, "I was a liar and would always be one, *sauve qui peut!* lay low and raid the enemy when possible, but the heroic gesture itself was not for me, though I had glimpsed the peaks and should never forget them." (27) Like much else in the *Autobiography,* this is an exaggeration. All of Williams's statements must be weighed against his unconscious deceptions, and luckily he furnishes enough material to let the reader judge versions of reality for himself. Finally, though, Williams's love of surface effects, which lets him convey "the speed of emotions," renders him incapable of a disinterested analysis of the emotions. The *Autobiography* is a classic case of multiplicity drowning unity in its honey.

VI

"WHAT IS time but an impertinence?" Williams once asked. Each autobiographer must answer the question in his own way; that is his duty, prerogative, and challenge. Through the writer's art, time—the past—can be mastered. If the poet thinks with his poem, as Williams said, then the autobiographer thinks with his autobiography. This requires finding a new, contrapuntal idiom that will reveal the hidden dimensions of a man's and a culture's experience. Williams had fashioned that multifaceted language brilliantly in *In the*

American Grain and more problematically in *Paterson;* he had wrestled with it valiantly in all his works. There is evidence of the struggle in the rich messiness of fact and impression that comprises the *Autobiography.* Why is the book so erratic?

The last chapter provides an anecdote that is an emblem of the book. In the middle of winter, in the company of his friend John Husband and his grandson Paul, Williams takes a trip to the Passaic Falls, the site of his epic poem. Poet, town historian, friend, and family man converge in this symbol of continuity. To amuse Paul, Williams takes a chunk of ice and heaves it into the icy waters below, where it hits with an"explosive bang." He chats with Husband about Sam Patch who jumped into the falls as part of his circus act, m daring feat. "Quite a story, quite a story," Husband remarks. Paul, overhearing, asks, "How deep is the water? I mean at the deepest place?" (394)

To this question Williams had no reply.

8

"Arise, Ye Pris'ners of Starvation": Richard Wright's *Black Boy* and *American Hunger*

"You take a man dat's got on'y one er two chillen; is dat man gwyne to be waseful o' chillen? No, he ain't; he cain't 'ford it. He know how to value 'em. But you take a man dat's got 'bout five million chillen runnin roun' de house, en it's diffunt. He as soon chop a chile in two as a cat. Day's plenty mo'."

—MARK TWAIN, The Adventures of Huckleberry Finn

I

*R*ACIAL CONFLICT has caused a permanent fissure in the American mind, and black autobiographers living insecurely on its dangerous fault lines have recorded the seismic shocks assiduously. From the slave narratives of Frederick Douglass, Harriet Jacobs, and the Reverend James Pennington to Richard Wright's *Black Boy* and Maya Angelou's *I Know Why the Caged Bird Sings,* autobiography has been a favorite form of deposition by American blacks about their experiences as members of a community of the despised and their struggles to solve what Angelou calls "the humorless puzzle of inequality and hate."[1] In their encyclopedia of social wrongs, blacks chronicle pernicious racism, economic serfdom, lynchings, and, perhaps worst of all, the emotional lesions wrought by constant belittlement: Douglass quotes in his *Narrative* a common saw that white boys used to taunt him with, "that it was worth half a cent to kill a 'nigger,' and a half-cent to buy one."[2] Although a few black autobiographers have subscribed, as Zora Neale Hurston did in some moods, to the belief that "I did not have to consider any racial group as a whole, God made them duck by duck and that was the only way I could see them,"[3] most minority writers musing over their past cannot help probing the historical realities that pressed upon them daily as well as "the stress and strain inside";[4] often they were indivisible. In telling the stories of their lives, blacks have not enjoyed the luxury of merely tracing the discovery and practice of a vocation as diplomat or mystic, painter or astronomer. They were too busy improvising ways to escape the white minotaur gorging on black flesh. Almost always they felt compelled to speak out for those, timid or silent, trapped in ghettoes or on plantations.

Slave narratives, the first black autobiographies, share a common physiognomy. Witness after witness, like muralists collaborating on an epic fresco, lays bare with vivid physical imagery the horrors of slavery:[5] whippings, cold-blooded murder for trivial offenses (with no legal redress), rags for clothes and foul, meager rations for desperate hunger (Douglass describes a girl named Mary "contending with the pigs for the offal thrown into the streets"[6]), exhausting toil from sunup to sundown, and the routine breaking up of families by selling a father to the Deep South or separating mothers from their children.

Against the "mental darkness" and systemic pathology of racism blacks forged various weapons of survival: armed insurrection, crime, wily accommodation, fearless self-assertion. Black autobiographies thus offer remarkable portraits of men and women under siege who create dynamic identities despite social handicaps that would have stopped less resolute persons in their tracks. The dominant pattern in these autobiographies, following the Augustinian model, is a triumphant reversal—from slavery to freedom, ignorance to understanding, follower to leader, and, sometimes, criminality to spirituality. Douglass's *Narrative* and Malcolm X's *Autobiography,* for example, demonstrate the possibilities of change through self-education and the direct sublimation of militant, reasoned anger into concrete political criticism of repressive author-

Richard Wright, 1945

ity—slaveowners and complicit clergy in antebellum America, leaders of government and industry in the 1960s—and the therapy of
action. Both grew into masters of political agitation, awakening the
"dozing consciences"[7] of whites and the political will of blacks dormant because of fears of reprisal. Their tenacious intellects and quick
charm singled them out for special attention by blacks and, within
limits, by whites. (Malcolm X, relishing confrontation, gave his rash
impulses and gift for sarcasm free rein, frightening whites and bringing an avalanche of criticism down on his head, as in the famous
"chickens come home to roost" quip after John F. Kennedy's assassination. Douglass, equally blunt, ruled his anger with canny patience; sure that his convictions and experiences mattered, he neither
jeopardized his alliances with whites nor ceded his independent
judgment to them.)

At the poetic heart of many black autobiographies, as the writers
seek to define both their black and their American identities, is a
profound meditation on shattered families, finally on a society that
is, as Jim says to Huck, "waseful o' chillen." Douglass's threnody
for his grandmother, who, having served her "old master faithfully
from youth to old age," is turned out to die in "perfect loneliness,"
illustrates the "fiendish barbarity" which perverted the relations that
should govern a family and, by extension, a civilized society:

The hearth is desolate. The children, the unconscious children, who once sang and danced in her presence, are gone.
She gropes her way, in the darkness of age, for a drink of
water. Instead of the voices of her children, she hears by day
the moan of the dove, and by night the screams of the hideous owl. All is gloom. The grave is at the door. And now,
when the head inclines to the feet, when the beginning and
the end meet, and helpless infancy and painful old age com-
bine together—at this time, this most needful time, the time
for the exercise of that tenderness and affection which children only can exercise towards a declining parent—my poor
old grandmother, the devoted mother of twelve children, is
left all alone, in yonder little hut, before a few dim embers.
She stands—she sits—she staggers—she falls—she groans—
she dies—and there are none of her grandchildren present to
wipe from her wrinkled brow the cold sweat of death, or to

place beneath the sod her fallen remains. Will not a righteous God visit for these things?[8]

Douglass's homily, stately in its biblical cadences, exposes the "base ingratitude" of the slaveholders, unable to practice even the rudiments of Christian charity. His status as a slave deprives him of the chance to perform the sacred office of tending his aged grandmother on her deathbed or burying her. She, the one close and reliable kin of his childhood, had instilled in him self-worth and that very loyalty so alien to the slaveholders. Douglass can cross this abysmal distance only by elevating her, posthumously, into a pietà without mourners, showing at the same time the casual methodized pettiness of the slaveowners who cast her out to die alone. This moral cruelty is far worse than the ravages of old age. She is a victim who symbolizes the recurrence of perfidy and powerlessness in racial and class relations and a hideous reality calling for immediate remedy. The space allotted slaves was minuscule and confined, a condition particularly dreadful in a country in which available space for self-betterment seemed to radiate out temptingly in all directions. This portable freedom was enshrined in American democratic folklore like a hallowed, efficacious text, which Douglass imbibed along with the "powerful vindication of human rights"[9] he had read in *The Columbian Orator*. Although he was barred from succoring his grandmother in her stooped old age, Douglass was not another of the "unconscious" children. He vigorously asserts and proves by example that there are ways out of this brutal impasse—"a glorious resurrection, from the tomb of slavery, to the heaven of freedom."[10] Knowledge, a word he strokes every time he uses it, is one route he takes, and principled defiance is a second: He teaches reading and writing to slaves in the woods despite the owners' prohibition of it, and he flees from bondage.

For Richard Wright, as for Douglass, Malcolm X, and Hosea Hudson, life was a war on "history's bloody road"[11] and autobiography a series of dispatches from the front lines documenting the casualties, the heroism and cowardice, the uproar and reek of the battlefield. Wright's memories were haunted by the dilemma of black Americans that W. E. B. Du Bois described in *The Souls of Black Folk:* "One ever feels his twoness,—an American, a Negro; two souls, two thoughts, two unreconciled strivings; two warring ideals in one dark body, whose dogged strength alone keeps it from being torn asunder."[12] Wright's childhood and young manhood, recreated in *Black Boy* and *American Hunger*,[13] were scarred by similar excesses: hunger, rage, family disruption, "crossed-up feeling,"[14] (AH, 7) a claustrophobic religiosity whose grim theme of "cosmic annihilation" (97) he struggled against but never quite got rid of, and above all, by the pathology and riddle of white racism. As Wright remembers his past, his consciousness was always in a state of siege, his emotions and spirit lacerated by a flagellant conscience like that of a Dostoyevskyan hero.

Yet miraculously, in the soil of a harsh, warped, and isolated milieu, an artist germinated, and this successful novelist with his "fiercely indrawn nature" (AH, 21) presides over the forensic dissection of his past. Because the life of the imagination was of problematic value to the world in which Wright grew up, a world scrambling for subsistence, he was a renegade, an embarrassment, an anomaly. Whites dismissed with jeering incredulity his ambition to be a writer, while blacks kept a bewildered distance from him, as if he were crazy for making up stories out of his head. "The Voodoo of Hell's Half-Acre," Wright's early attempt at a story, was as obscure to his family and friends as his self was to the author of the story. (This pattern hounded him throughout his formative years as a writer.) Not surprisingly—and in this Wright differs from such black artists as Langston Hughes, Claude McKay, and Zora Neale Hurston—he flirts with the fiction that he created himself as a writer out of nothing, though he acknowledges his debt to a host of literary mentors for awakening his intellectual curiosity.

The central motif of *Black Boy* and *American Hunger* is hunger. The word and the sensation stalk him like an assassin, but besides hungering for food, affection, justice, and knowledge (education was a garden on whose grounds blacks were mostly forbidden to trespass), Wright yearned for words. Like many black autobiographers—Douglass, Hurston, Malcolm X, Booker T. Washington—Wright felt that words possessed magical properties, in particular the power of conferring identity and erasing the stigma of inferiority. Although black words counted for little in America, even had no legal status, words promised to be the most effective weapon against the white man's efforts to subjugate blacks: Words could help extinguish a tenacious evil.

Like most children, Wright learned slowly and by trial and error that words were ambiguous, indeed had a baffling life independent of his intentions. They could maim and draw blood or place him like a leper in moral quarantine; they could rouse in adults, both black and white, anger, consternation, misunderstanding. Words would suddenly rise from dark corners of his mind and shock and offend his family, as when he impishly asks his Granny Wilson to kiss his anus or when at age six he scrawls obscenities on walls, unaware what these crude words mean (a street arab, he picked them up in saloons and playgrounds). Even as an adolescent he tried to puzzle out why a word like "prejudice," which all his life stood for the hideous deformity of racism, could, when used by H. L. Mencken, denote the opposite: a daring truth-telling. (From Mencken, who debunked the smug opinions and bigotry of white Southerners and the "booboisie" everywhere, Wright learned that words could be used as weapons.) Growing up in an environment where racial fears virtually mandated verbal subterfuges, where forgetting to say "sir" or to inflect a sentence in a deferent pitch might result in a lynching, Wright tried to teach himself to pick his words carefully.

Words also exerted a seductive appeal to console and delight. Like a carapace, they protected his nascent individuality and fantasy life from daily rebuffs, and in stories offered a welcome reprieve from the eternal vigilance and self-censorship needed to survive in the South. Wright hoarded words as he stuffed crackers in his pocket: to safeguard himself against deprivation. If he could decipher the hieroglyphs of race, poverty, dread, and insecurity and invest words with all the timbres of his thwarted feelings (his dream), his singularity would at last be manifest to all (and be applauded). But his ambition was also to speak for the black masses, who, like the dogs in a Chicago hospital laboratory, vocal cords severed, could only raise a soundless wail of protest. That he could make words mean what he wanted them to gave him a sense of tremendous power and mastery: With the right combinations of words, he might change the world. After storming and knocking down the walls American society had built to imprison his mind, he would put his chronic hurt and rebellion at the service of other oppressed blacks. This desire for community, for solidarity with his brethren, was genuine, not an extravagant romance. But it often met with resentment or incomprehension, because Wright could not rid himself of a tinge of contempt for those he would lead to victory. And so he remained a misfit.

The artful arrangement of words also signified a full-fledged style to Wright, and the process of acquiring one was, as for most artists, long and arduous. Looking back at his childhood, in *Black Boy*, Wright employs a militant style that reflects the extreme tension of growing up in his untrustworthy environment. That is why *Black Boy* opens with a cataclysmic event: The four-year-old boy sets his house afire and is viciously whipped by his mother. Here is how Wright describes the aftermath of that unintended act:

> I was lashed so hard and long that I lost consciousness; I was beaten out of my senses and later I found myself in bed, screaming, determined to run away, tussling with my mother and father who were trying to keep me still. I was lost in a fog of fear. A doctor was called—I was afterwards told—and he ordered that I be kept abed, that I be kept quiet, that my very life depended upon it. My body seemed on fire and I could not sleep. Packs of ice were put on my forehead to keep down the fever. Whenever I tried to sleep I would see huge wobbly white bags, like the full udders of cows, suspended from the ceiling above me. Later, as I grew worse, I could see the bags in the daytime with my eyes open and I was gripped by the fear that they were going to fall and drench me with some horrible liquid. Day and night I begged my mother and father to take the bags away, pointing to them, shaking with terror because no one saw them but me. Exhaustion would make me drift toward sleep and then I would scream until I was wide awake again; I was afraid to sleep. Time finally bore me away from the dangerous bags and I got well. But for a long time I was chastened whenever I remembered that my mother had come close to killing me. (6)

Wright takes the child's point of view, sketching his sensations and hyperactive fantasies with harrowing precision. There is a terrifying automatism to the brutal punishment his mother metes out to her son here (and elsewhere) in *Black Boy,* the product of some deep silent fury or frustration; Wright does not speculate on her reasons, as if they were beside the point. (Ralph Ellison has pointed out that "a homeopathic dose of the violence generated by black and white relationships . . . [was] administered for the child's own good,"[15] even if it obliged the mother to corrupt her nurturing instincts.) The style of this passage enacts the alternating rhythm of agitation and exhaustion, of fear and numbed hysteria, that accompanies Wright with every intake of breath in *Black Boy*. The passive voice controlling this description underscores the pathos of the child as victim; the regularity of the subject-verb construction hems in and intensifies the hallucinatory terror that seizes the boy; the patterned series of participles and clauses imposes an eerie order on an unnatural perversion of the parent-child bond. In language that is highly charged and febrile, the fire that burned down his house is transferred first to his own body and then to his nightmare. During Wright's delirium, the mother's milk of kindness and sustenance turns into a contaminating fluid, which might scald, poison, or drown him. Like a suppliant whose appeals for mercy and help are met by his captors' stony mien, Wright succumbs to an inconsolable anguish. The adults do not see his apparitions, cannot interpret his language or relieve his overstrained mind: Only time does that. The voice of the hurt child pierces the stoical demeanor of the autobiographer reliving the trauma of the charred rooms and his incendiary act.

"The house," Gaston Bachelard remarks in *The Poetics of Space*, "shelters day-dreaming, . . . allows one to dream in peace."[16] We become attached to a house for the "well-being it encloses," the stability and "protected intimacy"[17] it confers. But Wright seldom enjoyed such privileged solitude. His family lived in a succession of cramped and squalid tenements, in which domestic strife, not peace, flourished—and lurid, neurotic fantasies that drove him into deeper apartness (in Clarksville, sleeping in a dead child's bed so scares and unnerves him that he cannot shut his eyes and resists his uncle's rational explanations and pleas). Burning down his own house suggests irrational impulses, a rage so strong it cannot be suppressed; even play can unexpectedly grow out of control and nearly consume him. No adult guides him. What Erik Erikson calls "trust born of care,"[18] those circumstances that permit a child to pass, protected, through crucial periods of the life cycle, failed to reach Wright. He came to understand how the triple burdens of racism, poverty, and class destroy families, but in *Black Boy* he depicts his family as if it were the House of Atreus, its sins not to be forgiven. Yet even in their pinched and circumscribed selves, even when they are prisoners of degradation, ignorance, or casual cruelty, his family have an unforgettable physical and moral aura.

Here is the boy's early image of his father:

> I used to lurk timidly in the kitchen doorway and watch his huge body slumped at the table. I stared at him with awe as he gulped his beer from a tin bucket, as he ate long and heavily, sighed, belched, closed his eyes to nod on a stuffed belly. He was quite fat and his bloated stomach always lapped over his belt. He was always a stranger to me, always somehow alien and remote. (9)

This might be a drawing of Gluttony, in an allegory of the Seven Deadly Sins, caught at a moment of stupefying and repulsive satiety, or a George Grosz cartoon of a foul, grotesque bourgeois. The concrete words "slumped," "belched," "stuffed," "bloated," and "lapped" portray the father as an animal grossly feeding. The timid child stares at the oversized man, like Gulliver in Brobdingnag, disgusted by what he sees, every flaw writ large. Since Wright associates hunger with his father, this tableau of mindless debauchery is a profound indictment: His father is guilty of selfish unrestraint, of ignoring the clamor of his dependent children's empty bellies. We are not surprised that soon after, Mr. Wright deserts his family, thereby pitching them into a "sea of senselessness." (AH, 7)

The vehemence of Wright's disparagement of black culture for not nourishing the passional and intellectual lives of its children can perhaps be traced to his father's conduct. At the end of Chapter 1, Wright deliberately breaks narrative chronology and interpolates a long passage about a visit he took to the Mississippi Delta twenty-five years after his last glimpse of his father:

> A quarter of a century was to elapse between the time when I saw my father sitting with the strange woman and the time when I was to see him again, standing alone upon the red clay of a Mississippi plantation, a sharecropper, clad in

ragged overalls, holding a muddy hoe in his gnarled, veined hands—a quarter of a century during which my mind and consciousness had become so greatly and violently altered that when I tried to talk to him I realized that, though ties of blood made us kin, though I could see a shadow of my face in his face, though there was an echo of my voice in his voice, we were forever strangers, speaking a different language, living on different planes of reality. That day a quarter of a century later when I visited him on the plantation—he was standing against the sky, smiling toothlessly, his hair whitened, his body bent, his eyes glazed with dim recollection, his fearsome aspect of twenty-five years ago gone forever from him—I was overwhelmed to realize that he could never understand me or the scalding experiences that had swept me beyond his life and into an area of living that he could never know. I stood before him, poised, my mind aching as it embraced the simple nakedness of his life, feeling how completely his soul was imprisoned by the slow flow of the seasons, by wind and rain and sun, how fastened were his memories to a crude and raw past, how chained were his actions and emotions to the direct, animalistic impulses of his withering body. . . .

From the white landowners above him there had not been handed to him a chance to learn the meaning of loyalty, of sentiment, of tradition. Joy was as unknown to him as despair. As a creature of the earth, he endured, hearty, whole, seemingly indestructible, with no regrets and no hope. He asked easy, drawling questions about me, his other son, his wife, and he laughed, amused, when I informed him of their destinies. I forgave him and pitied him as my eyes looked past him to the unpainted wooden shack. From far beyond the horizons that bound this bleak plantation there had come to me through my living the knowledge that my father was a black peasant who had gone to the city seeking life, but who had failed in the city; a black peasant whose life had been hopelessly snarled in the city; and who had at last fled the city—that same city which had lifted me in its burning arms and borne me toward alien and undreamed-of shores of knowing. (30–1)

On first reading, Wright's father—he's never given his first name—seems to be posing for a genre painting as The Black Man with His Hoe, an example of how rural poverty grinds down and stunts black sharecroppers. His father is again (or still) a creature of appetite, shackled to the body and earth, the verbs "imprisoned," "fastened," and "chained" allowing him only a few square inches to move in. The gulf between the two men is immense, and nothing marks it so much as Wright's style. The father, an animal without awareness, is so unskilled he cannot even describe his own plight; the son is sophisticated and self-conscious, stiff and formal from his tension, but commanding the art to render and encompass their different lives.

Like a judge applying impersonal principles of law to the prisoner standing before him in the dock, Wright weighs his father's transgressions and finds him culpable. Wright's icy words of charity deny kinship as a mitigating factor. The closest he comes to embracing his father is with his mind's ache, not his heart's. They are still strangers. For a moment in this reverie, Wright's eye looks past his father's shambling figure to the dilapidated shack that is a palpable symbol of failure and grudgingly concedes that the racism of the white landholders cheated his father of his ethical birthright, his chance to learn and practice loyalty, that the primal victimizer was himself a hapless victim of systematic economic peonage. But his father's "easy, drawling" tone and hollow laugh, contrasting as they do with Wright's coiled, refined, and reserved speech, are audible tokens of their estrangement. In fact, the steely control of Wright's prose, its aloof style, checks the autobiographer's memories of a "crude and raw past" so they won't engulf him.

Though he speaks of his father in the manner of a minister at the gravesite of a man he doesn't know well, by lapsing into passive constructions Wright hints that he, too, was "swept" by historical forces: "there had come to me . . . ." Like his father, he had fled the red-clay country to better himself in the city; he had nearly failed there, but the city had become his foster father, lifting him in its sheltering arms above the feckless and earthbound destiny of his peasant father. Yet the embrace of the final image is equivocal and menacing: The fire of mystical exaltation and creativity, like the fire that opens the book, sets him apart in a state of "organic loneliness." Paradoxically, his father is "whole," Wright divided. Mr. Wright disappears from Black Boy, though not from his son's mind.[19]

By contrast, Wright portrays his mother with taciturn affection, as though reluctant to accuse her of the betrayal of maternal care he cannot forget or quite forgive. An intelligent, pensive, bookish woman of frail health, Ella Wilson Wright was brought up in a poor but genteel household and trained to be a schoolteacher, but after her marriage to Richard Nathan Wright, a farmer of poor soil, she gave up teaching. Her choice of husband was unsuitable—and disastrous. Perhaps this rough, sexual man, who shared none of her interests or manners, represented an escape from the prim respectability and dour faith of the Wilsons (Wright does not speculate). After her husband's desertion of his family, she tried bravely to support her two sons, but her guardianship became sporadic, then stolidly harsh, and finally prostrate. When she cannot feed her hungry children, she snarls and claws like a cornered animal, or turns the worst situation into an occasion for mocking laughter:

> "Mama, I'm hungry," I complained one afternoon.
> "Jump up and katch a kungry,"[20] she said, trying to make me laugh and forget.
> "What's a *kungry?*"
> "It's what little boys eat when they get hungry," she said.
> "What does it taste like?"
> "I don't know."
> "Then why do you tell me to catch one?"
> "Because you said that you were hungry," she said, smiling. (13)

Like a hapless bystander of her own fate, she puts the boys in an orphanage, a pestilential house of detention run by the "tall, gaunt" witchlike Miss Simon, from whom Richard flees in vain (he is returned by the police).[21]

When a series of strokes left Ella bedridden for months, Wright had to watch her suffer and receive wretched medical care: The South allowed no infractions of its segregated rules even in matters of life and death. His mother's prolonged ordeal became for Wright, as *his* mother's madness became for Malcolm X, a personal loss and grievance that was gradually enlarged into a humiliating symbol of the Negro's degraded status in America; and it engendered a resolve to strike back at the dread white phantom on behalf of the meek and disinherited black masses. Malcolm could reach them as Wright never could, because his years as a flamboyant hustler and criminal gave him the insider's expertise about the ghetto mind. A brilliant orator and debater, Malcolm throve on the uproar his polemics and preaching aroused (he talked as he lindy-hopped, with a mesmerizing theatricality); public notoriety and incessant action were therapeutic. But though Wright shared Malcolm's search for a system of perfection based on racial equity, he was essentially a mistrustful introvert, an evangelist of indirection, whose instincts as a writer drove him into a kind of private exile.

Wright recalls his convictions at age twelve:

> My mother's suffering grew into a symbol in my mind, gathering to itself all the poverty, the ignorance, the helplessness; the painful, baffling, hunger-ridden days and hours; the restless moving, the futile seeking, the uncertainty, the fear, the dread; the meaningless pain and the endless suffering. Her life set the emotional tone of my life, colored the men and women I was to meet in the future, conditioned my relations to events that I had yet to face. A somberness of spirit that I was never to lose settled over me during the slow years of my mother's unrelieved suffering, a somberness that was to make me stand apart and look upon excessive joy with suspicion, that was to make me self-conscious, that was to make me keep forever on the move, as though to escape a nameless fate seeking to overtake me. (87)

In Wright's methodical self-analysis and litany of abstract nouns can be detected the bedrock of his determinism (the antithesis of his declared self-creation). Each reiteration of the clause "that was to make me" is a blow that manacles his character. The gloomy parallelism of Wright's syntax, with its slow accretion of modifiers, imbues this passage with the impressive sobriety of a prisoner, condemned to die, taking stock of his life and expecting at every moment the executioner's tread outside his cell. Because this is not a time for cosseting illusions, the prose is without glamour or flair. Wright resigns himself, retrospectively, to a fixity of character.

The dry philosophical tone of Wright's accounting should not let us miss his close identification with his mother.[22] As a boy, he internalized her paralysis by becoming tongue-tied in school, an odd affliction for a future writer, or by blanking out all thoughts in tense situations. Despite such statements as "I knew that my mother had gone out of my life; I could feel it" and "That night I ceased to react to my mother; my feelings were frozen," (87) Wright obviously could not maintain that detachment, that amnesia. In the early chapters of *Black Boy,* Ella tutors Richard in the dual code of the streets, taunting him to fight with his fists against other black boys but "never, under any conditions, to fight white folks again"; her "Jim Crow wisdom,"[23] Wright sarcastically calls it in "The Ethics of Jim Crow," an early autobiographical sketch. She snappishly fends off his pesky questions about black-white relations as if trying to postpone indefinitely a grim day of reckoning and conflict.

What Ella does teach him is, in the words of the dedication to *Native Son,* "to revere the fanciful and imaginative." When Richard importuned her to show him how to read, she complied. And despite her being a part-time parent, she managed to instill in her son some self-esteem and tenacity of will. In her condition of ailing dependency she envies his breaking the draconian rules of Granny's house (her most assertive act is to join the Methodist Church, a blow to her mother's Seventh-Day Adventism).[24] Ella's unsteady mothering and invalidism left Wright with a permanent suspicion of women as weak creatures. During the approximately thirty-five years of his life covered by *Black Boy* and *American Hunger,* he entered into no intimacy with a woman, avoiding emotional complication and choosing only transient sexual partners.[25] In Memphis, when he rents a room from Mrs. Moss, who showers him with food and "simple, unaffected trust" and offers him her daughter Bess in marriage and her house, he is perplexed by her honeyed generosity and lack of unappeasable longings. At seventeen, his beleaguered childhood ended, Wright begins his quest for a creed, a vocation, which can redeem his mother's—and his own—"endless suffering." His final words of parting, though laconic, vibrate with tremulous guilt:

> "Mama, I'm going away," I whispered.
> "Oh, no," she protested.
> "I've got to, mama. I can't live this way."
> "You've not run away from something you've done?"
> "I'll send for you, mama. I'll be all right."

"Take care of yourself. And send for me quickly. I'm not happy here," she said. (181)

Historically, the black family has reacted to crisis by extending its protection to its abandoned children. As dutiful Christians, the Wilson family took Richard in as an act of charity, but Granny's house was the worst possible place for a nervous, dreamy boy. She dominated the household with unchallenged authority, the matriarch as Medusa. A fanatic Adventist whose cosmology was ruled by a jealous, punitive God, devils ready to work their evil, and an imminent apocalypse, which would sweep sinners into hell, she judged her wayward grandson's deeds with an absolute righteousness. She burned Richard's books because they were "the Devil's work," and she once "smashed the crystal radio he had made with outstanding ingenuity simply because she would not admit that the music coming out of it had a natural origin."[26]

Wright could not conform to a regime both strict and stingy. The daily fare of mush made from flour and lard, and a plate of greens, was, like the steady diet of bleak piety, impossible to swallow. So he blundered, broke taboos, could not keep up the pretense of worshiping his granny's angry God. He was an outlaw, a devil menacing the pious:

My position in the household was a delicate one; I was a minor, an uninvited dependent, a blood relative who professed no salvation and whose soul stood in mortal peril. Granny intimated boldly, basing her logic on God's justice, that one sinful person in a household could bring down the wrath of God upon the entire establishment, damning both the innocent and the guilty, and on more than one occasion she interpreted my mother's long illness as the result of my faithlessness. I became skilled in ignoring these cosmic threats and developed a callousness toward all metaphysical preachments. (90)

Against "cosmic threats" Wright might harden himself, but against the emotional blackmail that blamed him for his mother's suffering his spirit was helpless. It was another instance of the vast, mysterious injustice that proved his family misunderstood *his* wants. Of a

high-strung temperament, Wright experimented with multiple defenses: He withdrew into fantasy, furtively reading the delectable
forbidden stories; or unconscious protest, such as sleepwalking; or
mild delinquency. When in two separate incidents his aunt Addie
and uncle Tom assault him, Wright defends himself with violent
weapons (a knife and a razor blade) and wins a measure of respect.
Although his family, except for his mother, condemned and ostra-
cized him, he persisted in believing that he would achieve distinction
by relying solely on his native wit.

There is a precocious heroism in this plan, for as Wright remarks
in *Black Boy*, "Already my personality was lopsided; my knowledge
of feeling was far greater than my knowledge of fact." (107) With
the maturity of hindsight, the autobiographer in *Black Boy* brings
the two in balance, but the tension invests the book with its poetry;
the successful novelist has not lost touch with the wounded child.
And while he disdainfully rejects his family because "they were
chained by their environment and could imagine no other," that
clannish environment gave him the strength to mobilize his bruised
feelings and "deadlocking tensions."[27] He resisted coercion, servility,
inertia. Granny's looks did not turn him to stone. He did not perish.
Indeed, he inherited her discipline and fierce love of order, even her
tragic view of life, and on the wreckage of those early foundations
built his art. If he discarded her eschatology, he accepted her idea
of a friendless universe that might still embrace the principle of ultimate justice. Through the medium of art he could subvert tyrannical authority:

> It was possible that the sweetly sonorous hymns stimulated
> me sexually, and it might have been that my fleshly fantasies,
> in turn, having as their foundation my already inflated sen-
> sibility, made me love the masochistic prayers. It was highly
> likely that the serpent of sin that nosed about the chambers
> of my heart was lashed to hunger by hymns as well as dreams,
> each reciprocally feeding the other. The church's spiritual life
> must have been polluted by my base yearnings, by the leaping
> hunger of my blood for the flesh, because I would gaze at the
> elder's wife for hours, attempting to draw her eyes to mine,
> trying to hypnotize her, seeking to communicate with her
> with my thoughts. If my thoughts had been converted into a

concrete religious symbol, the symbol would have looked
something like this: a black imp with two horns; a long, curv-
ing, forked tail; cloven hoofs, a scaly, naked body; wet, sticky
fingers; moist sensual lips; and lascivious eyes feasting upon
the face of the elder's wife. (98)

Wright views with humor the faintly ridiculous figure he cut as an
infatuated young man, the thrill of the forbidden, the innocent sac-
rilege. Topics and sensations, like hunger, that before lashed him
with an accusatory tension here furnish an occasion for mild mockery. Under the austere eye of his granny and with the hymns of the
church as accessories, Wright turns into the very devil she has ful-
minated against. Wright embroiders the image of the serpent gaily
and playfully: The serpent is a friendly seducer gliding sinuously
through the garden of Wright's erotic fantasy, the elder's wife an
unsuspecting Eve, who does not yield to his temptations. Though
his hypnosis fails, for a few rare moments in *Black Boy,* Wright's
hunger is quelled, the "sweetly sonorous" language and his own
verbal imagery a sufficient feast to satisfy the flesh.

II

FROM EARLY childhood, the enigma of race disquieted Wright.
News of racial violence, of being caught by the "white death," first
reached him in the form of rumors of a monster, flashes of painful
light (the lynching of his uncle Hoskins because whites coveted his
thriving saloon), glimpses of a chain gang, hurried consultations and
midnight flights, tense whispers, weepings—and a fear whose presence was not the less awful for being unnamed.[28] In his earnest
naïveté, Wright thought the white father had a right to severely beat
the black child without being held accountable. The danger of violence, which even a chance innocuous remark might ignite, was the
more appalling for being routine: Police drew their guns on a young
black delivery boy in a white neighborhood, drunk joyriders
knocked Richard off the running board and kicked him simply for
the sadistic sport. Death lay in ambush everywhere.

But there were modes of racism as pernicious as these crude
redneck acts. For the status of black inferiority was institutionalized

in rigid law and enforced by custom. To the whites, as to the slave-owners before them, blacks were scarcely more than chattel or animals, to be taunted, manipulated, humiliated at will, and kept in their place at the bottom of society. Crossing the color line was an offense seldom tolerated and often severely punished both by the white majority and by the victimized black adult. For black parents, prudence dictated teaching their children to hide any evidence that they had private thoughts and ambitions; survival required self-control. The psychological toll was immense: rage directed at the self or blindly at other blacks, feelings of powerlessness and vengeance. To watch a black woman bloodied by a white shopkeeper for falling behind in paying her bill and to feel helpless to intervene, as Wright did, led to a deep sense of shame, self-hatred, and futility.

Though reared to do so, Wright could not adapt to the strain of shrinking into himself or turning his cheek to every insult and racial epithet aimed at him. He could not cringe or develop a "delicate, sensitive controlling mechanism that shut off [other black boys'] minds and emotions from all that the white race had said was taboo," (172) "any topic calling for positive knowledge or manly self-assertion on the part of the Negro." (202) When he was driven off a job and deprived of a chance to learn the optical trade, he felt that "he had been slapped out of the human race." (167) Wright learned the limited repertoire of roles available to blacks in the South (assigned and stage managed by whites), but he balked at playing them:

> In me was shaping a yearning for a kind of consciousness, a mode of being that the way of life about me had said could not be, and upon which the penalty of death had been placed. Somewhere in the dead of the southern night my life had switched onto the wrong track and, without my knowing it, the locomotive of my heart was rushing down a dangerously steep slope, heading for a collision, heedless of the warning red lights that blinked all about me, the sirens and the bells and the screams that filled the air. (148)

The prose, like the train, gets under way slowly, picks up speed, and then hurtles to a perilous crack-up. Wright savors the thrill of being out of control (there is no "I" at the throttle), of movement rather than stasis.

Black Boy capitalizes on the abnormal discords of his child-hood, which haunted his mind as proof of an omnipresent white malignity, against which he engraved on the tablets of his home-made law the words Resistance and Confrontation. This mood of surly defiance was a liability in his contacts with the white world, but it also set him uneasily apart from the majority of blacks. Wright deplores "the strange absence of real kindness in Negroes, how un-stable was our tenderness, . . . how bare our traditions," (33) carps at the prim, materialistic values of the black bourgeoisie (a small group) and the insipid, "will-less" pupils of Aunt Addie's religious school. In rejecting the fellowship of the black community because he believed it acquiesced too cravenly in its own subjection, Wright overstates the passivity and shallowness of black life.[29] He deliber-ately suppresses mention of those blacks who encouraged him.[30] Thus, in *Black Boy,* there is a dearth of competent black adults on whom the boy can model himself.[31] A milkman takes the time to teach Richard how to count; a newspaper editor good-naturedly explains the process of setting Wright's story into type; and a third man patiently points out that the tabloid the adolescent Wright was peddling to earn money was a Ku Klux Klan hate-mongering sheet (Wright devoured the pulp fiction serialized in its pages). More typical is his memory of roaming the streets, unsupervised, at age six, hungry and inquisitive, begging pennies from the patrons of a saloon:

> One summer afternoon—in my sixth year—while peering under the swinging doors of the neighborhood saloon, a black man caught hold of my arm and dragged me into its smoky and noisy depths. The odor of alcohol stung my nostrils. I yelled and struggled, trying to break free of him, afraid of the staring crowd of men and women, but he would not let me go. He lifted me and sat me upon the counter, put his hat upon my head and ordered a drink for me. The tipsy men and women yelled with delight. Somebody tried to jam a ci-gar into my mouth, but I twisted out of the way.
>
> "How do you feel setting there like a man, boy?" a man asked.
>
> "Make 'im drink and he'll stop peeping in here," some-body said.

"Let's buy 'im drinks," somebody said.

Some of my fright left as I stared about. Whisky was set
before me.

"Drink it, boy," somebody said.

I shook my head. The man who dragged me in urged me
to drink it, telling me it would not hurt me. I refused.

"Drink it; it'll make you feel good," he said.

I took a sip and coughed. The men and women laughed.
The entire crowd in the saloon gathered about me now, urg-
ing me to drink. I took another sip. Then another. My head
spun and I laughed. I was put on the floor and I ran giggling
and shouting among the yelling crowd. As I would pass each
man, I would take a sip from an offered glass. Soon I was
drunk. (18)

When he is pulled into the saloon with its odd smells and sounds,
the enchanted lair contains a beast: The mascot becomes the object
of the drunken crowd's thoughtless merriment. Putting an adult hat
on a child's head and sticking a cigar in his mouth are roughhouse
amusements that abuse the child's vulnerability and his hunger for
attention from people who might enjoy and pet him. Making him
drunk is pure sadism. The child's giggling behavior—he soon whispers obscenities into women's ears—pushes him into an adult role
he is incapable of acting, which is shown in the incongruous line,
"How do you feel setting there like a man, boy?" while the tipsy
men and women turn into irresponsible children. Wright offers no
commentary, no judgment. Since he cannot reconstruct the dialogue
literally, he embellishes the scene dramatically, negotiating the fine
line between "his younger self" and the autobiographer's memory.
He practices, in short, the art of autobiography, which entails a
subtle interplay of fact and imagination.

One of Wright's major goals in *Black Boy* is to shatter the stereotyped image of the "happy Negro" and to carefully distance himself from the defensive behavior and talk of the black boys he meets.
The most popular subject at lunch-hour meetings in the basement
of an office building in Memphis was "the ways of white folks toward Negroes," (206) "which formed the core of life for us." (200)
Their masks of smiling docility temporarily doffed, the black elevator operators and porters talked obsessively about whites, as of

cruel but remote gods who with impunity galled and controlled their lives; each slur, vicious caprice, and murder, each instance of being confined in economic serfdom, was entered into their ledger of stinging wrongs. Like an anthropologist studying an African tribe's cosmology, kinship system, rituals, jokes, and language, Wright jots down the data and his tentative analysis. He offers a rich sampling of the strategies of forgetting or numbing daily miseries, of blandly dissembling true feelings: curses, whiskey, "sex stories," numbers games, or the scatological humor of a piece of doggerel which barely contains the speaker's anger: "All these white folks dressed so fine/Their ass-holes smell just like mine . . ." (162)

Like the petty thievery that whites encouraged because it made them "feel safe and superior," (175) any defense that reduced blacks to infantilism disgusted and infuriated Wright, even when it was calculated and performed with the split-second timing of an artist. He tried to fathom how Shorty, an intelligent black man, could stoop to being kicked in the ass by a white man for the sake of a quarter. Shorty

> had tiny, beady eyes that looked out between rolls of flesh with a hard but humorous stare. He had the complexion of a Chinese, a short forehead, and three chins. Psychologically he was the most amazing specimen of the southern Negro I had ever met. Hardheaded, sensible, a reader of magazines and books, he was proud of his race and indignant about its wrongs. But in the presence of whites he would play the role of a clown of the most debased and degraded type. (198)

Shorty's patter and willingness to clown like a monkey on a string just to wheedle a pittance out of his enemy fascinated Wright by its perverse showmanship and repelled him by its masochism. When he once ventured to protest to Shorty, the following colloquy took place:

> "How in God's name can you do that?"
> "I needed a quarter and I got it," he said soberly, proudly.
> "But a quarter can't pay you for what he did to you," I said.
> "Listen, nigger," he said to me, "my ass is tough and quarters is scarce."[32] (200)

Though he recognizes that Shorty's role-playing was, in an oblique fashion, a way of manipulating the white man, of mitigating a position of weakness, Wright feels that it is unclean, like a whore offering her body for pay, and dehumanizing. He had refused a nickel from his father because it was tainted money, a bribe that would corrupt his integrity. (Later, for similar reasons, Wright would spurn a white man's offer of a dollar to buy food and the Communist party's offer that he drop his writing and go to Switzerland as a delegate to an international conference.)

The "gross environment" of the South exacted a heavy penalty from its black children, in ignorance, marginality, inertia, an idle or a paltry future. For Wright, a society that dictated such ignominious terms and separated blacks "by a vast psychological distance from the significant processes" (AH, 59) of life rested on the same demeaning principles as the slave auction. It forced even Wright with his stern conscience to violate his moral code, to lie and steal small sums of money for his flight to the North. A stubborn drive whose origins Wright broods over but never quite identifies pushes him to run away to the hazardous liberty of Chicago, with nothing to steer by but the dim North Star of self-direction. It was simply a question, he said, of his soul's life or death, of learning "who I was, what I might be," of not accepting white definitions. Uncertain whether to believe in the possibilities of change or in a tragic fixed character and fate, Wright leaves the South, dragging southern culture and its insidious discriminations with him like a ball and chain. He refuses to drug pain with illusions. And though his leave-taking is not the romantic rejection of Joyce's Daedalian artificer, he does half dare to put his faith in the power of his imagination to redeem his sufferings.

Books roused his imagination and became what the Emancipation Proclamation was for the masses of blacks: a "gateway to the world." (113) "Reading was like a drug, a dope," (219) which lifted him up and cast him down. The walls of prejudice had not tumbled at the trumpet call of a Mencken or a Dreiser; Jim Crow laws and the "white censor" still stood over him, barring the way to full identity. Arming himself with a new weapon, words, which he could eventually deploy in an insurrection testing the adamantine strength of those who oppressed blacks, exhilarated Wright, but he "carried a secret, criminal burden about with me each day." (221)

As a portrait of the black artist as a young man, *Black Boy* is unusual in presenting both raw experience and its refinement by a reflective imagination. The child who excitedly transformed a chain gang into a herd of elephants is and is not removed by time from the mature artist. Shearing off his childhood from the narrative of his artistic evolution, as Claude McKay had done in his autobiography,[33] would have meant for Wright an act of unthinkable repudiation. In descending into the hell of his past, Wright joins memory to his literary intelligence to display his mastery of the novelist's art. In contrast to the discursive autobiographies of McKay and Langston Hughes, *Black Boy* is intensely *composed*. Wright's first crude story had only atmosphere and a vague longing for death to recommend it, he recalls, and when he read it to a black girl she was confounded by it. That incomprehension thrilled him because it certified his own superiority, as if he had been anointed for a prophetic role, which remained hidden from those walking the streets on humdrum errands. He would cultivate his mind; he would study each gesture of whites and blacks; he would overcome the fits of shyness that rendered him unable to speak his own name; he would persevere.

He did. And the imagination is as much his instrument of control in *Black Boy,* his moral center, as his blackness is his destiny. Thus, despite his disparaging comments about the thinness of black culture, Wright continually draws on black folk tradition for stylistic variety: proverbs, coarse jokes and verses, pulpit rhetoric, and the blues.[34] (When as a boy Wright lived in a tenement near the railroad yards, he would climb into the engineer's seat and dream of bringing passengers safely to their homes. This fantasy of power and social responsibility, of mobility and freedom, a major theme of the blues, was denied by white racism, which restricted blacks to jobs as porters and waiters—both Claude McKay and Malcolm X held such jobs—and to riding in Jim Crow cars.) And in an extended section, Wright reproduces the street-corner banter known as the dozens, that spontaneous and bawdy verbal dueling in which attitudes, emotions, and dreams are aired and tested and in which insult, boasting, and homely philosophizing blend in a vernacular wit:

> "Hey." Timidly.
> "You eat yet?" Uneasily trying to make conversation.
> "Yeah, man, I done really fed my face." Casually.

"I had cabbage and potatoes." Confidently.

"I had buttermilk and black-eyed peas." Meekly informational.

"Hell, I ain't gonna stand near you, nigger!" Pronouncement.

"How come?" Feigned innocence.

"Cause you gonna smell up this air in a minute!" A shouted accusation. . . .

"Yeah, when them black-eyed peas tell the buttermilk to move over, that buttermilk ain't gonna wanna move and there's gonna be war in your guts and your stomach's gonna swell up and bust!" Climax.

"Man, you reckon these white folks is ever gonna change?" Timid, questioning hope.

"Hell, no! They just born that way." Rejecting hope for fear that it could never come true.

"Man, what makes white folks so mean?" Returning to grapple with the old problem.

"Whenever I see one I spit." Emotional rejection of whites.

"Man, ain't they ugly?" Increased emotional rejection. . . .

"They say we stink. But my ma says white folks smell like dead folks." Wishing the enemy was dead.

"Niggers smell from sweat. But white folks smell *all* the time." The enemy is an animal to be killed on sight. (68–71)

In revisiting this moment on the threshold of manhood, Wright links himself warily to his past. He had shared the code and comradeship of teenage gangs; the preoccupation with white bigotry and its crushing of the aspirations of black boys everywhere; the jokes about food, which still strike a tender nerve. Aesthetic distance does not immunize him from old pains. But by stylizing the swiftly moving talk and like a folklorist providing captions for an audience of outsiders, he pulls back disdainfully from the timid questions of these black boys. The phrase "Emotional rejection of whites" places Wright above the fray. Where they are trapped, he has access to different kinds of language and can consciously choose styles and discard them as the situation warrants. This is a precious but estranging liberty.

A similar motive underlies the set pieces Wright intersperses in the first five chapters of *Black Boy*. Each list appears immediately after an especially torturous ordeal:

> There was the delight I caught in seeing long straight rows of red and green vegetables stretching away in the sun to the bright horizon. . . .
> There was the yearning for identification loosed in me by the sight of a solitary ant carrying a burden upon a mysterious journey. . . .
> There was the aching glory in masses of clouds burning gold and purple from an invisible sun. . . . (7)

Wright goes to great lengths in these almanacs of marvels to suggest that much as the young boy was cut off by racism, poverty, lack of formal schooling, and family strife from a normal childhood, he had a sensibility that responded to beauty. These early visitations seeded his imagination with a sense of wonder. The parallelism of the entries and their rhapsodical language, even if self-consciously borrowed from the Bible and Whitman, impose an ecstatic order on an otherwise chaotic experience.

Black Boy is a great human document and an unforgettable autobiography because Wright succeeds in asserting his self against the sordid negations of his environment, which considered blacks such nonpersons that, as of September 4, 1908, Wright's birthday, it did not bother to issue an official birth certificate. Wright's weapon was his style—intuitive, lyrical, morose, tender, haughty, tormented, didactic—which mimes the rhythms of real men and women feeling, thinking, hating, acting, and brooding. The black and white citizens of Mississippi, Arkansas, and Tennessee bleed, weep, lust, work, pray, murder, laugh, hustle, and whine, but they never lose their quirky individuality. Wright's memory may distort events but always for the sake of imaginative accuracy; centered in his blackness, he renders the suffering of southern blacks and his stricken younger self in scenes that are dramatically fluent and pointed as a surgeon's scalpel, so that the reader winces at the pain of penetration. But he also crosses the color line and gets inside the skin of whites, exposing their vices, hypocrisies, mental habits, fitful generosity, and violent racism. He does not allow the reader the comforts of false optimism. We are fellow voyagers on his odyssey, sharing his scrapes with death, his struggle for autonomy, and his estimate of implacable limits and the means to surmount them. Intractable reality yields, in *Black Boy,* to the compensatory spiritual force of the imagination, which restores and validates identity.

III

LIKE THE slaves and freedmen before him who came North seeking asylum and husbanding an anxious wish to plant themselves in a new soil, Richard Wright arrived in Chicago. The year was 1927. Quickly the Promised Land disappointed him. Though he could walk the streets without being subject to racial abuse, he wondered how he would survive the city's coldly anonymous life. Chicago spoke in a cryptic tongue, and as he gazed distractedly at the maladjustment of the migrant blacks and their airless lives, Wright felt as though the gates of hell had clanged shut behind him: "I was going through a second childhood; a new sense of the limit of the possible was being born in me," (AH, 7) he remarks early in *American Hunger,* the second half of his autobiography. Being twice-born was a ghastly joke. Instead of a surge of energy and purpose, he was once again penned in by the familiar insecurities of his childhood—hunger, tension, timidity, friendlessness—and as dependent as ever on the companionship of his own thoughts and impressions. His initiatives stymied, Wright worked at an assortment of jobs, most poorly paying, some, like his menial job in the basement of a segregated hospital, reminding him that "America had kept us [Negroes] locked in the dark underworld of American life for three hundred years." (AH, 59)

Wright's image of a second childhood, however, is misleading, for despite his bouts of depression, he did not regress. Chicago was an ideal urban laboratory in which Wright, connoisseur of indignity, could study hunger not as a personal but as an *American* problem, part of a complex system of exploitation; could give proper names to the forces that trapped and diminished men and women; could probe the meaning of being black in a world dominated by whites. Wright took advantage of the opportunities and began educating himself; to his readings of Dreiser, Conrad, Dostoyevsky, and Sinclair Lewis he added the works of Marx and Veblen, constructing social theories out of their acumen and his experiences. Sensing the urgency of seeing his personal injuries in the light of wider forces and ideas, Wright seeks to "objectify" reality. The plight of blacks living on the fringes of an America "adolescent and cocksure, a stranger to suffering and travail, an enemy of passion and sacrifice," (AH, 14) was to be solved only by plumbing the aggressive authority of a white majority with its tawdry "lust for trash," the trivial prizes of a materialistic and superficial culture.

The Depression accentuated for Wright the crisis of a government that, because it was indifferent to the submerged underclasses, did not deserve their allegiance. Going from underemployment to unemployment, Wright shamefacedly had to apply for welfare in order to support his mother and brother, who had joined him in Chicago. He was desperate. It was therefore a logical step to enlist in the ranks of the Communist party, whose ideology promised to redress injustice, to find jobs, bread, and shelter for the needy of all races, and to foster an ethical consciousness. Wright was primed to commit himself to a noble cause. But given his temperamental caution, he proceeded slowly and circuitously, scrutinizing the members' words and deeds for signs of a subtle racism. His desire for kinship was shadowed by his mistrust of those who extended their hand to him. Wright called his decision to become a Communist one of the few "total emotional responses" he had ever made.[35]

But he had another motive, equally compelling: The party seemed prepared to encourage his writing talents. Under the spell of Gertrude Stein's *Three Lives,* he had been experimenting with "stream-of-consciousness Negro dialect," but he could not break out of his "subjective impressions." He merely produced lyrical fragments. He diagnoses his stumbling block as follows:

> I strove to master words, to make them disappear, to make them important by making them new, to make them melt into a rising spiral of emotional stimuli, each greater than the other, each feeding and reinforcing the other, and all ending in an emotional climax that would drench the reader with a sense of a new world. That was the single aim of my living. (AH, 22)

The repetition of the verb "make" suggests the strain of his compulsion to find an outlet for his overwrought feelings. At the same time, his readings in sociology propelled him "to use words to create religious types, criminal types, the warped, the lost, the baffled." For this pilgrim, with his faith that words reconstruct the world, the impasse was frustrating; he could not abide failure. So he fumbled his way toward party membership in the hope that his elusive "sense of a new world" would take on flesh.

Langston Hughes and Claude McKay were established men of letters when they encountered communism during their long sojourns in postrevolutionary Russia, what McKay called his "magic pilgrimage."[36] Despite their avowed pleasure at being able to breathe and move freely in a society that apparently ignored the color line— Hughes even rationalized the Soviet regime's purges and liquidation of political prisoners, including writers, as a necessary expedient— they backed away from enrolling in the party, out of a fear that ideology interfered with artistic freedom.[37] But Wright, an apprentice to his craft and a loner, hungered for a literary community, so that ideology looked like desirable discipline for his amorphous designs and homeless words. Before pledging himself to the party, Wright passed through several stages, temporarily allying himself with a group of cynical wits and then a Negro literary coterie "preoccupied with twisted sex," admiring the "emotional dynamics" of the Garveyites while rejecting their back-to-Africa nationalism as unworkable. Even the black Communists he heard haranguing on street corners he belittled for their simplistic, imitative slogans. These self-styled revolutionaries were toy soldiers marching backward, unthinking as blocks of wood, their voice boxes programmed to speak a few mechanical phrases: "An hour's listening disclosed the fanatical intolerance of minds sealed against new ideas, new facets, new feelings, new attitudes, new hints at ways to live." (AH, 38–9) Wright brandishes the word "new" like a fetishistic sword.

Disillusionment set in swiftly, but as with the planks of a seagoing vessel warped by dry rot, the damage was not immediately noticeable. Gazing at a "wild cartoon" of a worker followed by a raggle-taggle "horde of nondescript men, women, and children, waving clubs, stones, and pitchforks" on the cover of *The Masses,* Ella Wright asks, "What do Communists think people are?" Wright frankly admits that the cartoon "did not reflect the passions of the common people," and he had no answer to give. Like the fledgling writer, "they had a program, an ideal, but they had not yet found a language." (AH, 65) Flattered by the party's courtship of him, Wright was upset to discover that instead of his using or serving the party, the party was using him. Storm signals appeared early. When the party bigwigs decreed that *Left Front,* * a magazine designed to publish young leftist writers—Wright participated in editorial meetings—must cease publication, no rational protest could budge the inflexible leadership. The ludicrous episode in which a certified lunatic ran the John Reed Club for a while and leveled baseless charges that set one member against another in sniping factionalism dumbfounded Wright. If the party viewed dissent as an obstreperous desire to undermine authority, he grumbled, its idea of equality was a sham, a more insidious version of how whites had demagogically treated black assertiveness in Mississippi. An unspoken covenant had been shattered.

That the Communists did not respect individuality wounded Wright in his sorest spot: his ambition to be a writer. His touching hope was to mediate between the black proletariat, a potentially large political army waiting to be recruited, and the mythic power of the Communist system, which, with its "spirit of self-sacrifice," could tap the "emotional capacities" of men and thus destroy entrenched evil. Wright would be in the vanguard, his art no longer tongue-tied but fervently serving a collective ideal. Reluctantly he came to see that like the black soapbox revolutionaries, the Communists were remote from the black masses, did not care how they felt: They were fodder for revolution.[38] In its censorship of members' activities and thoughts, the party resembled the Seventh-Day Adventism of Granny Wilson. To be sure, the supernaturalism of his granny's salvational scheme was replaced by a materialistic theology, but both insisted that there was only one correct doctrine. Anybody who did not submit to it was a pariah. When he tried to explain his position, he blundered and "said the wrong things," sliding into the defensive role that plagued him in his quarrels with his family:

> Words lost their usual meanings. Simple motives took on sinister colors. Attitudes underwent quick and startling transformations. Ideas turned into their opposites while you were

---

*Wright contributed poems, sketches, and stories to *New Masses* and *Anvil,* other magazines published under Communist auspices.

talking to a person you thought you knew. I began to feel an emotional isolation that I had not known in the depths of the hate-ridden South. (AH, 86)

One of Wright's projects, innocently conceived, precipitates the crisis that ends with his expulsion from the Communist party:

In my party work I met a Negro Communist, Ross, who was under indictment for "inciting to riot." I decided to use him in my series of biographical sketches. His trial was pending and he was organizing support in his behalf. Ross was typical of the effective street agitator. Southern-born, he had migrated north and his life reflected the crude hopes and frustrations of the peasant in the city. Distrustful and aggressive, he was a bundle of the weaknesses and virtues of a man struggling blindly between two societies, of a man living on the margin of a culture. I felt that if I could get his story I would make known some of the difficulties inherent in the adjustment of a folk people to an urban environment; I would make his life more intelligible to others than it was to himself. I would reclaim his disordered days and cast them into a form that people could grasp, see, understand, and accept. (AH, 78–9)

Here was a proposal for which Wright was splendidly equipped. Ross was the prototype of those poor rural blacks who migrated from the South to the manufacturing cities of the North, where they met subtler and more dislocating forms of discrimination. That Ross had become an aggressive agitator directly and effectively confronting the inequities of the American political system was a socially significant fact. Wright's boast, "I would make his life more intelligible to others than it was to himself," may be excused as a young writer's conceit (he felt the same way about his father). Party officials, however, hearing of Wright's intentions, intervene and cross-examine him: "Who suggested that to you?" "Nobody. I thought of it myself." (This exchange echoes the suspicion of his motives he had thought a relic of his parochial past.) Next they insinuate that he is a police informer, smearing him with such cant terms as "smuggler of reaction" and "petty bourgeois degenerate."

Summoned before Buddy Nealson, "who had formulated the

Communist position for the American Negro" and "had spoken before Stalin himself," Wright vacillates but decides to go, hoping for
a truce. His sketch of Nealson is revealing:

> He was a short, black man with an ever-ready smile, thick
> lips, a furtive manner, and a greasy, sweaty look. His bearing
> was nervous, self-conscious; he seemed always to be hiding
> some deep irritation. He spoke in short, jerky sentences, hop-
> ping nimbly from thought to thought, as though his mind
> worked in a free associational manner. He suffered from
> asthma and snorted at unexpected intervals. Now and then
> he would punctuate his flow of words by taking a nip from
> a bottle of whisky. He had traveled half around the world
> and his talk was pitted with vague allusions to European cit-
> ies. I met him in his apartment, listened to him intently, ob-
> served him minutely, for I knew that I was facing one of the
> leaders of World Communism.
>   "Hello, Wright," he snorted. "I've heard about you."
>   As we shook hands he burst into a loud, seemingly cause-
> less laugh; and as he guffawed I could not tell whether his
> mirth was directed at me or was meant to hide his uneasiness.
> (AH, 101)

This "leader of World Communism" has clay feet. Nealson is a stage
Negro, a racist caricature, as though Wright deliberately set out to
portray him, as whites would, in an unflattering way. Wright's revulsion builds throughout the interview. He detests Nealson's guf-
faw, so like his father's, and Nealson's snorting joviality and patter,
smooth as a ward boss's. Wright dodges Nealson's injunction that
he stop writing and monitor the high cost of living, as he had rejected the school principal's plea that he read a graduating speech
that would not offend white educators. To Nealson's blunt assertion, "The party can't deal with your feelings," Wright replies,
"Maybe I don't belong in the party," (AH, 105) finally pushing his
secret doubt into the open. Nealson's impatient dismissal is crucial:
Any authority that usurps his liberty and brushes aside his feelings
is intolerable to Wright.

The stage is set for the show trial the party convokes—it occupies the last quarter of *American Hunger*—to make of Ross a cau-

tionary lesson and to reassert its binding rule. Despite misgivings and fears that he, too, will be tried for chimerical offenses, Wright attends, claiming that "my old love of witnessing something new came over me." (AH, 118) This is blatant rationalization. For Wright seems drawn unconsciously to enjoy Ross's public confession of guilt and plea for forgiveness, and to gather material for his stories. It is a kind of vicarious martyrdom.

The trial scene is pure political theater of the absurd, and Wright etches it with somber abstractness. He admires the "amazingly formal structure" of the prosecution, "a structure that went as deep as the desire of men to live together." (AH, 120) Ross's crimes are cleverly laid out against a backdrop that moves from the "world situation" to the Soviet Union, to America, and finally to Chicago's South Side (Wright's version is truncated paraphrase). The narrative meanders on as if Wright were embarrassed by what he hears[39]—Ross was accused of "anti-leadership tendencies," "class collaborationist attitudes," and "ideological factionalism," jargon that stuns Wright by its unreality—but he bestows one last ardent compliment on the party's "simple, elemental morality" and mission. Wright continually interrupts his account of the trial to debate with himself whether communism, which seemed to represent that quasi-divine power Historical Necessity, should demand that all members merge their selves in the collective will—as defined by the hierarchy.

Unflinchingly, Wright notes Ross's trembling body, his shaking hands, his sobs: "His personality, his sense of himself, had been obliterated. Yet he could not have been so humbled unless he had shared and accepted the vision that bound us all together."[40] That telltale "us" indicates that Wright's solidarity with the party has not yet loosened, and he adds, by way of analysis and partial extenuation:

> It was not a fear of the Communist party that had made him confess, but a fear of the punishment that he would exact of himself that made him tell all of his wrongdoings. The Communists had talked to him until they had given him new eyes with which to see his own crime. And then they sat back and listened to him tell how he had erred. He was one with all the members there, regardless of race or color; his heart was theirs and their heart was his; and when a man reaches

that state of kinship with others, that degree of oneness, or when a trial has made him kin after he has been sundered from them by wrongdoing, then he must rise and say, out of a sense of the deepest morality in the world:

"I'm guilty. Forgive me." (AH, 124–5)

What makes Ross's annihilation of self, a peril Wright had narrowly averted, acceptable to him? What permits him to call the trial a "spectacle of glory"? What glazes his critical judgment and incites him to adopt the view of the prosecutors and turn them into benefactors and custodians of morality? For elsewhere Wright concedes that Ross had committed no crime, that his confession on trumped-up charges was a ridiculous charade, and that the eyes the party had given Ross were implanted by a charlatan ophthalmologist.

The answer, I believe, is that Wright has fallen into a sentimental trance, as his imagery of kinship and oneness indicates, in which the party has become a loving family welcoming the prodigal son back to its fold. All his life Wright had craved this oneness, pursued it as the highest good, because it promised to embrace both his individuality and his blackness.[41] And this unity of self and other corresponded to his urgent impulse to sublimate his "balked emotion" (AH, 7) in the powerful satisfactions of his art. Wright's break with the party, a slow process, was an agonizing memory precisely because he had to relive his tragic betrayal: being cast out of an ideal family and falling from the grace of a fraternal idea. The phlegmatic prose, the guarded and evasive terms, of *American Hunger,* though free of self-pity, bespeak an unresolved mourning. It could not have been easy to renounce what promised to heal a lifelong rift between will and act.

There is no doubt that moral laxity invades the style of *American Hunger:*

Toward evening the direct charges against Ross were made not by the leaders of the party but by Ross' friends, those who knew him best! It was crushing. Ross wilted. His emotions could not withstand the weight of the moral pressure. No one was terrorized into giving information against him. They gave it willingly, citing dates, conversations, scenes. The black mass of Ross' wrongdoing emerged slowly and irrefutably. He could not deny it. No one could. (AH, 123)

Like most of the interrogation, this is all summary. Wright cannot bring himself to attach bodies and faces to the defilers of ideals still close to his heart. None of the scenes or conversations is recreated with dramatic fire or invention; the witnesses are all marionettes whose strings are pulled by the invisible leaders. The monotonous rhythm of Wright's simplistic recital almost makes him an accomplice in the spiritual havoc he watches unfolding, but awakening from this sleep of unreason, Wright calls the trial "a spectacle of terror," a "black mass," and a travesty of justice. The devils and frauds and villains the party conjures up for the captive audience are a burlesque of Granny's demonology and Last Judgment.

What saves Wright from capitulating to the party's despotism is his stubborn wish to be a writer and tell the truth as he sees it, not as others prescribe it. The party, he senses, is frightened by his "self-achieved literacy":

> The heritage of free thought,—which no man could escape if he read at all,—the spirit of the Protestant ethic which one suckled figuratively, with one's mother's milk, that self-generating energy that made a man feel, whether he realized it or not, that he had to work and redeem himself through his own acts, all this was forbidden, taboo. (AH, 120)

The Protestant tradition is a wet nurse borrowed to shore up Wright's shaky identity; by its betrayal of free thought, the Communist party becomes another poisonous mother who did not respect or nurture her children's need for autonomy. "Politics was not my game," Wright lamely concludes; "the human heart was my game, but it was only in the realm of politics that I could see the depths of the human heart." (AH, 123) Though this image of a game is mawkish and delivered with the tough-guy posturing of a Hemingway character, it nonetheless underlines the basic element of play that communism sought to outlaw or control and the novelist to liberate. It is paradoxically Wright's childhood experiences that enable him to resist the seduction of an authoritarian solution to his need for a unified self. Walking out of the trial room Wright vows, "I'll be for them, even though they are not for me." (AH, 125) There are magnanimity of spirit and loyalty, as well as political innocence, in Wright's statement. Only by practicing the art of fiction could he champion the cause of all the "pris'ners of starvation."

There is such a falling off in quality and style between *Black Boy* and *American Hunger* that one might suppose they were written by two separate people or by two sides of Wright's personality. *American Hunger* is a valuable historical document for the light it sheds on a black intellectual's participation in the Communist party during the 1930s, but as an autobiography it is prolix and circumspect to a fault. For long stretches in the narrative, the imagination is a dreary and pedestrian clerk writing his first political pamphlet; the novice ideologue steals off with the artist's brushes and palette. The grayness of the book's urban setting (Chicago) seeps into the style and anesthetizes it. Though *Black Boy* is not rich in spontaneous play, Wright ventures outside the invisible walls that enclose his character and reconnoiters the world in quest of an amnesty for his fears. Childhood is a nourishing placenta to his art, and he takes pleasure in the formal experiments, black vernacular, and cheeky verbal formulas that establish his right to be and to be black.

In *American Hunger,* however, while legitimately trying to widen the intellectual base of his inquiry into race, class, and economics (his cultural criticism), Wright succumbs to the blandishments of a specious objectivity; his sociological analysis is banal. "Sentences which run on without a body have no soul," William Gass remarks in "The Soul Inside the Sentence." "They will be felt, however conceptually well-connected, however well-designed by the higher bureaus of the mind, to go through our understanding like the sharp cold blade of a skate over ice."[42] Wright's sentences in *American Hunger* are boxed in by the laws of recurrence and by settling for the standard of regularity grammarians set forth in textbooks. The vice of explicitness, a kind of prosaic rambling, tampers with his feelings and leads Wright to compose a conventional and mediocre journalism:

> Party duties broke into my efforts at expression. The club decided upon a conference of all the left-wing writers in the Middle West. I supported the idea and argued that the conference should deal with craft problems. My arguments were rejected. The conference, the club decided, would deal with political questions. I asked for a definition of what was expected from the writers, books or political activity. Both, was the answer. Write a few hours a day and march on the picket

line the other hours. I pointed out that the main concern of
a revolutionary artist was to produce revolutionary art, and
that the future of the club was in doubt if a clear policy could
not be found. (AH, 89)

Wright's prose here drones on like a recording secretary reading the
minutes of an organization meeting. One expects such leaden speech
in the memoirs of public officials and bureaucrats when they recall
policy disputes, because they are accustomed to concealing the truth
in a dull style. Disconcertingly, Wright seems unaware that he has
slipped into the colorless and ambiguous pedantry of the apologist.
The demoralized tone[43] and standardized portraits of party members
in *American Hunger* may be traced in part to Wright's effort to be
impartial but more to Wright's pique at the party for being, like his
family, exasperatingly deaf to his beseechings, for not accepting his
self or his dreams on his terms. Faced with the alternatives of letting
himself be conscripted as an artistic mercenary or fighting, quixoti-
cally, as a free-lance knight, he could not but choose the latter
course. The issue was freedom for and from the self.

Perhaps because his disenchantment with the god that failed oc-
cluded his feelings, Wright's style in *American Hunger* falters. He
undervalues his sharp eye for the telling detail of dress, speech, or
psychic gesture that animated *Black Boy,* such as the way Aunt Addie kicked open doors to see what was in the room before she would
enter. There are a few scenes in *American Hunger* in which Wright
shelves the solemn preaching and blows away the vapory abstractions with a gust of clear invention (all precede his entanglement
with the party): the Finnish cook spitting into the soup pot and
Wright hesitating to notify the restaurant owner for fear she
wouldn't believe him; the white doctors at the hospital nastily step-
ping onto newly scrubbed steps and tracking dirt so that Wright had
to repeat the backbreaking work; and the violent fight between
Brand and Cooke, which breaks out over a trivial argument and
causes the release of laboratory animals from their cages. Wright
relishes the conclave of the unlearned that had to restore order by
guesswork because the doctors had contemptuously refused to im-
part any information about their research. Sarcasm and irony are
tonic to Wright's prose.

Wright's style in *American Hunger* does not inspire us with the vision that roused his hope that "out of my tortured feelings I could fling a spark into [the] darkness" of an atomistic world in which "man had been sundered from man." (AH, 134) At the book's climax, Wright's former comrades literally throw him out of the ranks of the Communist marchers during a May Day parade and treat him as a traitor. To this symbolic sundering he responds in a curious way:

> I had suffered a public, physical assault by two white Communists with black Communists looking on. I could not move from the spot. I was empty of any idea what to do. But I did not feel belligerent. I had outgrown my childhood. (AH, 132)

With the words of the Internationale ringing in his ears, "a better world's in birth," Wright vows to wait until his feelings will not stand in the way of words. But it was precisely the visions of his childhood and his belligerence that fueled his faith in words to alter reality. "The complete child must come forth in the whole man who invests and shapes a successful style,"[43] as it had in *Black Boy*. Its absence in *American Hunger* dampens the sparks before they can catch fire. In autobiography, it is a cardinal rule that, to borrow Blake's words, "The tygers of wrath are wiser than the horses of instruction."

9

Stoking the Oedipal Furnace:
Edward Dahlberg's *Because I Was Flesh*

*It is sin to believe in man's character. Man is continually
astonished at the moral weather of his identity.*
— EDWARD DAHLBERG, The Flea of Sodom

I

ONE OF THE blandishments of autobiography is that it permits
the "making of a marvelous mask."[1] From behind his mask of
complacent humility, Franklin could instruct his son and young
America in the prolific, rewarding virtues of self-discipline and civic
duty. Similarly, William Carlos Williams could adopt the persona
"Doc"—deliverer of babies, votary of the local gods, and suburban bumpkin—all the while demonstrating his poetic tenacity and
sophistication. If the memory of these two men is fallible, guileful,
selective, that is no fatal defect, as the artless style of their
autobiographies reassures us. They display little rancor against
themselves or their times; they lack the martyr's temperament. Their
versatility and useful vocations ensure a sort of democratic insouciance that informs the exuberantly haphazard structure of their autobiographies. Nevertheless, their supple opinions do not challenge
the premise that out of the welter of event and thought and feeling
some sense can be made of a man's life. They partially disprove
Tocqueville's contention that "democracy turns man's imagination
away from externals to concentrate it on himself alone."[2]

Such is not the case with Edward Dahlberg. "Autobiographical books are plain, honest perjury,"[3] he remarks in *Alms for Oblivion*. The present is an absolute sphinx and the past an equally grim riddle: "We never learn anything, but simply call old errors by new names." (28) Doomed to repetition, "we only do what we are," and what we are is hopelessly duplicitous. Man's nature is vicious, politics mutilates conscience and debases language,[4] and knowledge is intellectual pride, a deluded comfort, since it does not influence our behavior. Above all, we are the miserable prey of our erotic furies.

Character, Dahlberg insists like a hanging judge, is intransigently fixed; devious, murderous, guilty of eating his own nature, a Cain bearing the stigma of his separation, man seeks atonement in vain. This blunt determinism, gleefully condemning all explanations of motive as corrupt self-interest, is hardly an inducement for composing a memoir. Not surprisingly, Dahlberg calls *Because I Was Flesh* "an autobiography of my faults" (140) and, like a Missouri Rousseau, confesses his vices, defects, and "flinty heart," thus validating to himself that the self is an emotional Mojave Desert.

Dahlberg, reluctant to admit that he has much of a central consciousness ruling over the sequences of memories that could sort out his life, banishes the "I" until Chapter 4, when he leaves the orphanage in which he dwelt for seven years. His explanation is that "I was obscure to myself . . . [and] I was suffering locality rather than a person." (92) He substitutes a flexible structure for the inchoate self. *Because I Was Flesh,* he announces, is a "memoir of my mother's body." (4) The autobiography is written as though he has no life separate from his mother. Lizzie Dahlberg is perceived from the outside, with Edward Dahlberg's suffering shifted to the charged prose style. Strict chronology has nothing to do with the psychological poetry of the mother-son relationship; *that* exists in the timeless realm of myth and dream.

Finally, *Because I Was Flesh* is also a portrait of the American artist as Proteus: porcupine, vagabond, fox, saintly fool, and "crazy waif of the Muse." (128) By reviling himself for his shameful failings—inconstancy, unruly will, impotence of feeling—Dahlberg licenses his performance as the prophetic scourge of the world's follies. As he tells, ruefully and comically, the story of his (and his mother's) endless humiliations, he embroiders fact with fiction. He becomes the dervish of words, an author of wisdom literature for a world in which such wisdom is useless. A combative, peevish man, he plays

Edward Dahlberg, 1960

a repertoire of roles with self-delighting or nasty bravura: the huffy philosopher as clown, denying all our received opinions; Job, scratching his sores, railing at the injustice of his plight and excoriating the comforters; Ishmael, his hand against the world; the moralist, humbling man for his stupidity and shopkeeper mind. Only the "potent sanctified lies of art"[5] can redeem the galling contradictions of his life, and "ease" (a favorite word) the pains and social ugliness that affront him. *Because I Was Flesh* is thus a calculated leveling of our individual and collective self-esteem; heroism or a scrap of self-knowledge enters our consciousness only through the occasional windfalls of art. The morally examined life is a necessary fraud.[6]

Dahlberg hoards his wretched experiences as his mother did her orange peels and dog-eared postal cards. They are his bag of sacred relics containing the scattered clues to his blighted origins, and he fingers them remorselessly. "Why was it impossible for me to let go of the misery of my boyhood?" (220) he asks himself, expecting no suitable answer. If America is a "transient Golgotha," (208) Dahlberg is its suffering servant, stumbling from the heavy burden of his double cross: his Oedipal passion and his absent father. It is an ordeal and a pleasure he cannot—and does not want to—let go, because it is the major source of his creativity.

Because I Was Flesh is a masterpiece of Oedipal obsession, a poetic memoir of primal sunderings and rages.[7] At its heart, as at the heart of all Dahlberg's writings, lies his exasperated love for his mother, Lizzie, and his quest for knowledge of his father, Saul, a feckless womanizer, whose desertion is the other unappeasable demon of his childhood. His tainted birthright is an irrevocable, violent prologue—and he subsequently reaps the whirlwind. Cast out like Ishmael with the unreliable protection of his mother (Hagar), and soon abandoned by her, he roams America (and Europe), his own mortified condition a mirror of cosmic lawlessness and human disloyalty. As with Oedipus, the monstrous sphinx exacts its revenge: In memory he relives his grievances with a bitter compulsiveness. He, too, is blinded (in one eye); he turns disputatious, cranky, and self-pitying; he rants and complains that his guilt and punishment are out of proportion to his sin.

Where Oedipus at Colonus achieved a mysterious grace, Dahlberg's nomadic spirit remains bruised, defiant, wise in the lore of antiquity yet without that fundamental self-awareness that might reconcile him to his bereaved past. Yet paradoxically *Because I Was Flesh* converts Dahlberg's long internal exile into the consoling power of myth. A book of lamentations, it moves in a shower of aphorisms between comedy and prayer. For once, Dahlberg holds his frenetic egotism in check long enough to assemble and enshrine the tattered figure of his mother, proprietress of the Star Lady Barbershop, and to sketch her as Hogarth might have, against the raffish boom-town milieu of Kansas City, Missouri, in the early 1900s.

In the rich iconography of the autobiography, Lizzie acts Mary Magdalene and Mater Dolorosa to Dahlberg's Jesus, Hagar to his Ishmael, and Delilah to his Samson. She dominates the book as effortlessly as she does her son's emotions. The facts of her life are simple. The daughter of a large polyglot Orthodox Jewish family, she comes to America not to escape religious persecution but to flee a "loveless roof," only to undergo a series of unlucky episodes that would crowd a picaresque novel. (Hers is not the standard immigrant drama; as American as a cowboy, she feels no nostalgia for Europe.) A brother peddles her at sixteen to an older man, Harry Simonowitz. She bears him three sons in this dank marriage, one of whom dies. Dissatisfied with her lot, she gives up the two sons to an orphanage—a pattern to be repeated later with Edward and his half-brother Michael, not mentioned in the book—and takes up with Saul Gottdank, a stagy gigolo with waxed mustaches, curly hair, and a charlatan's smile, like Westervelt's in Hawthorne's *Blithedale Romance*. From this unpromising union Dahlberg was born on July 22, 1900, in a Boston charity hospital, the unwanted child of an impulsive error. His pedigree, Dahlberg says again and again, fatally engulfed him; it surely crippled his relations with his mother and with women throughout his life (he married seven times). Lizzie and Saul traveled from city to city for some months as itinerant barbers, Saul filching money from the till to spend on whores. The liaison couldn't last. Saul vanished in 1905, and Lizzie landed in Kansas City.

Saul flits through the book as a seriocomic ghost of an elusive paternity. For Dahlberg, he is humorously caddish, like the stockyards men and loafers who patronize Lizzie's barbershop. While not a King Saul or Saint Paul, he haunts his son's reveries. He is treated with a burlesque cheerfulness in the early pages of the book:

Whatever Saul was not even Saul knew; he was born corrupt, and what he did was natural to him. What was bad for others was good for him. A kind or charitable act on his part would have been gross deceit. He fobbed women when he desired to lie with them—which is nature. This is not hypocrisy because it is the way the world is made. Saul was some baleful seminal drop of a depraved rotting forefather; he lived solely to discharge his sperm. (44)

If Dahlberg begins by accepting his father's seedy sensuality with the satirist's amused tolerance—"Only a city could slake Saul's venery," (42) he observes—it is because Saul practices no moral dissembling. His sexual appetite may not have toppled the towers of Illium—he is, after all, just a faintly absurd philanderer—but that unalterable character, and the itch of sex when scratched, brings disastrous consequences: The wages of heedless nature is emotional destitution. As the passage builds, Dahlberg's charity runs out. His misgivings and his rage are directed at the way Edward Dahlberg is made; he is the product of that "baleful seminal drop," and he bitterly concludes that if nature involves such a thoughtless act of creation, kinship is itself depraved, comfortless, and selfish. What was good for Saul was bad for others.

In an adjacent passage, Dahlberg continues to muse on the problem:

The truth is that we can only perfect our vices, for we die with all our sins entire, and every wrong thought or vision in the child matures in the man. However, the moral combat against our flinty hearts must be waged: otherwise we eat ourselves in disgust and do nothing but feed and gender. There is nothing more important than this incessant warfare with our hard demons which makes men better thinkers but not better men. The only comfort that God can take in His Creation, after He has grown weary with the winds, India, the Cordilleras of the Andes, an earthquake or a tornado, is that man is a reflective beast. God caused men to die because He wanted them to think; our first parents ate of the tree of knowledge of good and evil though they knew it would cause them to die. All wisdom is sensual since it comes from the body. (43)

These brilliant tricky proverbs of Dahlberg's private hell, hammered into urgent moral universals, come close to being a recital of his Nicene Creed. And they provide a militant excuse for his own character. Eros and Thanatos are locked in an unstable marriage, a *folie à deux,* out of which impasse man can extract himself with only partially satisfying half-measures and ingenious compromises. "Sex absorbs all the functions of the soul," Dahlberg quotes Pascal; it is a temporary escape from loneliness.* Dahlberg celebrates the joys of an irresistible libido, like his mother's, identifying it with health; but he also adopts a puritanical contempt for man's sexual greed. Like Jonathan Edwards, he preaches sternly that Eros becomes Eris, the cause of strife and ultimately of death, the "skulking demiurgic glutton." (187) All sexual transports are a form of involuntary servitude. Indeed, Dahlberg often sounds like a Middle American Hamlet—registering disgust at his mother's carnal weaknesses, which cannot be controlled (as a young man in Los Angeles and Berkeley, he put on an "antic disposition" and practices a wild celibacy that does not last long) and which he takes as a betrayal of himself. His parents' sexual legacy is poisonous: faithlessness, he believes, is as inexorable as genes. No emotional reparations are possible for such acts. Dahlberg's parents, unlike our "first parents," were victims of moral muddle; their will "was too sick to love the child of their lust." (40) "Lizzie was guided by the laws of her body and the fear of any excesses that might curtail her days on the earth; Saul did not care how long he lived so long as he lived virile." (43)

Saul never struggled against his defect, never risked expulsion from the illusory Eden of sensual pleasure, so he never became that paradoxical creature "a reflective beast." (43) Lizzie did struggle and gains Dahlberg's deepest allegiance. Dahlberg's psychological hypotheses often appear in the guise of philosophical precepts; his reasoning is associative, gnomic, circular, not logical or linear: We must engage our demons in single combat, even though we know beforehand that it can have no effect on our moral conduct. Our "only comfort"—and glory—like the weary God's, is that we think, but our knowledge reduces to three bleak, fruitless propositions: Death is the mother of Truth, the child is the corrupt father of the man, wisdom comes from the body.

---

*Dahlberg's various sexual campaigns in the book always end in rebuffs and failure. His language of courtship is more bookish than Romeo and Juliet's; and he is as unlucky as the pair of star-crossed lovers.

THE FIRST ninety pages of *Because I Was Flesh* lovingly recreate the bawdy atmosphere of the Star Lady Barbershop, a tawdry sweatshop transfigured into a palace of pleasures, which railroad men, cowboys, and businessmen frequented for a shave, agreeable flirtation, and banter. So high do the sexual fevers run, heating the senses, that all of Kansas City seems to be in rut; even the flush of a toilet or smelly shoes excite desire. The coarse vitality of their amorous intrigues endears the lady barbers to Dahlberg, as though the Wife of Bath had set up shop in Kansas City and tutored the wild farm girls in how to speculate in men. These "virgins" trim their lamps as they trim their customers' hair—Daughters of Autolycus, fleecing and gulling the men. Breach-of-promise suits abounded. Though "vice was good for business"—lady barbershops were often fronts for brothels—the worship of Mammon was secondary to the worship of Priapus. Dahlberg savors the women's wanton genius at easing the woes and aches of the body. For them, money is health and sex generative: In seeking either, principles are a bother that their "homemade conscience" (29) cannot afford. Emma Moneysmith, the chief beauty, a sort of Mormon Venus,* "was good as she could be, and were she to try to be any better, she would be worse. . . . Emma would have believed in virtue had she found anybody else who used it. Lying, cheating, fornication and fleecing were contagious diseases she had caught from the most respectable folk who patronized the shop." (34) Prudes, Dahlberg scoffs, like scrawny poultry, not only were bad for business but had a mean spirit. Though Emma was murdered by a cowboy for her "amiable thievery," (45) she did not have a cold heart that plots with loveless malice the harm of others.

But Dahlberg's praise of these women is edged with mistrust. (He was a lifelong misogynist.[8]) His vocabulary for women, ransacked from dictionaries and Elizabethan slang, sounds like a recruiting officer's handbill for a whorehouse: tarts, wenches, trulls, whores, slovens, chits, chippies, prostitutes, trollops, strumpets, fil-

---

*Dahlberg sets up a hierarchy of Venuses, all of whom are out of reach: Venus Illegitima, "the goddess of various turpitudes"; (98) Venus Vulgivaga, "the patron saint of the house of ill fame"; (104) and Venus Urania, the goddess of exalted love. Language is Dahlberg's aphrodisiac.

lies, and jillflirts. Dahlberg would protest that the terms are affectionate and exact, not demeaning, for the lady barbers were as erotically stimulated, and stimulating, as Semiramis—and as dangerous. Women are natural,* a term that is, as we have seen, honorific but suspect:

> When the time came she would be a steadfast wife and provide a husband who cherished her with a jolly, bawdy bed and fat gammons. She would look just as legal and righteous as any other householder. Love restores the blind, the palsied and the virgin, and even if a lady barber smeared her wedding sheet with Heinz ketchup, no bridegroom should be so foolish as to examine it. A man who scrutinizes everything he does—or someone else does to him—will die swearing or live to run mad in the streets with no other cover for his nude soul but a syllogism. Besides, a woman is a marvelous chameleon creature, for she can cheat, lie and copulate, and still be the tenderest pullet. (27)

This sly and impudent tribute depicts women as alluringly fickle, gay roisterers who, properly appreciated, turn into jolly Griseldas (that ancient commonplace, the goodhearted prostitute!). But although Dahlberg finds their shams charming, he cannot follow his own chivalric advice: From paranoia, *he* would send his bride's sheet to a laboratory for chemical analysis, for he scrutinizes himself and others with a Calvinist's alertness to minute signs, and in Los Angeles and Berkeley runs mad in the streets with no cover for his nude soul—and shaved head—than a passel of Nietzschean syllogisms. He is a perjured witness.

These lady barbers, who might have been lifted from the pages of *The Beggar's Opera*, form a chorus of plebeian women and serve as a backdrop to the Oedipal drama with its theme: "Every mother, even while she lives, is the pit and grave of the son." (187) Although Lizzie is tormented by erotic longings and has a number of affairs, she is not, Dahlberg insists, the madam of a brothel; she is offended by the girls' sporting and calculating promiscuity. For Lizzie, sex is a "heart's balm," like her quack remedies, her enemas, and her pen-

---

*Only one woman in the book, Portia Kewling, is endowed with an intellect. At Berkeley, she becomes his tutor in Plato.

chant for useless surgery whenever life disappoints and threatens to crush her. Despite her henna-dyed hair, long nose, and unkempt appearance, she has a dignified air of "genteel breeding," (47) which the seamy barbershop cannot destroy. She is not common. She is an "angelic pariah," (227) whose string of "uninterrupted humiliations" (63) foreshadows and affects her son's own emotional destiny. He understands that "What she wished above all else was a place in society," (110) that "the asceticism of everyday toil" (61) was the one social pleasure she could count on. Bad luck dogs her and conspires with her faults of character—she is an irremediable dupe about men—to make "Kansas City the burial ground" (154) of his mother's hopes.

As a mature man, Dahlberg tries with a gallant idealism to cross the chasm between himself and his mother, conceding that she had what he lacked: sense, "sexual understanding and a charitable pity for others," (94) but black thoughts keep sabotaging his good intentions—the barely repressed returns. Foremost, he reproaches Lizzie for not providing him with a family or at least acknowledging, despite her muttered curses against *"Verdammter* Saul," that he was in fact the boy's father.

What infuriated Dahlberg as a child and continued to rankle him as an adult was his mother's combination of seductiveness and neglect. Dahlberg describes the young Edward as a puny, finicky, emotionally stunted boy, sensitive to vermin and subject to vomiting; he was like a character in Chaplin's films, the city his parent. He would hang all over the men who came to court his mother, a suppliant for a morsel of affection from these surrogate fathers (and rivals), but they usually rebuffed him, throwing him back onto his mother's whimsical care.

Lizzie seems to have chronically roused her son. As a child, he slept in bed with her. After a bath, she would rub her naked body in front of him, as if he were not there. She would urinate in doorways, while he shuffled, embarrassed, in the street. Most provokingly, he was supplanted by a series of men and agitated by the cries of lovemaking. She was a false Penelope with a makeshift morality who had given in to the importunities of the suitors while spurning his, thus betraying her tacit promises of forever suckling him. And when, finally, he was a nuisance, as with Captain Harry Smith, one of his mother's lovers, he was shunted off unceremoniously to the orphanage. This was the primal outrage, as if the Virgin Mary had refused to nurture the Infant Jesus. In a dream she appears to him as "two empty udders." (228) "She did not know what to do with herself or with him. She had reached the zero point in her freezing heart." (41)

Dahlberg's seven years at the Jewish Orphan Asylum in Cleveland institutionalized his profound sense of being cast off. He was an orphan in spirit if not in fact. Tyrannized and brutalized by monstrous mediocrities who failed to discharge their scriptural and ethical responsibility to care for them, these luckless boys and girls learned only the stratagems of survival. The regime was martial, the food foul, nature pinched or altogether absent. The orphans lived like prisoners in 'barracks, with numbers instead of names (some tried to escape before they were paroled), wore drab uniforms, and listened to treacly sermons exhorting them to be good. (Dickens's experience at the blacking factory was a mild lesion compared to Dahlberg's trauma.) "They had no manual skill in affections and were sore afraid of touching another except to harm or punish." (69) As if to wipe out the ignominy of their violated and injured selves, Dahlberg confers epic status on them, calling the rolls of heroes as worthy of remembering as warriors at Troy. The naming is a benediction: "Mugsy, Prunes, Shrimp, Bah, Mooty, Spunk, Bonehead Balaam, Moses Mush Tate, Phineas Watermelonhead, Mushmelonhead, Sachemhead." (69) Mush Tate, "the Socratic dialectician of the orphan home, . . . a liar, a thief, and a rhetor," (81) masterfully sums up the most terrifying experience of a "vacant" and affectionless world in *Because I Was Flesh*: "God humbles the proud and the lowly He raises. Think you're much? Know you're living?" (82) For Dahlberg, who was no stoic and pined for his mother and for the freedom to roam the streets, these seven years confirmed in him the pathology of the abandoned. Yet even as he speaks of betrayal and disgust, Dahlberg creates, through his style, a world of sensuality and enclosure that exists almost independent of the degrading events in the orphanage. It is as if the richness of language could return him to the lost warmth of his mother's body and erase all memories of deprivation.

III

IT TOOK Dahlberg four years of intensive work (1959–63) and the aid of four editors to finish *Because I Was Flesh*.[9] It is not hard to imagine the reason for his difficulty: He did not want to stoke the Oedipal furnace. But he made one of those artistic decisions that are strokes of genius. As he wrote to Jonathan Williams, "I am also using wit to relieve tragedy, and also because I have not the bravery to complete the book that in a way is being composed by my mother, without mining the comic veins. I must walk in comic socks or perish in buskined drama."[10] The "comic socks" were a fortunate purchase, since they afforded him some protection against both his tender feelings toward Lizzie and his grudge against her for his psychic maiming—and relieved his art of the shrill and monotonous diatribes that so often made his previous books brilliant half-ruins. The humor also enabled him periodically to judge her gently; he perceived the pathos and incorrigible romance of her failures. Though she is as eager for marriage as a young woman in Jane Austen's novels, some moral myopia seizes her, and she invariably chooses badly, ending up cheated of her savings and, worse, of her hopes. Unlike the other lady barbers, she lacks the hard practicality and relish of hustling, which permits them to trade their "lawless flesh" for the respectability of marriage.

As Lizzie grows older, her passion for security and her fear of death increase. The body turns a nasty gray. Dahlberg describes with a touching delicacy her preparations and manners when a new beau comes to call, yet he sees the comic incongruities: Lizzie's courteous set speeches, as if she had taken elocution lessons; her fiddling with her gold-embroidered dress and pince-nez; the cultured way she eats grapes; and her studied fingering of the piano, playing snatches of favorite light classics (to show that she is not ordinary), their lyrics poignantly emblematic of her caring for the beautiful— "Roses kissed by the golden dew" (195) or "Tell me something, tell me true, dear, tell me why you went away." (39)* Such refinement is lost on the wizened, miserly men who sized her up as a potential mate, but love and marriage is a game that requires gambling on

---

*"Her favorite semi-classic" had these lyrics: "I was jealous and hurt/When your lips kissed a rose,/Or your eyes from my own chanced to stray./I have tried all in vain/Many times to propose,/But at last I've found courage to say . . ." (47)

human character, even if the outcome is an emotional deficit. In these scenes, Mary Magdalene has become the Mater Dolorosa.

The epitome of these sallow, unsexual men is Tobias Emmeritch, who answers an advertisement Lizzie placed in a matrimonial gazette. This funny, complex episode, one of Dahlberg's finest inventions, is Lizzie's last, desperate fling before her death and mystical apotheosis. Though Tobias is a mouthpiece for Dahlberg's most acerb opinions,[11] he lives on the page. This creaky fop and Schopenhauerian cheapskate brings the smell of death in his galoshes and accentuates it with wan flourishes of his ubiquitous umbrella. His nihilistic proverbs are as sour as the pickles with which he has made a fortune; indeed, his contentious garrulity is oddly matched with a decrepit body, whose erotic energies, if they ever existed, have run down like a clock. He can only offer Lizzie the shelter of a wheezing romance. Strindberg, "who really abhorred life," is his bedtime reading, so he is appropriately cynical and preposterous while inflicting the last of Lizzie's major marital defeats:

> Besides, why should he heed what she was saying? What had he to do with woman's gaggling? The best conversation is a monologue in which no one else can meddle. He renewed his musings: My watchword is prudence. When a female folds you in her arms, she is winding a sheet around you, and knotting it too. Luckily there's no woman who can feast on my jaw, or gnaw my sunken temples, or dig her rotten amorous molar into my joints. I am grateful to admit that I have no marrow, and no wife will ever make a chronicle of my anatomy. No, it is positively clear: a bedfellow is a bailiff, a summons, a foreclosure, a pauper's oath and a hearse. (195)

Lizzie knows that Tobias is no cavalier but just a ridiculous, lonely old miser with "the knack of making money or of turning the worst into the best—while she always managed to turn every advantage into a loss." (183) Although she does not want to be taken for a scheming woman, she tries to inveigle him into making a financial settlement so she can pass her last years in comfort, without needing to call on her son for help. But Tobias is invulnerable to her pleas and wiles. In exasperation, Lizzie asks him, "Why don't you do something with your life besides save it?" (193) but he parries the question with such glum aperçus as "Think of having a suit cleaned; anybody with an ounce of intelligence knows that sooner or later it will pour." (200) Lizzie's campaign is conducted with a careful noble formality: "Frankly, I find more honor in being Lizzie Dahlberg; it's an educated name, and not common. I was born into my name and I didn't start from nowhere." (194–5) But although she denounces his fanatical thrift and furtive jealousy with the majestic scorn of Dr. Johnson, she ends, predictably, out in the cold—still defenseless, unprotected. The final irony of this misalliance *manqué* is that upon his death, the newspaper obituary refers to Tobias as a philanthropist! And he leaves his money to his aged invalid brother and sister.

Dahlberg has cunningly contrived it so that Lizzie's dwindling hopes force her into a close relationship with her son, as though their material and spiritual destinies converged to bring them to the brink of a shared carnage. As if contrite over her earlier neglect, she sacrifices herself and her money for her son's happiness. She beseeches him to be her shield against death, psychologically proposing he be her husband, but he cannot "go to her and kiss the latchets of her torn, grubby boots." (205) They both inhabit a desert of blighted souls, yet out of a perverse malice Dahlberg is driven to forsake her, to punish her for abandoning him as a boy. Her unbearable anguish and his sense of being irretrievably wronged are knotted like an umbilical cord that both strangles and gives life.

This remarkable woman, "this less than five-feet of relentless will," (162) "this shambles of loneliness," (232) who had made health her god, dies alone, her body not discovered for five days (in actuality, her body probably wasn't discovered for two weeks[12]). Dahlberg's explanation is that "all people have the automatic impulse to harm others, and while one is stroking the neck of the beloved he has an involuntary desire to break it." (206) His paralyzed will demonstrates for him the finality of our stricken, fallen natures. Our incestuous desires and guilt, our original trauma, like shrapnel in the soul, fester to the end of our days. The myth of recurrence triumphs. "Eros goes as far back as Chaos,"[13] Dahlberg tells us. Sex is force, not sentiment, as amorally destructive as Henry Adams's dynamo.

Confession, in autobiography, is a form of sincere equivocation. The author's tone may be complacent or brusque, but it usually implies a mobile self, one that chooses with difficulty among competing selves because, as George Eliot puts it in *Middlemarch,* "Character is a process and unfolding . . . character is not cut in marble—it is not something solid and unalterable. It is something living and changing, and may become diseased as our bodies do."[14] Dahlberg denies this somber faith in change. Man is too stupid to learn. Moral maxims fall on stony spirits, including his own. He cites Thoreau approvingly: "The heart is always inexperienced." (76)

The last chapter of *Because I Was Flesh* surpasses Rousseau's *Confessions* in its imperious solipsism and self-abasement. Instead of trying to exonerate himself of the most cruel acts, Dahlberg flays himself for filial ingratitude, as though he were an incarnation of Goneril and Regan: "It is hideous and coarse to assume that we can do something for others—and it is vile not to endeavor to do it. I had not the strength to handle her tragedy, for my will has failed me every hour of each day. It is said that a wise man falls down seven times a day and rises; I have fallen and never gotten up." (233) The inner man cries havoc. Enlightenment is a stab at a truth, the hopeless art of deciphering. Dahlberg, fluctuating, places blame "for making sport" of her life on his own ingrained evil habits, on Lizzie's passionate irregularities, and on Jehovah, the remote father.

If "the miracle of perception is involved with the miracle of love," (227) as Dahlberg claims, he is self-condemned "to dwell in the dungy caves of the Cyclops."[15] And indeed, Dahlberg's artistic career drew sustenance from an absolutist's dogma of impossibilism.[16] Loathing separation, he destroyed the intimacy he craved with a violent compulsiveness and lived in "boreal solitude."[17] With his genius for abuse and invective, Dahlberg sees perfidy everywhere, especially in his own heart, and barks at it like Thersites, Timon, Diogenes—and Job.[18] He is both the dragon—terrorizing himself and the world with its sting of gall, hoarding his treasures of rejection—and a failed Saint George, striking at the monster but not slaying it. "Nobody ever overcomes the phantasms of his childhood. The man is the corrupt dream of the child." (49–50) This self-fulfilling prophecy universalizes his destitution. It is the moralist's meager solace. The rhetoric is magnificent, but is it true?

Our reason may be deformed and our will enfeebled, and we may be estranged from ourselves as from others, but as Edwin Muir has remarked, "Without forgiveness our lives would be unimaginable."[19] Fortunately, Dahlberg's art is wiser than his philosophy. For like Muir, he has understood that the imagination is potentially an instrument of immortality. In the twinned life of mother and son, he has woven a web as subtle and intricate as the fatal pattern that tied Hippolytus and Phaedra. When "gibing Pilate," the spokesman for the moral average, counters Lizzie's angry question, "Why am I miserable, while others who are pitiless and contemptible are so fortunate?" with the retort, "What is Truth?" and she replies quietly, "My life," (233) the moment is one of the most heartbreaking in all the literature of autobiography.

Through the eloquence of his art, Dahlberg can set aside blame, self-laceration, and misanthropic humor and sing an anthem that bestows upon his mother the blessing of a conciliating grace:

> When the image of her comes up on a sudden—just as my bad demons do—and I see again her dyed henna hair, the eyes dwarfed by the electric lights in the Star Lady's Barbershop, and the dear, broken wing of her mouth, and when I regard her wild tatters, I know that not even Solomon in his lilied raiment was so glorious as my mother in her rags. *Selah*. (233–4)

This rapturous prose, the rise and fall and swelling of ecstatic revelation, and the intoning of the Psalmist's mysterious cadence bring aesthetic concord and a measure of peace to his wounded ego. His Oedipal obsessions have been subdued in the grandeur of reattachment, for he has finally been able to reassemble the image of his mother, which eluded him in the orphanage, in his wanderings, and in most of his books. *Because I Was Flesh* is Dahlberg's greatest act of expiation. The flesh may rot and perish, but the life of Lizzie Dahlberg cannot. Although society be as absent—or as much a bystander—as Saul Gottdank, in his art Dahlberg found the Cave of Machpelah and its long-sought conferral of identity. He found his name in writing Lizzie's epitaph.

IV

"Aesthetics is a style of living, enunciation—and affectation," (97) Dahlberg has said. The sheer flaunting artifice, the deliberate archaizing of his style—white bread becomes an "albic crust" and a cuspidor is "shaped like an Etruscan amphora," and he resembles the bookish jackanapes he makes fun of elsewhere—have stirred controversy and antipathy. Critics have derided him as an American Euphues, a poseur given to rodomontade. There is truth in these charges, but they miss the point, because his style is consonant with his moral vision. Despising the pedants, he became a ferocious compiler of literary texts, fables, and aphorisms. An autodidact, he offers lessons in the anthropological customs of primitive men, usually deemed superior to "civilized" men (a small group of savants is exempt from Dahlberg's strictures against the modern world) because they are not separated from nature and their testicles do not drive them mad—or at least much less so. Like Herodotus, Dahlberg is fascinated by odd customs, bits of natural lore. The clear contours of barbaric kings or eccentric sages appeal to his adversary imagination; they keep fresh his sense of wonder amid his moral disgust and become partners in his attack on the world's canting self-deceptions.

Dahlberg's style, though willfully invented, is a necessary outgrowth of his sense of self. Herbert Read, whose poised mind and sensible advocacy were a curious foil to Dahlberg's oracular stridencies, justly called him "a druid, hissing his imprecations into the dusty track of the marauder."[20] His style is a flamboyant procession of words, the verbal equivalent, say, of one of Montezuma's rituals. It is expensive but clear, even when he succumbs to a bout of tedious harangue. Dahlberg's defense is characteristic: "Long ago I resolved to be, like Crates, a jocose iconoclast, to see whatever my eyes compelled me to regard without blinking the worst by calling it the best, and to accept my hindrances as the founts of any perceptions I may be lucky enough to discover."[21]

But this rationale and its dependence on random inspirations cannot cancel the fact that Dahlberg often wears blinkers. His petty side is not pretty to watch. His vigilance to expose and correct error turns him into a vigilante. He engages, for example, in *ad hominem* arguments and specious polemics; he will quote Henry James's worst passages and ignore the formal perfection of the master's best; and he does not deign to refute logical critical objections. Spiteful and jealous, he has cultivated the art of denigration, as if by fiat he could demolish the truths of his artistic siblings and thus remove the threat to his aesthetic identity.[22] His stylistic excesses are the orphan's pugnacious defense.

All of Dahlberg's writings have been autobiographical. In his apprentice days, he followed uncritically the conventions of the naturalistic novel. The narratives of *Bottom Dogs* (1930), *From Flushing to Calvary* (1932), and *Those Who Perish* (1934) are oppressively literal, dazed transcripts of brutalized experiences, "consciousness in a state of repulsion,"[23] as D. H. Lawrence said of *Bottom Dogs*. The language of that book is bare of mythical adornments, a flat, morose voice moving over the terrain of memory, never straying from its tone of inert defeat, as the hero, Lorry Lewis, wanders across America. There is no connection among characters, just a drab amnesia, the stylistic counterpart of the Great Depression. Although the facts are the same as in *Because I Was Flesh,* the emotionally numbed center occurs in the lengthy recital of his seven years at the Jewish Orphan Asylum, which is condensed to one chapter in the autobiography. Mistreated by the authorities, given skimpy, rancid food, no affection, and heavy doses of hypocritical piety, the boys band together in the scrappy camaraderie of the forlorn. The asylum is a soulless, regimented place, a psychic Gehenna that formulizes Lorry's sense of being set apart. His subsequent adventures on the road as he drifts across a faceless America, from marginal jobs to a hobo's life, are a chronicle of mechanical survival.

Lorry's relationship with his mother is presented from a cold distance. Lizzie is merely a credulous, sour, hardworking woman, lost in vague reveries. She has no presence. Probably because Dahlberg had not begun to sort out his angry feelings for her, he muffled them and concentrated on the boy's life in the streets.

A comparison of two passages about the girls who were employed by Lizzie illustrates the difference in style:

> The girls, too, who worked for her were a trial. They were easygoing young kids from Wichita, Kansas City or St. Joseph, Missouri who wanted to learn a trade and become city

flirts. They wanted to be fast and to know how to take care of themselves in a tough town. She took them in, taught them the trade, lent them money when they were down on their backs, and when they got back on their feet again they'd primp up, run off with some well-perfumed guy who took dope or take a job in a competitive shop across the street because they thought it was closer to Walnut Street. (*Bottom Dogs,* 162–3)

Experienced lady barbers were now available. Often down and out, they came to Lizzie for work, and she would lend them money and take them in as free lodgers until they were on their feet. Among these was Gladys, who had Indian blood and a large bun of chestnut hair. She was a great drawing card for the shop. Emma Moneysmith, a Mormon with legs that quivered like a drawn bow, had the second chair; her boy, Marion, took violin lessons. The third was Miss Taylor's whose son, Noah, had the sexual habits of Ham. He claimed that Tisha, the daughter of the prostitute who kept light-housekeeping rooms above Basket's Lunchroom, had put a love potion in his cup of coffee. Sally Muhlebach, a good hairdresser but too seedy to bait trade, served the fourth chair. Her nine-year-old girl, Gizella, had ballooned, dropsical legs and once when she and Lizzie's boy were at the flat together, she told him some of the dark secrets of pleasure while fingering the keys on the Bach upright piano in the parlor so that none of the girl roomers could hear her. (*Because I Was Flesh,* 23–4)

The prose of *Bottom Dogs* has a "sapless complexion." (24) It is as riveting as one of Mary Baker Eddy's Christian Science tracts. The girls suffer from the ultimate Dahlbergian indignity: They have no name, no body, therefore no vivacious identity. The author parcels out information as if he were giving street directions to a stranger, betraying no feeling. He cannot carry a tune. The rhythm is slack, the rhetoric minimal, neutered, reductive, its dullness the "sign of a weak and stingy imagination."[24] In contrast, the prose of the autobiography is expansive, droll, animated, physical; the author shares his knowledge and enjoyment of the "dark secrets of pleasure," (24) improvising with a few deft images, while fingering the keys, the delicious, surreptitious, or brazen music of sex. The love potion has turned nearly everybody's head and legs; the girls are named and have children. Dahlberg's style has body and a robust flavor spiked with wormwood.

Dahlberg himself came to consider his early novels as mediocre manipulations of his childhood and young manhood, disfigured by self-pity—in short, dreary imitations of proletarian naturalism. Indeed, he repudiated them and refused to reread them.[25] In *The Flea of Sodom* (1950), Dahlberg describes his radical shift away from the linguistic void and gibbering of robots that he says marked much of the fiction and discourse of the thirties. He drastically revamped his style. His new ideal is expressed in a letter to Robert Hutchins: "A writer should employ a language that can pierce the heart or awaken the mind. Style ought to have some kinship with mountains, glens, furrows, orchards, if it is to have a symbolic and human value."[26]

To this end he rethought the role of the artist, shearing it of any overt political functions. "Art is sorcery,"[27] and the artist a hierophant ministering to the needs of the community with magical formulas, chants, and moral adages. Above all, he is a centaur guarding and adding to the stock of a nation's myths, by which it learns who and what it is. This task was particularly crucial for America, whose myths and legends had been neglected, or forgotten, or never acquired. Dahlberg thus recast himself as La Salle, Cabeza de Vaca, and William Bartram, solitary explorers willing to track the headwaters for samples of our autochthonous roots. In renouncing history,[28] that cluttered record of bloody and wasteful events, in favor of fable and prehistory, whose revivifying waters are "a surety of man's sanity,"[29] he converted his isolation into a virtue. In other words, he started making "a marvelous mask" and found a style manufactured half from the honey of books and half from his own venomous wit.

The new style emerged fully caparisoned in *Do These Bones Live* (1940). The title is exemplary: In a series of acrid, biblical, Brownean essays, he examines the American tradition and selects his own (narrow) usable past: Bartram, Thoreau, Melville, Sherwood Anderson, Dreiser. For the first time, he plays the *enfant terrible,* smashing idols with exhilarating swipes of the pen—and he indulges his love of pithy and provoking opinions. In the books that

came out in the years before he began writing *Because I Was Flesh,*
in 1959—*The Flea of Sodom, The Sorrows of Priapus* (1957)—he
refined his style and continued his didactic buccaneering: "like a
Grand Inquisitor," Read gently remarked to Dahlberg, "you would
send to the stake any author who in any respect offends your
dogma."[30] *The Flea of Sodom* is so violently turgid in its debunking
of left-wing attitudes—it is a private exorcism of old political demons and a purge of thirties apparatchiks—that it verges on inco-
herence.

Yet for all its superfluities, Dahlberg's baroque style has extraordinary energy, its bookishness balanced by a racy humor, its erudition as beautiful as carved lithic objects. And it suits the inner
man, whose planetary influences were so extreme. After all, he has
had only one story to tell, so that one should not seek any more
variety in his moral injunctions or his stiff-necked cries against the
stiff-necked—he packs the modern world off to hell with as much
skill as Dante's Cerberus—than in a hammer striking an anvil.

Dahlberg's style achieves consummate greatness in *Because I Was
Flesh.* And his imagination flourishes with a chaste ornateness. Sublimation and the sublime are cognates. There is no need for the
disarmingly casual explanation of why he wrote the book: "I have
nothing better to do with my life than to write a book and perhaps
nothing worse. . . . If this book is a great defect, then let it be; for
I have come to that time in my life when it is absolutely important
for me to compose a good memoir although it is a negligible thing
if I should fail." (4) Why? To empty his "sack of woe" (2) once
more? To cry *mea culpa* when his psychological premise is that guilt
is preordained? For unlike Saint Augustine, he does not find salvation in a system of truth that he avows it is his mission to expound
to other men. Saint Augustine's *Confessions* is a parable of spiritual
and psychological integration; *Because I Was Flesh,* of confusion
and partial transcendence.

Dahlberg tries to repair his broken world with mythic plumbing.[31] He extends the boundaries of his purview from Kansas City
to the heights of Lake Titicaca, as if his long pilgrimage in search
of his origins forced him back against the stream of time to the
child's dreams and the troglodytic world of the unconscious. The
quotations from his favorite authors, his authoritative geographers
of the spirit, are his lost father giving voice to, and glossing, the

text of his torn life.[32] The older man (and the better writer) of his private anthology rules with ironic scepter the reconstructed peonage of memory (again the parallel with Saint Augustine is startling).

The Word is Dahlberg's redeemer. In becoming flesh, it grants self-mastery. He no longer need guard himself against the world all the time; words guide his feelings to a taut harmony. Language may be "as unreasonable as life," (81) but in *Because I Was Flesh,* Dahlberg imbues it with heroic assurance—it is often all that stands between him and an infamous capitulation to nihilism. The profligacy of language, unlike that of sex, sustains him and enables him to overcome the vehement, coercive ideology he nursed from childhood. Words become his loving, nurturing parents, and *Because I Was Flesh* the wanted child of desire.

Notes

PREFACE

1. Walt Whitman, *Song of Myself,* Section 1, *Leaves of Grass, Complete Poetry and Selected Prose,* ed. James E. Miller, Jr. (Boston: Houghton Mifflin, 1959), p. 419.

2. Edwin Muir, *An Autobiography* (New York: The Seabury Press, 1968).

3. Konstantin Paustovsky, *The Story of a Life,* trans. Joseph Barnes (New York: Vintage Books, 1967).

4. Jean-Paul Sartre, *The Words,* trans. Bernard Frechtman (New York: George Braziller, 1964).

5. Benjamin Franklin, *The Autobiography of Benjamin Franklin,* ed. Leonard W. Labaree et al. (New Haven: Yale University Press, 1964).

6. Most autobiographers, bemused by the unpredictable flittings of images from the past, would agree with the novelist Paul West that "memory is fraught with drift, seepage, and distracted languor." Paul West, *Paul West 1930–,* Contemporary Authors Autobiography Series, Vol. 7 (Detroit: Gale Research Company, 1988), p. 165.

7. Nathalie Sarraute, *Childhood,* trans. Barbara Wright (New York: George Braziller, 1984), p. 154.

8. Henry James, "The Art of Fiction," *The Future of the Novel,* ed. Leon Edel (New York: Vintage Books, 1956), p. 14.

9. Albert Stone, *Autobiographical Occasions and Original Acts* (Philadelphia: University of Pennsylvania Press, 1982), p. 19.

10. V.S. Pritchett, "All about Ourselves," *New Statesman,* May 26, 1956, p. 602.

11. See Elizabeth Fox-Genovese, "Writings of Afro-American Women," *The Private Self,* ed. Shari Benstock (Chapel Hill: University of North Carolina Press, 1988), p. 83: "To write the account of one's self is to inscribe it in a culture that for each of us is only partially our own."

12. Robert F. Sayre, "Autobiography and America," *Autobiography: Essays Theoretical and Critical,* ed. James Olney (Princeton: Princeton University Press, 1980), p. 180.

13. John Adams, *Discourses on Davila* in *The Works of John Adams,* Vol. 6, ed. Charles Francis Adams (Boston, 1851), p. 233. Quoted in Sayre, op. cit., p. 153.

14. John Adams, op. cit., p. 234. Quoted in Sayre, op. cit., p. 153.

15. See, for example, Stephen Butterfield, *Black Autobiography in America* (Amherst: University of Massachusetts Press, 1974), p. 3: "The autobiographical form is one of the ways that black Americans have asserted their right to live and grow. It is a bid for freedom, a beak of hope cracking the shell of slavery and exploitation." Quoted in Susan Sanford Friedman, "Women's Autobiographical Selves," Benstock, op. cit., p. 43.

16. Walt Whitman, Preface to 1855 edition of *Leaves of Grass,* op. cit., p. 419.

17. Walt Whitman, *Song of Myself,* sec. 2, ibid., p. 25.

18. *Song of Myself,* Section 24, ibid., p. 41.

19. Ralph Waldo Emerson, "The Conservative," *Emerson* (New York: Library of America, 1983), p. 174.

20. Walt Whitman, *Democratic Vistas,* op. cit., p. 479.

21. Emily Dickinson, #228, *The Complete Poems of Emily Dickinson,* ed. Thomas Johnson (Boston: Little, Brown, 1960), p. 133.

22. Louis Sullivan, *The Autobiography of an Idea* (New York: Dover Books, 1957), p. 270.

23. Jane Addams, *Twenty Years at Hull-House* (New York: Signet Books/New American Library, 1960), p. 262, quotes the first verse of a poem called "Sweatshop," written by a Yiddish poet:
The roaring of the wheels has filled my ears.
 The clashing and the clamor shut me in.
Myself, my soul, in chaos disappears.
 I cannot think or feel amid the din.

24. Mark Twain, *Adventures of Huckleberry Finn,* ed. Walter Blair and Victor Fischer (Berkeley: University of California Press, 1986), p. 246.

25. John Jay Chapman, "Coatesville," *Selected Writings of John Jay Chapman,* ed. Jacques Barzun (New York: Farrar, Straus & Cudahy, 1957), p. 256.

26. I have reversed Estelle C. Jelinek's point here while retaining her words. See Estelle C. Jelinek, "Introduction," *Women's Autobiography,* ed. Estelle C. Jelinek (Bloomington: University of Indiana Press, 1980), p. 10.

27. Marcel Proust, *Swann's Way, Remembrance of Things Past,* trans. C. K. Scott-Moncrieff and Terence Kilmartin (New York: Random House, 1981), p. 11.

28. Wallace Stevens, "Esthétique du Mal," *The Collected Poems of Wallace Stevens* (New York: Alfred A. Knopf, 1954), p. 326.

1.

STYLE AND AUTOBIOGRAPHY

1. Jean-Paul Sartre, *The Words,* trans. Bernard Frechtman (New York: George Braziller, 1964), p. 120.

2. Virgil Thomson, *Virgil Thomson* (New York: Alfred A. Knopf, 1966), p. 16.

3. See Henry Adams, *The Education of Henry Adams,* ed. Ernest Samuels (Boston: Houghton Mifflin, 1974), pp. 4–5: "Although every one cannot be Gargantua-Napoleon-Bismarck and walk off with the great bells of Notre Dame, every one must bear his own universe, and most persons are moderately interested in learning how their neighbors have managed to carry theirs."

4. Ibid., p. 3.

5. Frederick Douglass, *Narrative of the Life of Frederick Douglass* (Cambridge: Harvard University Press, 1973), pp. 117–18.

6. Zora Neale Hurston, *Dust Tracks on a Road* (Urbana: University of Illinois Press, 1978), p. 56.

7. Ibid., p. 280.

8. Howard Nemerov, "Writing," *Collected Poems* (Chicago: University of Chicago Press, 1977), p. 203.

9. Henry James, "The Art of Fiction," *The Future of the Novel,* ed. Leon Edel (New York: Vintage Books, 1971), p. 12.

10. William Gass, "The Soul Inside the Sentence," *Habitations of the Word* (New York: Alfred A. Knopf, 1985), p. 126.

11. Thomson, op. cit., p. 24.

12. Ibid., pp. 3–4.

13. Ibid., p. 384.

14. Ibid., p. 13.

15. Ibid., pp. 47–8.

16. Otto Luening's autobiography, *The Odyssey of an American Composer* (New York: Charles Scribner's Sons, 1980), is another example of this American tradition of ingenuous narrative.

17. Edward Dahlberg, *Because I Was Flesh* (New York: New Directions, 1964), pp. 1–2.

18. Thomson, op. cit., p. 24.

19. Describing his literary method as a music reviewer on the New York *Herald Tribune* and his philosophy of writing in general, Thomson observes, "My literary method, then as now, was to seek out the precise adjective. Nouns are names and

can be libelous; the verbs, though sometimes picturesque, are few in number and tend toward alleging motivations. It is the specific adjectives that really describe and that do so neither in sorrow nor in anger." Ibid., p. 327. His adjectives in the autobiography do not call attention to themselves.

20. Peter Brown, *Augustine of Hippo* (Berkeley: University of California Press, 1967), p. 170.

21. Roland Barthes, *Empire of Signs,* trans. Richard Howard (New York: Hill & Wang, 1982), p. 63.

22. Saint Augustine, *Confessions,* trans. R. S. Pine-Coffin (Baltimore: Penguin, 1964), p. 214.

23. Cf. William C. Spengemann, *The Forms of Autobiography* (New Haven: Yale University Press, 1980), p. 9: "Even his language aspires continually to divinity, as he labors to maintain a level of discourse that will move smoothly in and out of Scriptural quotation with no syntactic break or tonal seam, and thus to demonstrate rhetorically the consonance of his own words with the divine Word." This essay offers an excellent interpretation of Saint Augustine's structure in the *Confessions.*

24. Ibid., p. 188.

25. Sol LeWitt, *Autobiography* (New York: Multiples Inc.; Boston: Lois and Michael K. Torf, 1980).

26. Gertrude Stein, *The Autobiography of Alice B. Toklas* (New York: Modern Library, 1955), p. 79.

27. Thomson, op. cit., p. 404.

28. Ibid.

29. Ibid.

30. Ibid.

31. Ibid., p. 417.

32. Henry James, *Autobiography,* ed. Frederick Dupee (New York: Criterion Books, 1956), p. 37.

33. Ibid., p. 156.

34. Ibid., p. 66.

35. Ibid., p. 70.

36. Ibid., p. 4.

37. Ibid., p. 81.

38. Ibid., p. 16.

39. Ibid., p. 149.

40. Ibid., p. 200.

41. Ibid., p. 21–2.

42. Conrad Aiken, *Ushant* (New York: Oxford University Press, 1971), p. 19.

43. Ibid., p. 3.

44. William Wordsworth, *The Prelude,* Book III, line 63. Ed. Ernest de Selincourt (Oxford: Oxford University Press, 1947), p. 35.

45. Jean Starobinski, "The Style of Autobiography," trans. Seymour Chatman, in *Autobiography,* ed. James Olney (Princeton: Princeton University Press, 1980), p. 73.

46. Aiken, op. cit., p. 244.

47. Ibid., p. 56.

48. One episode Aiken narrates that avoids the gussied-up language of an "interminable soliloquy" (Ibid., p. 94) tells of his father's enthusiastic plan to build a boat in his backyard. Despite the slightly overripe prose, when Aiken looks at his father's velleities, the daft schemes of a drydocked visionary, he evokes the scene beautifully. His father's "bright new boat of golden wood" is not a willed symbol but a disclosure of a character paddling in the shallows unable to bring projects to their completion, a trait that afflicts the autobiographer too. Ibid., p. 46.

49. Ibid., p. 191–2.

50. Paul Valéry, "Aesthetics," *The Problem of Style,* ed. J. V. Cunningham (New York: Fawcett Premier Books, 1966), p. 19.

51. Italo Calvino, *Six Memos for the Next Millennium* (Cambridge: Harvard University Press, 1988), p. 124.

52. Gass, "Emerson and the Essay," op. cit., p. 32. This essay lists and analyzes the range of styles American writers have used.

2

THE AUTOBIOGRAPHY OF BENJAMIN FRANKLIN

1. Letter of Thomas Jefferson to John Adams, Mar. 25, 1726. *The Adams-Jefferson Letters,* ed. Lester J. Cappon (Chapel Hill: University of North Carolina Press, 1959), vol, 2, p. 614. Though Jefferson was not thinking of Franklin, the terms apply.

2. Thomas Jefferson, Letter to Samuel Smith, August 22, 1798, *Jefferson* (New York: Library of America, 1984), p. 1052.

3. John Wesley, quoted in Philip Greven, *The Protestant Temperament* (New York: Alfred A. Knopf, 1977), p. 44.

4. Benjamin Franklin, *The Autobiography of Benjamin Franklin,* ed. Leonard W. Labaree et al. (New Haven: Yale University Press, 1964), p. 43. All parenthetical page references within the chapter are to this definitive edition.

5. "In plain Truth I was astonished at the grossness of his [General Lafayette's] Ignorance of Gover[n]ment and History, as I had been for years before at that of Turgot, Rochefoucault, Condorcet and Franklin." Letter of John Adams to Thomas Jefferson, July 13, 1813, op. cit., p. 355.

6. William Carlos Williams, "Poor Richard," *In the American Grain* (New York: New Directions, 1954), p. 145. The phrase is Franklin's.

7. Ibid., p. 156. Cf. Josephine Herbst, *New Green World* (New York: Hastings House, 1954): "The penny might be taken for Franklin's symbol; *thrifty,* the slogan to drive home an uneasy sense of insecurity. Stay put, dig in, hoe, save, be cautious. . . . Opposed to this was the beauty and fertility of the wilderness, the forbidden unknown . . .," p. 93.

8. C. A. Sainte-Beuve, *Portraits of the Eighteenth Century, Historic and Lit-*

erary, Vol. 1, trans. Katherine P. Wormeley (New York: Frederick Ungar Publishing Co., 1964), p. 322.

9. Williams, op. cit., p. 153. This is also Josephine Herbst's view: "In his own down-to-earth fashion, he did much toward chopping down the flowering wild thing in new world minds that tameness might grow. Thus he prepared the path for the Nineteenth Century and the conquest of man by machine." Ibid., p. 93.

10. D. H. Lawrence, "Benjamin Franklin," *Studies in Classic American Literature* (New York: Viking Press, 1969), p. 21.

11. Ibid., p. 14.

12. Ibid., p. 13.

13. Ibid., p. 9. "The gulf, of course, between types so opposite as Franklin and Lawrence," F. L. Lucas wryly notes, "remains unbridgeable. There can hardly be reconciliation between those who value, above all, 'fire in the belly' and those who value light in the brain. . . . As for 'subconsciously hating' that Europe in which he lived a quarter of a century, and several times considered settling for life, even were this pretty theory true, Franklin might have asked why it should be wicked for him to hate Europe, yet right for Lawrence to hate so much of America." F. L. Lucas, *The Art of Living* (New York: Macmillan Paperbacks, 1959), pp. 159–60.

14. John Woolman, *The Journal and Major Essays of John Woolman,* ed. Phillips P. Moulton (New York: Viking Press, 1971). p. 49.

15. Benjamin Franklin, *Poor Richard, The Almanack for the Years 1733–1758,* Library of America (New York, 1987), p. 1191.

16. Erik Erikson, *Young Man Luther,* 2nd ed. (New York: W. W. Norton & Co., 1962), pp. 53–4.

17. His father was actually a Congregationalist. Cf. Autobiography, pp. 145–6.

18. Cf. Carl Van Doren, *Benjamin Franklin* (New York: Viking Press, 1938), p. 647.

19. Henry Adams, *History of the United States of America During the First Administration of Thomas Jefferson,* (New York: Library of America, 1986), p. 81.

20. Herman Melville, *His Fifty Years of Exile (Israel Potter)* (New York: Sagamore Press, 1957), p. 75.

21. Benjamin Franklin, "Letter to a Young Man," 25 June 1745, Library of America, p. 302.

22. He once compared her to a "large fine Jugg for Beer." Quoted in John Updike, "Many Bens," *The New Yorker,* February 22, 1988, p. 107.

23. Franklin, *Poor Richard,* 1738, p. 1208.

24. As Updike points out, Deborah "was afraid of sea voyages and had twice refused to accompany him abroad." Op. cit., p. 108.

25. "Serve" was a favorite theological term of Cotton Mather's.

26. Melville, op. cit., p. 66.

27. Franklin, *Poor Richard,* 1735, p. 1197.

28. Cf. Frederick Tolles, *Meeting House and Counting House: The Quaker Merchants of Colonial Philadelphia, 1672–1763* (New York: W. W. Norton & Co., 1963), passim.

29. Albert Jay Nock notes in his biography of Jefferson (New York: Hill & Wang, 1960) that the Virginian "would have nothing to do with patents. He had no taste for money made out of any form of monopoly," p. 42.

30. Erik Erikson, *Young Man Luther,* p. 70.

31. Franklin, *Poor Richard,* 1737, p. 1204.

32. John Adams, diary, quoted in Van Doren, op. cit., p. 688.

33. Franklin, *Poor Richard,* 1735, p. 1198.

34. Claude-Anne Lopez and Eugenia W. Herbert, *The Private Franklin* (New York: W. W. Norton & Co., 1975), p. 25.

35. Van Doren, op. cit., p. 209.

36. In his pamphlet "A Narrative of the Late Massacres," Franklin protested vehemently against the Paxton Boys' massacres of the Conestoga Indians: "What had little Boys and Girls done; what could Children of a Year old, Babes at the Breast, what could they do, That they too must be shot and hatcheted?—Horrid to relate!—and in their Parents Arms! This is done by no civilized Nation in *Europe.* Do we come to *America* to learn and practice the Manners of *Barbarians?*" Library of America, p. 555.

37. Melville, op. cit., p. 63.

38. Long before Franklin freed his slaves, Keimer "proposed to teach blacks to read the Scriptures." Lopez and Herbert, op. cit., p. 20. Keimer published *A History of the Quakers* by William Sewell in 1728 and the first translation in America of Epictetus in 1729. Van Doren, op. cit., p. 94. This is another instance in which Franklin could not bear being the servant in a master-servant relationship. That Keimer was a stickler for a literal interpretation of the Mosaic law could not have endeared him to Franklin.

39. Franklin's polemics and pamphleteering are enlivened by his apt metaphors: "A great Empire, like a great Cake, is most easily diminished at the Edges," *Rules by Which a Great Empire May Be Reduced to a Small One,* Library of America, p. 689. Quoted in Lucas, op. cit., p. 233.

40. Franklin, *Autobiography,* p. 1402. See Franklin's letter to his sister, Philadelphia, June 19, 1730 [1731]. *The Letters of Benjamin Franklin and Jane Mecom* (Princeton: Princeton University Press, 1956), pp. 36–7.

41. Cotton Mather shared Franklin's position on the value of inoculation; John Woolman opposed it: "I have looked at the smallpox as a messenger sent from the Almighty to be an assistant in the course of virtue, and to incite us to consider whether we employ our time only in such things as are consistent with perfect wisdom and goodness. . . . It should be left to God's gift, not to be disposed of in our own wills." Woolman, op. cit., p. 102.

42. Jonathan Edwards, *Personal Narrative,* in *Basic Writings,* ed. Ola Elizabeth Winslow (New York: Signet Books, 1966), p. 88.

43. Greven, op. cit., p. 52.

44. Perry Miller, *Jonathan Edwards* (New York: W. Sloane Associates, 1949), p. 57.

45. Sacvan Bercovitch, *The Puritan Origins of the American Self* (New Haven: Yale University Press, 1976), p. 20.

46. Kenneth Murdock, "Introduction," Perry Miller, *Nature's Nation* (Cambridge: Harvard University Press, 1967), p. x.

47. "Of Experience," *Complete Essays of Montaigne,* trans. Donald Frame (Palo Alto, Cal.: Stanford University Press, 1965), p. 382.

48. Edwards, op. cit., p. 94.

49. Ibid., p. 101.

50. Cf. Daniel B. Shea, Jr., *Spiritual Autobiography in Early America* (Princeton: Princeton University Press, 1968), p. xi: "The spiritual autobiography of early America ought not be categorized exclusively, however, as a narrative of conversion."

51. Henry Adams, *The Education of Henry Adams,* ed. Ernest Samuels (Boston: Houghton Mifflin, 1974), p. xxx.

52. Karl Jackson Weintraub, *The Value of the Individual Self* (Chicago: University of Chicago Press, 1978), p. 251, argues that Franklin "is the Puritan personality without the Puritan motivation and the Puritan objective." The two concessive phrases, in my opinion, leave little of the Puritan personality intact.

53. It is wholly characteristic of Franklin that the exact nature and depth of his religious beliefs remain controversial. Professor Weintraub declares: "He was not an irreligious man. He surely did not present himself as such. He classed himself with the Deists; their trust in God as the necessary Creator and their trust in a general beneficial providence belong quite properly (and not hypocritically) to his intellectual outlook. He could not have held the positions he maintained had he been moved by an agnostic doubt about a providentially ordered creation." Ibid. Like many commentators, Weintraub defines Franklin's religious affiliations by what they are *not*. A few pages after the above statement, he observes that "the intense anxiety over God's acceptance furnished the energy for unifying the personality. Secularized man [Franklin], without the comfort of believing that God was working the true transformation, had to set his own law and implement it." Ibid., p. 255. Lopez and Herbert speak of Franklin's "ethically fortified deism," a phrase that suggests a wavering or weak faith.

54. Cotton Mather, *Bonifacius: An Essay Upon the Good,* ed. David Levin (Cambridge: Harvard University Press, 1966), p. 27.

55. Ibid., p. 17.

56. Ibid., p. 32.

57. Thomas Jefferson, Letter to John Adams, October 28, 1813, Cappon, op. cit., vol. 2, p. 391.

58. Letter of Thomas Jefferson to John Adams, August 22, 1813. Ibid., p. 368.

59. Cf. William C. Spengemann, *The Forms of Autobiography* (New Haven: Yale University Press, 1980), p. 53: "Franklin's idea of true being, the Life of Reason, is itself the product of history rather than its eternal governing law." And p. 54: "Franklin's *Autobiography* offers itself as a Scripture, the only available to an audience that had overthrown all forms of traditional authority and replaced them with the authority of personal conviction. By imitating his success men can fulfill his prophecy and bring about the rule of human Reason, that earthly heaven in which Franklin will have his immortality."

60. *Poor Richard Improved, 1753,* Library of America, p. 1278.

61. Jonathan Edwards, "Of Insects," *Selected Writings,* op. cit., p. 34.

62. Edwards, *Personal Narrative,* p. 91.

63. Ibid., p. 83.

64. Ibid., p. 87.

65. Miller, *Jonathan Edwards,* p. 197.

66. Edwards, *Personal Narrative,* p. 85.

67. Cf. Williams, op. cit., p. 155: "he didn't dare let it [lightning] go in at the top of his head and out at his toes, that's it; he *had* to fool with it."

68. V. S. Pritchett, "All About Ourselves," *New Statesman,* May 26, 1956, pp. 601–2.

69. "Franklin never, like Augustine, found one form and identity which could be made to stand for the whole life; he never even gives the appearance of having discovered one form and then written in it." Robert F. Sayre, *The Examined Self* (Princeton: Princeton University Press, 1964), p. 16.

70. Ralph Waldo Emerson, "Prudence," *Essays and Lectures* (New York: Library of America, 1983), p. 357. "Prudence," Emerson goes on to say, "is the virtue of the senses. It is the science of appearances. It is the outmost action of the inward life. It is God taking thought for oxen. It moves matter after the laws of matter. It is content to seek health of body by complying with physical conditions, and health of mind by the laws of the intellect." In a backhanded compliment, Emerson acknowledges that even "the wisdom of Poor Richard" can be helpful. Ibid., p. 364.

71. Ibid., p. 367.

72. Emerson, "Self-Reliance," Library of America, p. 268.

73. "Nor did Franklin feel much, apparently, for the loveliness of Nature. It is characteristic that he employed Wordsworth's Derwentwater, not as a theme for poetic feeling, but as a surface to cast oil on, in an experiment for calming troubled waters." Lucas, op. cit., p. 206.

74. Lawrence, op. cit., p. 10.

75. Emerson, "The American Scholar," op. cit., p. 60.

76. Ibid.

77. Henry David Thoreau, in *A Week on the Concord and Merrimack Rivers* (New York: Library of America, 1985), p. 59, discussing mythology, says: "And Franklin.—There may be a line for him in the future classical dictionary, recording what that demigod did, and referring him to some new genealogy. Son of —— and ——. He aided the Americans to gain their independence, instructed mankind in economy, and drew down lightning from the clouds." This conventional view of the "mythological" Franklin is belied by Thoreau's harsh attack in *Walden* on the American economy Franklin helped set up. There is a superficial resemblance between the two men in their fondness for moralizing proverbs and in their fascination with how much life can be sustained on meager material comfort. Thoreau, of course, came closer to living by this principle; Franklin ignored it. Perhaps Franklin, had he read *Walden,* might have called Thoreau a "Croaker," a pessimistic nay-sayer.

78. *Walden,* ibid., p. 378.

79. Ibid., p. 381.

80. Ibid.

81. Erik Erikson, *Childhood and Society,* 2d ed. (New York: W. W. Norton and Co., 1963), p. 304.

3.

LOUIS SULLIVAN'S *THE AUTOBIOGRAPHY OF AN IDEA*

1. Frank Lloyd Wright, *An Autobiography* (New York: Horizon Press, 1977), p. 112.

2. Louis Sullivan, *The Autobiography of an Idea* (New York: Dover Books, 1957). All parenthetical page references within the chapter are to this edition.

3. In a somewhat ambiguous judgment, Frank Lloyd Wright observed: "My old Master had designed for the old materials all alike; brick, stone, wood, iron wrought or iron cast, or plaster—all were grist for his rich imagination and his sentient ornament." Wright, op. cit., p. 172.

4. See my discussion of third-person narrative, pp. 102–4.

5. Wright, op. cit., p. 289.

6. Thomas S. Hines, *Burnham of Chicago, Architect and Planner* (Chicago: University of Chicago Press, 1979), p. 23.

7. Louis Sullivan, *Kindergarten Chats* (New York: George Wittenborn, 1965), p. 39. The book was written in 1901 and revised in 1918.

8. Ibid., p. 97.

9. Frank Lloyd Wright, *A Testament* (New York: Horizon Press, 1957), p. 33.

10. Tocqueville pointed out why genius or uncommon talent was suspect in America: "Democratic institutions awaken and flatter the passion for equality without ever being able to satisfy it entirely. This complete equality is always slipping through the people's fingers at the moment when they think to grasp it, fleeing, as Pascal says, in an eternal fight; the people grow heated in search of this blessing, all the more precious because it is near enough to be seen but too far off to be tasted. They are excited by the chance and irritated by the uncertainty of success; the excitement is followed by weariness and then by bitterness. In that state anything which in any way transcends the people seems an obstacle to their desires, and they are tired by the sight of any superiority, however legitimate." Alexis de Tocqueville, *Democracy in America,* ed. J. P. Mayer, trans. George Lawrence (Garden City, N. Y.: Doubleday/Anchor, 1969), p. 198.

11. Sullivan, *Kindergarten Chats,* p. 24.

12. Wright, *Testament,* p. 18.

13. Sullivan, *Kindergarten Chats,* p. 48.

14. Ibid., p. 39.

15. Sullivan is not interested in historical accuracy, so he neglects to point out that the classicizing impulse in American buildings can be traced back beyond Jefferson. The Capitol in Washington and the state capitols of Providence and

Boston are examples of the ancient grandeur American architects copied and adapted. Tocqueville points out that the taste of democratic peoples in their public buildings run to the monumental. De Tocqueville, op. cit., pp. 469–70.

16. Sullivan does not mention his brother in *The Autobiography of an Idea,* a signal omission.

17. Sullivan was more than fifteen years older than Margaret Hattabough, his wife, but he does not seem to notice that he has repeated his father's pattern.

18. Wright's father, a dreamer and musician-scholar, was somewhat remote from his son, though he did pass on a love of music. As in the Sullivan family, the mother was the favored parent. "After their son was born something happened between the mother and father. Sister Anna's extraordinary devotion to the child disconcerted the father. He never made much of the child, it seems. No doubt his wife loved him no less, but now loved something more, something created out of her own fervor of love and desire. A means to realize her vision." *An Autobiography,* p. 31.

19. Sullivan, *Kindergarten Chats,* p. 23.

20. Albert Stone, "The Childhood of the Artist," *Autobiographical Occasions and Original Acts* (Philadelphia: University of Pennsylvania Press, 1982), pp. 113–14. The entire passage reads: "His democratic philosophy with its intense but generalized ardor for mankind, his self-stylized role as the people's architect, his complete silence about any mature relationship with women—all suggest that Sullivan remained throughout his life a man whose capacities for strong universal emotions masked underlying ambiguities about personal ties."

21. Wright, *Autobiography,* p. 109.

22. Wright, *Testament,* p. 20.

23. Ibid., p. 19.

24. William Jordy, "Functionalism as Fact and Symbol: Louis Sullivan's Commercial Buildings, Tombs, and Banks," *American Buildings and Their Architects* (Garden City: Doubleday & Company, 1970), p. 120.

25. Wright, *Autobiography,* p. 93.

26. Wright, *Testament,* p. 180.

27. Wright, *Autobiography,* p. 109.

28. Ibid., p. 130.

29. Wright's roster of substitutes includes "he," "the boy," "his mother's son," "the minister's son," "the youth," "the urchin," and "the dreamer." There is an element of calculation in Wright's doling out and arrangement of the facts of his boyhood, which keeps the reader at arm's length. The linkage between the boy's early years and the middle-aged architect's opinions seems tenuously built. Wright offers an aerial perspective, sequences and all talk of the emotions controlled and muted by cerebral design.

30. Wright, *Autobiography,* p. 27.

31. Ibid., p. 114.

32. Stone, op. cit., p. 101.

33. Wright, *Autobiography,* p. 285. A surprisingly large number of Wright's sentences end in a question. Since he gives so much weight and prominence to his

polemics and his opinions—he is seldom beset by self-doubt—the rhetorical device seems an unconscious way of softening or modifying his egotism. The fiery sermonizing may be attributed to his family background. The garrulity and repetition often bring the narrative to a standstill, as if sand were thrown into its gas tank. The democratic ideologue doesn't know when to shut up.

34. Ibid., p. 125.

35. Frank Lloyd Wright is also given to long paragraphs of sentence fragments, as if substance, in a romantic style, pushed action out of the way. It becomes a tiresome mannerism, "a baying at the moon," a way of filling up the pages until a new idea comes. Wright casually admitted that *An Autobiography* was a "looseleaf" album (p. 533). The autobiographical narrative is shapeless, the laborious pronouncements poorly aligned with Wright's experiences, his harsh, angular side smoothed out by the cosmetician's art. Here is a sample:

> For three decades, the perfect mistress, Olgivanna, and I have lived and worked in luck and out of luck at Taliesin, in any case constantly together. This in sickness and in health. Mostly health. No fair-weather friend was Olgivanna. There was great work to be done now as well as a full life to be lived. But one that would have destroyed any human being less well trained for struggle for the better thing; less inspired by natural gifts, mutual love and understanding.
>
> Just to be with her uplifts my heart and strengthens my spirit when the going gets hard and no less when the going is good. (Ibid., p. 538)

Wright justifies his failures in *An Autobiography* by arguing that it's the autobiography of an architect, not a writer, that he is a verbal journeyman who can't cantilever his sentences, but that is a weak defense. The saccharine story of his cozy domestic life with Olgivanna is cloying and does not cancel the lingering bad taste from his indifference to his first family. *An Autobiography* is most brilliant in giving the lay reader a full sense of the romance and hard thinking that goes into designing a building like La Miniatura and solving problems of site, material, space, and use.

36. Vincent Scully, "American Houses: Thomas Jefferson to Frank Lloyd Wright," *An American Architecture,* ed. E. Kaufmann, Jr. (New York: Horizon Press, 1955), p. 186.

37. Wright, *Autobiography,* p. 293. Sullivan bequeathed to Wright a cherished daguerreotype of his mother and her two sons.

38. Louis Sullivan, *A System of Architectural Ornament* (New York: Eakins Press, 1967), unpaginated.

4.
JANE ADDAMS'S *TWENTY YEARS AT HULL-HOUSE*

1. Jane Addams, *The Long Road of Women's Memory* (New York: Macmillan, 1916), p. xv.

2. Ibid., p. 142.

3. "Jane Addams' efforts for peace cost her tremendous national prestige and led to accusations that she was a dangerous traitor." Lela B. Costin, *Two Sisters for Social Justice: A Biography of Grace and Edith Abbott* (Urbana: University of Illinois Press, 1983), p. 55. It is as if Addams went from being the mother ideal of the nation to being equated with Emma Goldman as an enemy of American patriotism.

4. Addams, op. cit., p. xiii.

5. Ibid., p. 147.

6. Ibid., p. 153.

7. Ibid., p. 152.

8. Ibid., p. 155.

9. Ibid., p. 157.

10. Ibid., p. xiii.

11. Ibid., p. x.

12. Florence Kelley, Jane Addams's friend and colleague at Hull-House, said of *her* father, Congressman William Darrah Kelley ("Pig Iron Kelley"), that "he welcomed me with enthusiasm which has enriched my whole life." *The Autobiography of Florence Kelley,* ed. Kathryn Kush Sklar (Chicago: Chester H. Kerr Publishing, 1985), p. 26. The original edition was published in 1898. See Elizabeth Cady Stanton, *Eighty Years and More* (New York: Schocken Books, 1975), p. 3: "My father was a man of firm character and unimpeachable integrity, and yet sensitive and modest to a painful degree. There were but two places in which he felt at ease—in the courthouse and at his own fireside. Though gentle and tender, he had such a dignified repose and reserve of manner that as children we regarded him with fear rather than affection." After the death of his only son, the bereft Mr. Stanton said to his comforting daughter: "Oh, my daughter, I wish you were a boy!" Ibid., p. 20. Elizabeth Cady Stanton came to rebel against the prevailing view that "a girl weighed less in the scale of being than a boy." Ibid., p. 21.

13. Kelley and Stanton also read through the well-stocked libraries of their fathers, who tacitly encouraged their intellectual talents.

14. Jane Addams, *Twenty Years at Hull-House* (New York: Signet Books/New American Library, 1961). All parenthetical page references within the chapter are to this edition. This volume originally appeared in 1910 (Macmillan), after being excerpted in the *Ladies' Home Journal,* to great popular and critical acclaim. Addams published a sequel in 1930, *The Second Twenty Years at Hull-House,* which is not so richly textured.

15. Stanton, op. cit., p. 160.

16. Because of his own hardships as a boy, William Darrah Kelley taught his daughter Florence responsibility to "less fortunate contemporaries," especially to widows and children. Kelley, op. cit., p. 26.

17. Allen F. Davis, *American Heroine: The Life and Legend of Jane Addams* (New York: Oxford University Press, 1973), p. 5.

18. Addams, *The Long Road of Women's Memory,* p. 95.

19. In the two decades after the Civil War, Florence Kelley pointed out, "Wom-

en's ancient concern for nurture, growth, and the stirring up of vigor was still limited to the home." Kelley, op. cit., p. 52. Christopher Lasch, *The New Radicalism in America,* 1889–1963 (New York: Vintage Books, 1965), p. 65, writes: "Women were the moral custodians of society. In a society that felt itself on the verge of chaos—a 'frontier' in the broadest sense of the term—they came to represent cohesion, decency, and self-restraint, and the cult of the home, over which they presided, became the national religion. Under those circumstances the rebellion against culture became a rebellion also against the definition of a woman's 'place' with which the nineteenth-century concept of culture was so closely bound up."

20. Carroll Smith-Rosenberg, "The New Woman as Androgyne," *Disorderly Conduct* (New York: Alfred A. Knopf, 1985), p. 256.

21. Ibid., p. 254.

22. See Davis, op. cit., pp. 6, 7: "Jane's stepmother, Anna Haldeman Addams, . . . was a high-strung, attractive woman who considered herself an aristocrat and intellectual. She had little formal education, but she had grown up in a family of intellectuals and was herself a talented musician and an avid reader, though she also never questioned the traditional belief that a woman's place was in the home." "Growing up in this relatively sophisticated environment, Jane Addams acquired a social assurance, a sense of position, an easy identity with those who represented wealth and culture, that would stay with her all her life."

23. The abbey of Port Royal in seventeenth-century Paris was the center of Jansenism and resistance against the Jesuits. It received the support of Pascal in his *Provinciales*. Jansenism at the abbey conflicted with the "monarchical absolutism of Richelieu and Louis XIV, since its adherents stood for the inviolable rights of the individual conscience." *Encyclopaedia Britannica,* 15th edition (Chicago, 1985), p. 623.

24. Florence Kelley was also brought up with "no fear of Hell-fire or eternal punishment of any kind." Kelley, op. cit., p. 30.

25. Elizabeth Cady Stanton told a reporter to "put it down in capital letters: SELF-DEVELOPMENT IS A HIGHER DUTY THAN SELF-SACRIFICE. The thing which most retards and militates against women's self-development is self-sacrifice." Quoted in Carol Gilligan, *In a Different Voice* (Cambridge: Harvard University Press, 1982), p. 129. George Eliot's novel *Romola* was the first fiction given a public reading at Hull-House. And the following moral sentiment from *The Mill on the Floss* might have been written by Addams: "The mysterious complexity of our life" cannot be bound by "general rules" but must instead be informed "by a life vivid and intense enough to have created a wide, fellow-feeling with all that is human." Quoted in Gilligan, op. cit., p. 130. *Middlemarch,* of course, is a masterly study of the seductive perils of self-sacrifice to an idealistic young woman.

26. *Oxford English Dictionary,* vol. I, p. 630.

27. Jackson Lears, *No Place of Grace* (New York: Pantheon Books, 1981), pp. 12–13.

28. C. L. R. James, *Beyond a Boundary* (New York: Pantheon Books, 1981), p. 115. The original edition of this book was published in 1963.

29. Czeslaw Milosz, *The Captive Mind* (New York: Doubleday/Anchor, 1957), p. 33. Cf. Emerson, "Politics," Library of America, p.565, quoting Fisher Ames: "a republic is a raft, which would never sink, but then your feet are always in water."

30. Jane Addams, "Practical Reform," *Democracy and Social Ethics,* ed. Anne Firor Scott (Cambridge: Harvard University Press, 1964), p. 222. Addams's book was originally published in 1902.

31. Ibid., p. 151.

32. Charlotte Perkins Gilman, *The Living of Charlotte Perkins Gilman* (New York: Harper Colophon, 1975), p. 184.

33. Letter of William James to Jane Addams, December 13, 1909: "You *inhabit* reality and when you open your mouth truth can't help being uttered." *William James: Selected Unpublished Correspondence, 1885–1910,* ed. Frederick J. Down Scott (Columbus: Ohio State University Press, 1966), p. 528. Jane Addams passionately believed that we should "learn from life itself." *(73)*

34. Addams's most influential books were *The Spirit of Youth and the City Streets* (Urbana: University of Illinois Press, 1972), originally published in 1909, and *Democracy and Social Ethics.* In a series of cogent, humanistic essays in *The Spirit,* Addams traces the connection between the monotony and dullness of factory work and the petty immoralities that are often youth's protest against such restrictions: "Puritan repression plus lack of any outlet for self-expression at drudging work make a lethal combination." She sympathizes with the problems generated by youth's "big primitive emotions," their appetite for sexual experience, which cannot be solved by moral exhortations or sermons. She wishes to shelter the tender susceptibilities of youth, not to censor them. Typically, she allows a beleaguered young woman to put the dilemma into concrete terms: "I just had to go to dances sometimes after pushing down the lever of my machine with my right foot and using both my arms feeding it for ten hours a day—nobody knows how I felt some nights." *(11)*

35. Abraham Cahan, *The Education of Abraham Cahan,* trans. Leon Stein et al. (Philadelphia: Jewish Publication Society, 1969), p. 254. Cahan attributes this remark to Michael Heilprin, an émigré from Poland and Hungary, who edited Appleton's *New American Cyclopedia* and wrote for *The Nation.*

36. See Lasch, op. cit., p. 37: "What she discovered at Hull-House was that the same thing was happening in immigrant families that she had already experienced in her own. The children of immigrants driven by the timeless longing of youth for broader horizons, restlessly roamed the streets of the city, avidly drinking in the new culture about them. Their parents sought to keep them in the old ways. The children, maddened by everything in their parents that now seemed alien and queer, turned on them with loathing. Thus there came into being another domestic tragedy, no less poignant for Jane Addams than her own; and the breakdown of immigrant families upon contact with conditions in America came to seem to her, indeed, the measure of the immigrants' general degradation."

37. The ethnic neighborhoods helped cushion the blow of cultural displacement for some immigrants. The church and other local institutions, even the hearing of Italian or Russian spoken, must have comforted many newcomers.

38. Rosa Luxemburg, "Reform or Revolution," *Rosa Luxemburg Speaks,* ed. Mary Alice Waters (New York: Pathfinder Books, 1970), p. 78.

39. Jane Addams, "The Thirst for Righteousness," *The Spirit of Youth and the City Streets,* p. 143.

40. Luxemburg, op. cit., p. 73.

41. See *Twenty Years at Hull-House,* p. 41, for an anecdote about her father's convincing tightfisted German farmers to buy stock in the Northwestern Railroad, so as to transport their crops to the Great Lakes via Chicago. The trust of a "high-spirited German matron who took a share to be paid for 'out of butter and egg money' " turned the tide in favor of the project.

42. Addams, *The Spirit of Youth,* p. 147.

43. See Jane Addams, "A Modern Lear," *Survey Magazine,* November 2, 1912, and Richard Sennett's brilliant analysis of the Pullman strike and of Jane Addams's acute understanding of issues and antagonists. *Authority* (New York: Alfred A. Knopf, 1980), pp. 50–83.

44. In *The Second Twenty Years at Hull-House* (New York: Macmillan, 1930), p. 266, Addams remarks: "We had learned that life is never logical and apparently not even reasonable."

45. "Women activists . . . transmuted Christian piety into moral politics." Mari Jo Buhle, *Women and American Socialism, 1780–1920* (Urbana: University of Illinois Press, 1981), p. xvi. Jane Addams had been influenced by the Social Gospel Movement from her visits to Toynbee Hall in London in the 1880s, but her Christian principles permeated her vision from youth, and she had decided to establish Hull-House before she visited Toynbee Hall.

46. Florence Kelley, a committed socialist, had no bias against "an agreeable woman of leisure and means" like Anna Farnsworth, who did volunteer work at Hull-House for long hours every day. "That was before the squalid, recent social convention had been set up, according to which everyone, however abundant and well-assured her income, must earn her own living or be censured as a parasite. Miss Farnsworth's gracious gifts of free time and abundant good will for counseling perplexed immigrants, finding comfortable quarters for old people who could do a little work but not find for themselves in the labor market, providing happy Saturdays in the parks for little groups of schoolchildren whose mothers worked away from home, were among the Settlement's early enrichments of the neighborhood life." Kelley, op. cit., pp. 78–9.

47. Alexander Berkman, quoted in Emma Goldman, *Living My Life* (New York: Dover Books, 1931), vol. I, p. 324.

48. "The idea of rights is nothing but the conception of virtue applied to the world of politics." Alexis de Tocqueville, *Democracy in America,* trans. George Lawrence, ed. J. P. Mayer (Garden City, N.Y.: Doubleday/Anchor, 1969), pp. 237–8. Jane Addams admired Prince Kropotkin and shared his belief that "Mutual aid is as much a law of nature as mutual struggle." Peter Kropotkin, *Memoirs of a Revolutionist* (New York: Horizon Press, 1968), p. 498. Kropotkin is quoting a Russian zoologist, Professor Kessler.

49. Barbara Sicherman, *Alice Hamilton: A Life in Letters* (Cambridge: Harvard University Press, 1984), p. 114.

50. See Lasch's fine chapter "Jane Addams," op. cit., pp. 3–37, and Davis, op. cit., p. 159: "Her autobiography is a conscious attempt to focus the reader's attention on Jane Addams. Her motives were not exclusively selfish, of course; she did want to promote her reform ideas and publicize Hull-House, but what better way to accomplish these goals than to write of herself as a heroine?" Professor Davis is right to demystify the legend of the saintly, self-sacrificing priestess, but he seems to expect autobiography to be a vehicle of unequivocal truths. Like Franklin and Stein, indeed like most autobiographers, Addams used the genre to "rediscover and confirm her own sense of identity and to give a new creative shape to her life." Ibid. Nor is *Twenty Years at Hull-House* the optimistic book Davis says it is: "Again and again throughout the book, Addams affirmed the superiority of American democracy, of American innocence and virtue when compared with the decadence and corruption of the old world." Ibid., p. 173. But this opinion is contradicted by Addams's refusal to gild all the ugly realities of America, its failure to practice its ideals.

51. See Kelley, op. cit., p. 78. Hull-House is "the place which Miss Addams' steadfast will has made and kept, through war and peace, a center of hospitality for people and for ideas." Costin, op. cit., p. 43: "Hull-House and Chicago provided a setting in which they [Edith and Grace Abbott] could find a creative solution to the restrictive status of women, meet their strong personal needs for work and achievement, and contribute to social reform." The years the Abbott sisters spent at Hull-House were seminal for them. Certainly Hull-House had a powerful and impressive list of residents, unsurpassed by any other settlement, and Jane Addams had an unusual ability to create a sense of unity, a sense of purpose among the residents. Edith Abbott stated the reason simply: "We were held together by the sincere and gracious liberalism of Miss Addams." Such tributes were spontaneous and nearly universal. Alice Hamilton was struck by Jane Addams's gentle but penetrating eyes. Sicherman, op. cit., p. 119.

52. Alice Hamilton, letter to Agnes Hamilton, October 13, 1897, ibid., p. 116.

5.

EMMA GOLDMAN'S *LIVING MY LIFE*

1. Emma Goldman "never saw the painting," but she enjoyed sitting for and conversing with Henri. "I should not have known it [the painting] was you, if your name had not been under it," her sister Helena reported to her. This was the prevailing opinion of her friends, but she says handsomely, "I was certain, however, that Henri had tried to portray what he conceived to be the 'real Emma Goldman.' " *Living My Life*, vol. II (New York: Dover Books, 1970), p. 529. The original edition was published in 1931. All parenthetical page references within the chapter are to the 1970 edition.

2. Goldman explained to her friend Alexander Berkman that she was "writing about the life of Emma Goldman, the public person"; though she wondered if she could *also* depict "the other side, the woman, the personality in quest for the unattainable—in a personal sense." Emma Goldman to Alexander Berkman, De-

345

cember 23, 1927, International Institute for Social History, Emma Goldman Collection, quoted in Candace Falk, *Love, Anarchy, and Emma Goldman* (New York: Holt, Rinehart & Winston, 1984), p. 3.

3. Letter of Emma Goldman to Ben Reitman, July 29, 1911 (University of Illinois—Chicago Circle). Ibid., pp. 3–4.

4. J. Edgar Hoover made his reputation hounding radicals in a zealous witch hunt. See Richard Gid Powers, *Secrecy and Power: J. Edgar Hoover* (New York: Free Press, 1987), pp. 80–1.

5. See letter to Gwyneth Roe, January 5, 1932. Quoted in Falk, op. cit., p. 9: "It was very painful to relive everything, and much more so than the actual living of my life. I was much younger then, and so cocksure that I would continue, till the end of my days, to serve the ideal I had chosen as my goal. It was different while I was writing my book. All my hopes for activity had been buried, really nothing to look forward to, and the past seemed oceans and miles away. To resurrect it was, indeed, a painful process; but it had to be done to make history real and vivid."

6. Berkman edited some of *Living My Life.* Although he was a better writer than she, she was reluctant to place herself in a dependent position with him. Doubtless his version of tumultuous events and painful emotions was different.

7. "Emma Goldman's forte is the platform, not the pen, as she knows very well." Letter of Alexander Berkman to Dr. Michael Cohn, October 10, 1922, Berlin. *Nowhere at Home: Letters from Exile of Emma Goldman and Alexander Berkman,* ed. Richard and Anna Mana Drinnon (New York: Schocken Books, 1975), p. 27. This collection is indispensable for understanding Berkman's and Goldman's lives, ideas, and historical importance. See Elizabeth Gurley Flynn, *The Rebel Girl* (New York: International Publishers, 1973), p. 50: Flynn expected Emma Goldman to be an Amazon, but was "surprised at the force, eloquence, and fire that poured from this mild-mannered, motherly sort of woman."

8. See Alice Wexler, *Emma Goldman: An Intimate Life* (New York, Pantheon Books, 1984), pp. 167–76.

9. Henry David Thoreau, *Walden* (New York: Library of America, 1985), p. 404.

10. See Patricia Meyer Spacks, "Selves in Hiding," *Women's Autobiography,* ed. Estelle C. Jelinek (Bloomington: University of Indiana Press, 1980), p. 125. Spacks points out that Goldman and Ed Brady tried to live out the fantasy that it must be possible for a man and a woman to have a beautiful love life and yet be devoted to a great cause: "But experience repeatedly offers Goldman a lesson which she never fully incorporates: devotion to the masses mixes badly with devotion to a man, conflicting responsibilities and conflicting desires for gratification proving impossible to reconcile. . . . Public commitment and activity manifestly feel necessary to Emma Goldman, but not altogether 'natural.' . . . Hence, perhaps, the strain in her prose as well as her life, her account of herself a sequence of poses, her writing an imitation of romantic and sentimental novels, secondhand in its phraseology. The uncomfortable artificiality of her style reiterates the impression of indistinct identity."

11. Goldman was often acutely clear about the quandary of the emancipated

woman. In a letter to Berkman, September 4, 1925, London, she writes: "We are still rooted in the old soil, though our visions are of the future and our desire is to be free and independent." She goes on to say: "It is a longing for fulfillment which very few modern women find because most modern men too are rooted in the old traditions. They too want the woman as wife and mother more than as lover and friend. The modern woman cannot be the wife and mother in the old sense, and the new medium has not yet been devised. I mean the way of being the wife, mother, friend and yet retain one's complete freedom. Will it ever?" *Nowhere at Home,* p. 133.

12. Walt Whitman, *Song of Myself,* sec. 25, in *Leaves of Grass, Complete Poetry and Selected Prose,* ed. Justin Kaplan (New York: Library of America, 1982), p. 53.

13. Spacks, op. cit., p. 112.

14. Ibid., p. 118.

15. *Living My Life,* vol. I, pp. 184–6.

16. *The Autobiography of Mother Jones,* ed. Mary Field Parton (Chicago: Charles H. Kerr Publishing, 1974), p. 154.

17. Ibid., p. 113.

18. Most attributed many of his anarchist views to his feelings of humiliation and shame at having a visible ugly scar on his face owing to an accident in his childhood and a botched operation. "It became the horror of his existence. It made him pathologically self-conscious particularly in the presence of women. . . . He was sure that a great deal of his fierce hatred of our social system, of the cruelty and injustice of life, was due to his own maimed condition, to the indignities and maltreatment it had caused him." *Living My Life,* vol. I, p. 64. By citing Most's experience, Goldman may be indicating that his point of view had validity, but she cannot undertake to analyze it.

19. Ibid., vol. I, p. 28. Kropotkin, op. cit., pp. 49–51, describes a scene in which his father ordered a serf punished by one hundred lashes with the rod. "Human feelings were not recognized, not even suspected, in serfs." Ibid., p. 51.

20. Three years before her father's death, after he had survived a dangerous operation on his throat, Emma Goldman had refused her sister Helena's request that she visit his bedside. " 'He should have died long ago,' I had wired back." In 1894, she feels "estranged, but no longer so hostile." She attributes this gentling to Helena's "beautiful spirit and my own development that gradually healed me of the bitterness I bore my father. I came to understand that it is ignorance rather than cruelty that makes parents do so many dreadful things to their helpless children.' " *Living My Life,* vol. I, p. 209.

21. Kate Simon, *Bronx Primitive* (New York: Harper & Row, 1982), p. 176.

22. Kate Richards O'Hare, a socialist and fellow "political" prisoner with Goldman in the Jefferson, Missouri, jail, called Emma "the tender, cosmic mother, the wise understanding woman, the faithful sister, the loyal comrade." Quoted in Richard Drinnon, *Rebel in Paradise* (New York: Harper Colophon, 1976), p. 202. Emma interceded with prison officials to improve conditions for the other women prisoners. See Wexler, op. cit., pp. 251–4.

23. See Emma Goldman, "The Child and Its Enemies," *Red Emma Speaks,*

compiled and edited by Alix Kates Shulman (New York: Schocken Books, 1983), p. 135: "As soon as the first rays of consciousness illuminate the mind and heart of the child, it instinctively begins to compare its own personality with the personality of those about it. How many hard and cold stone cliffs met its large wondering gaze? Soon enough it is confronted with the painful reality that it is here only to serve as inanimate matter for parents and guardians, whose authority alone gives it shape and form." For Goldman, the family is the child's primal experience of force. See also letter of Emma Goldman to Mary Leavitt, November 2, 1932, St. Tropez, *Nowhere at Home,* p. 175.

24. Elsa Morante, *History, A Novel* (New York: Alfred A. Knopf, 1977), p. 357.

25. In a letter to Havelock Ellis, November 8, 1925, Bristol, Emma Goldman reflected on her views of revolution, deepened by her disillusion with the Soviet revolution: "My Russian experience has made me see what I did not see before, namely the imperative necessity of intensive educational work, which would help to emancipate people from deep-rooted fetishes and superstitions. With many revolutionists I foolishly believed that the principal thing is to get people to rise against the oppressive institutions and that everything else will take care of itself. I have learned since that fallacy of this on the part of Bakunin—much as I continue to revere him in other respects—that the 'Spirit of Destruction' also contains the element of destruction." *Nowhere at Home,* p. 69.

26. Abraham Cahan, *The Education of Abraham Cahan,* trans. Leon Stein, Abraham P. Conan, and Lynn Davison (Philadelphia: Jewish Publication Society, 1969), p. 225.

27. Ibid., p. 282.

28. Ibid., p. 352.

29. Emma Goldman's chief reason for leaving Russia was "The bitter friction that existed between Father and me." *Living My Life,* vol. I, p. 11. She threatened to jump into the Neva if her father didn't consent to her leaving.

30. Rosa Luxemburg, *Rosa Luxemburg Speaks,* ed. Mary Alice Waters (New York: Pathfinder Books, 1970), p. 78.

31. Irving Howe, *World of Our Fathers* (New York: Harcourt Brace Jovanovich, 1976), pp. 104–5, notes that most of the deracinated radical immigrants felt "utterly adrift, without ties to the old world, or new, at home nowhere but in the regions of their thought."

32. The most comprehensive study of the Haymarket Affair is Paul Avrich, *The Haymarket Tragedy* (Princeton: Princeton University Press, 1984).

33. This is the title of an important essay by Emma Goldman, collected in *Anarchism and Other Essays* (New York: Dover Books, 1969), pp. 79–108.

34. See Drinnon, op. cit., p. 70: "Frick represented concentrated capitalistic power which was responsible to no public agency or group of outside individuals."

35. See James Joll, *The Anarchists* (New York: Grosset's Universal Library, 1972), p. 96: "The brief association of Bakunin and Nechaev had openly linked the doctrine of anarchism with the practice of individual terrorism, and with far-reaching results. From 1879 on there was always to be a section of the anarchist

movement ready to commit acts of terrorism, if not for their own sake at least to symbolize a total revolt against society. . . . All over Europe and elsewhere, terrorism was to be an accepted political weapon." For an important study of Russian anarchism, see Paul Avrich, *The Russian Anarchists* (New York: W. W. Norton & Co. 1978).

36. See Howe, op. cit., p. 107: "By the nineties it was becoming clear that anarchism would never win Jewish workers, simply because it had no answers to their immediate needs and, out of an ideological willfulness, denied their intentions as to what might be achieved in America. For all their claims to emancipation, the anarchists largely shared the feelings of lostness that were so heavy in the early immigrant world." Berkman had great difficulty translating his manifesto explaining his rationale for the *attentat* into plain English that the American workers could grasp.

37. Both Goldman and Berkman developed a contempt for the masses, who were supine before authority. In a letter to Berkman, November 18, 1931, Paris, she says: "I too have come to the conclusion, bitter as it is, that hardly anything has come of our years of effort, and that the mass is really hopeless as far as real progress and freedom are concerned." *Nowhere at Home,* p. 49. "No doubt, I shall be excommunicated as an enemy of the people," Goldman writes, "because I repudiate the mass as a creative factor." Preface to *Anarchism,* p. 44. See also the letter from Goldman to Berkman, January 5, 1935, Montreal: "Fact is, dearest, we are fools. We cling to an ideal no one wants or cares about. I am the greater fool of the two of us. I go on eating out my heart and poisoning every moment of my life in the attempt to rouse people's sensibilities." Ibid., p. 57.

38. Forty years after the failed *attentat,* Emma Goldman still remembers that "AB's act and his subsequent Calvary have been my cross and still are. That never again had I anything directly to do with an act of violence, though I have always taken my stand on the side of those who did. I have fought shy, all my life, from joining the cry of 'Crucify!' " Letter of Emma Goldman to Max Nettlau, January 24, 1932, Paris. *Nowhere at Home,* p. 100. She repudiated the idea that the end justified the means.

39. Angiolillo was the anarchist who in 1897 shot Canovas del Castillo, the repressive Spanish prime minister. Angiolillo had scruples his target lacked: He waited for a moment when he would not endanger the lives of del Castillo's innocent children. Angiolillo apologized to the widow: "I did not mean to kill your husband. I aimed only at the official responsible for the Montjuich tortures." *Living My Life,* vol. I, p. 190. Goldman does not dismiss this distinction as casuistry. Angiolillo's *attentat* was not meant as crude revenge or simpleminded "propaganda of the deed" but as symbolic protest against state murder.

40. Goldman, *Anarchism,* p. 90.

41. This phrase appeared in the anarchist journal *Free Society.* Quoted in Paul Avrich, *An American Anarchist: the Life of Voltairine de Cleyre* (Princeton: Princeton University Press, 1978), p. 133.

42. Goldman, "The Psychology of Political Violence," *Anarchism,* p. 91.

43. Wexler, op. cit., p. 111.

44. Jane Addams, *Twenty Years at Hull-House* (New York: Signet Books, 1961), pp. 281–2.

45. Estelle C. Jelinek, in her Introduction to the valuable collection of essays *Women's Autobiography,* p. 10, makes the puzzling statement: "Even so historical an autobiography as Emma Goldman's *Living My Life* (1930) dilutes the political activities of the anarchists with portraits of their personal lives and details of her own relationship with Alexander Berkman and other close friends." This is surely not Goldman's view. See her letter to Berkman, November 19, 1935, London: "As a greeting to your sixty-fifth birthday it is fitting that I should tell you the secret of my life. It is that the one treasure I have rescued from my long and bitter struggle is my friendship for you. Believe it or not, dear Sash. But I know no other value, whether in people or achievements, than your presence in my life and the love and affection you have roused." *Nowhere at Home,* p. 246.

46. Berkman's position was enunciated by Bakunin and Nechaev in 1869, in their *Revolutionary Catechism:* "The revolutionary despises and hates present-day social morality in all its forms. . . . All soft and enervating feelings of friendship, relationship, love, gratitude, even honour, must be stifled in him by a cold passion for the revolutionary cause. . . . Day and night he must have one thought, one aim—merciless destruction." Joll, op. cit., p. 95. See Edmund Wilson, *To the Finland Station* (New York: Doubleday/Anchor Books, 1953), p. 276.

47. Erik Erikson, *Young Man Luther* (New York: W. W. Norton & Co., 1962), p. 50.

48. See Emma Goldman, *Living My Life,* vol. I, p. 32: "Our poverty-stricken life in Königsberg had been made bearable to me only by the occasional outing with our teachers in the open. The forest, the moon casting its silvery shimmer on the fields, the green wreaths in our hair, the flowers we would pick—these made me forget for a time the sordid home surroundings. When Mother scolded me or when I had difficulties at school, a bundle of lilacs from our neighbor's garden or the sight of the colourful silks and velvets displayed in the shops would cause me to forget my sorrows and made the world seem beautiful and bright."

49. About anarchist men, Goldman remarks, in a letter to Alexander Berkman, February 20, 1929, St. Tropez: "Especially as regards women, they are really antediluvian." *Nowhere at Home,* p. 145.

50. Alexander Berkman, *Prison Memoirs of an Anarchist* (New York: Schocken Books, 1970), p. 489. The original edition of this autobiography was published in 1912.

51. See letter of Alexander Berkman to Tom Mooney, February 6, 1935, Nice: "It is far easier to die for one's faith than to suffer for it day in and day out, for long, endless years. And to suffer not only the persecution and humiliation by the enemy, but—worse yet—lack of understanding and sympathy on the part of some friends, as has always been the fate of martyrs." *Nowhere at Home,* pp. 237–8.

52. Berkman's romantic attachments tended to be with women intellectually inferior and much younger than he.

53. The name originated from a visit to a farm she stayed at in February 1906: "The soil was beginning to break free from the grip of winter, a few specks of

green already showing and indicating life germinating in the womb of Mother Earth. 'Mother Earth,' I thought; 'why, that's the name of our child! The nourisher of man, man freed and unhindered in his access to the free earth!' " *Living My Life,* vol. I, p. 378.

54. Berkman and Goldman disagreed about America's achievements and potentialities. Berkman derided the accomplishments of the American intelligentsia, arguing that except in architecture, "They have achieved absolutely nothing in any field that is worth mentioning." Letter to Emma Goldman, August 10, 1933, *Nowhere at Home,* p. 222. While conceding the political naïveté and immaturity of the American mind, Goldman declared, "It is nevertheless a fact that in the sciences, in psychology, education, architecture, the stage, the drama, poetry, yes, and literature, surgery, and many other fields, America can register very notable achievements since 1900." Letter to Alexander Berkman, August 12, 1933, St. Tropez, *Nowhere at Home,* p. 223. "America brings out adventure, innovation, experimental daring which, except for Russia, no European country does." Letter to Alexander Berkman, May 27, 1934, Toronto, *Nowhere at Home,* p. 235. It is significant that Goldman wanted to return to America, whereas Berkman vehemently declared, "I hate America now and don't want ever to see it again." Letter to Emma Goldman, December 21, 1933, Nice, *Nowhere at Home,* p. 232.

55. Falk, op. cit., p. 9.

56. The following is a brief sample of her erotic prose: "The day seems unbearable if I do not talk to you. I would prefer to do something else to you, to run a red hot velvety t over W and the bushes, so Hobo would go mad with joy and ecstasy. . . . I don't know what got into me, but never once in these two years did I want you so much, nor W. Oh for one S———at that beautiful head of his or for one drink from that fountain of life. How I would press my lips to the fountain and drink, drink, every drop. Really, Hobo, I am crazy with T-b. longings. I never knew myself to be that way." Letter of Emma Goldman to Ben Reitman, n.d. Quoted in Falk, op. cit., p. 79.

57. "The fantastic Ben R. wasn't too bad if you could hastily drop all your ideas as to how human beings should look and act." Margaret Anderson, *My Thirty Years' War* (New York: Horizon Press, 1960), p. 70.

58. Berkman's detestation of Reitman irked Emma Goldman. See letter of Alexander Berkman to Emma Goldman, December 22, 1931, Nice: "You object to [Joseph] Cohen emphasizing your love life. But, my dear, in your life your love life was of an emphatic nature and it is also emphasized in the book. Sex has played a very great role in your life and your book would have been lacking if that role had not been mirrored in it." *Nowhere at Home,* p. 167.

59. See Emma Goldman, "The Tragedy of Women's Emancipation," *Red Emma Speaks,* pp. 164–7: "The higher the mental development of a women, the less possible it is for her to meet a congenial mate who will see in her, not only sex, but also the human being, the friend, the comrade, and a strong individual who cannot and ought not lose a single trait of her character." "The demand for equal rights in every vocation of life is just and fair; but, after all, the most vital right is the right to love and be loved."

60. Like Emma Goldman, Voltairine de Cleyre grew up in a loveless family; a Catholic, she was sent away to a convent school. Her father was a petty tyrant, her mother emotionally ungenerous. Her life was marked by tragedy (the suicide of her lover, Dyer D. Lum, an assassination attempt on her life), deep poverty, and painful illness. Haymarket converted her to anarchism. In temperament she was the opposite of Goldman, reticent ("a secular nun in the Order of Anarchy," somebody said of her) rather than flamboyant; her later lovers "tended to be weak and undependable." Avrich, *An American Anarchist*, pp. 10, 53. "I never feel at home anywhere. I feel like a lost or wandering creature that has no place, and cannot find anything to be at home with," she once said of herself. Quoted in Emma Goldman, *Voltairine de Cleyre* (Berkeley Heights, N.J.: Oriole Press, 1933), pp.37–8.

61. Margaret Sanger was another friend and ally who grew apart from Goldman. See Drinnon, op. cit., pp. 170–1.

62. Leon Trotsky, *My Life: An Attempt at an Autobiography* (Harmondsworth: Penguin, 1984), p. xxxv.

63. Ibid., p. 348.

64. Ibid., p. 307.

65. Ibid., p. 422.

66. See letter of Emma Goldman to Freda Kirchwey, August 2, 1934, Toronto: "You see, my dear, my understanding of revolution is not a continued extermination of political dissenters. I was told once by Robert Minor that individual human life does not matter after all. I consider that an outrage of revolutionary ethics. Individual life is important and should not be cheapened and degraded into mere automaton. That is my main quarrel with the communist state." *Nowhere at Home,* p. 56. See letter of Emma Goldman to Alexander Berkman, June 28, 1928, St. Tropez, for a summing up of her revulsion from violence and its "process of destruction." She wants "the revolution to be understood as a process of reconstruction." *Nowhere at Home,* p. 87.

67. For Trotsky's evaluation of Lenin's personality, see *My Life,* pp. 352–3.

68. Makhnovtsky were followers of Nestor Makhno, "an anarchist, who with his peasant army . . . had helped to rout Denikin [a White general] and thus saved Moscow and the Revolution at the most critical period." *Living My Life*, vol. II, p. 734. *Ideiny* anarchists were philosophical anarchists.

69. This was Johann Most's phrase. *Living My Life,* p. 54.

70. Trotsky, op. cit., p. 167.

71. "And the only genuine revolution is ANARCHY! ANARCHY!, which means NO power, of NO sort for NO one, over NO one!" Such a pure view of revolution is doomed in the cruel world of history. Morante, op. cit., p. 484.

72. Joll, op. cit., p. 29.

73. Lincoln Steffens, *The Autobiography of J. Lincoln Steffens* (New York: Harvest Books, 1958), vol. II, p. 844.

74. Voltairine de Cleyre is also buried near them, in what anarchists considered sacred ground.

75. Joseph Conrad, *The Secret Agent* (New York: Bantam Books, 1984), p. 69.

76. Goldman published *The Social Significance of the Modern Drama* in 1914.

77. In "Afterwards," *My Disillusionment in Russia,* quoted in *Red Emma Speaks,* pp. 401–2, Goldman eloquently repudiates the political principle that the end justifies the means: "There is no greater fallacy than the belief that the aims and purpose are one thing, while the methods and tactics are another. This conception is a potent menace to social regeneration."

78. In an essay, "Was My Life Worth Living," *Harper's Magazine* CLXX (December 1934), *Red Emma Speaks,* pp. 433–4, Goldman concludes: "If I had my life to live over again, like anyone else, I should wish to alter minor details. But in any of my more important actions and attitudes, I would repeat my life as I have lived it. Certainly I should work for Anarchism with the same devotion and confidence in its ultimate triumph."

6.

GERTRUDE STEIN'S *THE AUTOBIOGRAPHY OF ALICE B. TOKLAS*

1. Vladimir Nabokov, *Speak, Memory,* rev. ed. (New York: G. P. Putnam's Sons, 1967), p. 126.

2. Ibid., p. 116.

3. Ibid., p.56.

4. Gertrude Stein, *The Autobiography of Alice B. Toklas* (New York: Modern Library, 1955). All parenthetical page references within the chapter are to this edition.

5. Richard Bridgman, *Gertrude Stein in Pieces* (New York: Oxford University Press, 1970), p. 26.

6. Gertrude Stein, *Three Lives* (New York: Signet Books, 1985), p. 89.

7. Ibid.

8. Gertrude Stein, *The Making of Americans* (New York: Something Else Press, 1966), pp. 792, 863, 903–4, 907. The sentence tolls like a funeral bell.

9. Paul Rosenfeld, "The Place of Gertrude Stein," *By Way of Art* (New York: Coward-McCann, 1928), p. 128. This early critical assessment of Stein's work is underappreciated.

10. Alexis de Tocqueville, *Democracy in America,* trans. George Lawrence, ed. J. P. Mayer (Garden City: Doubleday/Anchor Books, 1969), p. 482.

11. John Malcolm Brinnin, *The Third Rose: Gertrude Stein and Her World* (Boston: Little, Brown, 1959), p. xv.

12. Gertrude Stein, "The Gradual Making of *The Making of Americans,*" *Lectures in America* (Boston: Beacon Press, 1957), p. 243.

13. Stein, *The Making of Americans,* p. 284.

14. Ibid., p. 290.

15. Donald Sutherland, *Gertrude Stein: A Biography of Her Works* (New Haven: Yale University Press, 1951), p. 11.

16. Gertrude Stein, "Matisse," *Portraits and Prayers* (New York: Random House, 1974), p. 14.

17. James Mellow, *Charmed Circle* (New York: Praeger, 1974), p. 51.

18. Gertrude Stein, *Two: Gertrude Stein and Her Brother and Other Portraits* (New Haven: Yale University Press, 1951), p. 35.

19. Alice B. Toklas's opinions about Leo were, not surprisingly, acidulous. In a letter to Carl Van Vechten, July 4, 1950, she writes: "Of course he would mention Baby on every page just as she sincerely denied in '36 that she had another brother beside Mike in California when a man who was calling on her said he had just seen a brother of hers in Italy. She really had put him and the deep unhappiness he had caused her so completely out of her mind that finally he and it no longer existed." She adds that Leo had made her suffer too. *Staying on Alone: Letters of Alice B. Toklas,* ed. Edward Burns (New York: Liveright, 1973), p. 195. In a letter to Donald Gallup, July 31, 1950—she had read Leo's book of letters, journals, and papers—she says: "He was amongst the majority—the commonplace majority as Gertrude called him—of the sad and mistaken." Ibid., p. 199.

20. Stein, *Two,* p. 6. Edward Burns, letter to Herbert Leibowitz, December 17, 1983 (reprinted by permission of the author), has suggested that the second person/voice in *Two* belongs to Sarah Stein, Michael's wife and Gertrude's sister-in-law. "The Stein group was very inbred. None of them had work responsibilities and all their practical arrangements were made by Michael. Sarah Stein's role was to talk and to listen. Almost every day Leo and Gertrude, separately and together, would sit with her and go over, in excruciatingly minute detail, what had transpired the night before. . . . This is what one is getting a little in the *Two*—the problem is that at this time they all spoke in the same abstract, colorless terms—but terms that had meaning for them. Much of Gertrude's theoretical structure—that is the vocabulary for it—came from these passionate family conversations." That conjecture is interesting, but it is hard to imagine Gertrude Stein composing a portrait of such intensity about a person with whom she did not have the same conflicts as she did with Leo.

21. Gertrude Stein, "Ada," *Geography and Plays* (Boston: The Four Seas, 1922), p. 16.

22. Sutherland, op. cit., p. 82.

23. Stein, "Christian Bérard," *Portraits and Prayers,* p. 77.

24. Gertrude Stein, *Tender Buttons* in *Selected Writings of Gertrude Stein,* ed. Carl Van Vechten (New York: Random House, 1946), p. 463.

25. Ibid., p. 474.

26. Ibid., p. 483.

27. Cf. William H. Gass, "Gertrude Stein and the Geography of the Sentence," *The World Within the Word* (New York: Alfred A. Knopf, 1978), p. 100: "Words, of course, were tender buttons, to be sorted and played with, admired and arranged, and she felt that language in English literature had become increasingly stiff and resistant, and that words had to be pried out of their formulas, and allowed to regain their former Elizabethan fluidity, but it is now evident, I think, that she had other motives, indeed the same ones, which had driven her into writing in the first place: the search for and discovery of Gertrude Stein, and the recording of her daily life, her thoughts, her passions."

28. Stein, *Tender Buttons,* op. cit., p. 471.

29. Ibid., p. 488.

30. Ibid., p. 481.

31. Virgil Thomson, *Virgil Thomson* (New York: Alfred A. Knopf, 1966), p. 176, states that *The Autobiography of Alice B. Toklas* "is in every way except actual authorship Alice Toklas' book; it reflects her mind, her language, her private view of Gertrude, also her unique narrative powers. Every story in it is told as Alice herself had always told it." Gertrude Stein's "own way with narrative was ever elliptical, going into slow orbit around her theme." Ibid., p. 177. To my ear, Alice Toklas's own autobiography, *What Is Remembered* (New York: Holt Rinehart Winston, 1961), is less individual in prose rhythms.

32. Leo Stein, *Appreciation: Painting, Poetry and Prose* (New York: Modern Library, 1947), p. 124.

33. Gertrude Stein, *Everybody's Autobiography* (New York: Vintage Books, 1937), p. 13.

34. Gertrude Stein, *Narration: Four Lectures by Gertrude Stein* (Chicago: University of Chicago Press, 1935), p. 21.

35. Mellow, op. cit., p. 3.

36. F. W. Dupee, "It Shows Shine: Notes on Gertrude Stein," *The King of the Cats* (New York: Farrar Straus & Giroux, 1965), p. 70.

37. Steffens, *Autobiography*, II, p. 834.

38. Gertrude Stein, *Paris France* (New York: Liveright, 1940), p. 56.

39. Daniel-Henry Kahnweiler, *My Galleries and Painters* (New York: Viking Press, 1971), p. 128.

40. Leo Stein, letter to Albert Barnes, October 20, 1934, *Journey into the Self: The Letters, Papers, and Journals of Leo Stein*, ed. Edmund Fuller (New York: Crown Publishers, 1950), p. 148.

41. She "talked with anybody and everybody": "they were grist for her poetry, a relief from the solitudes of a mind essentially introspective." Thomson, op. cit., p. 170.

42. Leo Stein, op. cit., p. 134.

43. Gertrude Stein, *Everybody's Autobiography,* p. 65.

44. Guy Davenport, letter to Herbert Leibowitz, October 7, 1976. Reprinted by permission of the author.

45. Ralph Waldo Emerson, "Circles," *Essays and Lectures* (New York: Library of America, 1983), p. 406.

7.

THE AUTOBIOGRAPHY OF WILLIAM CARLOS WILLIAMS

1. "I'm no journalist and autobiography doesn't mean a thing to me. All I'm interested in—or almost all—is impersonally, as impersonally as possible, to get the meaning over and see it flourish—and be left alone." Letter of William Carlos Williams to Ronald Lane Latimer, November 26, 1934. *The Selected Letters of William Carlos Williams,* ed. John C. Thirlwall (New York: New Directions, 1957), pp. 150–1.

2. "But not autobiography just yet. That will have to be a monastic, brooding, gay sort of lonely thing that cannot be hurried—cannot even be put on the spot but will have to come about in the manner of the seasons." Letter of William Carlos Williams to Charles Henri Ford, March 30, 1938. *Selected Letters,* p. 169.

3. *Poetry* magazine published two installments in 1950.

4. William Carlos Williams, *The Collected Poems of William Carlos Williams,* ed. Christopher MacGowan, vol. 2 (New York: New Directions, 1988), p. 245.

5. Ibid., p. 284.

6. Doubtless the pressure to finish the manuscript by the deadline contributed to the stroke.

7. The original manuscript was written mostly in longhand in big letters, not too many words on a line. Each day's writing was dated and given to Kitty Hoagland to type up. There is not much crossing out, which indicates Williams had little hesitation or difficulty in conceiving or setting down his memories. When he did delete material, it was usually inert, stodgy, extraneous details, which retarded the narrative flow. Williams occasionally corrected dates, names, spelling errors, and facts, as, for example, when Franco came into the Spanish Civil War.

Some early titles he jotted down were: "Root and Branch (and Flower) or You are Lost"; "From the Ground Up"; "Rooted in the Sand"; "Rooted in Rot"; "Home Here"; and "Dock," of which he wrote to Norman Holmes Pearson in 1950: "[Dock] with us is a comparable weed growing unheralded about the edges of the dungheap. Of its root the practical Chinese make a delicacy." Unpublished letter, William Carlos Williams Collection, Beinecke Library, Yale University. Copyright © 1980 by The Estate of Florence H. Williams. Published by permission of New Directions, Agents.

8. Although the *Autobiography* was "good therapy," Williams flexing the muscles of survival, he suffered a nervous breakdown in 1953 that required his being hospitalized for two months. He underwent psychotherapy from 1953 to 1957.

9. William Carlos Williams, *The Autobiography of William Carlos Williams* (New York: Random House, 1951). All parenthetical page references within the chapter are from this text.

10. William Carlos Williams, *In the American Grain* (New York: New Directions, 1954), p. 155.

11. Cf. *Paterson* (New York: New Directions, 1963), Book III, p. 155: "only write carelessly so that nothing that is not green will not survive."

12. Cf. George Santayana, *Persons and Places* (New York: Charles Scribner's Sons, 1944), p. 247: "Dialectic merely throws a verbal net into the sea, to draw a pattern over the fishes without catching any of them. It is an optical illusion."

13. Letter of William Carlos Williams to John Riordan, October 13, 1926. Quoted in Mike Weaver, *William Carlos Williams: The American Background* (Cambridge: Harvard University Press, 1971), p. 164.

14. Ibid., p. 154–5.

15. *"La Vertue/ est toute dans l'effort,"* he observed with epigrammatic finality in *Paterson.*

16. "Williams' writings are laconic acclamations of the courage to swallow

bitter-flavored medicines, to bear unflinchingly the pain of violent cauterizations. They are the forms wherein a poet has given deep sober thanks to the principle by means of which he has managed to maintain his own spirit intact on a steep inclement bank of life, some Greenland on the verge of the Arctic Circle. And the homely magic he wishes to hold before men's eyes is light-hearted self-irony, relentless impersonality of regard, sense of the comic and grotesque in his own career, bald matter-of-factness, willingness to stand evil smells and not run from them. Life has tempted this man with dope of candies; urged glucose on him, cheap substitute for absent sweetness." Paul Rosenfeld, "William Carlos Williams," *Port of New York* (Urbana: University of Illinois Press, 1968), p. 104. The original edition of *Port of New York* was published in 1924. Rosenfeld's last image is curiously prescient in light of Williams's use of the candy image in the foreword to the *Autobiography:* "A thin thread of narrative remains—a few hundred pages— about which clusters, like rock candy, the interests upon which the general reader will spend a few hours, as might a sweet-toothed child, preferring something richer and not so hard on the teeth."

17. *View*, II, 3, Oct. 1942, p. 24.

18. Williams served as amanuensis for his mother's memoir, which appeared in a book titled *Yes, Mrs. Williams* (New York: McDowell Obolensky, 1959). Since there were two Mrs. Williamses, the wife and the mother, the title is ambiguous and telling. Bedridden for the last eighteen years of her life, his mother translated a Renaissance Spanish novel with her son. *Yes, Mrs. Williams* (was the poet being wryly obedient?) is the most diffuse of his books.

19. Once when H.D. fell into a trance she walked into a rough sea and nearly drowned. Williams notes without comment in the *Autobiography* that he carried around a nursing bottle until he was six years old, when he was shamed out of it on a boat trip to Connecticut with his grandmother.

20. Williams, *Paterson,* Book III. This phrase is used often, like a refrain, throughout Book III.

21. Arlo Bates, a professor of English at MIT, to whom Williams took his long Keatsian imitation, also had unpublished poems locked in his armoire, which he showed Williams as an example of the amateur poet's effusions. Williams understood Bates's delicate advice and threw his manuscript into the fire.

22. Ezra Pound, "Dr. Williams' Position," in *William Carlos Williams: A Collection of Critical Essays,* ed. J. Hillis Miller (Englewood, N.J.: Prentice Hall, 1966), p. 27.

23. In his youth, Williams threw himself into athletics with wild abandon, feeling sorrow if he won but driven so as not to lose.

24. William Carlos Williams, "The American Background," *Selected Essays of William Carlos Williams* (New York: Random House, 1954), p. 138.

25. Letter of William Carlos Williams to Ezra Pound, spring [1926], *Selected Letters,* p. 69.

26. Marianne Moore, "Three Essays on Williams" in *A Collection of Critical Essays,* p. 38. Miss Moore's phrase is used in her review of *Kora in Hell.*

27. This judgment is made in the context of a visit to Natalie Barney's salon

in Paris, a "remnant of Remy de Gourmont's (badly accoutered) old *salon,* one of the wonders of the last century." For Williams, it seemed "something preserved in amber from the time of the Renaissance." Williams plays the "primitive," the rube, in this cliquish old-world museum. Natalie Barney "could tell a pickle from a clam any day of the week" is his salty tribute. His contribution to the Parisian upper-class game of making a conspicuous exit is this: "I went out and stood up to take a good piss." Williams, who does not mention Pound's reaction to his "uncouth" behavior, seems to have been ill at ease among lesbians.

28. In a letter to his mother, March 30, 1904, Williams wrote about Pound: "He is really a brilliant talker and thinker but delights in making himself just exactly what he is not: a laughing boor." With an ambivalence that remained his whole life, Williams also applies the adjectives "artificial," "conceited," "untrusting," and "defensive" to Pound. *Selected Letters,* p. 6.

29. H. D. once explained to Williams that before sitting down to write, she sprinkled ink on her clothes in order to rid herself of the merely mundane side of creativity. His response to her silly ritual affectation was a satirical smile of tolerance: "Well, if you like it." Nonetheless Williams admired H. D.'s "provocative indifference to rules and order" and for a time was in love with her.

30. During the Spanish Civil War, Williams was active in a doctors' organization that sent medical supplies to the Republican forces.

31. Letter of William Carlos Williams to James Laughlin, December 14, 1940, *Selected Letters,* p. 192.

32. At a later visit, Pound's disheveled appearance and wild glances remind Williams of the beast in Cocteau's film *Beauty and the Beast.* This seems superficial. The beast in the film is ugly and scary on the outside but tender and vulnerable inside. Did Williams sense that or refuse to see it?

33. Williams's parting words to Pound are a gentle remonstrance spoken in his own voice: "Yes, what you say is quite true, but what you forget, Ez, is that logical as your elucidations may be, logic, mere logic, convinces no one." Williams's homily is lost on Pound, for he soon sends Williams "the usual semi-abusive letter." Pound cannot break out of the prison of his obdurate mind.

34. *Interviews with William Carlos Williams,* ed. Linda Wagner (New York: New Directions, 1976), p. 55.

35. William Carlos Williams, *I Wanted to Write a Poem* (Boston: Beacon Press, 1958), p. 6.

36. This phrase appears in the unpublished essay "The Baroness Elsa Von Freytag Loringhoven," p. 3. William Carlos Williams Collection, Beinecke Library, Yale University. Copyright © 1980 by The Estate of Florence H. Williams. Published by permission of New Directions, Agents. In the *Autobiography,* Williams tosses the word "love" about with sentimental largesse but can follow it immediately with a brusque remark, as with Marsden Hartley: "Maybe I hurt him. It couldn't be helped." Of his friend Robert McAlmon's poverty (before McAlmon married Bryher and came into enormous wealth), Williams remarks: "That was his racket, not mine."

37. This phrase is Nabokov's in *Speak, Memory.*

38. Williams mentions that Wallace Stevens was so scared of the baroness that he would not venture below Fourteenth Street.

39. Williams, "The Baroness Elsa Von Freytag Loringhoven," p. 6.

40. Ibid.

41. Of Williams's books written after their marriage, the *Autobiography* is the only one Floss did not read in manuscript.

42. R. W. Flint is surely right in saying that "For Floss he really had no metaphor that worked." See Flint's essay on Williams, "America of Poets," *Parnassus: Poetry in Review,* Fall/Winter 1976, p. 181.

43. With the immunity that the disguises of fiction confer, Williams treats his courtship of Floss at length in *The Build-up,* the third novel of his Stecher trilogy. There he makes no bones that he married Floss on the rebound after her artist sister, whose aura of "dreamy mystery" had enchanted him, rejected him in favor of his brother (she ended up not marrying Ed, either, but eloping with a dilettante, to the dismay and strong disapproval of the Stecher/Herman family), that he was an "insulting lover," and that marriage appealed to him because it would stiffen his wavering will. Williams's proposal to the Floss character in *The Build-up* is a classic document of the imagination's challenging the reluctant will to a duel: "There is a sort of love, not romantic love, but a love that with daring can be made difficultly to blossom. It is founded on passion, a passion of despair, as all life is despair." Repeating the word "passion," the Williams character sounds like a suburban Werther gloomily forcing himself to renounce love in order to marry an unexciting stranger. The strained logic is not all attitudinizing. Why Floss bowed to his persistent wooing (bullying?), despite her own and her family's misgivings, waits upon a statement from her. The evidence from the few published letters of Williams to Floss is skimpy. The entire correspondence will be published fifteen years after Floss's death.

44. Reed Whittemore, *William Carlos Williams, Poet from New Jersey* (Boston: Houghton Mifflin, 1975), p. 212.

45. Williams wanted to choose forestry as a career. "But Flossie said, 'As sure as shooting, you'd find an Indian up one of them [a tree], and she wouldn't be a man either!' [laughs]" *Interviews,* p. 10. In the *Autobiography,* Williams often presents himself as irresistible to women.

46. This phrase is from the late poem "To Be Recited to Flossie on Her Birthday," *Collected Poems,* vol. 2, p. 410.

47. In the play *A Dream of Love,* "Doc" (Williams) defends his infidelities with an image of the phoenix: "—to renew our love, burn the old nest and emerge transcendent, aflame—for you! Do you know any other way?" Myra, the Floss character in the play, scorns this explanation as sophistry; she resents and is unreconciled to Doc's conduct, which often estranges them. It is interesting to note that in the play Doc dies in a hotel room, where he had gone with another woman, which smacks of a punitive fantasy. *A Dream of Love* in *Many Loves* (New York: New Directions, 1961), p. 207.

48. This beautiful phrase comes from *Paterson,* Book III, p. 151.

49. *Paterson,* Book III, p. 167.

50. Williams's jingling slogan, "No ideas but in things," has damaged his reputation as a thinker. Taking the sentence as gospel, critics have sometimes claimed that Williams was nothing more than a sensualist or ephemeralist with no capacity for systematic thought. Yvor Winters argued that Williams was "a foolish and ignorant man, but at moments a fine stylist." A careful reading of *In the American Grain* should suffice to destroy that harsh judgment. In the foreword to the *Autobiography,* Williams says: "What becomes of me has never seemed to me important, but the fate of ideas living against the grain in a nondescript world have always held me breathless." A half-truth, perhaps, but worth pondering, especially in relation to the *Autobiography.*

51. Williams here exemplifies the eagerness of the children of immigrants to be taken as Americans. He says that he never forgave Pop for remaining a British citizen, and his mother never adjusted to American folkways. Williams's search for a consenting American environment may have originated in his parents' foreignness.

52. There are a number of incidents in the *Autobiography* of catastrophe narrowly averted: A bolt of lightning strikes close to him and he just misses the blows of a hurricane in 1938 while driving his mother from Connecticut to Rutherford. Williams tells a funny story of driving on the sidewalk in order to avoid a collision and then lurching back on the road, to be greeted by the Rutherford constabulary's cheerful, "Hi, Doc." These incidents are invariably told in a gleeful tone.

8.

RICHARD WRIGHT'S *BLACK BOY* AND *AMERICAN HUNGER*

1. Maya Angelou, *I Know Why the Caged Bird Sings* (New York: Random House, 1970), p. 168.

2. Frederick Douglass, *Narrative of the Life of Frederick Douglass* (Cambridge: Harvard University Press, 1973), p. 50.

3. Zora Neale Hurston, *Dust Tracks on a Road* (Urbana: University of Ilinois Press, 1978), p. 235.

4. Ibid., p. 234.

5. Numerous examples abound. See Frederick Douglass, *Narrative of the Life of Frederick Douglass,* originally published in 1845; *Five Slave Narratives* (Middletown, Conn.: Wesleyan University Press, 1968); *Great Slave Narratives,* selected and ed. by Arna Bontemps (Boston: Beacon Press, 1972); Harriet A. Jacobs, *Incidents in the Life of a Slave Girl,* edited by Jean Fagan Yellin (Cambridge: Harvard University Press, 1984), originally published in 1861; Charles Ball, *Fifty Years in Chains* (New York: Dover Books, 1970), originally published in 1836; *Reminiscences of Levi Coffin* (New York: Arno Press, 1968), originally published in 1876, 3d ed., 1898.

6. Douglass, op. cit., p. 61.

7. Primo Levi, *The Periodic Table,* trans. Raymond Rosenthal (New York: Schocken Books, 1984), p. 37.

8. Douglass, op. cit., pp. 77–8.

9. Ibid., p. 67.

10. Ibid., p. 109.

11. Richard Wright, *American Hunger* (New York: Harper & Row, 1977), p. 134.

12. W. E. B. Du Bois, *The Souls of Black Folk,* in *Three Negro Classics* (New York: Avon Discus Books, 1965), pp. 214–15. Du Bois's book, a brilliant wedding of poetry, history, music, sociology, and polemic, was originally published in 1903.

13. In 1945, Wright reluctantly went along with his agent's and publisher's expedient suggestion that *Black Boy* be separated from *American Hunger* and published independently. *Black Boy* was a selection of the Book-of-the-Month Club. Wright's original title for both halves was *The Horror and the Glory.* Portions of the second half appeared in periodicals during the 1940s. *American Hunger* was finally published in 1977. Each book is indispensable for an understanding of Wright's career and for what autobiography can and cannot accommodate. We still need an edition that combines both books in one.

14. "My environment contained nothing more alien than writing or the desire to express one's self in writing." *Black Boy,* p. 105. All parenthetical page references within the chapter are to the 1945 edition (New York: Harper & Row). Page references preceded by *AH* are to *American Hunger* (New York: Harper & Row, 1977).

15. Ralph Ellison, "Richard Wright's Blues," *Shadow and Act* (New York: Random House, 1972), pp. 85–6.

16. Gaston Bachelard, *The Poetics of Space,* trans. Maria Jolas (Boston: Beacon Press, 1969), p. 6.

17. Ibid., p. 4.

18. Erik Erikson, *Childhood and Society,* 2nd ed. (New York: W. W. Norton, 1963), p. 250.

19. Wright never mentions his paternal grandparents or family in *Black Boy,* and he assigns a minimal role to his younger brother, Leon, hinting that Leon was an ingratiating, obedient son, petted and preferred by the family, while Richard was saddled with the label of troublemaker. Their relationship was almost that of strangers, Wright notes (*Black Boy,* p. 152), and adds: "Slowly my brother grew openly critical of me, taking his cue from those about him, and it hurt." Wright never goes beyond such terse statements, as if the subject was too painful to dredge up.

20. Once again a word has vivid meaning for Richard, even though he cannot interpret it.

21. At the orphanage, the children were assigned the absurd and backbreaking task of pulling up blades of grass with their hands.

22. When, as a consequence of Ella's invalidism, the boys were parceled out to relatives, Richard chose to stay with his uncle Clark in Clarksville, Mississippi, because it was close to Jackson, where his mother was convalescing. To Richard's chagrin, Leon went north with their favorite, Aunt Maggie.

23. Richard Wright, "The Ethics of Jim Crow," *Uncle Tom's Children* (New York: Harper & Brothers, 1940), p. 4.

24. His mother had an ardent nature, Wright recalls in *Black Boy.* When he was a teenager, she begged and browbeat him to publicly announce that he was "converted."

25. There is an ascetic strain in Wright, which views the body as an enemy to be held in check. He looks upon Bess and the young woman in Chicago with whom he had sexual relations sporadically and whose only request was that Richard take her to the circus as pitiful, ignorant children with a craving to be stroked and cuddled like a kitten. Despite his contempt for such women, he almost married one in New York. In *American Hunger,* he guiltily slept with women who could not pay their insurance bills (he promised not to inform the insurance company). Wright admires a woman who, through guile, avenges the lynching of her husband by hiding a gun on her person and then killing several of the Ku Klux Klanners who were responsible for the crime.

26. Michel Fabre, *The Unfinished Odyssey of Richard Wright,* trans. Isobel Barzun (New York: William Morrow, 1973), p. 34.

27. Richard Wright, "How Bigger Was Born," *Native Son* (New York: Modern Library, 1940), p. xvi.

28. His mother either slapped him or took an irascible tone whenever he asked about white-black conflicts: "Again I was being shut out of the secret, the thing, the reality felt behind all the words and silences." *Black Boy,* p. 42.

29. Throughout *Black Boy* and *American Hunger,* Wright almost always puts parentheses around his diatribes against—and generalizations about—black culture, as if he could quickly repudiate them. See Ellison, op. cit., pp. 90–1, and James Baldwin, "Alas, Poor Richard," *Nobody Knows My Name* (New York: Dell, 1961), p. 212.

30. Charles T. Davis notes that Wright omits the names of teachers and peers who helped and encouraged him. To refer to them "would modify our sense of Richard's deprived and disturbed emotional life, a necessity for the art of autobiography, rather more important than any concern for absolute accuracy." Davis goes on to say, "Wright deliberately deprives his hero, his younger self, of any substantial basis for sensual gratification located outside his developing imagination." Charles T. Davis, "From Experience to Eloquence: *Black Boy* as Art," *Chant of Saints,* ed. Michael S. Harper and Robert B. Stepto (Urbana: University of Illinois Press, 1979), p. 431.

31. When his uncle Hoskins drives his horse and buggy into the Mississippi River, Richard is terrified (his piercing wail, "Naw," is disregarded by Hoskins). This rowdy horseplay is evidence of cruel insensitivity to Richard, and he never again trusts his uncle.

32. Richard takes nickels in the saloons and dimes from "Professor" Matthews, his aunt Maggie's lover, but he won't beg money from his father.

33. In *A Long Way from Home* (New York: Harvest Books, 1970, originally published in 1937), McKay begins his autobiography in adolescence. He scarcely mentions his father, mother, or brother and never acknowledges their influence on him.

34. *"Black Boy* is filled with blues-tempered echoes of railroad trains, the names of Southern towns and cities, estrangements, fights and flights, deaths and disappointments, charged with physical and spiritual hungers and pain. And like a blues song sung by such an artist as Bessie Smith, its lyrical prose evokes the paradoxical, almost surreal image of a black boy singing lustily as he probes his own grievous wound." Ellison, op. cit., pp. 78–9.

35. Cf. Hosea Hudson, *The Narrative of Hosea Hudson,* ed. Nell Irvin Painter (Cambridge: Harvard University Press, 1979), p. 180: "I found this Party, a party of the working class, gave me rights equal with all others regardless of color, sex or age or educational standards. I with my uneducation could express myself, without being made fun of by others who could read well and fast, using big words. I was treated with high respect. I had a right to help make policy." Hudson, a black proletarian steelworker, never left the party. His autobiography, an oral history, offers valuable glimpses of the attempts of the Communist party to recruit black industrial workers.

36. McKay, op. cit., p. 151.

37. Langston Hughes, *I Wonder as I Wander* (New York: Hill & Wang, 1964), pp. 68–235; McKay, op. cit., pp. 153–234.

38. In *Lawd Today* (New York: Walker & Company, 1963), an early Wright novel, written in 1936 but not published until 1963, the black postal workers ridicule the Communists with the phobic vehemence of right-wing fanatics.

39. Wright's silence is reminiscent of his refusal in *Black Boy* to tell his aunt Addie that the boy behind him in class, not Richard, was guilty of throwing nuts on the floor. He won't violate his schoolboy code of honor and tattle.

40. "American and British spectators were amazed at the complete and detailed testimony against themselves which the Russian prisoners gave without cajoling. It was interesting to witness in action that famous and perplexing pattern of self-confession that was to become a feature of many subsequent purge trials." Hughes, op. cit., p. 219.

41. Malcolm X, "the Man from Mars," also searched for this psychic concord and found it briefly during his pilgrimage in Mecca, where he was "embraced as a long-lost child." Malcolm X, *The Autobiography of Malcolm X* (New York: Grove Press, 1964), p. 332. Unable to speak Arabic, Malcolm felt helpless and dependent as a baby. Language was his primary instrument of control. He vowed to learn Arabic so as not to be disoriented ever again.

42. William Gass, "The Soul Inside the Sentence," *Habitations of the Word* (New York: Alfred A. Knopf, 1985), p. 122.

43. Langston Hughes caustically described Wright's personality during this period: "I have known a great many writers in my time and some of them were very much like [Arthur] Koestler—always something not right with the world around them. Even on the brightest days, no matter where they are. Richard Wright seemed like that in Chicago. . . . There are many emotional hypochondriacs on earth, unhappy when *not unhappy,* sad when not expounding on their sadness." Op. cit., p. 120.

44. Gass, op. cit., p. 135.

9.

EDWARD DAHLBERG'S *BECAUSE I WAS FLESH*

1. Edward Dahlberg, *Because I Was Flesh* (New York: New Directions, 1963), p. 97. All parenthetical page references within the chapter are to this edition.

2. Alexis de Tocqueville, *Democracy in America,* trans. George Lawrence, ed. J. P. Mayer (Garden City, N.Y.: Doubleday/Anchor Books, 1969), p. 484.

3. Edward Dahlberg, *Alms for Oblivion* (Minneapolis: University of Minnesota Press, 1964), p. 90. Dahlberg was referring to Sherwood Anderson's autobiographies, *Tar* and *A Story Teller's Story,* but the statement can be taken as standard Dahlbergian writ.

4. Edward Dahlberg agreed with Randolph Bourne, who "believed that, ultimately, politics, the serpent, would devour the word, the image, and the rebel who preserves the spirit of the nation." Ibid., p.81.

5. Edward Dahlberg, *Do These Bones Live* (New York: Harcourt, Brace and Company, 1941), p. 40.

6. Edward Dahlberg, *Epitaphs of Our Times,* ed. Edwin Seaver (New York: George Braziller, 1967), pp. 2–3, says of himself: "I am a passionate logician of the absurd."

7. Charles De Fanti, *The Wages of Expectation* (New York: New York University Press, 1978), p. 143, recounts that Clara Port, Harvey Breit's wife, believed that "the base of his [Dahlberg's] creativity was 'his tremendous anger against his mother.' Dahlberg once threatened to kill Miss Port for saying this."

8. Though he assigns women a central generative role as "orphic priestess" in the civilizing process, Dahlberg cannot avoid making caustic remarks about them. The following is typical: "Without woman, the Tree of Good and Evil cannot be tasted. Before the First Deception Adam is Primordial Clod: Women are guileful adepts at 'nature, custom, the past.' " *Do These Bones Live,* p. 110.

9. Dahlberg dedicated *Because I Was Flesh* to the poet Stanley Burnshaw, "for expunging much of the dross from the manuscript." In fact, James Laughlin, the publisher of New Directions, Rene Dahlberg, his wife at the time of publication, and Irving Rosenthal, the editor of *Big Table* (a literary magazine), all used pruning shears and editorial talents to improve the book's structure. See De Fanti, op. cit., pp. 233–7, for a discussion of this complicated process. In a letter to Allen Tate, October 8, 1962, Dahlberg called the book "a stale and withered mistress" and a "slut." This letter expresses Dahlberg's weariness with the many revisions he undertook. He admits that Laughlin "is doing his utmost to make a book perfect." *Epitaphs of Our Times,* pp. 242–3.

10. Letter of Edward Dahlberg to Jonathan Williams, March 12, 1962. Ibid., p. 102.

11. Lao-Tsu Ben is Dahlberg's alter ego in the Los Angeles section of the autobiography. Lao, who had "acquired a clandestine nature," is a flim-flam man, a voracious reader, a gambler, a "gourmet in female flesh," (135) and a Panurge, who sees laughter as consolation or temporary health. When Lao becomes involved in his business schemes, Dahlberg breaks with his mentor, the "one friend

of my soul," because he can't bear Lao's despotic acts and because Lao begins to smell of "the carrion of the herd." Lao-Tsu Ben was Max Lewis, a dissolute, shady schemer and surrogate parent who became a reclusive and misanthropic millionaire. De Fanti, op. cit., pp. 32–3, 140, 249.

12. Ibid., p. 158.

13. Edward Dahlberg, *The Sorrows of Priapus* (London: Calder & Boyars, 1970), p. 4. This book was originally published by New Directions in 1957.

14. George Eliot, *Middlemarch* (London: Penguin Books, 1965), pp. 790–1.

15. Dahlberg, *Do These Bones Live,* p. 25.

16. See Dahlberg, *Alms for Oblivion,* p. 80: "Randolph Bourne regarded himself as an impossibilist and made the most implacable exactions upon fate." This statement fits Dahlberg perfectly. "Long ago I would have perished had I not pined for absolutes, though they do not exist," Dahlberg remarks in *The Carnal Myth* (New York: Weybright & Talley, 1968), p. 4.

17. Letter to Lewis Mumford, September 9, 1953. *Epitaphs of Our Times,* p. 109.

18. "Maledictions are more instructive to man than man's blessings; for the latter always carry with them a tenuous treacle of holy unction." *Do These Bones Live,* p. 116.

19. Edwin Muir, *An Autobiography* (New York: Seabury Press, 1968), p. 235. The original edition was published in 1954.

20. Herbert Read and Edward Dahlberg, *Truth Is More Sacred* (New York: Horizon Press, 1961), p. 22.

21. Edward Dahlberg, *The Leafless American,* ed. Harold Billings (Sausalito, Cal.:Roger Beacham, 1967), p. 57.

22. See Dahlberg, *The Sorrows of Priapus,* p. 19: "Man is either too stupid or vain to know himself, and too self-loving to understand anyone. He cannot endure his own vices in others, and he is least just when he is railing at the faults of people."

23. D. H. Lawrence, introduction to Dahlberg, *Bottom Dogs* (New York: Minerva Press, 1976), p. 152. *Bottom Dogs* was first published in 1930.

24. Dahlberg, *The Flea of Sodom,* p. 12. ". . . the sign of a weak writer, who dares not take those risks which a parsimonious Imagination cannot sustain."

25. *Bottom Dogs* was "an energetic novel in the corrupt language of inertia," written in "a stunted, dry jargon." Edward Dahlberg, *The Confessions of Edward Dahlberg* (New York: George Braziller, 1971), p. 193.

26. Letter of Edward Dahlberg to Robert Hutchins, November 5, 1958. *Epitaphs of Our Times,* p. 24. See also *The Carnal Myth,* pp. 62–3: "Books should exhale affections, friendship, and good precepts and be redolent of the mulberry, osiers burning in the hearth, or lentils in the pot."

27. Dahlberg, *The Sorrows of Priapus,* p. 72.

28. See Dahlberg, *Do These Bones Live,* p. 6: "History, the ACT, is the sign of Cain. Terror is the lodestar and its mark is in the first blood-besmeared pictures in the Paleolithic cave, in human sacrifice, in murder and war." See also Edward Dahlberg, *Reasons of the Heart* (New York: Horizon Press, 1965), p. 109: "What

is history but a trance, a ghost of events that prowl through our aerated brains. Who can believe that the heifers of Abraham or the goats of Job ever existed? What we call time is only the apparel of the great god, Nothing. What is a dream but an etiological sigh?"

29. Dahlberg, *The Flea of Sodom,* p. 85.

30. Read and Dahlberg, op. cit., p. 143.

31. "Myths are sanctified customs, without which men are morose and slow-witted, and lack the learning to garb themselves suitably, or to bake a good loaf, and build a savory town." Dahlberg, *The Flea of Sodom,* p. 13. "Man must eat fables, or starve his soul to death." Dahlberg, *Reasons of the Heart,* p. 99.

32. See William Gass, "The Soul Inside the Sentence," *Habitations of the Word* (New York: Alfred A. Knopf, 1985), p. 134: "It [the art of fine writing] is, as in the case of Stephen Dedalus, the search for a verbal parent, an authority made of authors, a Leviathan which when constituted will prove as unremittingly hostile, implacably severe, impossible to please, equal, or even emulate, as any other God the Father, and who will henceforth receive, like mash notes written with a poisoned pen, all our scribbler's inner ambivalences: his love and fear and jealousy, her hope and hate and hallelujah."

Selected Bibliography

Abbott, Phillip. *States of Perfect Freedom: Autobiography and American Political Thought*. Amherst: University of Massachusetts Press, 1987.

Alkon, Paul K. "Visual Rhetoric in *The Autobiography of Alice B. Toklas*." *Critical Inquiry* 1, no. 4 (June 1975). pp. 849–84.

Andrews, William L. *To Tell a Free Story: the First Century of Afro-American Autobiography, 1769–1865*. Urbana: University of Illinois Press, 1986.

Berkin, Carol, and Norton, Mary Beth. *Women of America, A History*. Boston: Houghton Mifflin Co., 1979.

Blasing, Mutlu Konuk. *The Art of Life*. Austin: University of Texas Press, 1977.

Bontemps, Arna, ed. *Great Slave Narratives*. Boston: Beacon Press, 1972.

———. *Five Black Lives*. Middletown, Conn.: Wesleyan University Press, 1971.

Bosco, Ronald. " 'He that best understands the world, least likes it': The Dark Side of Benjamin Franklin," *Pennsylvania Magazine of History & Biography*, CXI, no. 4, pp. 525–34.

Bridgman, Richard. *The Colloquial Style in America*. New York: Oxford University Press, 1966.

Bruss, Elizabeth W. *Autobiographical Acts: the Changing Situation of a Literary Genre*. Baltimore: Johns Hopkins University, 1976.

Buckley, Jerome Hamilton. *The Turning Key: Autobiography and the Subjective Impulse since 1800*. Cambridge: Harvard University Press, 1984.

Burke, Kenneth, *A Grammar of Motives*. Berkeley: University of California Press, 1969.

———. *Language as Symbolic Action*. Berkeley: University of California Press, 1968.

———. *A Rhetoric of Motives*. Berkeley: University of California Press, 1969.

Chodorow, Nancy. *The Reproduction of Mothering*. Berkeley: University of California Press, 1978.

Coe, Richard N. *When the Grass Was Taller: Autobiography and the Experience of Childhood*. New Haven: Yale University Press, 1984.

Cooley, Thomas. *Educated Lives: The Rise of Modern Autobiography in America*. Columbus: Ohio State University Press, 1976.

Couser, G. Thomas. *American Autobiography*. Amherst: University of Massachusetts Press, 1979.

Cott, Nancy F. *The Bonds of Womanhood*. New Haven: Yale University Press, 1977.

Cox, James M. "Autobiography and America." *The Virginia Quarterly Review* 47, no. 2 (Spring 1971): pp. 252–77.

Croll, Morris W. *Style, Rhetoric and Rhythm*. Edited by J. Max Patrick, Robert O. Evans, John W. Wallace, and J. R. Shoeck. Princeton: Princeton University Press, 1966.

Davis, Allen F. *Spearheads for Reform: The Social Settlements and the Progressive Movement, 1880–1940*. New York: Oxford University Press, 1967.

Deutsch, Helene. *The Psychology of Women*, 2 vols. New York: Bantam Books, 1973.

Dillard, Annie. *An American Childhood*. New York: Harper & Row, 1987.

Douglas, Ann. *The Feminization of American Culture*. New York: Alfred A. Knopf, 1977.

Du Bois, W.E.B. *Dusk of Dawn*. New York: Schocken Books, 1968.

———. *Darkwater*. New York: Schocken Books, 1969.

Eakin, Paul John. *Fictions in Autobiography: Studies in the Art of Self-Invention*. Princeton: Princeton University Press, 1985.

Egan, Susanna. *Patterns of Experience in Autobiography*. Chapel Hill: University of North Carolina Press, 1984.

Elbaz, Robert. *The Changing Nature of the Self: A Critical Study of the Autobiographic Discourse*. London: Methuen Inc., 1988.

Erikson, Erik. *Gandhi's Truth*. New York: W.W. Norton & Co., 1963.

Flexner, Eleanor. *Century of Struggle*. rev. ed. Cambridge: Harvard University Press, 1976.

Freud, Sigmund. *The Interpretation of Dreams*. Translated by Dr. A. A. Brill. New York: Random House, 1950.

Gass, William. *Fiction and the Figures of Life*. New York: Alfred A. Knopf, 1970.

Genovese, Eugene D. *Roll, Jordan, Roll*. New York: Pantheon Books, 1974.

Goldman, Emma. *My Disillusionment in Russia*. Garden City, N.Y.: Doubleday, Page & Co., 1923.

——— *The Social Significance of the Modern Drama*. New York: Applause Theatre Book Publishers, 1987.

Gunn, Janet Varner. *Autobiography: Towards a Poetics of Experience*. Philadelphia: University of Pennsylvania Press, 1982.

Harding, Vincent. *There Is a River: The Black Struggle for Freedom in America*. New York: Harcourt Brace Jovanovich, 1981.

Hart, Francis R. "Notes for an Anatomy of Modern Autobiography." *New Literary History* 1, no. 3 (Spring 1970): pp. 485–511.

Hofstadter, Richard. *The Age of Reform*. New York: Vintage Books, 1955.

Howe, Irving. *The American Newness*. Cambridge: Harvard University Press, 1986.

Huggins, Nathan Irwin. *Black Odyssey: The Afro-American Ordeal in Slavery*. New York: Vintage Books, 1977.

Hughes, Langston. *The Big Sea*. New York: Hill & Wang, 1977.

Humphrey, William. *Farther Off from Heaven*. New York: Alfred A. Knopf, 1977.

Jakobson, Roman. *Language in Literature*. Edited by Krystyna Pomorska and Stephen Rudy. Cambridge: The Belknap Press of Harvard University Press, 1987.

James, Henry. *Autobiography*. Edited by Frederick W. Dupee. New York: Criterion Books, 1956.

Jay, Paul. *Being in the Text: Self-Representation from Wordsworth to Roland Barthes*. Ithaca: Cornell University Press, 1984.

Johnson, James Weldon. *Along This Way*. New York: Viking Compass Editions, 1961.

Kaplan, Louis, in association with James Tyler Cook, Clinton E. Colby, and Daniel C. Haskell, comps. *A Bibliography of American Autobiographies*. Madison: University of Wisconsin Press, 1961.

Kazin, Alfred. *A Walker in the City*. New York: Grove Press, 1958.

Kingston, Maxine Hong. *The Woman Warrior*. New York: Alfred A. Knopf, 1976.

Krupat, Arnold. *For Those Who Come After: A Study of Native American Autobiography*. Berkeley: University of California Press, 1985.

Lacan, Jacques. *The Language of the Self*. Translated by Anthony Wilden. New York: Delta Books, 1975.

Leiris, Michel. *Manhood*. Translated by Richard Howard. New York: Grossman Publishers, 1963.

Lejeune, Phillipe. *Le Pacte Autobiographique*. Paris: Editions du Seuil, 1975.

Levine, Lawrence W. *Black Culture and Black Consciousness*. New York: Oxford University Press, 1977.

Levi-Strauss, Claude. *Tristes Tropiques*. Translated by John and Doreen Weightman. New York: Atheneum, 1974.

Lopez, Claude-Ann, and Herbert, Eugenia W. *Mon Cher Papa Franklin and the Ladies of Paris*. New Haven: Yale University Press, 1966.

Lucas, F. L. *The Search for Good Sense*. New York: Macmillan Paperbacks, 1961.
———. *Style*. New York: Macmillan, 1955.

McCarthy, Mary. *Memoirs of a Catholic Girlhood*. New York: Harcourt, Brace & Co., 1957.

Mehlman, Jeffrey. *A Structural Study of Autobiography*. Ithaca: Cornell University Press, 1974.

Mitchell, Juliet. *Psychoanalysis and Feminism*. New York: Vintage Books, 1975.

Momaday, N. Scott. *The Names*. Tucson: SunTracks/University of Arizona Press, 1976.

Murray, Pauli. *Proud Shoes,* New York: Harper & Row, 1978.

Olney, James. *Metaphors of Self*. Princeton: Princeton University Press, 1972.

Pascal, Roy. *Design and Truth in Autobiography*. London: Routledge & Kegan Paul, 1960.

Paul, Sherman. *The Music of Survival*. Urbana: University of Illinois Press, 1968.

Pilling, John. *Autobiography and Imagination: Studies in Self-Scrutiny*. London: Routledge & Kegan Paul, 1981.

Poirer, Richard. *The Performing Self*. New York: Oxford University Press, 1971.

———. *A World Elsewhere: The Place of Style in American Literature*. New York: Oxford University Press, 1966.

Pole, J.R. *The Pursuit of Equality in American History*. Berkeley: University of California Press, 1978.

Rexroth, Kenneth. *An Autobiographical Novel*. New York: New Directions, 1966.

Rivera, Edward. *Family Installments*. New York: William Morrow & Co., 1982.

Rosengarten, Theodore. *All God's Dangers: The Life of Nate Shaw*. New York: Alfred A. Knopf, 1974.

Rowbotham, Sheila. *Women, Resistance, and Revolution*. New York: Vintage Books, 1974.

Simon, Kate. *A Wider World*. New York: Harper & Row, 1986.

Smith, Page. *Daughters of the Promised Land*. Boston: Little, Brown & Co., 1970.

Smith, Sidonie. *A Poetics of Women's Autobiography: Marginality and the Fictions of Self-Representation*. Bloomington: Indiana University Press, 1987.

Sontag, Susan. *Against Interpretation*. New York: Delta Books, 1966.

———. *Styles of Radical Will*. New York: Delta Books, 1970.

Soyinka, Wole. *Ake: The Years of Childhood*. New York: Aventura, 1983.

Spacks, Patricia Ann Meyer. *The Female Imagination*. New York: Alfred A. Knopf, 1975.

———. *Imagining a Self: Autobiography and Novel in Eighteenth-Century England*. Cambridge: Harvard University Press, 1976.

Stepto, Robert B. *From Behind the Veil: A Study of Afro-American Narrative*. Urbana: University of Illinois Press, 1979.

Sutherland, Donald. *On, Romanticism*. New York: New York University Press, 1971.

Taylor, Gordon O. *Chapters of Experience: Studies in 20th-Century American Autobiography*. New York: St. Martin's Press, 1983.

Toklas, Alice B. *What Is Remembered*. New York: Holt Rinehart Winston, 1963.

Twombley, Robert. *Louis Sullivan*. New York: Viking Press, 1988.

Welty, Eudora. *One Writer's Beginnings*. Cambridge: Harvard University Press, 1984.

Williams, Jonathan, ed. *Edward Dahlberg: A Tribute.* New York: David Lewis, Inc., 1970.

Williams, William Carlos. *The Build-Up.* New York: New Directions, 1968.

————. *A Voyage to Pagany.* New York: New Directions, 1970.

Index

Abbott, Grace and Edith, 126
"Ada" (Stein), 205
Adams, Abigail, 42
Adams, Henry, xvi, xvii, xviii, 3, 42,
    81, 320
  The Education of Henry Adams,
    xviii, 4–5, 103
  style of, 4–5
Adams, John, xx, 30, 33, 42, 44, 46,
    48–9
Addams, Jane, and *Twenty Years at
    Hull-House,* xvi, xviii, xxi, xxii,
    xxiv, 12, 27, 68, 69, 88, 115–55,
    175
  on capitalism, 148–52
  childhood themes, 116, 118–26,
    148
  death theme, 116, 118, 122–5, 135
  democratic principles, 126, 127,
    131, 138–40, 154
  filial relationships, 118–26, 127,
    135, 148, 154
  Hull-House work, 125–7, 135,
    138–40, 145–7, 151, 154–5

model of feminine identity in, 126–
    7, 147, 154
  moral intelligence of, 141–2
  religious attitudes, 129–33, 150–1
  on revolution and class conflict,
    147–8, 152–3
  Rockford Seminary education, 128–
    9
  social reform theme, 119, 120–1,
    123, 125–7, 129–55
  style of, 132–4, 136–7, 142–7,
    153–5
  and World War I, 115–16, 118
Addams, John, 118–21, 124, 126,
    127, 134, 135, 148, 154
Adler, Dankmar, 71, 74, 79, 83
  partnership with Louis Sullivan, 71–
    2, 84, 87–8
Adventures of Huckleberry Finn, The
    (Twain), 269
"Advice to a Young Poet" (Williams),
    238
Aesop, 252
Aesthetics (Valéry), 27

Aiken, Conrad, 24
  style of, 24–7
  Ushant, 5, 10, 24–7
Albany Conference (1754), 34, 55
Aldrich, Mildred, 222, 225
Alms for Oblivion (Dahlberg), 308
American Hunger (Wright), *see*
  Wright, Richard, and *American
  Hunger*
American Indians, 59
  Benjamin Franklin on, 49–51
Anarchism, 152, 170–3, 177–82, 192,
  193–4. *See also* Goldman, Emma
Anderson, Sherwood, 12, 326
Angelou, Maya, xvi
  I Know Why the Caged Bird Sings,
  269
Angiolillo, 173
Anthony, Susan B., 119
Anvil, 298n.
Apollinaire, Guillaume, 216, 222,
  227
Arensberg, Walter, 237
Armies of the Night (Mailer), 103
Armory show (1913), 237
Astaire, Fred, xxiii
Atlantic Monthly, 219
Auditorium building (Sullivan), 84,
  88
Augustine, Saint, xvi, xviii, 14, 270
  Confessions, xviii, 16–17, 327
  and Edward Dahlberg, compared,
  327, 328
Austen, Jane, 318
*Autobiographical Occasions and Orig-
  inal Acts* (Stone), xviii
Autobiography (Franklin), *see* Frank-
  lin, Benjamin, and *Autobi-
  ography*
Autobiography (Goldman), 68
Autobiography (James), 22–4
Autobiography (Kelley), xxiii
Autobiography (LeWitt), 17–19
Autobiography (Malcolm X), 270
Autobiography (Williams), *see* Wil-
  liams, William Carlos, and *Auto-
  biography*
Autobiography, An (Wright), 79, 84,
  88, 101, 103, 109–10

"Autobiography and America" (Sayre),
  xix
Autobiography of Alice B. Toklas, The
  (Stein), *see* Stein, Gertrude, and
  *The Autobiography of Alice B.
  Toklas*
Autobiography of an Idea, The (Sulli-
  van), *see* Sullivan, Louis, and *The
  Autobiography of an Idea*
Awkward Age, The (James), 210

Bacall, Lauren, xix
Bachelard, Gaston, *The Poetics of
  Space,* 277
Balabanoff, Angelica, 188, 191
"The Baroness Elsa Von Freytag Lor-
  inghoven" (Williams), 256, 257
Barthes, Roland, *Empire of Signs,* 15
Baumann, Frederick, 71
Beach, Sylvia, 255
Beaux-Arts (Paris), 87, 240
  Louis Sullivan at, 79–81, 91
Because I Was Flesh (Dahlberg), *see*
  Dahlberg, Edward, and *Because I
  Was Flesh*
Bérard, Christian, 206, 227
Berkman, Alexander, xxi, 152, 168,
  183, 185, 190, 191, 192
  and Frick assassination attempt,
  171–2, 180
  and Emma Goldman, 171–3, 174,
  176–82, 194, 196
Bessemer steel process, 83
Beyond a Boundary (James), 139
Bird, Sally, 255
Black autobiographies, 5–10, 269–75
  filial themes 272–3
  power of words in, 274–6
  of Richard Wright, 273–306
  slave narratives, xx, 5–8, 269, 270–
  3
  transformation themes, 270, 272,
  273
Black Boy (Wright), *see* Wright, Richard, and *Black Boy*
Blackwell, Elizabeth, 126
Blake, William, 306
Bolshevik Revolution (1917), 189–94

Bonifacius (Mather), 62
Boone, Daniel, 253
Boston, 62, 74
  fire of 1872, 72, 108–9
  Louis Sullivan in, 78, 89
Bostonians, The (James), 126, 224
Bottom Dogs (Dahlberg), 324–5
Bowen, Mrs. Louise DeKoven, 151
Brancusi, Constantin, 248
Braque, Georges, 221, 222, 224, 226,
  237
Brinnin, John Malcolm, 201
Bronx Primitive (Simon), 166
Broom and Others, 237
Browning, Elizabeth Barrett, 121
Bunyan, John, 252
  Pilgrim's Progress, 52
Burke, Kenneth, 237
Burnham, Daniel, 74, 77, 83
  Louis Sullivan on, 85–6
Burr, Aaron, 253, 254

Cahan, Abraham, 169
Calvino, Italo, 27
Captive Mind, The (Milosz), 140
Carson Pirie Scott & Co. Building
  (Sullivan), 88, 114
Cervantes, Miguel de, 252
Cézanne, Paul, 203, 218, 221
  Gertrude Stein on, 212–15
character, in autobiography, xvii–
  xviii, 15
  and style, 9–10
Chernyshevsky, Nikolai, *What Is To
  Be Done?,* 196
Chicago, 80, 121, 138, 152
  fire of 1871, 72
  Hull-House, 125–7, 135, 138, 139–
    40, 145–7, 151, 154–5
  Louis Sullivan in, 81–8
  Richard Wright in, 295–6, 304
Childhood (Sarraute), xvii
childhood themes, in autobiography,
  99, 306
  of Jane Addams, 116, 118–26,
    148
  of Edward Dahlberg, 308, 310–13,
    315–17, 324, 326

of Benjamin Franklin, 35, 36–9, 51
of Emma Goldman, 159, 164–8,
  177, 187, 193, 196
in slave narratives, 272–3
of Gertrude Stein, 209–10
of Louis Sullivan, 74, 75, 88–107,
  114
of William Carlos Williams, 232,
  234, 239–40, 261–2
of Richard Wright, 274, 276–86,
  288–9, 294, 295, 302, 303–4,
  306
chronology, in autobiography, 14–
  15
Civil War, xx, 67, 125
Cleyre, Voltairine de, 163, 187
Cocteau, Jean, 227
College of American Architectural
  Cardinals, 78
colonial autobiographies, xiv–xx
  of Benjamin Franklin, 29–70
Columbian Exposition (1893), 72, 74,
  77, 86–7
Communism, 193, 291
  and Richard Wright, 296–306
confession, in autobiography, 320–1,
  327
Confessions, (Rousseau), 321
Confessions (Saint Augustine), xviii,
  16–17, 327
Conrad, Joseph, 296
  The Secret Agent, 176
  Under Western Eyes, 188
consciousness in memory, 21–7
Constitution, U.S., xxii, 66
Crane, Hart, 25
Cubism, 211, 219, 222, 225, 226,
  227
Cunard, Nancy, 255
Czolgosz, Leon, 119, 152–3, 171,
  173–5

Dadaism, 227
Dahlberg, Edward, and *Because I Was
  Flesh,* xviii, xix, xxiii–xxiv, 9,
  10, 12–14, 68, 99, 232, 234,
  239, 307–28
  abandonment theme, 317, 320

Dahlberg, Edward (*cont.*)
  childhood themes, 308, 310–13,
    315–17, 324, 326
  confessional tone, 308, 320–2, 327
  Jewish roots, 311
  Oedipal theme, 308, 310–13, 315–
    22, 324
  orphanage years, 316–17, 324
  religious attitudes, 312
  and Saint Augustine, compared,
    327, 328
  on sexuality and women, 311, 313
    and *n.*, 314 and *n.*, 315 and *n.*,
    316–22, 324–6
  style of, 12–14, 308, 314–15, 317,
    323–8
Dahlberg, Lizzie, 308, 310–13, 315–
    22, 324
"To Daphne and Virginia" (Williams),
    240
Davenport, Guy, 228
Davis, Allen F., 121, 155
Debs, Eugene, 172, 194
Defoe, Daniel, *Essay upon Projects,
    An,* 62
democratic themes, in autobiography,
    xvi, xx–xxiii, 60, 67–8, 138,
    307
  of Jane Addams, 126, 127, 131,
    138–40, 148, 154
  of Benjamin Franklin, 66
  in black autobiographies, 273
  of Louis Sullivan, 74–8, 84–7, 89,
    101–2, 113–14
Derain, André, 224
"The Descent" (Williams), 230
Descent of Winter, The (Williams),
    233
"The Desert Music" (Williams), 230
Dewey, John, 147
Diary (Sewall), 42
Dickens, Charles, 8, 142, 317
Dickinson, Emily, xxi, 189
diction, 5
Dostoyevsky, Fëdor, 8, 296
Do These Bones Live (Dahlberg), 326
Douglass, Frederick, 269, 272, 274
  Narrative, 5–8, 270, 272–3
  style of, 5–8

Dreiser, Theodore, 196, 291, 296,
    326
Du Bois, W.E.B., *The Souls of Black
    Folk,* 273–4
Duchamp, Marcel, 236–7, 238, 256
Dunciad, The (Pope), 41
Dunkers, 56
Dust Tracks on a Road (Hurston), 8–
    9, 10

eccentricity, 27–8
Edelmann, John, 79
Education of Henry Adams, The
    (Adams), xviii, 4–5, 103
Edwards, Jonathan, 30, 57–8, 59–60,
    61, 63–5, 67, 313
  Personal Narrative, 60, 64–5, 66
Eighty Years and More (Stanton), 115
Eliot, George, xvii
  Middlemarch, 321
Eliot, T.S., 25, 238
  The Waste Land, 77, 246, 263
  and William Carlos Williams, 245–
    6
Ellison, Ralph, 277
"An Elucidation" (Stein), 202
Emancipation Proclamation, 291
Emerson, Ralph Waldo, xxi, 3, 67–8,
    69, 75, 100, 102
  "Circles," 228
  "Prudence," 67
Empire of Signs (Barthes), 15
Erikson, Erik, 69, 277
  Young Man Luther, 176
Essay upon Projects, An (Defoe), 62
"The Ethics of Jim Crow" (Wright),
    283
Evans, Walker, *Let Us Now Praise
    Famous Men,* 133
Everybody's Autobiography (Stein),
    226
external vs. internal experience, in
    autobiography, 15–21, 28

Falk, Candace, 184
fantasy, 7
Fauvism, 218, 221, 227

fiction, xvii
first-person narrative, 103–4
  of Jane Addams, 153–4
Flea of Sodom, The (Dahlberg), 307,
  326, 327
Florence, 81
Ford, Ford Madox, 223
form, 5
Franco, Francisco, 249
Franklin, Abiah Folger, 37, 43
Franklin, Benjamin, and *Autobiography,* xvi, xx, xxiii, xxiv, 12, 15–
  16, 27, 29–70, 99, 158, 253, 307
  attitudes on power, 44–7
  authority figures in, 35–9, 40, 44,
    47, 54, 58–9
  on capitalism, 30, 32
  childhood themes, 35, 36–9, 51
  criticism of, 30, 32
  early manhood themes, 38–44, 51,
    54
  emotion lacking in, 56–7, 64–6
  filial relationships, 36–9, 43, 51
  on Indians, 49–51
  influence of, 66–7
  intellect of, 47–8
  D.H. Lawrence on, 30, 32, 67
  Philadelphia years, 39–50, 62
  political themes, 34–5, 39, 45–6,
    47, 54–5, 66
  and printing business, 40, 44–7, 48
  religious attitudes, 33, 38, 58, 60–
    9, 129
  scientific and civic projects, 30, 34,
    47–8, 65–6
  self-improvement theme, 34–5, 49
  self-interest theme, 29–30, 32–3,
    35, 40, 43, 46, 48, 60–1, 66, 67,
    69–70
  style of, 33, 35, 41, 51–7
  time in, 33–5, 39
  use of rhetoric, 51–2
  William Carlos Williams on, 30, 32
  on women and sexuality, 39, 41–4
Franklin, Deborah Read, 43–4
Franklin, Francis Folger, 56–7
Franklin, Josiah, 37–9, 40
Franklin, William, 42
Franklin stove, 47

Freud, Sigmund, 164, 261
Freudian model for consciousness, 24–
  5, 261
Frick, Henry Clay, 171–2, 180
From Flushing to Calvary (Dahlberg),
  324
Furness, Frank, 72, 79, 83, 91

Gass, William, 10, 28
  "The Soul Inside the Sentence," 304
George III, King of England, 61, 66
Getty Tomb (Sullivan), 114
Gilman, Charlotte Perkins, xxi, 141
Goethe, Johann Wolfgang von, 147
Goldman, Abraham, 165, 166, 194
Goldman, Emma, and *Living My Life,*
  xvii–xviii, xxi, xxii, xxiii, xxiv,
  99, 125
  and Alexander Berkman, 171–3,
    174, 176–82, 194, 196
  on capitalism, 169, 172
  childhood themes, 159, 164–8, 177,
    187, 193, 196
  in exile, 158, 188–95
  femaleness of, 166–8, 178, 186–7
  filial relationships, 164–8, 177,
    187, 193, 194–5
  idealism of, 168, 169, 170, 173,
    175, 178, 190, 193, 195
  Jewish roots, 164–5, 169
  on love and sex, 158, 162–4, 177,
    183–7
  and McKinley assassination, 173–5
  in New York City, 171–2
  platform oratory in, 159–62
  political views, 158, 160–2, 168,
    170–5, 178–9, 182, 189–96
  and Ben Reitman, 182–7
  religious attitudes, 164–5, 193
  and Russian Revolution, 189–95
  self-inflation of, 163–4, 196
  style of, 158, 162–4, 179–80, 184–
    5, 192, 193, 196
  use of rhetoric, 159–62
  violence theme, 164–8, 172–4, 185
  and World War I, 182
  written in past tense, 179–80
Goldman, Taube, 166, 167, 194–5

Gorky, Maxim, 191, 193, 196
Gottdank, Saul, 310, 311–13, 316
"The Gradual Making of *The Making
     of Americans*" (Stein), 201
Great American Novel, The (Wil-
     liams), 233
Great Awakening, 63
Great Depression, xix, 296
Greie, Johanna, 170
Greven, Philip, 58
Gris, Juan, 221, 222
Guaranty Trust skyscraper (Sullivan),
     114

Hamilton, Alice, xxi, 126, 153, 154,
     155
Hartley, Marsden, 216, 237
Harvard University, 78
Hauptmann, Gerhart, 196
Haymarket Affair, 138, 164, 170,
     171, 173, 183, 195
Hemingway, Ernest, 12, 223, 227,
     238
Henri, Robert, 157
Hewitt, George, 112
Hewitt, John, 79
history, in autobiography, xix, xxiii,
     4, 15
   vs. invention, xvii–xix, 3
Homestead Strike of 1893, 171–2,
     180
Hudson, Hosea, 273
Hughes, Langston, 274, 292, 297
Hugo, Victor, 81
Hull-House. *See* Addams, Jane
Hurston, Zora Neale, 270, 274
   Dust Tracks on a Road, 8–9, 10
Hutchins, Robert, 326

Iacocca, Lee, xix
Ibsen, Henrik, 196
I Know Why the Caged Bird Sings
     (Angelou), 269
immigration, xxi, 169–70, 175, 311
Impressionism, 212
inaccuracies, in autobiography, 230
industrialization, xxi, 138

internal vs. external experience, in
     autobiography, 15–21, 28
In the American Grain (Williams),
     233–4, 242, 253, 255, 267–8
invention vs. history, in autobiogra-
     phy, xvii–xix, 3
Iroquois confederation, 50
Israel Potter (Melville), 42, 51
Ives, Charles, 102
"I Wanted to Write a Poem" (Wil-
     liams), 230

Jacob, Max, 218
Jacobs, Harriet, 269
James, C.L.R., *Beyond a Boundary,*
     139
James, Henry, 10, 19, 222, 323
   Autobiography, 22–4
   The Awkward Age, 210
   The Bostonians, 126, 224
   A Small Boy and Others, 21
   style of, 21–4, 26
James, William, 22, 142, 260
Jefferson, Thomas, 29, 62
Jenney, Le Baron, 79, 82
Jim Crow laws, 283, 291, 292
John Reed Club, 298
Johns, Katherine, 254–5
Joll, James, 194
Jones, Mother, 172
Jordy, William, 100
Joyce, James, 222, 238, 254, 291
Judaism:
   and Edward Dahlberg, 311
   and Emma Goldman, 164–5,
     169
Junto, 48, 57

Kahnweiler, Daniel-Henry, 221,
     222
Keats, John, 242
Kelley, Florence, xxi, xxii, 154
   Autobiography, xxiii
Kennedy, John F., 272
Kersner, Jacob, 170
Kindergarten Chats (Sullivan), 75,
     77–8, 84–5, 92, 104

Kora in Hell (Williams), 232, 233, 256
Kropotkin, Pyotr, 191
Ku Klux Klan, 288

Lane, John, 223
Lasch, Christopher, 155
Lathrop, Julia, 126, 154
Lawrence, D.H., 33
    on Edward Dahlberg, 324
    on Benjamin Franklin, 30, 32, 67
Lears, Jackson, *No Place of Grace,* 138–9
Leaves of Grass (Whitman), xx
Left Front, 298 and *n.*
Lenin, Nikolai, 176, 188, 189, 191–4
Let Us Now Praise Famous Men (Agee), 133
Lewis, Sinclair, 12, 296
LeWitt, Sol, 17
    Autobiography, 17–19
    style of 17–19
Lincoln, Abraham, xx, 121
Lingg, Louis, 183
Lives (Plutarch), 62, 118
Living My Life (Goldman), *see* Goldman, Emma, and *Living My Life*
Long Road of Women's Memory, The (Addams), 115
Loy, Mina, 255

Mailer, Norman, *Armies of the Night,* 103
Making of Americans, The (Stein), 200–2
Malcolm X, 99, 272, 273, 274, 281–2, 292
    Autobiography, 270
Marin, John, 237
Marx, Karl, 296
Masses, The, 297
Mather, Cotton, 69
    Bonifacius, 62
Matisse, Henri, 202–3, 216, 219, 221, 226
McAlmon, Robert, 223, 260
McBride, Henry, 214

McKay, Claude, 274, 292, 297
McKinley, William, assassination of, 119, 152–3, 171, 173–5
Mellow, James, 204
Melville, Herman, 46, 326
    Israel Potter, 42, 51
    Moby Dick, 8, 113
Memories (Xenophon), 62
memory, 99
    consciousness in, 21–7
    and inaccuracies, 230
Mencken, H.L., 275, 291
Meredith, Hugh, 41, 44
Michel, Louise, 163, 164
Michelangelo, 147
    Louis Sullivan on, 111–12
Middlemarch (Eliot), 321
Miller, Perry, 58, 64
Milosz, Czeslaw, *The Captive Mind,* 140
Moby Dick (Melville), 8, 113
Monnier, Adrienne, 255
Montaigne, 59
Moore, Marianne, 247, 255
Most, Johann, 159, 164, 173, 177, 178
Mother Earth, 182, 196
Mots, Les (Sartre), 3
Muir, Edwin, xvi, 230, 321–2
Murdock, Kenneth, 59
Mussolini, Benito, 249
My Life (Trotsky), 176, 188
My Life (Wagner), xxiii

Nabokov, Vladimir, 88, 230
    Speak, Memory, 99, 197–8, 232
Narrative (Douglass), 5–8, 270, 272–3
Native Son (Wright), 283
Nealson, Buddy, 299–300
Nemerov, Howard, 10
New Masses, 298*n.*
New York City:
    Emma Goldman in, 171–2
    William Carlos Williams, 235, 253, 254
New York *Sun,* 214
Nixon, Richard, *Six Crises,* 5

No Place of Grace (Lears), 138–9
Norris, Isaac, 46
Notes Toward an Autobiography
(Williams), 229
Novelette, A (Williams), 233

oedipal theme, in Dahlberg's *Because I
Was Flesh,* 308, 310–13, 315–22,
324
O'Hara, Frank, 261
Olivier, Fernande, 224

pacing, 8
Paris, 79–81
Gertrude Stein in, 211–12, 218,
219–25
William Carlos Williams in, 235,
244–6, 255, 262, 265–7
Paris Commune, 163, 164
Paris France, 220
Pascal, Blaise, 313
Paterson (Williams), 230, 246, 259,
268
Paul, Elliot, 223
Paustovsky, Konstantin, xvi
Pennington, Reverend James, 269
Personal Narrative (Edwards), 60, 64–
5, 66
Philadelphia, 91
Centennial Exposition of 1876,
100
1873 panic, 72
Benjamin Franklin in, 39–50, 62
Picasso, Pablo, 203, 212, 219, 220,
221, 222
and Gertrude Stein, 211, 218, 224,
225, 227
Pilgrim's Progress (Bunyan), 52
Pissarro, Camille, 214
Plutarch, *Lives,* 62, 118
Poetics of Space, The (Bachelard),
277
political biographies, xxi–xxiii, 15
political reform, nineteenth century,
126–7, 138–41
Poor Richard's Almanac (Franklin),
32, 44, 48

Pope, Alexander, *The Dunciad,* 41
Pound, Ezra, 25, 222–3
Villon, 248
and William Carlos Williams, 236,
238, 245, 247–53, 254
Powderly, Terence, 177
Pritchett, V.S., xviii, 3, 66
Progressive Era, xxi–xxiii, 69, 125,
168
Provincetown Playhouse, 237, 248
Pullman, George, 148
Puritan autobiographies, xix–xx, 16,
58–61, 64
Puritanism, 58–69, 255–6

Quakers, 49, 56, 119

Ralph, James, 41
Ray, Catherine, 44
Read, Herbert, 323, 327
Reed, John, 194
Reitman, Ben, 157, 182–7
Reitzel, Robert, 157, 163
religion, 58
Jane Addams on, 129–33, 150–1
Edward Dahlberg on, 312
Benjamin Franklin on, 33, 38, 58,
60–9, 129
Emma Goldman on, 164–5, 193
Richard Wright on, 284, 294, 298,
303
Revolutionary War, 33, 54
Rheingold (Wagner), 264, 266, 267
rhythm, 5
Richardson, H.H., 72, 78
Riis, Jacob, xxi, 148, 168
Riordan, John, 233
Roché, H.-P., 222
Roosevelt, Franklin, 250
Root, John, 82–3
Rosenfeld, Paul, 237
Rousseau, Douanier, 19, 216
Rousseau, Jean Jacques, *Confessions,*
321
Royal Society, 48
Russia, 169, 188–95, 251, 297
Russian Revolution (1917), 189–94

Sappho, 252
Sarraute, Nathalie, *Childhood,* xvii
Sartre, Jean-Paul, xvi
  Les Mots, 3
Sayre, Robert F., "Autobiography and
  America," xix
Secret Agent, The (Conrad), 176
Sewall, Samuel, *Diary,* 42
show-biz autobiographies, xxiii
Simon, Kate, *Bronx Primitive,* 166
Six Crises (Nixon), 5
Six Nations, 50
slave narratives, xx, 5–8, 269, 270–3
Small Boy and Others, A (James), 21
Smith, Mary Rozet, 126, 151
Smith-Rosenberg, Carroll, 127
Socialism, 148, 177
social reform, nineteenth-century,
  126–7, 138–41, 168, 182. *See
  also* Addams, Jane; Goldman,
  Emma
Song of Myself (Whitman), xv–xvi,
  xx–xxi, 28, 66
Sorrows of Priapus, The (Dahlberg),
  327
"The Soul Inside the Sentence" (Gass),
  304
Souls of Black Folk, The (Du Bois),
  273–4
Sour Grapes (Williams), 263, 264
Spacks, Patricia Meyer, 163–4
Speak, Memory (Nabokov), 99, 197–
  8, 232
Spectator (Addison and Steele), 51–2
Spring and All (Williams), 233, 262
Stalin, Joseph, 176, 251, 300
Stanton, Elizabeth Cady, 118
  Eighty Years and More, 115
Starobinski, Jean, 26
Starr, Ellen, 126, 137, 154
steel frame, 83–4
Steffens, Lincoln, xxi, 194, 220
Stein, Gertrude, and *The Autobiogra-
  phy of Alice B. Toklas,* xviii, xix,
  xxiv, 5, 12, 16, 19, 99, 103,
  197–228, 253
  on art world, 220–2, 224, 226, 227
  and Cézanne, 212–15
  childhood themes, 209–10

introspection lacking in, 198, 225–
  7, 261
and Matisse, 202–3, 226
narrative time in, 211–12
in Paris, 211–12, 218, 219–25
and Picasso, 211, 218, 224, 225,
  227
popularity of, 219–23, 226
relation of insides to outsides in,
  204–8, 225, 226
on sexuality, 198, 206, 218–19,
  220
and Leo Stein, 204–5, 223, 226
style of, 5, 19–20, 200–17, 219,
  224, 228
transposed consciousnesses in, 217,
  261
use of repetition, 201–2, 205, 213,
  216
and William Carlos Williams, 244–
  5, 260, 261
and World War I, 224*n.,* 225
Stein, Leo, 198, 204–5, 212, 215,
  219, 223, 226
Stevens, Wallace, xxv
Stevenson, Polly, 44
Stieglitz, Alfred, 237
Stock Exchange Building (Chicago),
  87
Stone, Albert, xviii, 94
  *Autobiographical Occasions and
  Original Acts,* xviii
Stravinsky, Igor, 20
Strindberg, August, 196, 319
style, autobiographical, xxiii–xxiv,
  3–28, 230
  of Henry Adams, 4–5
  of Jane Addams, 132–4, 136–7,
    142–7, 153–5
  of Conrad Aiken, 24–7
  and character, 9–10
  and consciousness in memory,
    21–7
  of Edward Dahlberg, 12–14, 308,
    314–15, 317, 323–8
  of Frederick Douglass, 5–8
  elements of, 5, 7–8
  and external vs. internal experience,
    15–21, 28

style, autobiographical (*cont.*)
    of Benjamin Franklin, 33, 35, 41,
        51–7
    of Emma Goldman, 158, 162–4,
        179–80, 184–5, 192, 193, 196
    of Henry James, 21–4, 26
    of Sol LeWitt, 17–19
    of Gertrude Stein, 5, 19–20, 200–
        17, 219, 224, 228
    of Louis Sullivan, 5, 72, 102–12
    of Virgil Thomson, 11–12, 20–1
    of William Carlos Williams, 5, 232–
        4, 236, 242, 244, 259, 260–7
    of Richard Wright, 276–7, 280,
        282, 287, 289, 292–4, 296–7,
        301–6
stylus, 8
"The Subjective Necessity for Social
    Settlements" (Addams), 129–30
Sullivan, Andrienne List, 89, 92–5
Sullivan, Louis, and *The Autobiogra-*
    phy of an Idea, xxi, xxii–xxiii,
    xxiv, 5, 9, 68, 71–114, 223
    architectural ideas and innovations,
        79–80, 83–8, 92, 104, 111–14
    Beaux-Arts training, 79–81, 91
    Boston years, 78, 89
    career decline, 71, 74, 99,
        112–14
    Chicago years, 81–8
    childhood themes, 74, 75, 88–107,
        114
    democratic principles, 74–8, 84–7,
        89, 101–2, 113–14
    disillusionment theme, 85–7, 99,
        112–14
    filial relationships, 88–98
    idealism theme, 72, 74–8, 84–7,
        89, 99–100, 113–14
    on Nature, 88, 100–1
    partnership with Adler, 71–2, 84,
        87–8
    on power, 112–13
    sentimentality of, 92–3, 96–7, 105–
        8, 111–12
    style of, 5, 72, 102–12
    on women and sexuality, 92–7
    Frank Lloyd Wright on, 74, 79,
        104, 113–14

Sullivan, Margaret Davies Hatta-
    bough, 74
Sullivan, Patrick, 89–92
Surrealism, 227
Sutherland, Donald, 202, 205
syntax, 5, 7–8
System of Architectural Ornament, A
    (Sullivan), 104, 114

Tarkington, Booth, 12
Tchelitchew, 227
Tender Buttons (Stein), 206–8, 209,
    218
Testament, A (Wright), 71
third-person narrative, 103–4
    of Louis Sullivan, 72, 102–3
Thomas, Dylan, 247
Thomson, Virgil, 3, 10, 226, 228
    style of, 11–12, 20–1
    Virgil Thomson, 10–12, 20–1
Thoreau, Henry David, 68–9, 162,
    321, 326
    Walden, 68–9
Those Who Perish (Dahlberg), 324
Three Lives (Stein), 198, 200, 202,
    223, 296
Tinayre, Yves, 248
Tocqueville, Alexis de, 307
Toklas, Alice, *see* Stein, Gertrude, and
    The Autobiography of Alice B.
    Toklas
Tolstoy, Leo, 154
Transcendentalism, 67, 100, 113
Tree, Iris, 255
Trotsky, Leon, 193
    My Life, 176, 188
Truman, Harry, 12
Twain, Mark, 12, 27, 183, 235
    The Adventures of Huckleberry
    Finn, 269
Twenty Years at Hull-House
    (Addams), *see* Addams, Jane, and
    Twenty Years at Hull-House
Two (Stein), 204–6, 226
Tzara, Tristan, 226

Under Western Eyes (Conrad), 188
Ushant (Aiken), 5, 10, 24–7

Vail, Clotilde, 255
"A Valentine for Sherwood Anderson" (Stein), 202
Valéry, Paul, 28, 246
 Aesthetics, 27
Van Doren, Carl, 49–50
Vaughan, Benjamin, 35, 51
Veblen, Theodore, 296
Vietnam War, xxiii
Villon (Pound), 248
Virgil Thomson (Thomson), 10–12, 20–1
Vollard, Ambroise, 212–15, 222
"Vollard and Cézanne" (Stein), 214
"The Voodoo of Hell's Half-Acre" (Wright), 274
Voyage to Pagany (Williams), 236

Wagner, Richard:
 My Life, xxiii
 Rheingold, 264, 266, 267
Wainwright Building (Sullivan), 71, 84, 88, 114
Wald, Lillian, 168
Walden (Thoreau), 68–9
Ware, William, 78
Washington, Booker T., 274
Waste Land, The (Eliot), 77, 146, 263
Way to Wealth, The (Franklin), 32
Weaver, Mike, 233
Wells, Ida, xxi
Welty, Eudora, 27
Wesley, John, 30
Wexler, Alice, 174
What Is To Be Done? (Chernyshevsky), 196
Whistler, James Abbott McNeill, 212
Whitefield, George, 63
Whitman, Walt, xv–xvi, xx, 66, 75, 93, 102
 Leaves of Grass, xx
 Song of Myself, xv–xvi, xx–xxi, 28, 66
Whittemore, Reed, 258
Williams, Elena, 240
Williams, Florence (Floss), 236, 239, 250, 258–9

Williams, Jonathan, 318
Williams, William Carlos, and *Autobiography,* xvii, xxiv, 5, 77, 229–68, 307
 childhood themes, 232, 234, 239–40, 261–2
 distance vs. intimacy in, 238–44, 247
 dual profession theme, 241–4, 254, 259
 and Marcel Duchamp, 236–7, 238
 and T.S. Eliot, 245–6
 filial relationships, 232, 239–40, 257, 262
 inaccuracies in, 230, 232–3
 innocence theme, 234, 235–8
 intellect of, 238
 introspection lacking in, 260–2
 medical career, 235, 236, 240, 241–4, 259–60
 mistrust of pattern, 233, 267
 in New York City, 235, 253, 254
 in Paris, 235, 244–6, 255, 262, 265–7
 popularity of, 246–7
 and Ezra Pound, 236, 238, 245, 247–53, 254
 relation of insides to outsides in, 260–7
 and Gertrude Stein, 244–5, 260, 261
 style of, 5, 232–4, 236, 242, 244, 259, 260–7
 unity lacking in, 267–8
 on women and sexuality, 253–9
Winthrop, John, 58
Woolman, John, 33
Woolson, Moses, 78, 83, 89, 91
Wordsworth, William, 26
World War I, xix, 166, 263
 and Jane Addams, 115–16, 118
 and Emma Goldman, 182
 and Gertrude Stein, 224*n.*, 225
World War II, 247, 250
Wright, Ella Wilson, 276, 281–3
Wright, Frank Lloyd, 77, 78, 81, 93, 100, 223
 An Autobiography, 79, 84, 88, 101, 103, 109–10

Wright, Frank Lloyd *(cont.)*
  on Louis Sullivan, 74, 79, 104,
    113–14
  A Testament, 71
Wright, Richard, and *American Hun-
    ger,* xviii, xxiv, 30, 99, 274,
    295–306
  childhood themes, 295, 302, 303–4,
    306
  Communist involvement, 296–306
  hunger theme, 274, 295
  moral laxity of, 302–5
  racial themes, 295–306
  religious attitudes, 298, 303
  style of, 296–7, 301–6
Wright, Richard, and *Black Boy,* xviii,
    xxiv, 30, 99, 269, 274–95, 304,
    305
  black folk tradition in, 292–4
  childhood themes, 274, 276–86,
    288–9, 294, 304, 306

  early manhood themes, 291–4
  filial themes, 274, 276–86
  hunger theme, 274, 278, 281, 286,
    288
  racial themes, 281–3, 286–95
  religious attitudes, 284, 294
  style of, 276–7, 280, 282, 287,
    289, 292–4, 304, 306
  transformation theme, 294–5
  violence theme, 276–7, 286
  on women and sexuality, 283, 285–
    6
Wright, Richard Nathan, 278–80,
    281

Xenophon, *Memories,* 62

Yeats, William Butler, 249
Young Man Luther (Erikson), 176

Permissions Acknowledgments

Grateful acknowledgment is made to the following for permission to reprint previously published material:

Cambridge University Press: Excerpt from William Carlos Williams' October 13, 1926, letter to John Riordan from *William Carlos Williams, The American Background* by Mike Weaver. Reprinted by permission of Cambridge University Press.

Harper & Row, Publisher, Inc.: Excerpts from *American Hunger* by Richard Wright. Copyright 1944 by Richard Wright, © 1977 by Ellen Wright; excerpts from *Black Boy* by Richard Wright. Copyright 1937, 1942, 1944, 1945 by Richard Wright. Reprinted by permission of Harper & Row, Publisher, Inc.

NAL/New American Library: Excerpts from "Personal Narrative" from *Jonathan Edwards: Basic Writings,* edited by Ola Elizabeth Winslow. Reprinted by permission of NAL/New American Library.

New Directions Publishing Corporation: Excerpts from William Carlos Williams: *The Baroness Elsa Von Freytag Loringhoven*, from the Collection of American Literature, Beinecke Rare Book and Manuscript Library, Yale University. Copyright © 1989 by William Eric Williams and Paul H. Williams; excerpts from William Carlos Williams: *The Autobiography of William Carlos Williams.* Copyright 1951 by William Carlos Williams; excerpt from William Carlos Williams' letter to James Laughlin from William Carlos Williams: *The Selected Letters of William Carlos Williams.* Copyright 1957 by William Car-

A NOTE ON THE TYPE

The text of this book was set in Sabon, a type face designed by Jan Tschichold (1902–1974), the well-known German typographer. Because it was designed in Frankfurt, Sabon was named for the famous Frankfurt type founder Jacques Sabon, who died in 1580 while manager of the Egenolff foundry.

Based loosely on the original designs of Claude Garamond (c. 1480–1561), Sabon is unique in that it was explicitly designed for hot-metal composition on both the Monotype and Linotype machines as well as for film composition.

Composed by Creative Graphics, Inc.,
Allentown, Pennsylvania
Printed and bound by Fairfield Graphics,
Fairfield, Pennsylvania
Designed by Mia Vander Els